Transnational Encounters between Germany and East Asia since 1900

This volume contributes to the emerging field of Asian German Studies by bringing together cutting-edge scholarship from international scholars working in a variety of disciplines. The chapters survey transnational encounters between Germany and East Asia since 1900. By rejecting traditional dichotomies between the East and the West, or the colonizer and the colonized, these essays highlight instead connectedness and hybridity. They show how closely Germany and East Asia cooperated and negotiated the challenges of modernity in a range of topics, such as politics, history, literature, religion, environment, architecture, migration, and sports.

Joanne Miyang Cho is professor and chair of History at William Paterson University of New Jersey. She is co-editor of *Transcultural Encounters between Germany and India* (2014), *Germany and China* (2014), *Transnational Encounters between Germany and Japan* (2016), *Gendered Encounters between Germany and Asia* (2017), and *Transnational Encounters between Germany and Korea* (2018). She has also published book chapters and articles on the politics of civilization as related to a number of German intellectuals and writers. She is co-editor of the Palgrave Series in Asian German Studies.

Routledge Studies in Modern History

Understanding the City through Its Margins
Pluridisciplinary Perspectives from Case Studies in Africa, Asia and the Middle East
Edited by André Chappatte, Ulrike Freitag and Nora Lafi

The Style and Mythology of Socialism
Socialist Idealism, 1871–1914
Stefan Arvidsson

Capitalism and Religion in World History
Purification and Progress
Carl Mosk

Michael Collins and the Financing of Violent Political Struggle
Nicholas Ridley

Censuses and Census Takers
A Global History
Gunnar Thorvaldsen

America and the Postwar World
Remaking International Society, 1945–1956
David Mayers

Transnational Encounters between Germany and East Asia since 1900
Edited by Joanne Miyang Cho

The Institution of International Order
From the League of Nations to the United Nations
Edited by Simon Jackson and Alanna O'Malley

For a full list of titles in this series, please visit www.routledge.com/history/series/MODHIST

Transnational Encounters between Germany and East Asia since 1900

Edited by Joanne Miyang Cho

LONDON AND NEW YORK

First published 2018
by Routledge
2 Park Square, Milton Park, Abingdon, Oxon OX14 4RN

and by Routledge
711 Third Avenue, New York, NY 10017

Routledge is an imprint of the Taylor & Francis Group, an informa business

© 2018 selection and editorial matter, Joanne Miyang Cho; individual chapters, the contributors

The right of Joanne Miyang Cho to be identified as the author of the editorial material, and of the authors for their individual chapters, has been asserted in accordance with sections 77 and 78 of the Copyright, Designs and Patents Act 1988.

All rights reserved. No part of this book may be reprinted or reproduced or utilised in any form or by any electronic, mechanical, or other means, now known or hereafter invented, including photocopying and recording, or in any information storage or retrieval system, without permission in writing from the publishers.

Trademark notice: Product or corporate names may be trademarks or registered trademarks, and are used only for identification and explanation without intent to infringe.

British Library Cataloguing-in-Publication Data
A catalogue record for this book is available from the British Library

Library of Congress Cataloging-in-Publication Data
Names: Cho, Joanne Miyang, 1959– editor.
Title: Transnational encounters between Germany and East Asia since 1900 / edited by Joanne Miyang Cho.
Description: Abingdon, Oxon ; New York, NY : Routledge, 2018. | Series: Routledge studies in modern history ; 37
Identifiers: LCCN 2017051590 | ISBN 9780815378402 (hardback : alk. paper) | ISBN 9781351232517 (ebook)
Subjects: LCSH: East Asia—Relations—Germany. | Germany— Relations—East Asia | East Asia—Foreign relations—Germany. | Germany—Foreign relations—East Asia
Classification: LCC DS518.3 .T73 2018 | DDC 303.48/24305—dc23
LC record available at https://lccn.loc.gov/2017051590

ISBN: 978-0-815-37840-2 (hbk)
ISBN: 978-1-351-23251-7 (ebk)

Typeset in Sabon
by Apex CoVantage, LLC

Contents

List of illustrations	vii
List of contributors	viii
Introduction JOANNE MIYANG CHO	1

PART I
German missionaries and German-speaking Jews in China   21

1   One family, two systems: how German missionary mothers
    and their Chinese "daughters" challenged the late Qing
    Confucian family model   23
    JULIA STONE

2   Working with disaster: Weimar Mission responses to the
    Boxer catastrophe (1900–1901)   45
    LYDIA GERBER

3   Representations of Jewish exile and models of memory in
    Shanghai Ghetto and *Exil Shanghai*   62
    SHAMBHAVI PRAKASH

PART II
Japanese images of Germany and transnational flow
between Germany and East Asia   83

4   A close country in the distance: Japanese images of
    Germany in the twentieth century   85
    TORU TAKENAKA

vi *Contents*

5 The Lex Adickes in its East Asian contexts:
the introduction of land readjustment
and its spatio-political effects   101
JIN-SUNG CHUN

6 A nuclear fall-out turning political: the German-Japanese
relationship and the consequences of the Fukushima
nuclear incident   123
VOLKER STANZEL

PART III
German and Austrian intellectuals/writers and East Asia   143

7 Max Weber and East Asian development   145
KEUMJAE PARK

8 "History as a poet": Stefan Zweig's historical and
biographical writing in Maoist China   162
ARNHILT JOHANNA HOEFLE

9 Ming Ying transreads women: Christa Wolf and Chen Ran   176
ROBERT COWAN

PART IV
Politics and sports during the Cold War era   191

10 From war to peace: the Allied occupation of Germany
and Japan   193
DAVID M. CROWE

11 War by other means: dynamics of sport in divided Germany
and divided Korea   216
AARON D. HORTON

Index   235

Illustrations

5.1	Ground plan for the Donam District Readjustment (1939)	117
10.1	Allied occupation zones of Germany after World War II	197
10.2	The principal political subdivisions of Japan after WWII	204

Contributors

Jin-Sung Chun is Professor at Busan National University of Education. His dissertation (Humboldt University in Berlin), which thematized the West German *Strukturgeschichte*, was published by R. Oldenbourg Verlag (2000). He is also the author of two books in Korean – *The Conservative Revolution: A Nihilistic Ideal of German Intellectuals* (2002) and *History Tells Memory* (2005). His latest book, *Sang Sang ui Athene, Berlin-Tokyo-Seoul* (Imagined Athens, Berlin-Tokyo-Seoul, 2015), deals with transcontinental urban history.

Robert Cowan is Professor of English at Kingsborough Community College and Assistant Dean at Hunter College, both of the City University of New York, as well as a volunteer instructor at Rikers Island Correctional Facility. He is the author of *The Indo-German Identification* (2010), *Teaching Double Negatives* (2018), and is completing a novel and a hybrid-genre manuscript.

David M. Crowe is a Presidential Fellow at Chapman University and Professor Emeritus of History at Elon University. He is the author of many books, including *Soviet Law and Justice: The Pathway to Nuremberg and Beyond, War Crimes, Genocide, and Justice* (2014), *Crimes of State, Past and Present* (2010), *The Holocaust* (2008), *Oskar Schindler* (2004), and *A History of the Gypsies of Eastern Europe and Russia* (1994 and 2007). He is currently writing *Raphael Lemkin: The Life of a Visionary*.

Lydia Gerber studied Sinology in Hamburg, Germany and at Shandong University in Jinan, PRC. She received her Ph.D (1998) from Hamburg University. She is currently Director of the Asia Program at Washington State University, Pullman. Her research and publications focus on Sino-German relations before WWI. She is the author of *Von Voskamps 'heidnischem Treiben' und Wilhelms 'höherem China'* (2002). In recent years, she has published several book chapters on German-Chinese relations and German sinologists.

Contributors   ix

Arnhilt Johanna Hoefle is a researcher at the Austrian National Library and a lecturer at the University of Vienna. She received her Ph.D from the University of London in 2014. Her publications include *China's Stefan Zweig: The Dynamics of Cross-Cultural Reception* (2017) and several articles on German-Chinese literary relations. She was awarded the Erwin Schrödinger Mobility Fellowship (2014–2017) in order to undertake research at the University of California, Berkeley, the University of Hamburg, and the University of Vienna.

Aaron D. Horton is an Associate Professor of History at Alabama State University. He earned his Ph.D in history from Louisiana State University. His research interests include the intersection of sports with politics, as well as with national and cultural identities. He is the author of *German POWs, Der Ruf, and the Genesis of Group 47* (2014) and of two forthcoming book chapters on the North Korean soccer team in the 2010 World Cup and a comparative analysis of East German and North Korean stereotypes.

Keumjae Park is Professor of Sociology at William Paterson University of New Jersey. Her research explores migration, transnationalism, gender, and identity, with a focus on Asian immigrants in the US, and migration in East Asia. She authored *Korean Immigrant Women and the Renegotiation of Identity* (2009) and co-authored *Student Research and Report Writing* (2016). She is currently conducting a qualitative research project on immigrant advocacy movements in South Korea and in the US.

Shambhavi Prakash is Assistant Professor at the Center of German Studies, Jawaharlal Nehru University, in New Delhi, India. She received her Ph.D from Rutgers University. Her dissertation explored ethnographic experimentalism in the works of filmmaker Ulrike Ottinger and writer Hubert Fichte. Her interests include the intersections of literature and anthropology, travel literature, and transnational cinema. She is currently working on textual and filmic representations of the Jewish exile community in Shanghai during the Second World War.

Volker Stanzel studied Japanese Studies, Sinology, and Political Science in Frankfurt, Cologne, and Kyoto and received his Ph.D in 1980. As a German diplomat (1979–2013), he served as German Ambassador to China and German Ambassador to Japan. In 2014, he taught at Claremont McKenna College and at UCSC. He published several books, including *Aus der Zeit gefallen* (2016), *Doitsu-taishi mo nattoku shita, Nihon ga sekai de aisareru riyu* (2015), *Chinas Außenpolitik* (2002), and *Im Wind des Wandels. Ostasiens neue Revolution* (1997).

Julia Stone is an independent scholar in Berlin, Germany. She studied Modern History at Hertford College, Oxford and subsequently worked as a x *Contributors*

journalist in London and Berlin. She completed her Ph.D in Sinology at the Freie University Berlin in 2012. She is the author of *Chinese Basket Babies: A German Missionary Foundling Home and the Girls It Raised, 1850s–1914* (2013). Her current research is on unwanted children in nineteenth century Europe and China.

Toru Takenaka received a Ph.D at Kyoto University. His specialty is modern German history and cultural transfer between Japan and Germany. He taught at Osaka University from 1993 until he moved to his current position at NIAD-QE in 2017. He is the author of *Siemens in Japan: Von der Landesöffnung bis zum Ersten Weltkrieg* (1996) and *Meiji no Waguna Bumu: Kindai Nihon no Ongaku Iten* [Wagner Boom in the Meiji Period: Music Transfer in Modern Japan] (2016).

Introduction

Joanne Miyang Cho

The present volume surveys transnational encounters between Germany and East Asia from 1900 to the present. This relationship in the first half of the twentieth century took a somewhat distinctive shape, which differentiates it from the typical power configuration between the West and a non-Western region. Whereas most Western and non-Western relationships were defined in colonial terms, this picture was more complex in the case of Germany and East Asia. Germany was a colonial power in China, not only along with other Western powers but also with Japan. By the same token, not only was Japan not colonized by the West, but it even challenged Western powers militarily, and later formed a military alliance with Nazi Germany during World War II. Also unusual is the fact that, although Korea was colonized, it was by Japan and not by a Western power. Such unusual dynamics can also be found in the post-1945 German–East Asian relationship. Since the 1970s, East Asian economies have grown at a faster rate than those of other parts of the world. Japan, in particular, overtook the West German economy in 1968. Consequently, while the flow of culture and information was clearly from Germany to East Asia during the first half of the century and in the early postwar period, this relationship has, of late, become much more equal. East Asia and Germany increasingly see each other as equal partners in trade, economic affairs, and international politics. Moreover, there have been substantive cultural and intellectual flows between them. Yet again, whereas during the first half of the twentieth century the direction of these flows was much more from Germany to East Asia, it has been shifting in recent years. Currently, this flow moves in both directions and there have been many cases of transnational cooperation between Germany and East Asia on multiple levels.

In addressing the somewhat exceptional relationship between Germany and East Asia, the chapters in this volume bring together cutting-edge scholarship by international scholars from three continents. This volume's diverse perspective is further underscored by the multiple disciplines represented by the contributors, which include history, sociology, comparative literature, German literature, Sinology, and Japanology. As a thematically organized volume, this book considers German influences on East Asia as well as the

2 Joanne Miyang Cho

East Asian impact on Germany. This mutual influence has been significant to both regions' culture and identity. The chapters in this volume explore entanglements, exchanges, and hybridity between Germany and East Asia. It is important to remember that the results from these transnational contacts are not exact duplicates of the original, but involve instead a creative process.

In order to situate this present volume in a historical, theoretical, and historiographical context and to present its key findings, this introduction explores the following four points of inquiry. The first part provides a brief sketch of transnational relations between Germany and three East Asian countries (China, Japan, and Korea) from their diplomatic beginnings in the second half of the nineteenth century to the present. The second part explores the main characteristics of the book's transnational framework. It rejects the idea of a dichotomy between the East and the West and instead questions the narrow national and local focus of earlier work. Instead, it emphasizes interrelatedness between nations. The third part highlights the historiographical landscape in German–East Asian relations. This review focuses on examining edited volumes similar to the present volume in its comprehensive scope and interdisciplinary approach. The last part highlights key findings of the chapters in this volume. They cover a rich variety of topics in history, politics, literature, environmental studies, urban planning, mission, migration, and sports. Through a careful examination of these topics, the editor hopes that this volume contributes to a better understanding of German–East Asian relations.

A brief survey of German–East Asian relations

This brief sketch of German relations with China, Japan, and Korea will provide an overview of these relationships from the start of their diplomatic relations in the second half of the nineteenth century (China in 1861, Japan in 1860, and Korea in 1883) to the present. This overview, which is clearly not comprehensive, will highlight some key events and markers in these relationships. Although formal diplomatic relations started only about 150 years ago, relations between Germany and East Asia subsequently became quite active and multifaceted, touching not only economic, political, and military aspects, but also cultural and intellectual areas. Since these East Asian nations share some common cultural views, one can identify common responses toward Germany, such as their enthusiasm for German culture and scientific knowledge. But their respective relationships with Germany also show their unique characteristics.

In respect to German-Chinese relations, although some Germans, such as Gottfried Leibniz, were interested in Chinese thought as far back as the seventeenth century, Sino-German relations truly began in 1861, when Prussia and the Qing Empire concluded the Treaty of Tianjin during the Eulenburg Expedition.[1] This occurred during the aftermath of the Second Opium War

(1856–1860). In so doing, Germany joined Britain and France as an imperial power. Prussia sent its first minister to China in 1862, and in 1869 three Qing diplomats visited Otto von Bismarck in Berlin. German military and business interests worked to expand German relations with China.[2] China was similarly interested in the Prussian military, especially after the latter won the Franco-Prussian War. Wang Tao's 1873 work, *Pu Fa zhan ji* [*Franco-Prussian War*], suggested using Germany as a model in reforming China's military. This book inspired Li Hongzhang, a general and politician at the Qing court, to promote the purchase of German arms and German-built ships.[3] He also hired German military officers when he founded a military academy in Tianjin.

Yet there were also serious snags in Sino-German relations. When two German missionaries were murdered in Shandong in 1897, Germany used the murders as a pretext to seize Kiaochow in Shandong, later formalized through a 99-year lease with the Qing dynasty in 1898.[4] After the death of Clemens von Ketteler in 1900, a German minister at Beijing, during the Boxer Rebellion, the Kaiser secured the appointment of Field Marshall Count von Waldesee as commander-in-chief of the Allied forces in China.[5] German troops joined six other Western and Japanese forces in fighting the Boxers. At the start of World War I, Germany lost its colonial holding in Shandong to Japan and about 5,000 German POWs were interned in a series of POW camps spread across Japan.

After concluding a 1921 peace treaty, Germany and China began a period of close cooperation. Germany needed China's raw materials, whereas General Chiang Kai-shek wanted German weapons and German military advisers to modernize China's military. In this, he was assisted by Colonel Max Bauer (from 1928), General Hans von Seeckt (from 1933), and General Alexander von Falkenhausen (from 1935).[6] This close cooperation continued, even after the rise of Nazi Germany. Its first foreign minister, Freiherr von Neurath, advocated "a strong pro-China and pro-Chiang Kai-shek foreign policy."[7] Germany and China still needed each other; Germany wanted to sell its exports in order to have access to foreign currency and Chiang desired German military advisers and weapons to fight the emergent Chinese communist movement. But their close relationship came to an end following a series of pro-Japanese acts by the Nazi state – the anti-Comintern Pact (1936), the German recognition of Japan-dominated Manchukuo (1938), the Tripartite Pact (1940), and Germany's recognition of Wang Jingwei's regime in Nanjing (1941).[8] Ribbentrop, who replaced Neurath in 1938, also favored a pro-Japanese policy.[9]

After World War II, East Germany initially worked with the People's Republic of China (PRC), but their relations became strained due to growing tensions between the PRC and the Soviet Union during the 1960s, which forced East Germany to side with the Soviet Union. West Germany maintained its distance from the PRC under Mao, "even though left-wing radicals in the [Federal Republic of Germany in the 1960s] began to look to the

4   *Joanne Miyang Cho*

PRC as an ideological role model."[10] When China embarked upon reforms under Deng Xiaoping, however, West Germans began to see the PRC as a potential market. "By the end of the 1970s, the PRC had become an international partner like many others."[11] In the present, these two countries maintain vibrant economic, technological, and cultural relations, despite their clear differences politically, especially in the area of human rights. In addition, a growing Chinese presence in Germany (slightly over 100,000 Chinese citizens, now the largest Asian population in Germany) is further proof of their growing cooperation.[12]

Compared with Sino-German relations, German-Japanese relations in the first half of the twentieth century were more egalitarian, but racism against Japan still played a role.[13] Many scholars have observed a striking degree of convergence between Germany and Japan in the twentieth century, despite their very different historical pasts. A small minority of scholars, however, still reject any meaningful partnership between these two nations. They point to the "significant diplomatic breaches" between them, such as the German participation in the Triple Intervention (1895), the conflict over the German leasehold in Qingdao (1914), and the Hitler-Stalin Pact (1939). They also question the true strength of the Berlin-Rome-Tokyo wartime alliance.[14] Bernd Martin also cautions against overestimating the similarities between them, seeing more differences between them than similarities.[15] Still, a majority of scholars present a close relationship between these two nations. In supporting this argument, they point to Germany and Japan as "two modern nation-states with limited democratic features of a similar type, [sharing] a belated entry into the imperialist struggle for space in the late 19th century, a drive for supremacy over its neighbors, and ensuing joint defeat in World War II."[16]

Although their formal alliance ended in 1945, Germany and Japan continued to follow similar paths in the postwar period. Both nations were subjected to Allied occupation, Germany by four occupying powers, whereas Japan was occupied primarily by the US. But there was also a difference, specifically as it concerned their respective war crimes trials. "The Tokyo Trials have not received the approval accorded those in Germany," although both they and the Nuremberg Trials had applied the same principles of international law.[17] The two countries' similar paths are particularly obvious in respect to their economies. Although both were devastated by the end of the war, they soon experienced what were dubbed at the time the "economic miracles" of the 1950s and 1960s, with Japan's growth outpacing even that of Germany. In 1951, both the German GNP (28.5 billion) and the Japanese GNP (14.2 billion) were smaller than those of Great Britain and France. But by 1980, the German GNP was 816.5 billion and Japan's GNP was 1,040.01 billion, whereas the British GNP was half that of Japan, and French GNP was about 65 percent of Japan's. By 1970, Japan and Germany became the third and fourth largest economics in the world, respectively, which remains the case today.[18] Yet these former pariah

Introduction   5

nations have been received differently by their neighbors. While Germany was accepted by its neighbors after admitting its responsibility for the war, Japan's lack of admission regarding its guilt still deeply offends its neighbors, in particular Korea, Taiwan, and China. Despite this difference on the question of war guilt, one can, in general, argue that Germany and Japan "shar[ed] a similar fate politically, militarily, and economically" across the twentieth century.[19]

The significant flows in several cultural and intellectual areas between Germany and Japan should also be noted. Yet this was not a truly equal relationship until the postwar period. During the second half of the nineteenth century, as is well known, there was significant Japanese borrowing from Germany in law, philosophy, history, music, and so on, and both groups visited each other's land.[20] During the Taishō era, Japanese scholars were well acquainted with German philosophy, since "virtually all of the major works of European philosophy" had been translated into Japanese. During the interwar period, "hundreds of Japanese, perhaps over one thousand" traveled to the West, mostly to Germany, to study. A number of German scholars taught in Japan as well. After 1945, Japanese scholars continued to read German authors, much as they had before the war, including Goethe, Nietzsche, Thomas Mann, and Hermann Hesse, and to listen to German composers, such as Beethoven and Wagner. But Germans have shown a greater interest in Japanese culture as well in recent years. For instance, Japanese authors, such as Ōe Kenzaburō, Murakami Haruki, and Tawada Yoko, have been well received in Germany.[21] German and Swiss artists and writers, such as Doris Dörrie and Adolf Muschg, demonstrate a strong interest in Japanese culture. Japanese *manga* and *anime* both enjoy a sizable number of followers in Germany. Given their very different historical and cultural backgrounds and the relatively short history of their diplomatic relationship, the extent of their similarities and transnational cooperation is "unusually close for a European and an Asian nation."[22]

Compared against Germany's diplomatic relations with China and Japan, the German-Korean diplomatic relations were concluded two decades later in 1883.[23] The Treaty of Friendship, Commerce, and Navigation was signed between the German empire and the Joseon dynasty. Paul Georg von Möllendorff, who was Korea's First Vice-Minister of Foreign Affairs, was present at this event, and he was responsible for inviting several Germans to Korea to work in various industries.[24] The composer Franz Eckert and the medical doctor Richard Wunsch spent time in Korea.[25] But with the signing of the Protectorate Treaty with Japan in 1905, Korea lost control over its diplomatic relations and, as a result, the German mission to Korea was closed.[26] In 1910, Korea became a colony of Japan until the end of World War II. During the colonial period, some Koreans managed to go to Germany to study. Since they were considered Japanese citizens, they did not need visas. One of these students was Li Mirok, who received a Ph.D in 1928 and composed his *Der Yalu fließt* [*The Yalu River Flows*, 1949] in

6 *Joanne Miyang Cho*

German.[27] Other Korean students studied medicine, philosophy, law, or natural sciences at German universities.[28]

After the end of World War II, both Germany and Korea shared the tragic fate of being divided. South Korea and West Germany, on the one hand, and North Korea and East Germany, on the other, began to develop separate and divergent relationships with each other. The communist partners established diplomatic relations in 1949, with East Germany supporting North Korea with economic aid and accepting some orphans and students in the 1950s. In 1955–1964, the East German state dispatched advisers to North Korea to help rebuild the city of Hamhŭng.[29] However, in the early 1960s East Germany suspended its credits to North Korea due to its own economic difficulties. This relationship also started to falter as a result of the growing Sino-Soviet split after 1958, but there was some improvement in 1966 after North Korea realigned itself with the Soviet Union because of China's Cultural Revolution.[30] The relatively good relationship between East Germany and North Korea can be observed in the visits made by General Secretary of the Socialist Unity Party of Germany, Erich Honecker, to Pyongyang in 1977 and by Kim Il-Sung to East Berlin in 1984, when he signed a treaty of friendship with the German Democratic Republic, although this agreement was later invalidated due to German reunification. The reunified German state established diplomatic relations with North Korea in 2001.[31]

The government of West Germany was initially "more reserved when it came to providing aid to the ROK [Republic of Korea]."[32] West Germany and South Korea entered into diplomatic relations in 1954, which was five years after their communist counterparts. West Germany did eventually come to support South Korea economically. It assisted the Park Chung-Hee government in achieving its first five-year plan for the economy.[33] West Germany's recruitment of South Korean *Gastarbeiter* in 1963–1977 also helped the South Korean economy. Their relationship was strained, however, as a result of the [South] Korean Central Intelligence Agency's kidnapping of seventeen South Korean students and intellectuals from West Germany, the so-called Berlin Affair, in 1967. The relationship normalized in 1979, when leaders on both sides visited each other. But the pivotal turning point of their improved relationship was South Korea's democratization in 1987.

Since 1990, as South Korea has rapidly developed into an industrialized country, economic exchange with Germany has increased. The German Chancellor Helmut Kohl visited South Korea in 1993, and later chancellors – Gerhard Schröder and Angela Merkel – did so as well. In addition, all democratically elected South Korean presidents have visited Germany.[34] Among these visits, Kim Dae-Jung's in March 2000 stands out. He gave an address at the Freie University of Berlin on "Lessons of German Reunification and the Korean Peninsula." In solidarity with the South Korean Sunshine Policy toward North Korea, German Foreign Minister Joschka Fischer decided to open diplomatic relations with North Korea.[35] German–South Korean bilateral relations today are comprehensive. Thus, like China and Japan, South

Introduction 7

Korea has also overcome its disparities with Germany, which characterized the beginning of their relationship. Currently they maintain an amicable bilateral relationship.

Main characteristics of transnational and global history

Multiple historians in North America have located the emergence of global history and transnational history as a field to the 1990s. According to Pierre-Yves Saunier, "the expression 'transnational history' is recent," although a number of historians were already interested in it prior to the 1990s.[36] According to Lynn Hunt, there had already been a trend toward the globalization of history before the 1990s, but it took "a fundamentally different shape" in the 1990s because of "the collapse of the Soviet Union and the end of the Cold War." This reshaping allowed scholars to become more engaged in global history.[37] Historians in Germany also point to the 1990s as the starting point of transnational history as a field. It is no coincidence that German specialists in East Asian history and African history have been among the most active researchers in transnational and global history, given the extent of their critique for the focus on the nation by the German social history dominant in the 1980s.[38] Sebastian Conrad explains that the end of the Cold War stimulated Western scholars to transcend national perspectives and investigate transnational entanglement.[39] Osterhammel and Petersson argue that "in the 1990s, globalization was embraced by a wider public and has since skyrocketed to terminological stardom."[40] In East Asia, as Conrad observes, interest in global history has also "appreciably increased" since the 1990s, which "complements the still dominant national history." These historians look beyond their national parameters and see the potential in East Asian regional history. In South Korea, some have begun discussing "East Asia as a cultural realm." In Japan, some began to "place the Japanese past more firmly in an Asian context." In China, some have shown interest in "networks between Chinese coastal cities and Korean and Japanese cities."[41] Scholars in all three countries have identified new topics, such as migration, cultural globalization, and diaspora.

Most scholars today refer to global history or transnational history, whereas others use related expressions, such as hybridity, entangled history, connected history, intersectionality, transculturality, transfer history, cross-cultural history, and *Verflechtungsgeschichte*, or *histoire croisée*.[42] Some prefer to position their work as transcultural, which emphasizes flows of culture, rather than transnational, which tends to focus on politics.[43] They argue that post–Cold War developments, in particular, favor transcultural over transnational methodologies, for "national ideologies" have been deemphasized and "religion and civilization" have become more prominent categories.[44] In the following, I will use the terms *transnational history* and *global history* interchangeably in exploring their common characteristics. At the end of the discussion, I will briefly explain this volume's

8 Joanne Miyang Cho

slight preference for the methods associated with transnational history over transcultural and/or global history.

In defining transnational and global history, the following three characteristics are particularly worthy of attention. First, transnational history does not emphasize the differences between nations, but instead focuses on points of contact between them. It does not see a given society as a closed unit, but instead as constantly interacting with and being impacted by other nations. It explores contacts and circulation as well as tensions and disputes.[45] Global history also explores "the numerous dependencies and interferences, the interweaving and interdependencies."[46] Its emphasis on interactions between various societies differentiates it from world history, which focuses more on comparing them. Moreover, transnational history rejects the assumption that cross-cultural influences move in one direction only, as is often the case with colonial history, which sees influences primarily as moving from the center to the periphery. Instead, it identifies bi- or multidirectional cultural flows. As Thomas Adam points out, although it can appear that cultural influences are one-directional in the short term, they often become bi- or multidirectional if viewed in a longer timeframe like a century. Transnational history also sees cultural flows as a creative process, not just as a repetition or copy of the original culture.[47]

Secondly, transnational historians reject both international history and social history in engaging with the local and domestic. Various American historians have occupied themselves with international history since the 1970s, with Akira Iriye among them. However, Iriye has, in recent years, turned away from international history and is now a strong advocate of transnational history. In his discussion of their difference, transnational history seeks "cross-national connections," whereas international history studies "relations among nations as sovereign entities."[48] Although both types of history initially appear to have a global scope, since both study other nations, the focus of international history is "on the nation as the key unit of analysis," as exemplified by Paul Kennedy's *The Rise and Fall of the Great Powers* (1987).[49] By contrast, transnational history looks at players from both sides and their interactions.

Iriye has similarly criticized US social history for being overly nation focused. American social historians have "accentuated the exceptionalist interpretation of the national past."[50] If their tendency has been to frame American exceptionalism in a positive light, it has generally been the opposite for German social historians such as Hans-Ulrich Wehler, who criticized the unique qualities of the German past as responsible for the rise of Nazism. Andrew Zimmerman's *Alabama in Africa*, which studies connections between the US, Germany, and Togo, thus chastises both American social historians for acting as boosters for American exceptionalism and German social historians for focusing excessively on domestic politics (the German *Sonderweg*). Unlike the latter, he rejects domestic politics as having been the main determinant of German overseas expansion.[51] Despite

Introduction 9

their good intentions of interrogating the German past critically, these German social historians narrowed the scope of German historical scholarship. Their critics, on the other hand, have highlighted strong globalizing tendencies in Germany during the late nineteenth and early twentieth centuries.[52]

Third, global history and transnational history are critical of the comparative approach. In contrast to Hans-Ulrich Wehler, who regarded "comparison as the highest form of social historical research," advocates of transnational history reject civilizational comparisons as leading to "essentializing models or purely impressionistic observations and generalizations."[53] There is one caveat to this critique, which a number of historians have recently suggested. While they accept that transnational and comparative history are quite different, they do not see them as being necessarily exclusive of each other and even see the potential benefits of comparative history. As Saunier has pointed out, "both approaches can be combined with proof because they help to answer different questions."[54] Indeed, comparative history can be quite useful in regard to some historical topics. After all, transnational historians "have to understand what happens to the ties and flows they follow through different polities and communities."[55] According to Heinz-Gerhard Haupt and Jürgen Kocka, comparative and entangled history are "compatible and have many points of contact."[56] Thus comparisons are acceptable when framed within a global context.

The present volume, *Transnational Encounters between Germany and East Asia*, uses global history and transnational history mostly interchangeably. That said, there is a slight preference for transnational over global, given that this volume's focus is the interrelatedness between countries within two regions, namely Germany and three East Asian countries. While they are important locations in and of themselves, they do not represent the world. By the same token, since the chapters in the volume focus on entanglements between these areas, the emphasis on *trans* in transnational is preferable to global. Also, while transcultural and transnational history are quite similar, this present volume places a bit more emphasis on transnational history, since several chapters in this volume examine the period before 1945, when the category of the nation still remained important. This volume also accepts the aforementioned caveat regarding comparative history as compatible with transnational history, so long as it is properly contextualized. While nine chapters in this volume adopt a transnational approach, the final two chapters take largely a comparative approach, but they do so within clearly defined global contexts.

A historiographical landscape

In recent years, there has been growing interest in German-Asian studies. Since one can find detailed bibliographies on Sino-German, German-Japanese, and German-Korean relations elsewhere,[57] this review of historiography will focus on edited books published since 2000. To start, there

10 Joanne Miyang Cho

are edited volumes that examine German relations with China, Japan, and Korea individually. Secondly, there are edited volumes that treat German relations with East Asia as a whole. In both cases, the edited volumes that cover a century or more will receive particularly close attention in this review, for they are similar to this present volume in terms of chronological coverage. It is exciting to see that more than a dozen such volumes have been published in the last ten years.

In respect to German-Chinese relations, several edited volumes in the *Berliner China Studien* series (published by the Freie University of Berlin) treat diverse topics mostly in German, including politics, culture, missions, colonialism, diplomacy, and military history. Since 2000, two edited volumes have been published in the series. *Deutsch-chinesische Beziehungen im 19. Jahrhundert* [German-Chinese Relations in the Nineteenth Century] (2001), edited by Mechthild Leutner and Klaus Mühlhahn, treats German-Chinese relations in 1890–1910 in the areas of missionary activity and economic relations. *Beiträge zur Geschichte der Beziehungen der DDR und der VR China* [Contributions to the History of the GDR and the PRC Relationships], edited by Joachim Krüger (2002), highlights the broad and intense cooperation between the GDR and the PRC in the political, economic, and cultural arenas. This work includes several authors describing their experiences in the 1950s as diplomats and students.[58] Another series by Freie University, China Hefte/Chinese History and Society, has an edited volume on the topic. *Deutsch-chinesische Beziehungen* (German-Chinese Relations) (2011), edited by Katja Levy, examines the bilateral relationship between China and Germany in the twentieth century.[59]

In English, two edited volumes are of particular interest to this volume due to their long chronological coverage and diverse topics. The first is *Sino-German Relations since 1800* (2000) by two Chinese scholars based in Hong Kong, Ricardo K. S. Mak and Danny S. L. Pau.[60] The second is *Germany and China: Transnational Encounters since 1800* (2014) by two US-based historians, Joanne Miyang Cho and David M. Crowe. While the first book suggests that its time coverage extends to the year 2000, its strength lies in the pre-1945 period, with only one chapter covering the post-1945 period. The second volume has four chapters dealing with post-1945 topics. While the former has one chapter dealing with Sino-German relations prior to the mid-nineteenth century, the latter has three chapters. The former volume has three chapters on Hong Kong but does not include some key topics, such as German-speaking Jewish refugees in Shanghai, whereas the latter manages to present a more diverse range of topics, such as politics, diplomacy, military history, culture and literature, and philosophy.[61]

In German-Japanese relations, two volumes dealing with the topic have appeared in German and English since 2000 in the series Deutsche Gesellschaft für Natur- und Völkerkunde Ostasiens [German Society for Natural and Cultural Studies of East Asia]. *Gelebte Partnerschaft; Deutschland und Japan* [A Living Partnership: Germany and Japan] (2014), edited by

Ruprecht Vondran, examines how Germans and the Japanese learned to appreciate each other's scholarship (*Wissenschaft*) between 1964 and 2014.[62] *Global Governance*, edited by Saori N. Katada, Hanns W. Maull, and Takashi Inoguchi, compares the foreign policy of Germany and Japan in a comprehensive manner.[63]

The following four edited volumes, which have appeared in English since 2006, are of particular interest for this present volume due to their comprehensive approach. *German-Japanese Relations, 1895–1945. War, Diplomacy and Public Relations* (2006), edited by Christian W. Spang and Rolf-Harald Wippich, offers a range of interpretations on bilateral relations between Germany and Japan, but the book's coverage only extends to 1945, and a majority of the chapters focus on military and political aspects of the relationship.[64] *Japan and Germany* (2009), edited by Kudō Akira, Nobuo Tajima, and Erich Pauer, emphasizes economic relations but has little cultural coverage.[65] *Transnational Encounters between Germany and Japan: Perceptions of Partnership in the Nineteenth and Twentieth Centuries* (2016), edited by Joanne Miyang Cho, Lee M. Roberts, and Christian W. Spang, covers the period from the late nineteenth century to the present and includes a variety of well-balanced topics.[66] The latest edited volume, *Mutual Perceptions and Images in Japanese-German Relations, 1860–2010* (2017), edited by Sven Saaler, Kudō Akira, and Tajima Nobuo, presents nuanced interpretations on German-Japanese relations, instead of focusing simply on their similarities, as has been repeatedly the case.[67]

In the field of German-Korean relations, there are some edited volumes in both German and Korean that focus on specific themes. Bonghi Cha and Siegfried J Schmidt's *Interkulturalität* [Interculturality] (2004) examines the idea of interculturality, using examples between Korea and Germany.[68] Three chapters in Klaus Stüwe and Eveline Hermannseder's *Migration und Intergration als transnationale Herausforderung* [Migration and Integration as Transnational Challenges] (2015) probe South Korea and Germany on the related questions of migration and integration.[69] Martin H. Schmidt's *Franz Eckert – Mirok Li – Yun Isang* (2008) discusses the musician Franz Eckert in Korea and the musician Yun Isang and the writer Mirok Li in Germany.[70] In Korean, Chun-Sik Kim's edited volume *Han'guk kwa dog'il, Tong'il yŏksa kyo'yuk ŭl malhada* [Korea and Germany Talk About History Education for Reunification] (2016) analyzes a popular topic in German-Korean relations, namely political division.[71]

In English, Eun-Jeung Lee and Hannes B. Mosler's two volumes appeared in 2015, but they are primarily comparative. *Civil Society on the Move: Transition and Transfer in Germany and South Korea* (2015) examines civil societies in South Korea, Eastern Europe, and the reunified Germany. Likewise, *Lost and Found in "Translation"* (2015) does not deal with transnational exchange but only draws representative examples from Korea and Germany.[72] San-Jin Han's edited volume, *Divided Nations and Transitional Justice* (2012), includes chapters by the Korean president Kim

12 *Joanne Miyang Cho*

Dae-jung and the German president Richard von Weizsäcker concerning the lessons that Germany, Japan, and South Korea can teach the world.[73] However, the first comprehensive examination of German-Korean relations from a transnational perspective can be found in *Transnational Encounters between Germany and Korea*, edited by Joanne Miyang Cho and Lee Roberts (2017). This book attempts to provide a comprehensive examination of German-Korean relations from the 1880s to the present, while covering literature, history, politics, films, architecture, and *manhwa* (Korean comics).[74]

As this overview shows, there are now multiple edited volumes with relatively comprehensive coverage on German relations with these three individual East Asian countries. In the last five years, several edited volumes discussing German relations with all three of these East Asian countries in a single volume have appeared, not including the present volume. There are points of similarity, but also differences between them. *Imagining Germany Imagining Asia* (2013), by Veronika Fuechtner and Mary Rhiel, treats German relations not only with East Asia, but also with South Asia and Southeast Asia, and as a result, East Asia receives only partial attention. Likewise, in *Gendered Encounters between Germany and Asia* (2017), edited by Joanne Miyang Cho and Douglas McGetchin, East Asia receives only partial attention. In addition, this work's focus is narrowly on gender.[75] The work that comes closest to this present volume in respect to scope is *Beyond Alterity: German Encounters with Modern East Asia* (2015), edited by Qinna Shen and Martin Rosenstock.[76] While both volumes are interdisciplinary, cover the period since 1900, and discuss several exciting topics, their respective scholarly emphases and the backgrounds of their contributors are somewhat different. In respect to *Beyond Alterity*, a majority of the contributors are literary specialists, while three of them are historians. All contributors, with the exception of one, are affiliated with North American institutions. In contrast, a majority of the contributors to this volume are historians, while other contributors come from the fields of literature, sociology, Japanology, and Sinology. They are additionally affiliated with institutions in six different countries and thus lend a more diverse perspective to the volume.

Chapter summaries

The volume is organized topically in three parts. Part I ("German Missionaries and German-speaking Jews in China") includes chapters on Chinese "daughters" at the German foundling home Findelhaus Bethesda in Hong Kong, the critical views of two liberal Weimar German missionaries on the Boxer Rebellion, and the German-speaking Jews who came to Shanghai as exiles from Nazi persecution. In Chapter 1, Julia Stone suggests that reconsideration of the role of late Qing transnational encounters is needed in order to understand broader social changes in twentieth-century China.

Introduction 13

One such transition, the erosion of the traditional Confucian family and the growth of the nuclear family, is generally ascribed to indigenous intellectual and political developments. However, the lives of abandoned baby girls raised by German Protestant missionaries at the foundling home Findelhaus Bethesda from the early 1850s to 1919 exposed other forces at work. They highlight the crucial role played by what Henri Lefebvre termed transformative spaces. The parallels between the lives of the missionary-reared foundlings and the "unusual women" in southern Guangdong shed light not just on familial change but also on the processes enabling the emergence of new roles for women in Republican China.

In Chapter 2, Lydia Gerber presents examples of Richard Wilhelm's and Wilhelm Schüler's private letters and published reports, including a sermon that Schüler delivered in Qingdao to commemorate fallen German soldiers. It argues that, through a careful process of editing and selective publication of some of this material in the home board's signature journal, _Zeitschrift für Missionskunde und Religionswissenschaft_, the Weimar Mission was able to deflect the potential impact that the Boxer Uprising might have had otherwise on its missionary enterprise. Instead of excusing the violence of the foreign response as a means of chastising the Chinese in preparation for the gospel, as other missionaries had done, the Weimar Mission ultimately positioned itself as a source for peace and cross-cultural understanding within a context dominated by violence and racism. In particular, Richard Wilhelm's significant role as a cross-cultural communicator between China and Germany began with his mission as peacemaker in the midst of the Boxer unrest.

In Chapter 3, Shambhavi Prakash explores questions of memory and the representation of exile in the two documentaries _Exil Shanghai_ (1997) by Ulrike Ottinger and _Shanghai Ghetto_ (2002) by Dana Janklowicz-Mann and Amir Mann. The two documentaries use interviews with survivors to record the experiences of the Jewish community in Shanghai, including some of the 20,000 central European Jews who fled to Shanghai from Europe during the Second World War. In addition to being the site of multiple colonial administrations, the Shanghai of that time was also flooded with internal refugees fleeing military conflict and natural disasters in other parts of China. Following Michael Rothberg's question, "Does the remembering of one history erase others from view?", this chapter analyzes how these two histories and their memories emerge and intersect in the two cinematic accounts. The theme is further explored by analyzing how the documentaries frame these recollections and representations of Shanghai differently, thus revealing two distinct approaches to history, identity, and memory.

Part II ("Japanese Images of Germany and Transnational Flow between Germany and East Asia") examines how Japanese images of Germany have significantly changed over the past 150 years. It also probes German–East Asian transnational relations related to the questions of urban planning and the environment. In Chapter 4, Toru Takenaka argues that the

14 *Joanne Miyang Cho*

Japanese image of Germans went through significant changes over the past 150 years. Its history can be divided into five periods. In the initial period (1860s–1918), Germany was primarily regarded as a superb model of modernization. In the second period (1918–1945), the Japanese wanted to see in Germany a peer instead of a teacher. In the third period (1945–1980s), relations between the two countries weakened. Around the 1980s, which is the beginning of the fourth period, a remarkable shift occurred; Japan praised Germany as the heartland of ecology and for its quality of life. This was followed by an increasingly sober outlook in the fifth period (since the 2000s). The Japanese have ceased to think highly of Germany. Germany had finally become a normal country in their eyes.

In Chapter 5, Jin-Sung Chun argues that land readjustment, or Lex Adickes, emerged as a model of urban planning specific to the German context. This subsequently provided an effective means of comprehensive urban restructuring in East Asian countries. The so-called German turn in the process of the Westernization of Japan has already been under way since the 1880s, but this method of land readjustment was only partially implemented on the Japanese mainland; indeed, it proved its greatest utility in Japan's overseas colonies. In Seoul, the Japanese authorities instrumentalized this European technique for colonial domination. These trends continued unabated in post-liberation Seoul. The land policies of the Park Jŏng-Hee military government focused on supporting state-dominated economic development rather than the equitable distribution of ownership, and thereby the authoritarian culture of Prussian provenance pervaded the urban milieu of postcolonial Korea in the form of undisguised market economic exploitation.

In Chapter 6, Volker Stanzel analyzes the effect of the Fukushima nuclear accident on German-Japanese relations. Following the accident on March 10, 2010, Japan shut down all of its reactors until it gradually restarted them beginning in 2013. The German government also decided to completely shut down all reactors earlier than they had planned – specifically, by 2022. On this issue, both sides showed marked interest in the decisions taken by the other. Japanese industry interested in regenerative energies and anti-nuclear activists frequently visited Germany. German industry, for its part, tried to sell renewable energy technologies to Japan, and German activists and members of the Green Party tried to influence political decision making in Japan. It is rare that modern democratic societies try to influence each other to this extent; this was due to the emotional shock experienced as a result of the nuclear accident, to the established industrial relationship between both countries, and to the high level of mutual sympathy and interest in both societies.

Part III ("German and Austrian Intellectuals/Writers and East Asia") considers representations of East Asia in the works of four German and Austrian intellectuals and writers. One of these German writers is compared to a Chinese writer. These chapters examine East Asian capitalism, a bourgeois

Introduction   15

writer in Mao's China, and the idea of "transreading women" in literature. In Chapter 7, Keumjae Park reexamines Max Weber's historical analysis of economic institutions and the rationalization of culture, and explores the ways in which the recent success of East Asian capitalism may inspire more complex approaches to analyzing connections between economic systems and culture. Max Weber's conclusion that East Asia's traditional societies and cultures were inadequate in providing the preconditions necessary for the rise of modern capitalism must be reconsidered, in light of the spectacular growth of East Asian economies. The chapter critically examines Weber's concept of "Asian values" as a key formula of economic success and argues that Weber's preoccupation with European society resulted in an ethnocentric oversight as to Asia's potential. At the same time, it cautions against relying upon an ahistorical and reified conceptualization of culture as the key to East Asia's economic success. Instead, the chapter focuses on the ways in which culture was strategically appropriated and mobilized by the state and economic entities for their development and nation-building agenda.

In Chapter 8, Arnhilt Johanna Hoefle shows how, despite being a bourgeois Austrian writer, several historical and biographical texts by Stefan Zweig (1881–1942) were published in China only a few months after the founding of the People's Republic in 1949. Why these translations could still be published under communist censorship is closely linked to the specifics of the literary genre Zweig had devised. In his lecture "History as a Poet" ("Die Geschichte als Dicterin," 1939), he devised a poetology of historical and biographical literature that resonated with ancient Chinese theories of life writing. Moreover, it was also purposefully employed by intellectuals during turbulent times in the 1920s and, in revised form, in the early 1950s. The genre of the biography, in particular, as a hybrid form between literary and historical work, thus played a crucial role in the Chinese reception of Zweig's work.

In Chapter 9, Robert Cowan discusses a thirty-year-old student in his class, Ming Ying, who had a bachelor's degree from a university in Beijing but still found English to be a challenge. When she read Christa Wolf's 1968 novel *Thinking about Christa T.* in his modern European literature class, she was struck by the ways that people in East Germany tried to function ethically within the tremendous limitations imposed upon them. Ming Ying then juxtaposed Wolf's novel to Chen Ran's 1992 novella *Sunshine Between the Lips*, emphasizing the transgressive nature of *fin-de-siècle* Chinese literature. Her "transreading" of Wolf's and Chen's respective versions of the GDR and the PRC prompted her to wonder about the relationships between the individual and the collective, in terms of agency, freedom, and fulfillment. Ming Ying took an approach that was neither pro-Western nor pro-Chinese, but critiqued the dystopic globalization of each, wondering whether women are better able to self-define in one system, or the other, or both, or neither.

16 *Joanne Miyang Cho*

Part IV ("Politics and Sports during the Cold War Era") examines the Allied occupation in West Germany and Japan as well as the nexus of politics and sports in divided Germany and divided Korea. Unlike the earlier chapters, these two chapters are primarily comparative in their approaches, yet they are still firmly anchored in the global contexts of postwar Allied occupation and Cold War politics. In Chapter 10, David M. Crowe examines the Allied occupation of Germany and Japan. Occupation policies varied considerably in each zone, although Britain, France, and the US worked to denazify their zones with an eye toward creating a viable democracy in what would become West Germany. Stalin followed a different path in East Germany, seeing it as a cornerstone of his efforts to create a Soviet empire in Eastern and Central Europe. Yet all of the occupying forces, with the exception of France, adopted aggressive efforts later in bringing German war criminals to justice. The situation in Japan was quite different because the US government, and more importantly, Gen. Douglas MacArthur, was more concerned with encouraging democracy in Japan as a bulwark against the growing communist threat in East Asia than with the question of Japanese war criminality. This, coupled with the collective Japanese horror over Hiroshima and Nagasaki, led Japan to follow a very different path historically when it came to the question of war guilt.

In Chapter 11, Aaron Horton argues, using divided Germany and Korea as examples, that sports are often an extension of political divisions and tensions. Sporting encounters between the two Germanys, primarily in Olympic competition but also occasionally in pan-European soccer club tournaments, were also often politically charged affairs, as was East Germany's famous 1–0 upset of West Germany in the 1974 World Cup, hosted by West Germany. North and South Korea have met numerous times in various sports, and the encounters have often been marred by political issues. In Korea, tensions surrounding sports closely paralleled contemporary diplomatic relations between North and South Korea; in times of reduced tensions, matches passed largely without incident, but in periods of heightened animosity, political differences often manifested on the field. By examining sports competition in divided Germany and divided Korea, the chapter examines the ways in which states use sports as a political tool for promoting their preferred narratives.

In sum, this edited volume seeks to shed new light on German–East Asian relations from 1900 to the present. It explores topics that have already received scholarly attention as well as largely untouched issues in German–East Asian relations, in presenting some of the most recent scholarship on the topics that it treats. It covers topics not only related to politics, literature, history, sociology, and missionary activity, but also in urban planning, migration, and the environment. This volume has endeavored to present both German perceptions of East Asia and East Asian perceptions of Germany in terms of cross-cultural cooperation. Although cultural and informational flows were mostly one-sided, from Germany to East Asia, at the

Introduction   17

beginning of this relationship, it has since become truly bidirectional in recent years, with these countries cooperating actively in many areas. It is surprising how these two geographic spaces, which were so different, could have become so entangled in only around 150 years. With its emphasis on transnational perspectives, this book reflects the shift from nation-focused social history during the 1970s and 1980s to the transnational and global forms of history that have become popular since the 1990s. It is hoped that this volume will stimulate a broader dialogue among readers not only in Germany-speaking countries, North America, and East Asia, but also in other parts of the world.

Notes

1 For a brief overview of German-Chinse relations, see "Introduction," in *Germany and China: Transnational Encounters since 1800*, ed. Joanne Miyang Cho and David M. Crowe (New York: Palgrave MacMillan, 2014), 2–6; David M. Crowe, "Sino-German Relations, 1871–1917," in *Germany and China: Transnational Encounters since the Eighteenth Century*, ed. Joanne Miyang Cho and David M. Crowe (New York: Palgrave MacMillan, 2014), 71–96; Christian Swanson and David M. Crowe, "Sino-German Relations, 1918–1941," in *Germany and China: Transnational Encounters since the Eighteenth Century*, ed. Joanne Miyang Cho and David M. Crowe (New York: Palgrave Macmillan, 2014), 115–38.
2 Cho and Crowe, "Introduction," 2.
3 Ibid., 2–3.
4 Immanuel C.Y. Hsü, *The Rise of Modern China* (New York and Oxford: Oxford University Press, 2000), 348.
5 Ibid., 394, 400.
6 Ibid., 557–58.
7 Irene Eber, *Wartime Shanghai and the Jewish Refugees from Central Europe: Survival, Co-Existence, and Identity in a Multi-Ethnic City* (Berlin: de Gruyter, 2012), 44.
8 Ibid., 44–45.
9 Ibid.
10 Sebastian Gehrig, "Friend or Foe? The People's Republic of China in West German Cold War Politics," in *Germany and China: Transnational Encounters between Germany and China*, ed. Joanne Miyang Cho and David M. Crowe (New York: Palgrave Macmillan, 2014), 224.
11 Ibid., 245.
12 Statisches Bundesamt, "Bevölkerung und Erwerbstätigkeit: Ausländsiche Bevölkerung Ergebnisse des Ausländerzentralresigsters," Fachserie 1, Reihe 2, accessed on August 15, 2017, www.destatis.de/DE/Publikationen/Thematisch/Bevoelkerung/MigrationIntegration/AuslaendBevoelkerung2010200157004.pdf?__blob=publicationFile.
13 For a brief overview of German-Japanese relations, see "Introduction," in *Transnational Encounters between Germany and Japan: Perceptions of Partnership in the Nineteenth and Twentieth Centuries*, ed. Joanne Miyang Cho, Lee M. Roberts, and Christian W. Spang (New York: Palgrave MacMillan, 2016), 1–3.
14 Ibid., 1.
15 Bernd Martin, *Japan and Germany in the Modern World* (New York: Berghahn Books, 1995), xii.

18 *Joanne Miyang Cho*

16 Cho, Roberts, and Spang, "Introduction," 2.
17 Marius B. Jansen, *The Making of Modern Japan* (Cambridge, MA: The Belknap Press of Harvard University Press, 2000), 673.
18 Andrew Gordon, *A Modern History of Japan: From Tokugawa Times to the Present* (Oxford: Oxford University Press, 2014), 244–45.
19 Cho, Roberts, and Spang, "Introduction," 2.
20 The influence of Germany on Meiji Japan can be identified in multiple fields. For instance, the Meiji Constitution was based to a large degree upon the Prussian Constitution of 1850. Its primary author, Itō Hirobumi, consulted German scholars during his visit to Germany in 1883–84 and invited a leading German scholar in law, Herman Roesler, to Japan in 1878. German historical science influenced Japan as well, with Ludwig Riess, a student of Leopold von Ranke, arriving in Japan in 1887. Jansen, *The Making of Modern Japan*, 390–91, 397.
21 Cho, Roberts, and Spang, "Introduction," 2.
22 Ibid.
23 For an overview of Korean-German relations, see Eun-Jeung Lee and Hannes B. Mosler, "130 Years of German-Korean Relations," in *Transnational Encounters between Germany and Korea: Affinity in Culture and Politics in the Long Twentieth Century*, ed. Joanne Miyang Cho and Lee M. Roberts (New York: Palgrave Macmillan, 2018).
24 Eun-Jeung Lee, *Paul Georg von Möllendorff: Ein deutscher Reformer in Korea* (Munich: Iudicium, 2008), 21.
25 Cf. Hans-Alexander Kneider, "Franz Eckert and Richard Wunsch: Two Prussians in Korean Service," in *Transnational Encounters between Germany and Korea: Affinity in Culture and Politics in the Long Twentieth Century* (New York: Palgrave Macmillan, 2018); Kneider, *Globetrotter, Abenteurer, Goldgräber: Auf deutschen Spuren im altern Korea* (Munich: Iudicium, 2010).
26 Lee and Mosler, "130 Years of German-Korean Relations," 31–2.
27 cf. Martin H. Schmidt, ed., *Franz Eckert - Li Mirok - Yun Isang: Bortschafter fremder Kulturen. Deutschland-Korea*, 2nd ed. (Oberursel/Ts., Regardeur, 2010 [2008]).
28 Lee and Mosler, "130 Years of German-Korean Relations," 34.
29 Ibid., 36.
30 Ibid., 39
31 Ibid., 39.
32 Ibid., 36.
33 Ibid., 36–7.
34 Ibid., 40.
35 Ibid., 40–1.
36 Pierre-Yves Saunier, *Transnational History: Theory and History* (New York: Palgrave Macmillan, 2013), 4.
37 Lynn Hunt, *Writing History in the Global Era* (New York: Norton, 2014), 45–46. Ann-Christina L. Knudsen and Karen Gram-Skjoldager (2009) argue that it was only in the 1990s "that the transnational perspective has gained ground in historical research more broadly." "Historiography and Narration in Transnational History," *Journal of Global History* 9, no. 1 (2014), 145.
38 Jürgen Osterhammel, *Die Verwandlung der Welt* (Munich: C. H. Beck, 2009); Dominic Sachsenmaier, *Global Perspectives on Global History: Theories and Approaches in a Connected World* (Cambridge: Cambridge University Press, 2011); Sebastian Conrad, Andreas Eckert, and Ulrike Freitag, eds., *Globalgeschichte* (Frankfurt a. M.: Campus Verlag, 2007); Sebastian Conrad, *Globalisation and the Nation in Imperial Germany* (Cambridge: Cambridge University Press, 2010).

Introduction 19

39 Sebastian Conrad and Andreas Eckert, "Globalgeschichte, Globalisierung, multiple Modernen: Zur Geschichtsschreibung der modernen Welt," in *Globalgeschichte: Theorien, Ansätze, Themen*, ed. Sebastian Conrad, Andreas Eckert, and Ulrike Freitag (Frankfurt am Main: Campus Verlag, 2007), 17. Conrad and Eckert observe that area studies and "a non-Eurocentric and empirically-based world and global history are increasingly approaching each other." Ibid., 13.

40 Jürgen Osterhammel and Niels P. Petersson, *Globalization: A Short History* (Princeton, NJ: Princeton University Press, 2003), 1. The authors published another on the topic in Germany in 2017. *Geschichte der Globalisierung: Dimensionen, Prozesse, Epochen* (Munich: C. H. Beck, 2007).

41 Sebastian Conrad, *Global Geschichte: Eine Einführung* (Munich: C.H. Beck, 2013), 73–74.

42 Madeleine Herren, Martin Rüesch, and Christiane Sibille, *Transcultural History: Theories, Methods, Sources* (Heidelberg: Springer Verlag, 2012), 5; Andrea Komlosy, *Globalgeschichte: Methoden und Theorien* (Vienna: Böhlau, 2011), 63.

43 Dirk Hoerder, "Losing National Identities or Gaining Transcultural Competence: Changing Approaches in Migration History," in *Comparative and Transnational History: Central European Approaches and New Perspectives*, ed. Heinz-Gerhard Haupt and Jürgen Kocka (New York: Berghahn Books, 2009), 258; Thomas Adam, *Intercultural Transfers and the Making of the Modern World, 1800–2000: Sources and Contexts* (New York: Palgrave Macmillan, 2012), 5.

44 Jon Thares Davidann and Marc Jason Gilbert, *Cross-Cultural Encounters in Modern World History* (Upper Saddle River, NJ: Pearson, 2013), 9.

45 See Herren, Rüesch, and Sibille, *Transcultural History*, 6; Komlosy, *Globalgeschichte*, 61.

46 Sebastian Conrad and Shalini Randeria, "Einleitung: Geteilte Geschichte – Europa in einer postkolonialen Welt," in *Jenseits des Eurozentrismus: Postkoloniale Perspektiven in den Geschichts-und Kulturwissenschaften*, ed. Sebastian Conrad, Shalini Randeria, and Regina Römhild, 2nd ed. (Frankfurt a.m.: Campus Verlag, 2013), 39.

47 Adam, *Intercultural Transfers*, 4–5.

48 Akira Iriye, *Global and Transnational History: The Past, Present, and Future* (New York: Palgrave Macmillan, 2012), 15.

49 Ibid., 6–7.

50 Ibid., 14.

51 Andrew Zimmerman, *Alabama in Africa: Booker T. Washington, the German Empire, and the Globalization of the New South* (Princeton, NJ: Princeton University Press, 2010), 1, 3.

52 Sebastian Conrad and Dominic Sachsenmaier, "Introduction," in *Competing Visions of World Order: Global Moments and Movements, 1880s–1930s*, ed. Sebastian Conrad and Dominic Sachsenmaier (New York: Palgrave Macmillan, 2007), 3; Andreas Eckert, "Germany and Africa," in *Comparative and Transnational History: Central European Approaches and New Perspectives*, ed. Heinz-Gerhard Haupt and Jürgen Kocka (New York: Berghahn, 2009), 227.

53 Monica Juneja and Margrit Pernau, "Lost in Translation? Transcending Boundaries," in *Comparative History and Transnational History: Central European Approaches and New Perspectives*, ed. Heinz-Gerhard Haupt and Jürgen Kocka (New York: Berghahn Books, 2009), 107, 110.

54 Saunier, *Transnational History*, 5.

55 Ibid., 8.

56 Heinz-Gerhard Haupt and Jürgen Kocka, "Introduction," in *Comparative and Transnational History: Central European Approaches and New Perspectives*, ed.

20 *Joanne Miyang Cho*

Heinz-Gerhard Haupt and Jürgen Kocka (New York: Berghahn Books, 2009), 2, 19.

57 For Sino-German relations, see Cho and Crowe, "Introduction," 9–11. For German-Japanese relations, see Cho, Roberts, and Spang, "Introduction," 5–7. For German-Korean relations, see Cho and Roberts, "Introduction."

58 Mechthild Leutner and Klaus Mühlhahn, eds., *Deutsch-chinesische Beziehungen im 19. Jahrhundert – Mission und Wirtschaft in interkultureller Perspektive*, vol. 38 of Berliner China Studien (Münster: LIT, 2001); Joachim Krüger, ed., *Beiträge zur Geschichte der Beziehungen der DDR und der VR China: Erinnerungen und Untersuchungen*, vol. 41 of Berliner China Studien (Münster: LIT, 2002).

59 Katja Levy, ed., *Deutsch-chinesische Beziehungen*, vol. 39 of Berlin China Heft/Chinese History and Society (Münster: LIT, 2011).

60 Ricardo K.S. Mark and Danny S.L. Pau, eds., *Sino-German Relations since 1800: Multidisciplinary Explorations* (Frankfurt a. M.: Peter Lang, 2000).

61 Cho and Crowe, *Germany and China*.

62 The associations that were founded to maintain German-Japanese friendship joined forces in 1964 through the VDJG. This is their 50th anniversary volume.

63 Saori N. Katada, Hanns W. Maull, and Takashi Inoguchi, eds., *Global Governance: Germany and Japan in the International System* (Aldershot: Ashgate, 2004).

64 Christian W. Spang and Rolf-Harald Wippich, eds., *German-Japanese Relations, 1895–1945: War, Diplomacy and Public Relations* (London and New York: Routledge, 2016).

65 Kudō Akira, Nobuo Tajima, and Erich Pauer, eds., *Japan and Germany: Two Late Comers on the World Stage, 1890–1945* (Folkestone, UK: Global Oriental, 2009).

66 Cho, Roberts, and Spang, *Transnational Encounters between Germany and Japan*.

67 Sven Saaler, Kudō Akia, and Tajima Nobuo, eds., *Mutual Perceptions and Images in Japanese-German Relations, 1860–2010* (Leiden: Brill, 2017).

68 Bonghi Cha and Siegfried J Schmid, eds., *Interkulturalität: Theorie und Praxis: Deutschland und Korea* (Münster: Lit, 2004).

69 Klaus Stüwe and Eveline Hermannseder, eds., *Migration und Intergration als transnationale Herausforderung: Perspektiven aus Deutschland und Korea* (Wiesbaden: Springer, 2015).

70 Schmidt, *Franz Eckert - Li Mirok - Yun Isang*.

71 Chun-Sik Kim, ed., *Han'guk kwa dog'il, Tong'il yŏksa kyo'yuk ŭl malhada* [Korea and Germany Talk About History Education for Reunification] (Seoul: Nutisup, 2016).

72 Eun-Jeung Lee and Hannes B. Mosler, eds., *Civil Society on the Move: Transition and Transfer in Germany and South Korea* (Frankfurt a. M.: Peter Lang, 2015); Lee and Mosler, *Lost and Found in "Translation": Circulating Ideas of Policy and Legal Decision Processes in Korea and Germany* (Frankfurt a. M.: Peter Lang, 2015).

73 Han Sang-Jin, ed., *Divided Nations and Transitional Justice: What Germany, Japan and South Korea Can Teach the World* (New York: Routledge, 2012).

74 Cho and Roberts, *Transnational Encounters between Germany and Korea*.

75 Veronika Fuechtner and Mary Rhiel, eds., *Imagining Germany, Imagining Asia: Essays in Asian-German Studies* (Rochester, NY: Camden House, 2013); Joanne Miyang Cho and Douglas McGetchin, eds., *Gendered Encounters between Germany and Asia: Transnational Perspectives since 1800* (Cham, Switzerland: Palgrave Macmillan, 2017).

76 Qinna Shen and Martin Rosenstock, *Beyond Alterity: German Encounters with Modern East Asia* (New York: Berghahn, 2014).

Part I

German missionaries and German-speaking Jews in China

1 One family, two systems

How German missionary mothers and their Chinese "daughters" challenged the late Qing Confucian family model

Julia Stone

Imperial China's Confucian family structure is traditionally understood to have fallen victim to attacks initially from the Republican-era New Culture Movement and subsequently from the post-1949 Communist regime. These ensured the rise of the *xiao jiating* (nuclear family, literally small family) model. Recent studies are beginning to question this narrative, redirecting attention to developments in the late Qing.[1] So far, scholars have neglected to investigate the influence of transnational encounters on this process, particularly those involving Western missionary activity. The purpose of this article is to examine the role played by a German Protestant institution whose aim was to introduce the Western nuclear family. It will study the contestation between the two family systems by focusing on a foundling home established in the late Qing by the Pietist *Berliner Frauen-Missionsverein für China* (Berlin Women's Missionary Association for China, or BFM), known as Findelhaus Bethesda (shortened to Bethesda). The lives of girls raised in the institution will be used to explore the erosion of the traditional Confucian family. The extent to which they broke away from the family unit, either with their husbands or alone, will be analyzed. Which couples did so and what may have motivated others to stay? Their choices in terms of places of residence, religion, and economic and social security will be used to measure this. For those breaking away, the factors involved will be isolated, in particular the roles played by Bethesda and its allied Western missionaries in facilitating this step. Widowhood provides a particularly apposite focus for revealing the processes at work. In order to assess whether the findings are applicable to other segments of Chinese society, the specific contexts in which home and the girls it raised were embedded will be considered. The parallels revealed to unorthodox familial practices among the rural non-elite will demonstrate how changes already under way in the late Qing catalyzed the Confucian family's reinvention in the Republican era.[2]

Such a relatively unknown home as Bethesda with an active life span of almost seventy years makes an excellent lens because it reveals details of the lives of the transcultural mediators themselves. From the early 1850s, BFM missionaries in Hong Kong took unwanted infant girls into their care. They raised and then reintegrated them into Chinese society through marriage to indigenous converts. Existing research on the social aspects of missionary work with children in late Qing China has largely concentrated on the replication of the domestic ideal among those educated in Christian institutions such as boarding and day schools.[3] While the conservative and patriarchal BFM's idealized role envisioned girls raised at Bethesda becoming wives and mothers, its goal was more revolutionary – the establishment of Western nuclear families. Ostensibly, this was not the BFM's prime purpose, which was to spread Christianity and to combat female infanticide. Yet its foundling home was constructed as a Western family and the girls, as its "daughters," were trained to reproduce this. The extent to which they and their ethnic Chinese husbands broke away from the traditional Confucian family reveals much about the processes driving social change in China at the turn of the twentieth century.

Married Bethesda girls' lives and their marital relations form a largely untold chapter of entangled transnational history, highlighting the contribution of various spaces to the unraveling of the Confucian family. An analysis of the girls' interactions reaches beyond a pure impact-response perspective to uncover the interwoven nature of German missionary involvement in social change in late Qing China. Bethesda girls married into a number of different settings, both social and geographic. Most girls returned to their region of origin, southern Guangdong, many to the non-elite. Others settled overseas, marrying pastors in Australia and the United States or emigrating with groups to destinations including Borneo and Demerara. In later years, many were able to remain in Hong Kong where Bethesda was situated. Entanglements were created as the girls sought individually and together with their husbands to position themselves in these communities. The different life patterns which emerged show the importance of both finances and space in undermining the traditional family system.

Henri Lefebvre's concept of "transformative space" is crucial in analyzing the processes unleashed by Bethesda in relation to the Confucian family. He argues that space is both a place of conflict for power as well as the object of struggle itself. Lefebvre defines such a space as the meeting point (historical and/or geographical) of two different cultures and their discourses, which jostle with each other. Their contestation produces transformation with the potential for positive change – for individuals, identities, and social hierarchies.[4] In this case, the cultural encounter and disputation over family involves three main groups: the German missionaries who ran Bethesda, their German-socialized Chinese charges and ethnic Chinese socialized to the Confucian family system. Several different spaces were involved: Bethesda and mission stations as walled institutions, the families into which Bethesda girls married, as well as southern Guangdong, Hong Kong, and the overseas Chinese communities in which a number lived. In this chapter, the primary emphasis will be on the Bethesda girls' relations with their new families, which illuminate the grassroots outcome of the contestation in late Qing China. However, first it is important to understand the key differences

One family, two systems   25

and characteristics of the two spaces, Bethesda and the Chinese Confucian family which dominated these transnational mediators' lives.

While not a monolith, the traditional Confucian family did feature certain cultural norms which differed profoundly from Bethesda's. For financial reasons, few families achieved the ideal of five generations under one roof. So most late Qing families were large joint ones (*da jiazu*).[5] Confucian families were patrilineal in structure and patriarchal in power relations, which tied sons into filial obligations. Families in southern Guangdong belonged to larger groups or lineages, and their aims were collective.[6] None of these attributes lend themselves well to measuring the degree to which couples departed from this pattern and established a smaller unit with independent aims resembling a Western nuclear family. Therefore, a more precise description of the traditional Confucian family is required.

Historian Lloyd Eastman's classic definition is applied here. He isolated three different ways in which the late Qing family operated: as a religious unit, an organized form of social security, and an economic unit.[7] By examining how Bethesda's "daughters" (as the BFM termed them) and their husbands affected each of these, the forces either directly or indirectly promoting a retreat from the traditional Confucian family structure become apparent. The easiest area to determine is the religious aspect: to what extent did the girls implement Bethesda's religious unit? Answering this involves examining whether or not the Bethesda dream of its "daughters," not just proselytizing but also creating Christian family dynasties, was realized. The other two questions, relating to the family as an economic and social security unit, are to some degree interrelated. Did the couples choose to stay in the family unit or to leave it? If they did leave, did they turn to Bethesda for help? The couple's/girl's place of residence is a general indicator for all three questions to some degree. Although not totally conclusive, if girls (and/or their spouses) stayed in the husband's native village, they were likely to have remained part of the family's religious, economic, and social security units. Before considering their acceptance or rejection of each of these aspects, the position of Bethesda and the girls it raised in relation to the Chinese family must be understood.

Girls raised at Bethesda occupied an anomalous position in relation to the Chinese Confucian family system and society since they were effectively outsiders. As foundlings, they did not belong to society's main building block, the family unit. Although not genuinely abandoned as the home's narratives suggested, they had been physically excluded from their natal families.[8] Instead, they belonged to a German institution built in a British colony. BFM missionaries believed that Bethesda was a superior replication of indigenous foundling homes known as *yuyingtang*. However, this was not the case, as most late Qing, indigenous child welfare institutions intended the stays of children and babies to be temporary. They worked to rapidly reintegrate infants into families by arranging adoptions or selling baby girls as "daughters-in-law." In contrast, Bethesda had no interest in this circulation and kept its "daughters" outside Chinese society.

26 Julia Stone

BFM missionaries, however, were not aiming to create an institution, as familial models had replaced institutional ones in German child welfare practice and discourse.[9] BFM writings constantly constructed Bethesda as a family. A married couple, known as housefather and housemother, managed the home. The remaining staff, all single women, saw themselves as "mothers." BFM newsletters adopted this language and referred to the girls Bethesda raised as "daughters."[10] Bethesda understood itself in terms of the nuclear family. This was in essence the one (known as *xiao jiating*) demanded by China's New Culture Movement intellectuals in the early decades of the twentieth century.[11] It was characterized by individual choice in marriage, companionate relationship, and economic independence.[12] This was very much at odds with the families most Bethesda "daughters" joined upon marriage.[13]

Marriage formed the meeting point between the two systems and the method of the Bethesda "daughters'" reintegration into Chinese society. Possibly because family was the bastion of this society, indigenous actors constructed the home as such in their dealings. Girls wanting to wed needed to belong to a family, since marriage in the late Qing was still a business arrangement between two families. Therefore, Bethesda both embraced and was ascribed the social role of the bride's family. This paralleled the role accorded to *yuyingtang*, which also brokered marriages.[14] In negotiations with Bethesda, the bridegroom's family recognized the girls, who initially all bore the surname of the current housefather, as his daughters. Other native actors also seem to have accepted the housefather in loco parentis. Rebels in Canton, for example, who captured one Bethesda girl in the wake of the Boxer Rebellion released her immediately when the housefather arrived to request her return.[15] Once married, Bethesda girls became part of their husbands' family, thus making the traditional Confucian family itself a transformative space. Details of these complex interrelations have been sifted from missionary sources, which presents a methodological challenge.

Information used in this analysis is drawn from a study of the BFM's newsletters and annual reports between 1850 and 1919, when the home was closed by the British. Since no Chinese sources with the original voices of the girls and their husbands exist, where present their voices are mediated by the missionaries. They are also subject to the interpretative filter of European languages. In order to overcome these difficulties, the missionary writings are viewed as data following the suggestion of anthropologist Clifford Geertz.[16] Bethesda's reports become sources of raw data from which to reconstruct the girls' lives before and after marriage. Biographies have the advantage of concentrating on actions which are not so directly affected by mediation. These represent a voice in their own right, which gender historian Gail Hershatter terms "an audible trace."[17] Sufficient data for biographies exists for 143 girls reaching the age of nineteen before Hong Kong authorities restricted the home's activities following the outbreak of World War I.[18] Records extend further until Bethesda's closure in 1919, but these provide insufficient details of the girls' married lives. Viewed as a sample, the biographies clearly show the subversion of the Confucian family system on a number of different levels. Before the behavior of Bethesda "daughters" is studied in relation to the three roles of the Confucian family, the part played by their Western socialization in impeding integration must be understood.

While marriage had ensured that Bethesda "daughters" belonged to Chinese society again, their upbringing created conflict which would have made them want to leave their new families. The main flashpoints are all illustrated by the life of On Yi, who married a poor "merchant" (who turned out to be a barber) from southern Guangdong in 1889. Soon after the wedding, the nineteen-year-old wrote to BFM missionaries complaining about being left with her mother-in-law in a remote village far from other Christians. She told them that her mother-in-law had thrown her Bible into the fire.[19] Just two and a half years into the marriage, her husband died and On Yi was forced to flee the family's attempts to sell herself and her baby. By this time, she had unexpectedly developed such a close bond to her mother-in-law that she took her along, creating a new family unit. However, within two years, On Yi was earning so little that she decided to remarry and emigrate.[20] Her life highlights three important factors hindering the incorporation of Bethesda "daughters" into the Confucian family: poverty, relations with their mothers-in-law, and their Christianity.

Two of the forces driving Bethesda "daughters" out of the family were common to late Qing women from the non-rural elite. Poverty was endemic in southern Guangdong and forced many to emigrate as On Yi did. Mothers-in-law were so notorious for abusing daughters-in-law at that time that the problem featured in Republican-era periodicals. However, Bethesda's upbringing had exacerbated this tension by teaching a different model of power in the family. Missions' Inspector Gabriel Sauberzweig Schmidt noted: "Our daughters have difficulty in adopting the correct attitude toward their mothers-in-law, who often live in their son's home, since they have mostly only rendered obedience to Europeans. Furthermore, they have never lived in a Chinese family and have never even had the opportunity of observing the relationship between a mother- and a daughter-in-law."[21] These difficulties could, however, be overcome, as the example of On Yi shows. While power struggles combined with poverty were hampering female participation in many late Qing families, religion, the third factor impeding integration, was not. For Bethesda "daughters," however, this was potentially a huge obstacle.

Bethesda and its girls challenge the Confucian family model: religious, economic, and social security aspects

Bethesda, as a Christian institution, was most conspicuous and deliberate in its assault on the Confucian family as a religious unit. BFM missionaries

28 Julia Stone

expected their "daughters" to form the first generation of Christian families. To this end, Bethesda wed each girl to a native convert. The only ones to avoid this fate were those who died before marriage or, in later years, expressed a wish to remain single. Thus, all first husbands were Christians, at least at the time of the wedding.

Christian beliefs created barriers to integration not just for Bethesda "daughters" into their husbands' family but for them and their husbands into the surrounding community. In addition to being members of a marginalized group, Bethesda "daughters" and their husbands were often both settling into a new community, as the husbands were missionary employees posted to a new location. Rural communities in late Qing China were, as tight cultures with a strong sense of common identity and values tend to be, less welcoming of divergent views.[22] Anti-Christian sentiment was rising in the late Qing, and some Bethesda "girls" had to flee for their lives in "missionary incidents" (*jiao'an*) and in the Boxer uprising.[23] They faced hostility in their everyday lives such as threats against mixed Christian worship and stones thrown at women going to chapel.[24] One couple was fined by village elders for not contributing money to a communal religious service and not worshipping their ancestors.[25] For those Bethesda "daughters" moving into their husbands' non-Christian family, life was also very tough.

Interfamilial clashes arose between some girls and their "heathen relatives," making their refusal to adopt the religious elements of the family unit a major problem. In one particularly severe incident, a Bethesda "daughter" had to hide to escape assault by angry visiting aunts after she pushed over their idol to demonstrate it was dead.[26] As the Bethesda "sons-in-law" also faced opposition from their families, the establishment of a new religious unit was an obvious choice.

Religious conviction is one of the most difficult things to assess from the sources, particularly due to its subjective nature. This is compounded here by the lack of egodocuments, leaving missionary judgments as one of the main extant tools of assessment. Raising the girls in a walled institution, BFM staff were able to shield them from Confucian thinking, which was considered superstitious and idolatrous. The instilling of what was believed to be pure Christianity produced a socialization in German Protestant culture. For this reason, even though Bethesda workers considered few "daughters" had a genuine faith, their strongest identities were, nonetheless, Protestant and Christian.[27]

In order to avoid reliance on missionary judgments, missionary employment is used as a yardstick of religious affiliation. While not full-proof, it can be considered as evidence of adherence to Christianity or at least affiliation to the Christian community.[28] The vast majority of husbands worked for missionary societies and, of those in secular jobs, most were reported to have been good Christians.[29] Even if a lapsed husband left, Bethesda "daughters" remained in Christian circles.[30] Of the sample, only nine girls may have turned their backs on them.[31] Four of these clearly opted out, but

One family, two systems   29

the other five lost contact (and are included since they may have turned their backs on Bethesda).[32] So Bethesda was successful in at least starting (if nominally) Christian families which would fill Protestant churches and send their children to missionary schools.[33] While the odds were against the home being able to realize its vision of family, the behavior of its "daughters" with regard to establishing a new economic unit, the second aspect of the traditional Confucian family, was far less predictable.

Although traditionally rural non-elite women are considered to have little autonomy, fewer than half of Bethesda "daughters" actually remained inside their new families' economic unit.[34] Of these, two major groups with differing motivations are apparent. The biggest, comprising more than half of those staying (23), had married into Christian families. This means that they were perpetuating the Christian dynasties of which the BFM dreamed, except that they were joining the second or even third generation rather than forming the first as anticipated. For such couples, there was less pressure to leave, providing the family was functioning well as an economic unit. The second identifiable group consisted of those who were forced to rely on the family economically because the husbands were poorly paid Hakka Christian workers. Men employed by German missionary societies did not earn enough as sole breadwinners to feed their families, particularly since Bethesda girls were not skilled in household management and work.[35] Therefore, these Bethesda "daughters" integrated into the family economy and performed agricultural jobs. One housefather was rather chastened to find "daughters" married to men considered ideal "sons-in-laws" carrying grass for miles.[36] However, those staying were in the minority.

The majority (49), who did decide to leave the family, turned their backs on its economic unit primarily because of the groom's life choices. In many cases, these had been made prior to marriage (21). Historian Kenneth Pomeranz has noted the importance of geographical separation in enabling Chinese men to escape family control of their finances.[37] Most Bethesda "sons-in-law" came from southern Guangdong, an area of high emigration due to its poverty. Many men, especially Hakkas, had left to seek work elsewhere. Missionaries from Germany's Basler Mission noted that their church in Lilong, one of the villages from which Bethesda had originally received many abandoned girls, was populated by grass widows.[38] Just under half of the Bethesda "sons-in-law" who had left their families had previously lived and made money abroad (9). For the remainder, religious conversion itself may have been the trigger, as it was a springboard to jobs in the growing Protestant subculture.

The lure of professional training and employment opportunities offered by missionary societies was strong enough for many couples to cut their economic ties with the Confucian family. American and British missions had established medical facilities where men could train as doctors, chemists, dentists, or in other medical roles. All missionary societies including the German ones allied to Bethesda were seeking potential pastors, teachers,

30 *Julia Stone*

and evangelists. For the less able, they provided jobs such as chapel overseers and colporteurs (to distribute Bibles and tracts). Since they also offered support to their converts, such societies effectively represented an alternative economic unit to the traditional Confucian family.[39] Bethesda offered a similar possibility of economic support to its "daughters," thereby enabling them to leave their new families both with their husbands and individually.[40]

It was Bethesda's construction of itself as a Western nuclear family which opened the door to the possibility of autonomy for its "daughters." It refused to accept the Confucian system whereby, upon marriage, girls became the property of their husbands' family. Instead, Bethesda considered them its responsibility until their deaths.[41] The cradle-to-grave support Bethesda felt it owed its "daughters" effectively turned the home into a social security unit. They could not have left the traditional family without an alternative. Departing Bethesda "daughters" adopted one of two avenues: firstly, relying exclusively on Bethesda, or secondly, creating their own support network from the Bethesda "family" and the wider missionary/Western community.

Bethesda's own offer of assistance and welfare was available to and used by several different groups of "daughters." This support ranged from finding jobs and providing accommodation to caring for Bethesda "grandchildren." Married "daughters" or their husbands who either had lost their jobs or were in financial difficulties frequently sought Bethesda's help. For those who remained single, the home's aid was equally important – just as natal families were for a special type of single woman in Guangdong (see discussion to follow).[42] Even married "daughters" who were effectively separated from their husbands received help.[43] Therefore, rather than treating their new families and in-laws as the source of their security, most Bethesda "daughters" continued to rely on the home for this. The extent to which the home's self-understanding placed it in direct competition with the Confucian family is most apparent for widowed girls.[44] The options available to this group of women highlight the social changes promoting the erosion of the Confucian family.

Widowhood was a common dilemma for women from poor families in the late Qing as it left them at the mercy of their in-laws. China historian Matthew Sommer notes that remarriage was frequent among the non-elite, where women were effectively sold by their late husbands' family. The latter wished to avoid being left with a financial burden and therefore ignored the Qing-promoted ideal of chaste widowhood.[45] Often the remarriage was against the woman's will. Widows' vulnerability and their poverty were such prominent social issues that many charitable institutions opened for them in the late Qing using names like *qingjietang* (chaste widow hall).[46] While scholars have shown that widows from poor families did seek assistance from outside their husbands' family, sometimes from their natal ones, they remained in a precarious position.[47]

While they often experienced poverty, Bethesda "daughters" had alternatives, unlike many impoverished non-elite widows. Suicide was prevalent among the latter group in the late Qing, as it was perceived to be their only form of agency in the face of pressure to remarry. Although Bethesda's twenty-eight widows were vulnerable, none took their own life. One potentially at risk was On Yi, whose biography has been outlined. Yet when her late husband's family attempted to sell her, she found shelter at a mission station.[48] Since Bethesda's construction of family was based on the autonomous actions of individuals, its "daughters" were never made to remarry against their wishes. Widowed "daughters" could choose to remain single, which the majority (eighteen) of the twenty-eight widows did. Only seven remarried.[49] It was the economic backing of Bethesda which made it possible for them to forge a different path – career widowhood.

Career widows could select from three degrees of dependence on their "natal" family (Bethesda): turning to the home or its allies (extended family), or going their own way. The multiplicity of options was largely due to the training they had received, either directly from the home or through the work experience it had arranged. Potential employers thus included not just Bethesda but also missionary societies from various countries or Western non-Christian employers. The girls made ideal employees as nannies and servants for all three groups, since their socialization had accustomed them to Westerners' emotions and to complying with their rules. Those choosing the latter route were either the most adventurous or possibly less attached to Bethesda.

Not only was it easiest to rely exclusively on Bethesda economically (which could find jobs or provide them within the home), but some "daughters" also developed emotional bonds. Feelings of closeness either to particular staff or to the home itself were exactly what Bethesda had envisaged. Staff had sought wherever possible to maintain ties and correspondence with the girls. One such "daughter" was Yat San (II), who followed Chinese custom by visiting the home with presents on the third day after her wedding (as she would have done for her parents), spending time with each European staff member.[50] A Eurasian girl whose father had placed her at Bethesda as a boarder visited the missionaries repeatedly and sent presents despite leaving on reaching adulthood.[51] By the twentieth century, some of the women who had spent their childhoods at Bethesda treated BFM staff as friends, visiting them for tea or asking them to act as godparents.[52] However, the infrequency with which these bonds are mentioned in BFM reports suggests that such attachments were the exception rather than the rule. For many "daughters," the maintenance of the bonds to Bethesda and the wider missionary community may have been pragmatic, as these constituted their support network.

As girls sought to build a personal network, their "sisters" from the home were a prime focus. Adult "sisters" established a quasi alumni network, offering each other financial, practical, and emotional support. One widow, Ameng, had saved enough money from her own work to loan another widowed "sister" the money to open a school. Others provided assistance

32   *Julia Stone*

in times of illness. In later years, married "daughters" became mediators when tension grew between missionaries in the home and the ever-growing number of unmarried adult "daughters" living there. The married "daughters" sheltered those who had run away from the Bethesda compound and then liaised with the home to resolve the crisis. Unmarried girls also used their "sisters" outside in the community as matchmakers to help them find husbands without Bethesda mediation.[53] Many girls were eager to work or join grooms in areas where there were married "sisters." The ones who had been wed longer assisted newcomers in overcoming homesickness and adjusting to their changed lives.[54] This mutual aid explains why married "daughters" were active in supplying grooms to Bethesda. It gave them a new potential friend/ally nearby. Generally, those men for whom they acted as go-betweens were friends or a husband's relatives, further strengthening their own networks. Given that recent research shows that these women did not sever ties to their natal families upon marriage, attempts by Bethesda "daughters" to build support networks through their "natal" family were not quite as unconventional as they first appear.

The girls' networks extended across a variety of different spaces. In their local operations, they functioned similarly to native place associations. But the "jungle telegraph" reached beyond Hong Kong and southern Guangdong. Two married "sisters," for example, came to greet a newly married girl when her boat stopped in the north of the province en route to her new home in southern Jiangxi.[55] Emigration posed no obstacle to this networking. One émigré to Hawaii, Tai Heong, took the initiative in contacting married "sisters" and missionaries upon arrival.[56] Another, living in the US, wrote to Bethesda that she was sad that her husband would not let a nearby "sister" join in reading the Bible and praying with them.[57] Such mutual support delighted Bethesda staff. Housefather Johannes Müller remarked: "And it is a constant joy to us to see how loyally they stick together, how the better off support the needy, give them work, take them into their homes and how they comfort each other when they are in distress due to tragedy or death."[58] He attributed it to the success of the home's family building. However, the reciprocal aid was also spurred by other factors less pleasing to the home, but of its own making, all relating to integration.

The detachment of Bethesda "sons-in-law" from their families (mainly due to emigration, conversion, and job opportunities), either before or after marriage, had left them and their wives in need of new networks. Many men had chosen to approach the home for a bride as part of this strategy. Deepening their links with Bethesda increased their options in times of difficulty and reduced reliance on the missionary society employing them. They strengthened bonds with the home by getting brides for relatives or friends and maintained ties beyond their wives' deaths. Before the home's closure, a second generation "grandson" was marrying a Bethesda bride.[59]

Unwittingly, Bethesda's own selection of grooms from among those applying for brides had further fueled the need to build independent networks. In the early years, BFM missionaries had based their selection on a man's individual qualities rather than his family's reputation. Furthermore, they had a predilection for men separated from their Confucian unit, as they did not want "heathen" relatives making life hard for the newlyweds.[60] It was not until the 1890s that Bethesda staff fully accepted that this detachment was not advantageous for the girls. However, from this time onward, another factor influenced the increase in the proportion of "sons-in-law" without family ties.

Once again, the BFM'S definition of the ideal groom was the difficulty, generating a degree of pre-programmed social alienation. Bethesda desired and was most likely to accept potential husbands if they were pastors, evangelists, or in other Christian work. Increasing numbers of single male Christian converts gave BFM missionaries a greater choice of grooms and the ability to select those who best fulfilled their ideal. While all Christian converts faced a degree of ostracism, the most fervent were the most marginalized.[61] The correlation between the jobs of husbands and Bethesda girls leaving the families into which they married confirms this. More than two thirds of those exiting had husbands who worked for missionaries. Of these, more than half were pastors/preachers at one point.[62] The remainder worked in Christian medical service or in more menial jobs such as chapel overseers. Therefore, Bethesda's chosen "sons-in-laws" were the least likely to be able to remain in their village communities and Confucian families.

The ostracism Christians faced amplified the need of Bethesda "daughters" and "sons-in-law" for a self-supportive network. As one scholar of Protestant converts in Guangdong, Joseph Tse-Hei Lee, observed, Christian converts needed a strong, supportive community to live out their faith amid such general hostility.[63] Bethesda "sons-in-law" and their wives demonstrate not only the importance of China's Christian subculture but also the spaces it formed in facilitating breakaways from the traditional Confucian family system.

Three spaces for Bethesda "daughters" to shape new lives: Hong Kong, Guangdong, and the mission station

Three spaces highlight the way in which specific locations enabled Bethesda "daughters" to shape new lives and family patterns. In each one, altered power relations enabled departures from Confucian patriarchal norms. The most obvious example was Hong Kong, the site chosen by BFM missionaries, which was one of the most malleable and open in southern China. Among the earliest treaty ports, Hong Kong had developed a diverse culture under the colonial rule of a secularizing but still Christian British power. Physical protection was just one of the benefits enjoyed by Chinese Christians. Much more important for the challenge to the traditional family was the lack of official backing for Confucian orthodoxy. By the early twentieth century, the Christian subculture was sufficiently large for Chinese believers

34 *Julia Stone*

to create their own structures.[64] It provided the best surroundings, not just for career widows, but also for Christian couples. Of the girls married from 1896 to the end of 1916, just under 30 percent lived in Hong Kong.[65] The colony's greater attraction with its increasing numbers of job opportunities and grooms may explain the decrease in emigration among Bethesda girls marrying at this time.[66] Its nature as a treaty port created a society much more cosmopolitan and well suited to "sons-in-law" who had previously lived abroad.[67] A more egalitarian attitude toward women also assisted the autonomous lives of Bethesda's career widows.[68] However, Hong Kong's influence on the life and family choices of Bethesda "daughters" was not as significant as neighboring southern Guangdong.

New social practices emerging from the turn of the twentieth century in southern Guangdong offer signs that all three aspects of the Confucian family were breaking down. Still part of the Qing empire, though on its margins, Guangdong was the region from which most Bethesda "daughters" originated and to which most returned.[69] Its geographical position meant that Confucian orthodoxy was not so easily imposed on social relations. Particularly evident from the 1890s onward was what one anthropologist has termed a "highly un-Confucian range of marital and residential choices" for women there.[70] These ranged from delayed transfer and compensation marriages to other practices more clearly identifiable as marriage resistance. The former behavior termed *bu luo jia* involved women not switching to their husbands' home directly after the wedding, as was the norm. Instead, they waited months or even years, often until the first pregnancy. Due to the unusual opportunities it provided for alternative lifestyles among women, southern Guangdong fits Lefebvre's definition of a transformative space.

Social acceptance also emerged in the region for a new family pattern enabling single women to establish their own economic unit and become self-supporting.[71] This was variously referred to as *zishunü* or *gupo* and involved a public ceremony declaring a woman's desire not to marry.[72] While some of these women in southern Guangdong stayed in their natal homes and contributed to their biological families' economic unit, others left it. They took advantage of female-only spaces such as vegetarian halls (*zhai tang*) and girls' houses (*nüjian/nüwu*). The latter existed throughout Guangdong, and girls aged ten years and upward were allowed to move there before marriage.[73] The vegetarian halls provided networks upon which single women could build in order to support themselves financially.[74] Thus, they acted as a form of social security organization. Such was the strength of the status of single women in the Pearl River Delta region that the traditional male-dominated Confucian religious unit was forced to accept the worship of single women.

Although there is some disagreement over their origins, scholars concur that new forms of female agency were promoted by the Pearl River Delta area silk boom from the late nineteenth century to the early 1930s. Marxist anthropologist Hill Gates makes a strong case that the emergence of more independent women was connected to the demand for female labor and notes similar unusual marriage patterns in northern Taiwan, where girls worked in the tea industry.[75] Other scholars have suggested that spinsterhood and delayed marriage transfer were linked to non-Han peoples, had a longer tradition predating the silk boom, and may have existed in other areas.[76] It is difficult to assess the extent to which population issues and non-Han peoples affected or mutually reinforced each other in contributing to female autonomy and the erosion of the traditional Confucian family in the region.[77] Whatever the root causes, women in southern Guangdong were challenging the economic and social security elements of the family.

Seen in this context, Bethesda's proximity to and connections with southern Guangdong was propitious for single "daughters" seeking to exploit new spaces. From the turn of the century a growing number of them went to the Pearl River Delta region, where, starting in 1906, a former BFM missionary, Lydia Borbein, was working.[78] In this case, developments in the region and those among Bethesda girls were probably self-reinforcing. Bethesda, for example, followed the lead of a nearby German mission in borrowing the *zishunü* ceremony for what it called its "sworn spinsters."[79] These were girls who had pledged not to marry but to devote themselves to their work.[80] The major difference between the two was that the work of Bethesda "daughters" was seen as having a spiritual, not purely financial, end. Similarly, Bethesda's career widows present a parallel to the area's widows who joined vegetarian halls. Another highly significant space, from which Bethesda "daughters" benefited but which lay beyond the reach of southern Guangdong's (non-Christian) non-elite, was the mission station.

Due to the levels of rejection we have discussed and problems with non-Christian families, the mission station provided the third key space for the autonomy of Bethesda "daughters" and "sons-in-law." While the husbands' moves there were often enforced because of their Christian work, wives joining them represented a break with Confucian family norms. Spouses usually stayed in the husband's village if he emigrated to find work. Bethesda girls welcomed making homes at mission stations. Among the advantages was living alongside Westerners from whom Bethesda "daughters" sought friendship and emotional support.[81] One extreme example of this was Tschung Tscheng, who chose to spend her first Christmas after marriage there, apart from her husband, after having a major falling-out with her mother-in-law.[82] The mission station most closely resembled the home in which Bethesda girls had been brought up. One missionary described it as "a small world of its own. It is like a piece of Europe in the midst of the Chinese world."[83] Fellow residents were the type of Chinese with whom Bethesda "daughters" were most likely to bond – indigenous believers from mission backgrounds with Western socialization.[84] Apart from being fertile ground for network building, mission stations also provided a base for believers to develop family patterns which ran against Confucian norms. Here, Christian culture and the concept of the Western nuclear family were dominant. The significance

36 Julia Stone

of such spaces becomes apparent when common features shared by both Bethesda "daughters" and the female ground-breakers in southern Guangdong are examined to determine catalysts for the erosion of the traditional Confucian family.

Unorthodox family patterns: transnational forces and transformative spaces

Breaches in Confucian family norms were not restricted to Bethesda "daughters" and *zishunü/gupo* but were also exhibited by other members of the non-elite. As governmental authority became more difficult to enforce at the local level in the late Qing, Confucian norms developed greater fluidity among the poor. Deviations like unusual male marriage patterns as part of poverty survival strategies are now coming to light. China historian Matthew Sommer has even suggested that the judicial evidence for polyandry (a woman having more than one husband) and wife-selling that he has uncovered may be the tip of the iceberg. Magistrates accepted the need for such strategies and tacitly allowed non-elite families to peacefully negotiate their own non-conforming norms.[85] Research on these strategies is in its infancy and the contribution here is to isolate the triggers for the unorthodoxy of Bethesda "daughters" and the rural non-elite in southern Guangdong by considering what they had in common.

Poverty stands out as the reason for unorthodoxy in Sommer's sample and was a salient characteristic prevalent within both groups. However, it cannot account for all the un-Confucian marriage patterns and lifestyle choices discussed here. For both Bethesda's "offspring" and families with *zishunü/gupo*, other factors were at play. Anthropologists have suggested that the unusual marriage practices may have initially developed as status markers.[86] Furthermore, the uncommon marital forms in the Pearl River Delta were not linked to poverty. The region was actually flourishing economically in the midst of a silk industry boom, which paid well the young unmarried women who became *zishunü/gupo*. Their unorthodox behavior benefited both themselves and their natal families financially, which is why such un-Confucian practices and delayed marriage transfer were supported. The prospect of well-paid jobs was also what encouraged many Bethesda girls and their husbands to leave the family's economic unit. Similarly, Bethesda's lifelong support package gave widows the opportunity to free themselves from the family and resist remarriage, if they so wished. Therefore, factors other than poverty common to southern Guangdong's non-elite and Bethesda "daughters" must be sought.

Marginalization constitutes one such shared characteristic, which played a major role in the detachment of Bethesda "daughters" from the Confucian family. Both they and the area's non-elite women were of low social status (which was compounded by their gender) and lived on the margins of the Qing empire. The degree of marginalization experienced by Bethesda "daughters" was especially profound due to their foundling background, Christianity, and Western socialization. As ill-fitting outsiders never firmly embedded in the traditional family, their chances of breaking from Confucian norms were high.

Combining with extreme marginalization in the case of Bethesda "daughters" was another divisive element created by their transnational exposure: individualism. BFM missionaries had inculcated this unintentionally with their Pietist brand of Protestantism. Central to Pietism was the anti-establishment belief in the importance of the individual Christian and his/her relationship with God. It was up to each person to hear God for her/himself and act according to the particular plan carved out for that person. These tenets explain why Bethesda curtailed its own power monopoly and allowed its "daughters" to take decisions against the staff's wishes and vision of creating wives and mothers. Grown-up "daughters" were seen as autonomous actors and therefore granted vetoes for the most important decisions in their lives – first to Bethesda's proposed groom and later to getting married or remarried.[87]

Such individualistic thinking increased the likelihood of Bethesda "daughters" taking decisions in their own best interests rather than that of the larger family into which they had married. They applied the BFM belief into which they had been socialized which made God's plan paramount rather than the continuation of the family. Therefore, they did not see the necessity to sacrifice their own personal needs to this end. Their individualism led to a readiness to think in smaller, nuclear family units and was the force propelling so many to develop unusual family patterns such as those of career widows. Bethesda "daughters" clearly possessed an unusually high degree of individualism, one which could possibly have been shared by the mould-breakers in southern Guangdong.[88] Individualism alone, however, would not have been sufficient to cause the erosion of the Confucian family, particularly in the case of Bethesda "daughters," had transformative spaces not existed.

Transnational influences and their contestation in late Qing China created transformative spaces both directly, as with treaty ports, and indirectly. Metropolises, which were growing both in size and number, are an example of the latter. They underwent cosmopolitanization through the influences of both Western colonial powers and émigrés returning from North America and Australia. Such settings fostered the weakening of the social control of the Chinese government, thus assisting the development of nuclear families, independent of the larger Confucian family. Hong Kong, for example, facilitated the birth of new kinds of family dynasty, not just Bethesda's desired Christian one, but also Eurasian family dynasties.[89] Mission stations provided a similar opportunity for new family forms on Chinese soil as they

38   *Julia Stone*

enjoyed de facto extraterritoriality. All these spaces also affected the native region of *zishunü/gupo*.

Southern Guangdong had close links to extraterritorial spaces, possessing both mission stations (many rural), the treaty port of Canton, and good boat links to Hong Kong. Anthropologist Helen Siu notes the effect of both the multi-ethnic British colony and city culture on the Pearl River Delta.[90] It too was contested space inhabited by three different Han peoples, Punti, Hakka, and Dan (sometimes called Tanka).[91] Thus, southern Guangdong's intercultural and transnational entanglements provided fertile soil for transformation.[92]

The potential of the transitive space of southern Guangdong for positive change in the late Qing is demonstrated through the lives of both *zishunü/gupo* and Bethesda "daughters." They show the innovation and restructuring which was possible for individuals, identities, and hierarchies, particularly in marginalized groups (in this case, women). Given Bethesda's own patriarchal beliefs and desire to form Christian families, sworn spinsters, career widows, and separated women were not first choices for its "daughters." They blossomed due to cultural borrowing – both from Bethesda and from the new forms created by women in southern Guangdong. Bethesda girls adopted networks similar to those in the area's vegetarian halls whose sisterhood model they copied in their adaptation of the Bethesda family. The Bethesda sisterhood also bore a close resemblance to the form operated by *zishunü/gupo*. Southern Guangdong thus highlights the key role of transformative spaces played as breeding grounds for new forms in the erosion of the traditional Confucian family.

The fusions patterned by Bethesda girls in southern Guangdong demonstrate processes that were under way but rarely featured in official historiographies. They lend weight to Helen Siu's supposition that apparent gender anomalies to a Confucian mindset may turn out to be more widespread than currently believed. Like Matthew Sommer, she suggests that the perceived unorthodoxy, in this case delayed marriage transfer, may have been the regional norm.[93] While further research is needed on this, Bethesda girls' lives clearly provide another example of individuals and groups who transgressed boundaries without articulating a conscious challenge to normative behaviors in the late Qing.

Ultimately Bethesda girls and the *gupo/zishunü* of southern Guangdong were able to adopt unorthodox lifestyles because of the transformative spaces they inhabited. These transformative spaces were like the Petri dishes of a laboratory where new cultures can grow in a specific atmosphere. The lives of Bethesda "daughters" exhibit the emergence of one such culture, promoted by their missionary "parents." They also help to explain the silent revolution in southern Guangdong and other spaces in late Qing China, which led to the sudden toppling of Confucian family norms in early Republican China.

Notes

1 Susan Glosser, *Chinese Visions of Family and State 1915–53* (Berkeley: University of California Press, 2003), 1.
2 This paper is not arguing that the structure collapsed but that the norms and the family were permanently altered.
3 Dana Robert, "The 'Christian Home' as Cornerstone of Anglo-American Missionary Thought and Practice," in *Converting Colonialism, Visions and Realities in Mission History, 1706–1914*, ed. Dana Robert (Grand Rapids, MI: Eerdmans, 2008), 141. See also Marjorie King, "Exporting Femininity, Not Feminism: Nineteenth-Century US Missionary Women's Efforts to Emancipate Chinese Women," in *Women's Work for Women: Missionaries and Social Change in Asia*, ed. Leslie Flemming (Boulder, CO: Westview Press, 1989), 128.
4 Henri Lefebvre, *La production de l'espace* (Paris: Editions Anthropos, 1974), 8. Lefebvre stressed the importance of a historical analysis of space, which he carried out from a Marxist perspective. His concept of space is particularly relevant because it is designed to help understand processes of modernization and urbanization-which southern China was undergoing during the period studied. I would like to thank Maria Jaschok for drawing the importance of this work to my attention.
5 Joint families are ones where many generations live together in one household.
6 Most Chinese men and women were not independent actors but part of family strategies. See Bryna Goodman and Wendy Larson, "Introduction: Axes of Gender: Divisions of Labor and Spatial Separation," in *Gender in Motion: Divisions, Cultural Change in Late Imperial and Modern China*, ed. Bryna Goodman and Wendy Larson (Lanham, MD: Rowman & Littlefield, 2005), 19.
7 Lloyd Eastman, *Family, Fields and Ancestors: Constancy and Change in China's Social and Economic History, 1550–1949* (New York: Oxford University Press, 1988), 15.
8 In many cases, particularly from the 1890s onward, it is clear that parents were strategically placing their daughters at Bethesda.
9 These were popularized in Protestant circles by the *Rettungshausbewegung* and *Rauhes Haus* started by Johann Hinrich Wichern (1808–1881) in 1833.
10 In this work, the terms "daughters" and girls are used because they are more appropriate than more neutral terms such as products or inmates, which do not give the correct impression of the institution.
11 The New Culture Movement can be considered to have lasted from 1915–23.
12 Gender historian Susan Glosser defines it as predicated on free marriage choice, economic independence and physical separation from the joint family, promising the fulfillment of individual potential. Glosser, *Chinese Visions*, 9.
13 See below for further details of the grooms. The only exceptions were the four who married pastors abroad whose families had adopted the nuclear model.
14 For example, "育嬰善局遺議" "Yuying shanju yiyi" [Outstanding Suggestions on Benevolent Bureaus for Nurturing Children], *Shenbao*, January 25, 1889, 1. A girl from Shanghai who had been involved in prostitution was sent to the *yuyingtang* to be married off.
15 M 01, 3:90–1. Annual reports (*Jahresberichte des Berliner Frauen-(Missions-)Vereins für China*, shortened to *JB*) and quarterly newsletters (*Mitteilungen des Berliner Frauen-(Missions-)Verein für China*, shortened to *M*) are numbered from 1850 using that as year 1. For newsletters, the second number is the quarter of the year. Hence the third quarter of 1871 for the above report.
16 Clifford Geertz, *The Interpretation of Cultures: Selected Essays* (New York: Basic Books, 2000).

40 *Julia Stone*

17 Gail Hershatter points out that the traces are present but that the women involved are unable to represent themselves in the discourse, see *Dangerous Pleasures: Prostitution and Modernity in Twentieth-Century Shanghai* (Berkeley: University of California Press, 1997), 26, 4.

18 The sample represents those born up to the end of 1895. They would have been 19 by the time war broke out when records became patchier as they could no longer be directly sent to Germany. Certain samples have been reduced slightly in size where insufficient information existed. The data used for this paper is based on biographies compiled as part of research for my dissertation thesis published as *Chinese Basket Babies: A German Missionary Foundling Home and the Girls It Raised (1850s–1914)* (Wiesbaden: Harrassowitz, 2013).

19 *JB* 39:116–118, *M* 90, 3:84.

20 The fate of her mother-in-law is not recorded. *JB* 42:94, 96 & 100 and *M* 94, 1:15.

21 *bmw* 1/6602, 1905–10, China Allgemeines Band 1, *Visitationsbericht des Missionsinspektors Sauberzweig Schmidt*, Hong Kong, May 23, 1905, 17 (held in the Archiv des Berliner Missionswerkes and abbreviated to *SS* in future references). All quotes have been translated by the author from the original German.

22 Other marginalized groups, such as the Hakkas and religious sects, were the most open to Protestantism.

23 Seven had to flee mission stations at Sheklung and Tungkun (*M* 72, 1:30, *JB* 21:12, 14 & 19 and *M* 94, 2:32). Three married women took flight in the Boxer uprising (*M* 00, 3:86).

24 *JB* 36:110.

25 *M* 86, 3:88.

26 *M* 83, 1:17.

27 For more on the girls' socialization, see Stone, *Chinese Basket Babies*, 160–64 and on their nominal Christianity, ibid., 63–64.

28 The number of girls with a fervent Christian faith was small and most were nominal Christians, see Stone, *Chinese Basket Babies*, 63–64.

29 Seventy-five were in missionary employment and only 42 in secular positions. Of these, all but nine were said to be good Christians.

30 Their use of these as support networks will be considered in what follows.

31 One example of the difficulties of escaping from the Christianity inculcated by Bethesda is the rebel A-Tschung. At fourteen, she tried to run away and compared herself to a "lost sheep" (see *M* 79, 2:55). However, later in life, her letters to missionaries clearly show a Christian mindset and her relationship to her husband became strained after he lapsed in his faith; see Stone, *Chinese Basket Babies*, 105.

32 Of the five who lost contact, two had emigrated. Of the nine, two ran away before marriage.

33 There are only a handful of cases where "daughters" are described as "lost souls," their salvation is doubted, or they are accused of "heathen" practices like selling their children.

34 Forty out of a sample of eighty-nine (reduced after excluding all those with insufficient details or who never married due to premature death, runaways and those staying single for other reasons).

35 Anglo-Saxon missionary societies paid nearly three times as much (see *SS*, 20 & 16). Twelve women stayed in Hakka families throughout their lives, but a further six left only together with their husband for emigration or upon widowhood.

36 *M* 89, 2:53–54 & 56. Bethesda staff used the term "sons-in-law" to apply to the husbands of their "daughters."

37 Kenneth Pomeranz, "Women's Work and the Economics of Respectability," in *Gender in Motion: Divisions of Labor and Cultural Change in Late Imperial*

and Modern China, ed. Bryna Goodman and Wendy Larson (Lanham, MD: Rowman & Littlefield, 2005), 257. He discusses the curbs preventing men from controlling their own income.

38 One of the standard works on the society notes skewed sex ratios among converts as early as 1875 and blamed Lilong's small congregation size in 1915 on male emigration. Wilhelm Schlatter, *Geschichte der Basler Mission 1815–1915* (Basel: Missionsbuchhandlung, 1916), 317–18, 387.

39 Although the social status is not known for all Bethesda "sons-in-law," the attraction of missionary employment appears unconnected to the family's social standing. Of the twenty-two men whose social status is apparent, twelve were high and ten were low (although another seven could be added to the low classification because of their Hakka identity).

40 Sometimes personal missionary accounts reveal the hidden background, such as women who were effectively living separated from their husbands.

41 This had led the home in 1869 to refuse to take blind girls or those with other physical and mental challenges.

42 For the importance of natal families for sworn spinsters (*zishunü*) in Guangdong, see Maria Jaschok and Suzanne Miers, "Women in the Chinese Patriarchy System: Submission, Servitude, "Escape and Collusion," in *Women and Chinese Patriarchy: Submission, Servitude and Escape*, ed. Maria Jaschok and Suzanne Miers (Hong Kong: Hong Kong University Press, 1994), 47.

43 Stone, *Chinese Basket Babies*, 134–36.

44 Girls struggling financially while their husbands were still alive also received help. However, the vast majority did not use it to actually leave their husbands but rather to find jobs to supplement their income.

45 See Matthew Sommer, *Polyandry and Wife-Selling in Qing Dynasty China, Survival Strategies and Judicial Interventions* (Oakland: University of California Press, 2015), 9–10. Qing officials were pushing for not only elite but also non-elite widows to remain in the deceased husband's family in what was constructed as fidelity to him. Despite the mushrooming of rewards for chaste widows, families frequently took a more pragmatic approach.

46 In addition to providing welfare, their function was to try to enforce Qing sexual mores.

47 Both the affines and the uterine family (i.e., mother and siblings) were important to poor women. Wing-hoi Chan suggests that the power of patriliny may have been exaggerated. See "Women's Work and Women's Food in Lineage Land," in *Merchants' Daughters, Women, Commerce and Regional Culture*, ed. Helen Siu (Hong Kong: Hong Kong University Press, 2010), 81.

48 *JB* 42:94, 96.

49 Three widows were excluded due to a lack of detailed records. Age was clearly also a key factor in remarriage decisions.

50 *M* 09, 2:75.

51 For example, see *JB* 37:135 & *M* 89, 1:14.

52 There were also social visits like that of the house parents to Sun Yeung and Tak Shin *M* 87, 2:58. Indeed, there is evidence that girls took ownership of Bethesda, making financial contributions to the work and giving opinions on the school.

53 See Stone, *Chinese Basket Babies*, Chapter 4. Married girls appear to have also acted as go-betweens to ensure Bethesda's acceptance of the match already made by the girl herself, for example in *M* 13, 2:83.

54 Newly-married Tsin Koi, for example, was comforted by visits from A Seng. *JB* 39:116.

55 *M* 03, 2:99.

56 Other married "daughters" in the US also kept in touch (*M* 92, 3:50) and one, A Teng, visited all girls in Honolulu (*M* 09, 3:104).

42   *Julia Stone*

57 *JB* 24:41–42.

58 *M* 06, 4:146.

59 *M* 13, 3:79. This wedding may never have taken place as nothing more was mentioned. One widowed "son-in-law" continued to actively cultivate the relationship and still sent prospective grooms to the home (*M* 16, 2:38). Several sets of brothers got brides from Bethesda, some applied together (*M* 87, 2:66) or younger siblings would follow the example of older ones (*M* 74, 1:7 & *M* 92, 1:9–10).

60 Men applying to Bethesda for brides were first judged on their Christian and character credentials based on the references provided. If deemed acceptable, staff decided together which girl would be most suited. Against Chinese notions of propriety, the pair then had the opportunity to see each other at a missionary-mediated meeting where each was questioned by staff in the hearing of the other. Both the man and woman could then decide whether to go ahead with the marriage.

61 One such fervent groom asked questions about the state of his wife's soul and prayer life during the engagement process (*M* 91, 2:47). Another wrote asking his bride to serve God "with a fiery heart" (*M* 88, 1:31).

62 Thirty of forty-four were married to Christian workers. Almost all girls married to Christian workers after 1893 left their husband's families, at the latest upon widowhood.

63 Joseph Tse-Hei Lee, "Gospel and Gender: Female Christians in Chaozhou, South China," in *Pioneer Chinese Christian Women: Gender, Christianity, and Social Mobility*, ed. Jessie Lutz (Bethlehem, PA: Lehigh University Press, 2010), 191.

64 The man who served as Chinese pastor at the foundling home, Wong Yuk-cho, became pastor of the To Tsai Church (Independent Chinese Church of Hong Kong). Many Protestant missionary societies had bases in the colony as did Catholic groups.

65 Too little information exists for marriages after 1916. The sample of girls marrying between these dates, excluding those for whom there was too little information (four, due in all but one case to late marriage) is 62. Of those, 18 settled in Hong Kong or Kowloon.

66 The plentiful nature of educated Christian grooms in Hong Kong seeking brides like Bethesda's was one of the arguments used by an RM missionary in 1906 (*RMG* 3.043:21 at Vereinte Evangelische Mission in Wuppertal) for the home not moving to mainland China.

67 Overseas Chinese often found it too difficult to readjust to life in their home communities and preferred to live in Hong Kong.

68 The growing importance of women is evidenced by the listing of daughters and granddaughters on the grave stones of Hong Kong Christians, see Carl Smith, *Chinese Christians: Elites, Middlemen and the Church in Hong Kong* (Hong Kong: Hong Kong University Press, 2005), 207 & 202.

69 At some point in their lives, 88 of the 129 girls born before 1896 for whom information is available did return to southern Guangdong.

70 Rubie Watson, "Girls' Houses and Working Women: Expressive Culture in the Pearl River Delta, 1900–41," in *Women and Chinese Patriarchy: Submission, Servitude and Escape*, ed. Maria Jaschok and Suzanne Miers (Hong Kong: Hong Kong University Press, 1994), 26. For a discussion of the timing see Li Shuping and Gong Huihua, "Qianxi Qingmo Minchu Zhujiang Sanjiaozhou zishunü de hunyinguan" [A Brief Analysis of the Attitudes to Marriage of the Late Qing and Early Republican Era Pearl River Delta Sworn Spinsters], *Guizhou Shehui Kexue* 238, no. 10 (2009): 118 and Helen Siu, "Where Were the Women? Rethinking Marriage Resistance and Regional Culture in South China," *Late Imperial China* 11, no. 2 (1990): 36–37.

One family, two systems 43

71 Prior to this, only girls who became Buddhist or Daoist nuns (or Catholic virgins) or who were sold to brothels remained unmarried. For family support of their daughters' un-Confucian behavior, see Siu ("Where Were the Women?" 33, 38–39) and Watson (*Women and Chinese Patriarchy*, 36).

72 The term *gupo*, was also used for sworn spinsters, often interchangeably with *zishunü*. Sometimes a distinction was made between the former, defined as women who had experienced limited non-sexual contact to men, and those who had not (*zishunü*), see Maria Jaschok, "On the Lives of Women Unwed by Choice in Pre-Communist China: Research in Progress," *Republican China* 10, 1a:42–55 (1984): 45–46.

73 Spinster houses were often referred to as *gupowu*. The girls' houses also served the function of preparing teenage girls for marriage.

74 Women who had previously been married could join vegetarian halls, which were lay religious sisterhoods where members enjoyed more freedom than nuns and earned their own living. For more on their roles see Hill Gates' discussion of previous scholarship. *China's Motor, a Thousand Years of Petty Capitalism* (Ithaca, NY: Cornell University Press, 1996).

75 Gates, *China's Motor*, 94. The position of women may also have been strengthened by male emigration as Wing-hoi Chan has shown for their economic roles in Chaozhou, eastern Guangdong, see Siu, *Merchants' Daughters*, 77–100.

76 Anthropologist Helen Siu and other scholars believe that the delayed transfer practice may well have developed among indigenous peoples in southwestern China. Siu argues that it spread to part of Guangdong's Han population in the late eighteenth/early nineteenth century and acted as a status marker until it became more widespread during the silk industry boom ("Where Were the Women?" 48–53). Liu Zhiwei has concluded that female-centered cultural tradition, which she calls indigenous culture, extended beyond Guangdong and Guangxi to marginal areas of central and northern China. "Women's Images Reconstructed: The Sisters-in-Law Tomb and Its Legend," in *Merchants' Daughters, Women, Commerce and Regional Culture*, ed. Helen Siu (Hong Kong: Hong Kong University Press, 2010), 34–37. More research is needed on this.

77 For consideration of these various aspects see Liang Qizi, "Pingjie youguan Zhujiang sanjiaozhou hunyin zhidu de liang zhong jinzuo" [Review of Two Recent Works on Marriage Systems in the Pearl River Delta], *Xin Shixue* 2, no. 4 (1991): 163–68; Li Ningli and Zhou Yurong, "Zhujiang Sanjiaozhou "zishunü" xingqi beijing tanxi" [Investigating the Rise of the Pearl River Delta 'Sworn Spinsters'], *Yunnan Shehui Kexue* 4 (2004): 89–93; Siu, *Merchants' Daughters*, 34–36.

78 Twenty-three of the sixty-two girls married between January 1896 and December 1916 went there.

79 Bethesda girls fit both Jaschok's description and example of a *zishunü* ("On the Lives of Women," 46–47). See M 98, 3:73 for the ceremony undergone by one Bethesda girl. The Basler Mission (Basel Missionary Society) had previously held one in 1889 (M 90, 1:23).

80 This breach in Bethesda's policy of compulsory marriages for girls began in the early 1890s when several were sent to Canton for expensive training as doctors.

81 Bethesda was happy with this, see M 05, 3:97–8. Female Western missionaries and adult Bethesda girls such as Mrs Leonhardt and A Yan and Tschung Schang and Anna Zahn formed friendships which were recorded. See Anna Zahn, *Schwesternarbeit in China* (Gütersloh: Bertelsmann, 1907) and M 98, 1:4–5.

82 M 03, 2:104–5.

83 Zahn, *Schwesternarbeit*, 19.

84 For example, one Bethesda "daughter" immediately struck up a close friendship with a girl who had grown up in the Basel Missionary Society's boarding school upon arrival at her nurses' training school (M 96, 1:14).

44 *Julia Stone*

85 Sommer argues that only the cases where conflict arose were actually documented, otherwise magistrates did not intervene. *Polyandry and Wife-Selling*, 11–18.
86 Siu, "Where Were the Women?" 53.
87 While it could not have stopped the adult "daughters" from getting remarried, Bethesda could have hindered their lives as career widows by refusing to help them find jobs or to provide any kind of support.
88 More research is needed to establish whether this is the case.
89 For Eurasian ones, see Emma Jinhua Teng, *Eurasian, Mixed Identities in the United States, China and Hong Kong, 1842–1943* (Berkeley: University of California Press, 2013), 107–11 and Josephine Kai-kuen Wong, "The Eurasian Way of Being a Chinese Woman: Lady Clara Ho Tung and Buddhism in Prewar Hong Kong," in *Merchants' Daughters, Women, Commerce and Regional Culture*, ed. Helen Siu (Hong Kong: Hong Kong University Press, 2010), 143–63.
90 Siu, *Merchants' Daughters*, 7.
91 Helen Siu and David Faure David, eds., *Down to Earth, the Territorial Bond in South China* (Stanford, CA: Stanford University Press, 1995), 11.
92 This is highlighted by Siu's excellent collection, *Merchants' Daughters*.
93 She is referring to southern Guangdong. Siu, "Where Were the Women?" 32–62.

2 Working with disaster

Weimar Mission responses to the Boxer catastrophe (1900–1901)

Lydia Gerber

> What has been accomplished at least is that we are no longer justified before God in considering ourselves above the Chinese. All inhumanity and cruelty have been repaid with interest in the name of culture.
>
> (Richard Wilhelm, letter to Weimar Mission President Arndt, January 29, 1901)

In the summer and fall of 1900, two young Protestant German missionaries, Richard Wilhelm (1873–1930) and Wilhelm Schüler (1869–1935), witnessed the cruelty of the German response to the Boxer Uprising from the vantage point of the new German Lease Kiaochow in the province of Shandong. Both men were academically trained theologians sent to China by the liberal-Protestant Weimar Mission (WM). Wilhelm had arrived in Qingdao in the spring of 1899, and Schüler followed in the spring of 1900 to serve as pastor for the German residents and troops. Newcomers to China, the two men observed the events surrounding the Boxer Uprising without guidance from senior China missionaries and developed a perspective that differed significantly from that of other German Protestants. In the relative safety of the German settlement of Qingdao, Wilhelm and Schüler were confronted not with Chinese, but rather with German acts of continued violence and hostility. At a time when the world declared China to be barbaric and inhumane, these two men saw the Chinese population as victims of German imperialism.

Both men recognized that an open critique of German brutality and barbarism would not be understood, and could potentially limit their ability to work productively and perhaps even to protect the Chinese. Yet both eventually shared their concerns with the WM home board. This chapter presents evidence to this effect from Wilhelm and Schüler's private letters and published reports, including a sermon that Schüler delivered in Qingdao in commemoration of fallen German soldiers. It argues that through a careful process of editing and piecemeal publication of some of this material in the home board's signature journal, *Zeitschrift für Missionskunde und Religionswissenschaft* (ZMR), the missionary society was able to deflect the potential impact that the Boxer catastrophe might otherwise have had on its missionary enterprise. Instead of excusing the violence of the foreign response as a means of chastising the Chinese in preparation for the gospel,

46 *Lydia Gerber*

as other missionaries had done, the Weimar Mission effectively positioned itself as a source for peace and cross-cultural understanding within a context dominated by violence and racism. In particular, Richard Wilhelm's significant role as a cross-cultural communicator between China and Germany began with his mission as peacemaker in the midst of the Boxer unrest.

Historical background: the Boxer threat of 1900

The Boxer Uprising, which gripped public attention worldwide with its acts of violence against Chinese Christians and foreigners in the spring and summer of 1900, began as a local movement in northern Shandong in 1898/99.[2] The movement was spurred by elements of traditional Chinese spirit beliefs, the influence of secret societies, in particular the Big Sword Society, the martial arts practiced by members of village militias, and the conviction that foreign influence was responsible for the catastrophic cycle of floods and droughts causing widespread famine across the region. As historian Paul A. Cohen suggests, Western imperialism, including the German takeover of the Kiaochow Lease and the growing influence of missionaries in the interior of Shandong, would easily have suggested this connection to the Chinese populace.[3] In a sense, the Boxer Uprising can therefore be seen as the popular response to a crisis that had also brought about the failed 100-Day Reform movement in the summer of 1898, which had been introduced as the elite solution to China's obvious weakness and unrest. While the newly appointed Shandong governor, Yuan Shikai, quickly suppressed the movement there, support by the central government under the Empress Dowager Cixi, though not unequivocal, contributed to its spread across northern China with devastating loss of life, predominantly among Christian communities. Over 30,000 Chinese Christians, mostly Catholics, as well as more than 200 missionaries, including children, lost their lives in the summer of 1900. The Boxer Uprising also resulted in the destruction of property associated with Western encroachment, most prominently telegraph and railway lines. In June, Boxer militias, supported by Chinese regular troops, took control of the cities of Beijing and Tianjin, placing the consular and legation quarters there under siege. In Beijing, 473 foreign civilians, 451 foreign soldiers, and more than 3,000 Chinese Christians had to hold out for 55 days until foreign troops from an eight-nation relief force finally lifted the siege on August 14.[4]

The fact that telegraph communication and railway lines between Beijing, Baoding, Tianjin, and Shanghai had been interrupted not only slowed down the foreign military response, but also added to worldwide uncertainty, fear, and speculation about the extent of the violence. The most outrageous widely reported rumor, published by the London *Daily Mail* on June 16, 1900, claimed that all the foreigners in the legation quarter in Beijing had already been murdered.[5] Lurid rumors such as these only served to further exacerbate public perceptions of the Chinese as barbarians and enemies of all civilization. Perhaps the best-known image of China was conveyed by the German Kaiser, who, in his infamous "Hunnenrede" held on July 27, encouraged German troops preparing to join the war to use extreme violence to teach the Chinese a lesson about German might. As historian Yixu Lü demonstrates in his article "Germany's War in China: Media Coverage and Political Myth," the German media largely aligned itself with the images of German brutality as the necessary civilizing force promoted by the Kaiser in response to Chinese barbarism.[6] By the time the majority of Germany's troops had arrived in China in September, the Boxers were almost defeated. The Chinese imperial court had fled. Beijing and Tianjin were occupied by foreign troops, who engaged, along with other foreigners, including missionaries, in looting and other acts of violence against Chinese civilians. From October to December of 1900 and into 1901, Field Marshal Count von Waldersee, who first led German troops and soon assumed supreme command over the allied troops, enacted collective punishment in areas known to have been hotbeds of Boxer violence.[7] The number of Chinese killed in these retaliatory missions is unknown but extends into the thousands, and may even equal the number of the Boxers' victims.[8] The Boxer Protocol, signed by China and representatives of the eight-nation force on September 7, 1901, officially ended the Boxer wars. Beijing was returned to Chinese control in early 1902, but Tianjin remained under foreign military control until 1906.

The Boxer Uprising as a challenge to the Weimar Mission's aspirations in Kiaochow

Following Germany's occupation (1897) and subsequent Lease of the Kiaochow Territory, the Protestant Swiss-German Weimar Mission (founded in 1884) aspired to unite all its goals in one grand missionary enterprise. Schools and hospitals for the Chinese population would support the spread of Protestant Christianity and lead to the first WM congregations in China. The WM's first China missionary, the eminent scholar Ernst Faber (1839–1899), would continue with his literary work as the basis for a sophisticated intellectual exchange with China's elites. But in Kiaochow the WM would simultaneously support German colonial endeavors, as promised in its foundational document, by providing a Protestant theologian as pastor for the German Protestant residents and marines stationed there. Overruling concerns raised by some of its Swiss members, the home board of the WM in Berlin expected a surge in popularity and financial support for its new endeavor, particularly from the so-called colonial circles representing the global aspirations of the young German empire.[9]

The Boxer summer of 1900 challenged the foundational rationale for the WM's work in Kiaochow. The widely publicized real and imagined Boxer atrocities against Chinese and Western victims contradicted the image of an enlightened and sophisticated Chinese culture at the heart of the WM enterprise. Accusations that the German occupation was at least partially to blame for the violence also implicated the WM's active support for this colonial endeavor. Other voices blamed some or all of the missionaries in China

48 Lydia Gerber

for having caused anti-Western feelings there. The WM's plan to serve both the colonizers and colonized seemed impossible in the face of the violence and overt racism of the German occupation. Following the untimely death of Faber in 1899, it was left to two young men with less than two years of China experience between them, Richard Wilhelm and Wilhelm Schüler, to respond to this escalating crisis. The challenge was at least two-fold: to contribute to the restoration of peace in the German Lease; and to reassure a concerned missionary society that there were reasons the work in China should continue.

Beginning with its August 1900 issue, articles in the ZMR offer a sense of the options the WM was contemplating in response to the Boxer crisis. Paul Kranz, a self-supporting missionary affiliated with the WM, wrote about the situation in China while vacationing in Germany. Kranz blamed the Manchu government, rather than foreigners or natural disasters, for the crisis, in particular the suppression of the 1898 Reform Movement through the Empress Dowager. Foreign powers, he argued, had been "appointed by God to lead throughout modern history," and were therefore responsible for the challenge of modernizing China. In order to safeguard the inevitable process of modernization from further attacks, Kranz suggested that China be divided into spheres of interest.[10] In its September issue, August Kind, home board member and a future WM president (elected within the year), summarized current media debates regarding the responsibility of missionary societies for the China crisis. While highly critical of Catholic missionaries, Kind concluded that China still urgently needed missionaries to "help it out of its darkness and isolation and to connect it with the rest of the world in the spirit of Jesus." In contrast to the explicitly high regard the WM had previously expressed for Chinese culture, Kind suggested that "[t]he notion that China was an old civilization and Confucianism an excellent doctrine and a fortunate example of an a-religious moral system should now be relinquished for ever."[11]

The ZMR's October and November issues were devoted to the annual WM meeting held September 25–27 in Hamburg, and naturally considered the situation in China. In the keynote address and in a sermon, speakers reaffirmed that missionary work was the duty, not just a right, of Christians, and that setbacks such as the events in China should not be a deterrent, particularly in view of the many challenges missionary work had encountered and mastered over the centuries. Notably, the keynote sermon identified opposition to Christianity as the one unifying attitude of all Chinese, whether Boxers or not. The sermon also reflected the broader German understanding of the punitive excursions already under way in China: "Our brothers in arms, jointly with the armies of the civilized nations, have an earnest and terrible task to accomplish, so that the defiled honor of our country, so that justice and morale will find atonement and protection."[12] This view of the events unfolding in China was well received. Whether in their discussion of the military or of the missionary conquest of China, these voices shared the conviction that Western powers were called upon to impose and enforce what was judged to be divine justice upon the unwilling Chinese, who had, through the Boxer Uprising, forfeited their claim to be representatives of a notable culture and civilization in their own right. These perceptions of the Boxer crisis expressed by WM members in Germany contrasted strongly with Wilhelm and Schüler's experience of anti-Chinese violence in and around the Kiaochow Leasehold. A significant gap needed to be breached in returning to a shared understanding of the situation in China and the role of the WM.

Defending China, accusing Germany: Richard Wilhelm's response to the Boxer crisis

Violence between German troops and the Chinese population in areas surrounding the German Lease had begun before 1900. When Richard Wilhelm[13] arrived to serve as missionary to the Chinese and pastor to German Protestants in May of 1899, these two groups were already engaged in conflict. Issues surrounding the construction of a railway into the interior had caused local unrest, and German troops had responded with excursions to district towns beyond the borders of the Lease, leading to violent confrontations.[14] The German marines demonstrated a pervasive lack of regard for Chinese culture and traditions during these early months, most notably in the indefensible act of burning the library of the Confucius Academy in Gaomi in September 1899. The immense difficulties Wilhelm encountered as he tried to connect with both the Germans in Qingdao and the local Chinese population are implied in his cheerful observation that "in contrast to the frequent emphasis on racial differences . . . the common human bond outweighs whatever might be separating [us]."[15] Wilhelm's firsthand experience with the brutality of German behavior against the Chinese soon convinced him that the Boxer Uprising was understandable as a response to the treatment of China and the Chinese. But he also knew that this was an unpopular perspective to share publicly in the German Lease.

His background and training had prepared Wilhelm to take an unusually critical stance against the spirit influencing public opinion in the German Lease. Born, raised, and educated in Württemberg, Wilhelm was largely indifferent to the German navy, as well as the northern German enthusiasm for trade and colonial enterprise. Moreover, his key mentor and soon-to-be father-in-law Christoph Blumhardt (1842–1919) understood Wilhelm's mission in China primarily as a means of bringing the Blumhardtian vision of God's kingdom to China and later, through China, to the entire world. This vision explicitly did not recognize differences of race, culture, and religion. In his letters to Wilhelm, Blumhardt freely expressed his concerns about Western imperialism, but also encouraged Wilhelm to exercise caution in his own activities and communications, both with the home board and with the Qingdao public, to avoid unnecessary rifts.[16]

50   Lydia Gerber

Wilhelm followed Blumhardt's advice in his public stance in Qingdao, where he apparently avoided speaking out against German violence. In communicating with the home board, however, Wilhelm chose to use a two-pronged approach. Comparing Wilhelm's quarterly reports published in the mission journal ZMR against the personal letters accompanying them, significant differences emerge. Cautious in his official reports, Wilhelm expressed his frustration with German behavior against the Chinese more freely in letters to the WM president. In two such letters from September 19, 1900 and January 29, 1901 Wilhelm gave vivid accounts of German abuses against the Chinese civilian population. In a letter from November 1900, however, Wilhelm offered such a hopeful report of his ability to bring about an end to a military conflict between German troops and Chinese villagers that the WM chose to include it in the February edition of the ZMR, albeit in a censored version. These missives do not only show how Wilhelm perceived and described the Boxer events to his Weimar Mission audience. They also illustrate how the ZMR, through careful editing and timing, guided its readers toward a more balanced understanding of the conflicts surrounding the new German Lease.

In the September letter accompanying his official quarterly report, Wilhelm freely shared his sense of outrage about abuses committed by German troops in Shandong, as well as those by foreign troops in the fighting around Tianjin. This letter was not publicly shared, but it did offer the home board a view of the situation that was vastly different from those held by most of the German public at the time. Wilhelm wrote: "It is mainly the actions of the Catholic missions and the foreign powers that have added fuel to the general dislike of foreigners present among the Chinese. As the gentleman Dr. Krebs, who played a key role as interpreter, told me confidentially, the so-called conquest of Kiaochow was 'mean-spirited without equal, an act every German should be ashamed of.'"[17] Describing the Chinese uprising as the understandable response to foreign aggression, Wilhelm even challenged the Western assumption that there were differences in the way Chinese Boxers and foreign troops were conducting themselves during the recent battles: "Also when it comes to Tianjin and so forth we can see our so-called civilization shipwrecked, since Europeans engaged in the torture and killing of those they had captured or wounded just as much as the Chinese did."[18] While Wilhelm was not an eyewitness to these events, he may have received this information from participants or immediate observers. Wilhelm also expressed his frustration with the public discourse, and with the Kiaochow government in general: "But who dares to speak publicly these days of such causes? Nobody would hear them in the current climate of intoxication. But I have experienced just about everything that could possibly occur. Among the men who are responsible here for the Chinese there is not one, not a single man who has love for the people. What good can be accomplished with such governing?"[19] Lastly, Wilhelm assured the home board that he would refrain from making his views public: "But I can assure you, that in spite of this insight I am striving to avoid being tactless."[20]

In contrast, Wilhelm's quarterly report published in the December issue of the ZMR contained only a very oblique criticism of foreign occupation and behavior against the Chinese, and ignored the role played by Germany. Having traced the Boxers and similar movements, like the Big Sword Society, back to the beginning of the Manchu dynasty, Wilhelm described them as originally intended to restore the Ming dynasty and therefore strongly suppressed by the ruling Manchu dynasty. He also mentioned the societies' roles as social networks in Chinese settlements abroad, which included engagement in a certain amount of violence: "They [the Chinese secret societies] used to have a neutral attitude toward the Europeans. Things changed, however, in recent years, when Europeans, through their actions in China turned into the foremost enemy to be fought in China. . . . The enmity against the dynasty faded into the background compared to th[is] shared goal."[21]

Rather than dwelling on the roles of specific foreign actors in provoking the Chinese, Wilhelm argued: "There is no point in considering who is responsible for this. To me, this seems like a call to atonement and self-reflection for those who are able, and who recognize that we are spiritual children, as a renewed incentive to persist in helping these people to understand that God loves the world."[22] Both in the introduction and in the conclusion of this report, which covered other topics as well, Wilhelm expressed his hope that the Boxer catastrophe might lead to real change. He also emphasized his compassion for the suffering of the Chinese. Compared with his personal letter, Wilhelm's published report seemed dispassionate and even slightly patronizing, a rather effective disguise of his true feelings amidst the "climate of intoxication" he witnessed in Qingdao.

In November 1900 Wilhelm sent a personal letter to the home board that offered a frank and disturbing eyewitness account of the activities and attitudes of German marines engaged in an anti-Boxer mission in the Gaomi district. This letter also suggested a new role for the WM in Qingdao, namely as an intermediary and peacemaker in a region that had already seen severe disturbances during the construction of a German railway line into the interior. Wilhelm's letter was published immediately in the ZMR, but in a carefully edited version that did not implicate the German marines to the same degree. The passages in italics below appear in the original letter but were excised from the published version. In his missive, Wilhelm explained his reasons for visiting the area and described what he discovered. First, he described his interaction with the Germans, which led to the softening of their attitude toward the Chinese:

> Our troops in Gaomi, who are there to restore order, *have been engaged in excesses that I refuse to mention. I have been able to look deeply*

52   *Lydia Gerber*

into an unbelievable abyss. Less friendly [in comparison to the welcome I received from the district official] was the reception in the German garrison, *since until then there had been looting in an unspeakable manner and the presence of a European was therefore viewed as embarrassing. Gaomi was quite deserted when I arrived.* I did succeed eventually, however, in convincing the [German] officers that I had no political goals and only came in order to help. They would not believe that the Chinese *dogs* would be willing to see me. But I was gradually able to soften the anti-Chinese attitudes in the camp. [23]

His letter then described his interaction with the Chinese and Governor Jaeschke, illustrating his role as a cultural intermediary between the Chinese and the Germans:

> The Chinese themselves welcomed me with open arms. Yuan Shikai personally sent Colonel Ma to me to express his gratitude. The Gaomi populace gradually returned to town. *The looting also became less frequent. . . .* Upon my return [to Qingdao] I found our governor [Jaeschke] to be very eager to hear my account, *which surprised and distressed him.* He told me to use the sum collected as fines . . . to ease the suffering of the innocent, and begged me to go back [to Gaomi].[24]

Even in its censored version, this letter conveyed a strong impression of the nature of Germany's so-called expeditions into the interior of Shandong. It appeared in the February 1901 edition of the ZMR together with the text of a sermon Wilhelm Schüler had delivered in July of 1900 in Qingdao (to be discussed), which also challenged the public to reconsider its view of the Boxer wars. Beginning with August Bebel's remarks during a debate in the German Reichstag in November 1900, voices critical of the international and more specifically the German response to the Boxer Uprising were already present in the German public arena, making Wilhelm's letter and Schüler's sermon less surprising or disturbing to the readership of the ZMR. But a third letter Wilhelm wrote to the home board dated January 29, 1901 goes even further in its indictment of the German occupation and remained unpublished. Here Wilhelm recounted:

> [Through my travels to Gaomi] I have seen and experienced much I cannot even talk about. I am surprised that at home apart from the opposition parties nobody is raising his voice against such appalling behavior. . . . Even military courts and such are a sham. The *obviously* guilty are declared innocent – I myself served as a witness in such a case – and afterward there is always an announcement that "based on an in-depth investigation it was found that there is no case" and so on.[25]

Working with disaster   53

Wilhelm reflected further on the double standard and how "demands of the most basic justice" were readily dismissed and never extended to the Chinese.[26] The end effect, for Wilhelm, was that it was no longer possible for the Europeans to consider themselves superior to the Chinese. Wilhelm concluded this letter with thoughts about his own options: "Much wisdom and caution are needed. Direct action against all that occurs here is of no value. It would only lead us to be simply ignored, and opportunities to be of help would diminish even further. So it is necessary to find a *modus vivendi* to be able to at least occasionally do something."[27]

Wilhelm's official report covering the four-month period from September 1 to December 31 was published in the March 1901 edition of the ZMR, at a time when public debates on the Boxer Uprising and the Western punitive actions had long shifted away from outright condemnation of the Chinese side exclusively. Wilhelm's vivid descriptions of the suffering of the Chinese people could now be freely shared. Contrary to his expectation that it would be difficult for him even to interact with the Chinese population, which was "generally described as stupid and cruel," he instead found "the main difficulties" to lie with the German troops who committed brutal acts against them:

> The German troops and their behavior had caused a panic. The women and a large number of men had fled, and the city was deserted. . . . Shortly before our arrival one of the villages had been the target. When we arrived, we found the houses and the granaries burnt down, survivors had fled. . . . Soon after news of our arrival had spread, the injured were brought to us, and we did what we could. Most of them were women, children, and the aged, who had been hit by machine gun fire while attempting to flee. Some were horribly injured, and it was a miracle that they had not perished.[28]

Wilhelm also shared his findings about the connection the village had made with local Boxers:

> Some unruly elements had entered into relationships with Boxers in the area. These had appeared in the village and promised the help of eight million spirit soldiers, who would at the right time fall from the sky. . . . The Germans arrived and began shooting a breach. The people defended themselves courageously. But the outcome was never in question. The spirit soldiers did not come, and the old cannons and rampart rifles would explode and hurt their own people rather than the German soldiers, who had not a single casualty.[29]

Later in this account Wilhelm, who credited the Chinese general Ma for having eradicated the Boxers in their main lair near Pingtu on Chinese-held territory, stated that he considered the threat to be essentially over. Wilhelm

54 Lydia Gerber

also reported that he had succeeded in having one hundred village leaders come together to listen to his explanation of the situation and compose and sign a letter declaring their willingness to submit to the Germans. This they presented, in Wilhelm's presence, to the German major in charge of the excursion, who sent them home with words of reassurance. During a second trip to Gaomi Wilhelm brought his wife with him, whose presence encouraged the residents of Gaomi to also have their wives return to town, a reminder that rape was clearly an issue with the German occupation.[30]

While this report did not accuse the German side of complete disregard for the basic rights and needs of the Chinese, as Wilhelm's letters did, or dispute the German strategic decision to target the village, it offered a deeply compassionate account of the plight of the Chinese victims. It also described the Chinese authorities, district officials, and General Ma as rational, helpful, capable, and engaged in effectively addressing the challenges of both the Boxers and the German excursion into Chinese territory beyond the Lease. By focusing on his own experiences and firsthand information, Wilhelm avoided any discussion of the larger military situation in China, including Waldersee's much-debated punitive excursions, or a discussion of victims among the Western missionaries and Chinese Christians. This focused discussion of a single village's fate (including details about individual victims) humanized the Chinese. While these vignettes offered little detail compared with the well-publicized accounts of the experiences of Western missionaries, Wilhelm's report helped to correct the imbalance in reporting on Western versus Chinese victims. Wilhelm's contacts with Gaomi would continue for more than a decade and have a lasting impact on his own perceptions of China and the WM's work there.[31] In 1906 Wilhelm was the first German Protestant missionary to receive the Chinese literary degree of Daotai (Circuit Intendant) in acknowledgment of his contributions to peace and his educational work.[32] To this day, Wilhelm is respected in Germany and China as a bridge-builder between the two countries, first as missionary and educator in Qingdao, and later as the founder of the China Institute and professor of Chinese Studies at the University of Frankfurt.[33]

A plea on behalf of China: Wilhelm Schüler's sermon commemorating fallen German soldiers

Richard Wilhelm's cautious approach to confronting the public with information about German atrocities contrasts strongly with a public sermon commemorating fallen German soldiers delivered by Wilhelm Schüler[34] on July 1, 1900. This eloquent sermon, which was eventually published in the February 1901 edition of the ZMR, stands alone among Schüler's public texts as a bold and explicit challenge to his German audience to treat the Chinese with kindness and as equals, even amidst the Boxer crisis. Texts he later published in the ZMR parallel Wilhelm's published accounts in their references to German violence, which were admittedly oblique. Schüler's

Working with disaster 55

initial task in Qingdao was to serve as the Protestant pastor and to bridge the cultural divide that existed between the Christian missionaries and the residents and military in the colony. He arrived in Qingdao in April of 1900 at a time when the widespread unrest culminating in the Boxer Uprising was already under way. This violence heightened tensions and precipitated an influx of European refugees, including many missionaries, into the new settlement. On June 17, in a military operation lasting only a few hours, troops from the newly formed eight-nation alliance, including German marines from the Third Battalion stationed in Qingdao, succeeded in capturing the Dagu Forts near Tianjin. Seven German soldiers lost their lives, while others, including the commander, were seriously injured and later recognized for extraordinary valor. Further German lives were lost during the advance toward and occupation of Tianjin. On June 21, China declared war.[35] When Qingdao's governor Jaeschke asked Wilhelm Schüler to hold a memorial service, Schüler knew what was expected of him. He described his dilemma later in a personal letter to the WM president:

> I do believe, though, that one should not especially emphasize consideration for the military and patriotic [perspective], because the greatest danger for the spread of the gospel of Jesus would be to go too far in such consideration. . . . "You hypocrites," Jesus would say; but then a word of contrition spoken by his disciples should not be avoided, and [would be] particularly effective if spoken at an occasion when nobody wants to hear it, when the preacher is only invited so that he can glorify the warrior as divine. Such an occasion for me was the memorial service. It is difficult for me at such moments to speak, but it would go against my conscience if I gave in.[36]

In choosing to follow his conscience, Schüler risked the WM's aspiration of finding recognition among the German supporters of colonialism, and quite possibly his own standing in the colony as well. In his sermon commemorating fallen German soldiers in the midst of the Boxer Uprising, he not only called on his exclusively German audience to work toward an enduring peace. He even went so far as to call the uprising "understandable" in the context of China's situation. The text of the sermon must have arrived in Berlin in time for the September edition of the ZMR.[37] But the editor of the ZMR did not publish it until months later, in the February edition of 1901, after it had lost its incendiary potential and the Boxer wars were essentially over.[38]

A brief summary of Schüler's sermon illustrates the difficulty of his position, facing a German audience fearful of an attack while simultaneously attempting to prevent the Germans from exacting revenge on the Chinese in the name of civilization. This was in fact the first and most public statement on the Boxer conflict made by the Qingdao missionaries of the WM within the German Lease. As is the nature of sermons, particularly those

56 Lydia Gerber

presented to military units required to attend, this event offered Schüler a rare opportunity to make a complex argument and to present it without being interrupted. A letter Schüler wrote only days after he delivered his sermon, on July 4, illustrates how tense and uncertain his German audience in Qingdao was of its own fate. "The situation is very serious," Schüler claimed, "and one anticipates that the Boxer masses will also move toward Qingdao itself."[39]

Schüler set the tone for his unwelcome message with his choice of 1. Peter 5:6 as the sermon's biblical text, "humble yourselves therefore under the mighty hand of God, that in due time he may exalt you." By using this quote to identify suffering as a universal experience, Schüler presented the fallen Germans being commemorated as only a small group among the "hundreds and thousands" who had died along with them. These numbers already suggest that Schüler included the Chinese among the victims worthy of note. As he described the fallen, he focused on the impact of death on their bodies. He spoke of human life, youth, and optimism forever silenced and pointed again to the universal rather than specific nature of this loss. With these observations, Schüler effectively removed the uniform and all it implied from these young men. Instead Schüler emphasized the similarities between the characteristics of good soldiers and the values at the heart of Christianity, namely selflessness, devotion, courage, sobriety, and wakefulness, as well as persistence in the face of danger. Noticeably, Schüler chose not to include service to one's country or sacrifice for one's nation, the mainstays of memorials to the fallen. What he acknowledged and praised instead are the qualities of soldiers worldwide, regardless of the particulars of a specific cause or battle. This epitaph could just as easily have been for the Chinese who died in the battle along with everyone else.[40]

In the third paragraph of the sermon, Schüler described China as a victim of centuries of mismanagement and crisis, exploitation and suppression, superstition and betrayal. Reverting again to imagery of the body, Schüler challenged his audience to abandon concepts of China as the permanent other and as the enemy of civilization. The "we" of this sermon now included all of mankind as one body, Christian or not, European or not, supposedly "civilized" or not. The suffering of a member of this body of mankind, including China, Schüler claimed, should naturally be of concern to all. Schüler dared to take this claim even further. He called the decision of individual Chinese to rise up against foreigners quite understandable, especially when considering China's past and current occupation and ongoing exploitation from the Chinese perspective. Still, acknowledging the inherent lunacy of the Boxers as a mass movement, he concluded these provocative statements with one that might have actually been shared by his audience, namely the hope that the people of Europe who were attempting to quell the Boxer movement might soon be successful.[41] Schüler continued, however, that a lasting peace could not be achieved through bloodshed, but only through what he called the "instruments of peace" inspired by the spirit

Working with disaster 57

of Jesus, which extended beyond the imagined barriers of nationhood or race. Schüler now challenged his listeners to actually show evidence of their own assumed superiority over the Chinese through actions and attitudes in accordance with Christ's spirit of love and peace. In his final statement he presented an even greater challenge, as he called on his unwilling audience to be inspired to work for a united world in which young lives would no longer be sacrificed in war.[42]

Among the published texts in which Schüler directly addressed the Boxer wars, this sermon stands alone as a fairly explicit critique of the status quo, and as a direct appeal to his German audience to treat the Chinese with compassion and as equally human. In his later travelogue, for example, which described his visit to a younger brother who was stationed with the Second Sea Battalion in occupied Beijing, Schüler only alluded to the Chinese costs of this occupation, when he mentioned briefly that articles of value had gone missing, or that very few Chinese would dare to emerge after dark. Direct accusations of looting or random violence were reserved for the "Cossacks."[43] Another account of a visit to the marines in barracks in the interior of Shandong mentioned evidence of problematic behavior, such as the disrespect the soldiers demonstrated toward Chinese religious statuary in an occupied temple. But again, Schüler made the observation only in passing. Suggestive of much more significant abuse was a small comment included in Schüler's description of a visit to soldiers stationed in Gaomi. He described how "[t]he atmosphere at the time was that of a merry excursion, made even more attractive by the appeal that marksmanship must have for a soldier."[44]

Schüler's sermon can be viewed primarily as evidence of his inexperience as a newly appointed pastor in a complex colonial setting. Heinrich Hackmann (1864–1935), by comparison, who served as the WM's Protestant pastor for Germans in Shanghai beginning in 1894, delivered a sermon on the same day (July 1, 1900), which according to the ZMR's editors gave evidence of "the true Christian point of view during this time of unrest." It was published immediately in the September issue. Hackmann skillfully avoided all judgment of the current crisis, arguing in general terms instead that God allowed both the constructive and destructive tendencies in human nature to manifest themselves, though neither were representative of God's will.[45]

Two particular points, though, suggest that Schüler knew exactly what he was doing when he delivered his sermon. First of all, the sermon itself is a masterpiece of rhetoric, carefully crafted with the knowledge that he was facing a hostile crowd. Secondly, the sermon was an opportunity to try at least to make a difference in an ongoing disaster. In contrast to Hackmann's congregation of Shanghai business people and consular officials, Schüler faced soldiers and officers about to join battle, as well as government officials who had to decide what methods they would use to safeguard the German Leasehold with its mixed Chinese and German population. This particular audience, whether hostile or thoughtful, was about to have a

58   Lydia Gerber

direct and immediate impact on the fate of Sino-German relations and the lives of countless Chinese. In contrast to this unique opportunity to make an argument for peace and compassion, Schüler's more general texts about visits with soldiers in the field, written for German readers of the ZMR, were comparatively inconsequential. These other texts still suggest, however, his personal distaste for the way the international forces, including the Germans, acted toward and spoke of the Chinese.

In conclusion, aided by a more general shift in public opinion, Wilhelm and Schüler submitted material to the WM home board and to the ZMR that successfully and gradually transformed the views of Western superiority that had characterized earlier texts in the ZMR discussing the Boxer summer of 1900. On the one hand, Wilhelm's personal observations from the Gaomi district presented the majority of the Chinese population as the perhaps deluded, but fundamentally innocent, victims of a minority of unruly elements and Boxers. Most importantly, he saw that once trust had been established, cooperation by those in leadership positions was willingly offered, a notable contrast to the forceful imposition of divine or Western will suggested in earlier comments in the ZMR. Wilhelm's stinging indictment of the German occupation, however, remained unpublished. Schüler's argument in his sermon, on the other hand, offered a fundamental challenge to the notion of the Chinese as distinct "others" to be chastised or punished for this perceived alterity. He also reframed ideas about what Christians were called upon to do, from that of imposing the Christian message even in the face of resistance to performing acts of kindness and working toward a lasting peace. Subsequent developments in Gaomi as well as in the German Lease supported the view that service to those in need and collaboration on the basis of mutual trust offered new promise for the work of the WM.[46]

Notes

1 Letter, Richard Wilhelm to Weimar Mission President Arndt, dated Qingdao, January 29, 1901; Weimar Mission Archives DOAM acta 276, 175–77.

2 The English name "Boxers" referenced both the original Chinese name of the movement – Yihequan, Fists of Righteousness and Harmony – and its use of martial arts. Among the many studies of the Boxer movement Joseph Esherick, *The Origins of the Boxer Uprising* (Berkeley and Los Angeles: University of California Press, 1987) and Paul A. Cohen, *History in Three Keys: The Boxers as Event, Experience and Myth* (New York: Columbia University Press, 1997) are classics. For the German experience specifically, see, among others, Mechthild Leutner and Klaus Mühlhahn, eds., *Kolonialkrieg in China: Die Niederschlagung der Boxerbewegung 1900–1901* (Berlin: Ch. Links Verlag, 2007). Robert Bickers and R.G. Tiedemann, eds., *The Boxers, China and the World* (Lanham, MD: Rowman & Littlefield, 2007) offer fresh insights from both a regional and a global perspective.

3 Paul A. Cohen makes this argument. "Humanizing the Boxers," in *The Boxers, China and the World*, ed. Bickers and Tiedemann (Lanham, MD: Rowman & Littlefield, 2007), 179–97, 186–90.

4 See Diana Preston, *The Boxer Rebellion: The Dramatic Story of China's War on Foreigners that Shook the World in the Summer of 1900* (New York: Berkley

Working with disaster 59

Publishing Group, 1999) for a detailed account of the siege in Beijing based on multiple primary accounts.

5 Ibid., 172.

6 Yixu Lü, "Germany's War in China: Media Coverage and Political Myth," *German Life and Letters* 61, no. 2 (April 2008): 202–14.

7 Bernd Martin argues that the extent of the violence enacted by German troops at this time was at least in part a result of the propaganda at home describing the Boxers as "subhuman." "Soldatische Radikalisierung und Massaker: Das deutche Erste und Zweite Seebataillon im Einsatz im 'Boxerkrieg' in China 1900," *Militärgeschichtliche Zeitschrift* 69 (2010): 221–41.

8 Daniel Bays suggests this in his *A New History of Christianity in China* (Chichester, UK: Wiley-Blackwell, 2012), 86. See also Preston, *The Boxer Rebellion*, 283–95, for examples of looting during the occupation of Beijing.

9 For a brief English-language account of the Weimar Mission's philosophy and work in Qingdao, see George Steinmetz, *The Devil's Handwriting: Precoloniality and the German Colonial State in Qingdao, Samoa, and Southwest Africa* (Chicago: University of Chicago Press, 2007), 479–81. For a more in-depth analysis of its goals for and work in Qingdao, see Lydia Gerber, *Von Voskamps 'heidnischem Treiben' und Wilhelms 'höherem China': Die Berichterstattung deutscher protestantischer Missionare aus dem deutschen Pachtgebiet Kiautschou 1898–1914* (Hamburg: Hamburger Sinologische Gesellschaft, 2002), 73–103.

10 Paul Kranz, "Der Krieg in China und die Mission," *Zeitschrift für Missionskunde und Religionswissenschaft* (hereafter abbreviated as *ZMR*) (1900): 241–46, 244.

11 August Kind, "Die chinesische Mission im Gerichte der deutschen Zeitungspresse," *Zeitschrift für Missionskunde und Religionswissenschaft* (1900): 264–69, 269. These and all subsequent quotes from the ZMR are translated from the German by the author.

12 H. Schulz, "Die Liebe Christi dringet uns also – Predigt bei der 16. Jahresversammlung in Hamburg," *ZMR* (1900): 289–96.

13 Salome Wilhelm's biography *Richard Wilhelm: Der geistige Mittler zwischen China und Europa* (Düsseldorf, Köln: Diederichs, 1956) still offers the most complete rendering of Wilhelm's life and work. For examples of more recent scholarship on Wilhelm's work and influence see Klaus Hirsch, ed., *Richard Wilhelm: Botschafter zweier Welten* (Frankfurt am Main: IKO Verlag, 2003) and Dorothea Wippermann, Klaus Hirsch, and Georg Ebertshäuser, eds., *Interkulturalitaet im fruehen 20. Jahrhundert: Richard Wilhelm – Theologe, Missionar und Sinologe* (Frankfurt am Main; London: IKO Verlag, 2007).

14 For a concise description of these conflicts, see Klaus Mühlhahn, "Negotiating the Nation: German Colonialism and Chinese Nationalism in Qingdao, 1897–1914," in *Twentieth-Century Colonialism in China: Localities, the Everyday and the World*, ed. Bryna Goodman and David Goodman (London and New York: Routledge, 2012), 37–56, 46–47.

15 "Bericht von R. Wilhelm über 1. Juli bis 1. November 1899," *ZMR* (1900): 29–31.

16 Letter, Blumhardt to Wilhelm, dated February 6, 1900, in Christoph Blumhardt, *Christus in der Welt: Briefe an Richard Wilhelm*, ed. Arthur Rich (Zürich: Zwingli Verlag, 1958), 47–48. For an English-language account describing Wilhelm's relationship to Blumhardt, see Lydia Gerber, "Christianity for a Confucian Youth: Richard Wilhelm and His Lixian Shuyuan School for Boys in Qingdao, 1901–1912," in *A Voluntary Exile: Chinese Christianity and Cultural Confluence Since 1552*, ed. Anthony E. Clark (Lanham, MD: Lehigh University Press and Rowman and Littlefield, 2014), 117–43.

17 Annette Biener describes how Diederichs and the German troops tricked the Chinese battalion stationed in Qingdao into relinquishing their hold on the military basis. This was not widely known at the time. *Das deutsche Pachtgebiet Tsingtau*

60   Lydia Gerber

in Schantung 1897–1914: Institutioneller Wandel durch Kolonialisierung (Bonn: Wilhelm Matzat, 2001), 29–33.

18 Letter, Wilhelm to Arndt, dated Tsingtau, September 19, 1900 (Weimar Mission Archives, Speyer: DOAM Acta 236, 155–58).

19 Ibid.

20 Ibid.

21 "Bericht des Pfarrers und Missionars R. Wilhelm über die Zeit vom 1. Juni bis 31. August 1900," *ZMR* (1900): 377–79.

22 Ibid.

23 Letter, Wilhelm to home board, dated November 26, 1900, original in the Weimar Mission Archives, DOAM acta 236, 159–60, the published version *ZMR* (1901): 59–61. The underlined passages appeared in the original, but were not published.

24 Ibid.

25 Letter, Wilhelm to Arndt, dated Qingdao, January 29, 1901; Weimar Mission Archives, DOAM acta 276, 175–77. Wilhelm underlined words in the original letter for emphasis.

26 Ibid.

27 Ibid.

28 "Bericht des Pfarrers und Missionars R. Wilhelm über die Zeit vom 1. September–31. Dezember 1900," *ZMR* (1901): 90–92.

29 Ibid.

30 Ibid.

31 For evidence of this continued impact, see Lydia Gerber, "Mediating Medicine: Li Benjing, Richard Wilhelm, and the Politics of Hygiene in the German Leasehold Kiaochow (1897–1914)," in *Germany and China: Transnational Encounters since the Eighteenth Century*, ed. Joanne Miyang Cho and David Crowe (New York: Palgrave Macmillan, 2014), 97–112.

32 *Tsingtauer Neueste Nachrichten*, May 17, 1906.

33 Suzanne Marchand describes Wilhelm's influence in both China and Germany under the heading "Richard Wilhelm German Mandarin" based on recent German scholarship. *German Orientalism in the Age of Empire: Religion, Race, and Scholarship* (Cambridge: Cambridge University Press; Washington, DC: German Historical Institute, 2009), 463–73. Weizhi Su, "Chuanjiaoshi – Gongzheng Yulun – Jiaoan: You Yihetuan shiji Wei Lixian suo Xiangdaode" [Missionary, Righteous Public Opinion, and Anti-Missionary Incidents: Richard Wilhelm's View of the Boxers], *Qingshi Yanjiu*, Issue 2 (May 2003): 89–94 is one of several recent examples of China's continued appreciation for Richard Wilhelm's advocacy on behalf of China.

34 Wilhelm Schüler (1869–1935) devoted his professional career to cross-cultural understanding between Germany and China. A trained theologian, he served as pastor and missionary for the WM in Qingdao and Shanghai between 1900 and 1913. He spent his remaining career as a professor at the Institut für Orientalische Sprachen in Berlin. Ferdinand Lessing offers a detailed and highly appreciative account of Schüler's life in "Dem Gedächtnis Wilhelm Schülers," *Ostasiatische Rundschau*, no. 3 (February 1, 1935). See also Gerber, *Von Voskamps heidnischem Treiben*, 196–200 for a description of Schüler's contributions to the WM's work in Qingdao.

35 For a detailed account, see Wolfgang Petter, "Die Deutsche Marine auf dem Weg nach China," in *Das Deutsche Reich und der Boxeraufstand*, ed. Susanne Kuß and Bernd Martin (Munich: Iudicium-Verlag, 2002), 145–64. For an in-depth and highly appreciative description of German contributions to the conquest of the Dagu Forts, see Wolfgang Nöcker, "Kampf um die Taku-Forts for 70 Jahren,"

Working with disaster 61

Marine-Rundschau 67 (June 1970): 349–61. For an account of the occupation of Tianjin see Lewis Bernstein, "After the Fall: Tianjin under Foreign Occupation, 1900–1902," in *The Boxers, China and the World*, ed. Robert Bickers and R.G. Tiedemann (Lanham, MD: Rowman & Littlefield, 2007), 133–46.

36 Letter, Schüler to Arndt, dated Qingdao, April 2, 1901, Weimar Mission Archives, DOAM acta 227, 134.

37 The September issue of the *ZMR* quoted a letter Schüler wrote on July 4th in "Die gegenwärtige Lage unserer Missionare in China," *ZMR* (1900): 285–87.

38 The edition of the *Deutsch-Asiatische Warte* of July 8, 1900 (missing in a microfilm reel of the newspaper) may actually have included the sermon, since it published two of Schüler's sermons in the following year, including the sermons he delivered in January 1901 at the funeral of Governor Jaeschke.

39 Quoted in "Die gegenwärtige Lage unserer Missionare in China," 285–87.

40 "Rede des Pfarrers Lic. Schüler in Tsingtau bei der Gedenkfeier am 1. Juli 1900 für die bei Taku und Tientsin Gefallenen," *ZMR* (1901): 61–63.

41 "Ihm gegenüber stehen im Augenblick die Völker Europas vereint, um diesen Geist zu dämpfen; wir hoffen zuversichtlich, dass es bald gelinge." Schüler does not include Japan or the United States in this image.

42 "Rede des Pfarrers Lic. Schüler in Tsingtau bei der Gedenkfeier," 61–63.

43 "Bericht des Pfarrers Lic. Schüler in Tsingtau über die Zeit vom 1. April bis 30. Juni 1901," *ZMR* (1901): 282–87.

44 "Bericht des Pfarrers Lic. Schüler in Tsingtau vom 1. August bis 31. Oktober 1900," *Zeitschrift für Missionskunde und Religionswissenschaft* (1901): 92–95, 94.

45 "Die gegenwärtige Lage unserer Missionare in China," *ZMR* (1900): 285–87.

46 Steinmetz sees the WM, and in particular Richard Wilhelm, as significant contributors to a shift from a "sinophobic" to a "sinophilic" attitude in Germany around 1905. *The Devil's Handwriting*, 470–507.

3 Representations of Jewish exile and models of memory in *Shanghai Ghetto* and *Exil Shanghai*

Shambhavi Prakash

Shanghai, between the mid-nineteenth and mid-twentieth centuries, was a place where various histories converged. Following the brutal Opium Wars (1839–42, 1856–60), Shanghai had become a colonial port city with multiple administrations. The victories of Britain, France, and other colonial powers ensured their territorial concessions and administrative control over parts of China, including parts of Shanghai that came to be called the International Settlement and the French Concession. These enclaves were governed by various colonial powers through separate legal, educational, and administrative systems.

Colonial Shanghai counted amongst its residents a mix of Chinese and European groups, masters and subjects, "natives" and migrants. This paper concerns itself with one particular migrant group: namely the Jewish refugees who made their way to the city. The city had seen multiple waves of migration by Jews, beginning from the late nineteenth century – Sephardic Jews arrived in Shanghai for the trading opportunities it presented, while Russian Jews were fleeing from pogroms. Another wave of Russian Jews arrived in Shanghai after the October Revolution of 1917.[1] Between 1937 and 1941, with National Socialism tightening its grip on Europe, another group of Jews, around 20,000 central European Jews, managed to flee to Shanghai. They were to live there for almost a decade before they were able to procure visas enabling them to immigrate to other parts of the world. Shanghai was not the first choice for many of them. It was, however, the one destination still open to them at a time when other nations had firmly shut their doors to Jewish refugees.[2]

Accounts of this topic within the history of the Holocaust only started coming to light half a century after 1945, even though the themes of migration and exile had already been well explored with the boom in memory and Holocaust studies.[3] Although still not commonly known, this episode of history has come to be well recorded through archival documentation, biographical and historical accounts, as well as fictionalized ones. Both the memoirs and the historical accounts that have been published in the last few decades have provided us with overviews as well as the details of this history.[4] Especially revealing among these varied works are the collections of interviews. They present a variety of vivid oral narratives that portray the uniquely cosmopolitan yet fiercely stratified society of Shanghai of that period and describe how newly arrived central European refugees survived. Although there exist multiple published compilations, this chapter deals with collections of interviews presented through film. It focuses on two documentaries that were released within a few years of each other – *Exil Shanghai* (1997) by Ulrike Ottinger, and *Shanghai Ghetto* (2002) by Dana Janklowicz-Mann and Amir Mann.[5]

This chapter is not interested in judging the comprehensiveness of historical accounts in these two documentary films. Rather its interests lie in the modes through which this history is remembered in oral narratives and represented through the filmic medium, especially with respect to the depiction of Shanghai encountered by central European refugees. In addition to being the site of multiple colonial administrations, the Shanghai of this period was flooded with internal refugees fleeing military conflict and natural disasters in other parts of China.

Reflecting on these intersecting histories of violence and deprivation is crucial if we are to imagine "other ways of thinking about the relation between histories and their memorial legacies."[6] Amidst the terrible existential threat and experiences of exclusion, how do European Jewish refugees in Shanghai frame other experiences of exclusion affecting the local non-Jewish population they encountered? How is their "culture shock" in Shanghai described in these accounts, and what do they reveal about intersecting histories of exclusion?[7] As we shall see, amidst the "collective memory" of the Jewish exile community in Shanghai, another history is remembered: that of the semi-colonial Shanghai of the 1930s and 40s and the Japanese occupation of the city.[8] In the sections below, we will examine whether and how other histories of exclusion figure in accounts of and about central European refugees in Shanghai. We will do this by discussing representations of Shanghai and its local inhabitants in oral accounts presented in the two documentaries. The theme is further explored by analyzing how the two documentaries frame these recollections and representations of Shanghai differently. By attending to the particular cinematic strategies employed by the two documentaries, the chapter seeks to reveal two distinct approaches to history, identity, and memory.

Models of memory

Since Maurice Halbwachs drew attention to the interaction between individual memory and social networks and to the role of representational forms such as literature in creating our collective memory of historical events, scholars have come to recognize the growing dominance of the visual medium in our collective engagement with history.[9] This has recently been underscored by scholars such as Robert Rosenstone, who writes, "Each day it becomes clearer to even the most academic of historians that the visual

64   *Shambhavi Prakash*

media are the chief conveyor of public history in our culture. [. . .] We live in a world shaped, even in its historical consciousness, by the visual media."[10] In the last few decades, the democratization of filmmaking technologies as well as that of the dissemination of films of varying formats through the internet has added to the importance of visual media. At the same time, as has often been pointed out, the aging of the population that experienced these historical traumas has also brought home the urgency of preserving individual oral accounts that shed more light on how these ruptures left imprints on the everyday lives of people. This has in turn contributed to a flourishing of autobiographical and biographical accounts of these histories in both textual and visual forms. If we are to explore the dynamic character of memory's interaction with identities and multiple histories of violence, it is pertinent that we examine how various media represent history and create collective memories. We also must pay attention to the peculiarities of each medium, as "[each] has its specific way of remembering and will leave its trace on the memory it creates."[11]

My discussion of the two films relies upon Michael Rothberg's and Max Silverman's recent explorations of a poetics of memory that is attentive to multiple histories of violence and not contained by exclusivist identities.[12] Both scholars have analyzed how different works of art, both literary and visual, promote a different way of remembering. In so doing, they have proposed models of memory that pay attention to the interaction of different temporal traces, as well as to its associative aspects that reveal how "one buried memory turns out to be an investigation into another."[13] The two films discussed below will be read in the light of their respective models and conceptualizations of multidirectional memory and palimpsestic memory, which emphasize the importance of a form of remembering that goes beyond group identities to explore intersecting histories of violence.

Rothberg examines how multiple histories confront each other in the public sphere and challenges two primary assumptions of the current understanding of collective memory and group identity: "that of their notion of public sphere as a pre-given, limited space in which already established groups engage in life and death struggle" and that of "the notion that the boundaries of memory parallel the boundaries of group identity."[14] Such assumptions limit collective memory within a competitive memory model: "As I struggle to achieve recognition of *my* memories and *my* identity, I necessarily exclude the memories and identities of others."[15] Rothberg critiques such a model and instead proposes a multidirectional model of memory, which does not limit itself to individual group identities: "The model of multidirectional memory posits collective memory as partially disengaged from exclusive versions of cultural identity and acknowledges how remembrance both cuts across and binds together inverse spatial, temporal, and cultural sites."[16]

Likewise, Max Silverman highlights the associative nature of memory and explores a poetics of memory that connects disparate historical events and cuts across cultural and national identities. For Silverman, with palimpsestic memory "[t]he relationship between present and past therefore takes the form of a superimposition and interaction of different temporal traces to constitute a sort of composite structure, like a palimpsest, so that one layer of traces can be seen through, and is transformed by another."[17] A palimpsestic approach to memory is thus described as a process wherein "[f]irst, the present is shown to be shadowed or haunted by a past which is not immediately visible but is progressively brought into view. [. . .] Second, the composite structure in these works is a combination of not simply two moments in time (past and present) but a number of different moments, hence producing a chain which draws together disparate spaces and times."[18] In this approach, as Silverman shows through an attentive analysis of a number of films and literary works, a memory, instead of remaining attached to a singular historical event or confined within a particular group identity, can instead turn out "to be an investigation into another."

Both Silverman and Rothberg thus explore the anachronistic aspect of memory, and its potential for constructing solidarities by connecting different historical experiences of exclusion. As Rothberg states, "Memory's anachronistic quality – its bringing together of now and then, here and there – is actually the source of its powerful creativity, its ability to build new worlds out of the materials of older ones."[19] For documenting Shanghai of this time period, with the histories of colonialism and of the Holocaust intersecting in its diverse population of the time, this model of memory could have interesting implications for the manner in which these collective histories are framed through interviews, such as in the documentaries under discussion here. Both the films discussed below rely heavily on interviews of survivors who spent their childhood or youth in Shanghai and then relocated, mainly to the United States. The individual memories of the interviewees, therefore, are of primary importance to the two films. As we shall see below, the two films have slightly varying approaches to the interviews as well as in the choice of individuals who have been selected to narrate this episode of history. Memory, however, is associative. And as Rothberg points out, this makes it difficult to contain it within group identities.[20]

Memory as a "mirror" of the past in *Shanghai Ghetto*

The 2002 documentary film *Shanghai Ghetto* follows an overarching chronology in the way it presents this history through individual memories, archival material, and historians' accounts. The directors Dana Janklowicz-Mann and Amir Mann based this film upon extensive research and archival sources drawn from various public and private archives in the United States, Israel, and China. However, the on-camera interviews with five former refugees now residing in the United States play a very central role in the film as well.

66 *Shambhavi Prakash*

All five survivors presented in the film were children or young adults at the time that their families had to flee Germany in the aftermath of *Kristallnacht*.[21] As Janklowicz-Mann points out in the directors' commentary in the DVD version of the film, almost all of the individuals interviewed during the making of the film had already written memoirs about their experiences of exile.[22] As is common with many of the memoirs, as well as historical accounts dealing with this episode of history,[23] the film is divided into various stages based on its subjects' lived experiences, which are grouped together and interspersed with archival and historical material.[24]

The resilience and innovation demonstrated by the interviewed narrators and their families are clearly evident in their accounts, which take us through their struggle for survival in a new city. The five interviewees begin by describing their childhoods in Germany, which were eclipsed by experiences of escalating anti-Semitism in their hometowns, culminating in memories of *Kristallnacht*. This is followed by descriptions of a hurried escape from Europe, journey to Asia by sea, initial impressions upon arrival in Shanghai, and the invaluable assistance received from the Jewish community in Shanghai.

Two elements tend to dominate the descriptions of Shanghai as a place – the cosmopolitan culture of the colonial port city and its miserable living conditions, especially in the poor Hongkew district (now Hongkou), where many Jewish refugees had to live. In descriptions of Shanghai's cosmopolitan culture, we also come to know the Jewish refugees' persistent attempts to start from scratch and carve out a living, as well as to rebuild – by opening cafes, bakeries, theater groups, newspapers, etc. – a semblance of the cultural life they had left behind. The presence of European powers and their influence on the culture of the city helped in this, although many struggled to overcome the language barrier. However, the colonial context of Shanghai is primarily mentioned with respect to the cosmopolitan culture and employment options in the International Settlement, and there is only a brief reference to the other implications of this context for the various groups inhabiting the same locales.[25] Although we hear much about Shanghai's cosmopolitan culture at the time, the existing colonial hierarchies which engendered brutal racial violence rarely come up in the oral accounts in the film. While the non-Western population bore the brunt of much of this colonial violence, these hierarchies also affected the newly arrived central European refugees in different ways.[26] We do not hear much about the social hierarchies that existed between European refugees and the poorer Chinese, some of whom were employed by wealthier refugees to help with domestic chores. We hear even less about colonialism's role in the destitution of the Chinese population or the effect of everyday violence of colonial structures on Chinese as well as Jewish refugees. One exception to this, however, is a scene involving Harald Janklowicz' moving description of the plight of the Chinese which is interspersed with archival images supporting the narrative. We see a close-up shot of Janklowicz narrating the struggles of "coolies" and

Jewish exile and models of memory 67

rickshaw pullers. As he remarks on the difficulty of witnessing "a human being lugging a wagon with rich people through the streets for hours and days," we are shown a black and white image of a couple of two-wheeled rickshaws carrying a European family. The contrast between the European man wearing a suit and hat and the emaciated Chinese rickshaw runner highlights the oppressive colonial relations that do not otherwise find much mention in these narratives. A few scenes earlier, another survivor, Alfred Kohn, also recalls the Chinese as "very poor, very hardworking and under [the] direct oppression of the Japanese." Such accounts reveal the possibilities of multidirectional memory. Although the focus in the interviews is on the struggles of the Jewish community in Shanghai, memory's associative nature does not completely lend itself to a single group's identity.

Aside from fondly recalled descriptions of Shanghai's uniquely cosmopolitan International Settlement, those interviewed in this film also chronicle their memory of the city in relation to its difficult living conditions. All of them describe their initial shock at being confronted by the crowds, smells, and heat upon arrival at the port in Shanghai. Before their descriptions of the eventual end of the war and departure from Shanghai come the most grueling accounts of life in the Hongkew district. All of them recall vividly the lack of hygiene and the terrible sanitary conditions they encountered in the city, the overpowering smells, non-flushing toilets, the lack of kitchen facilities. We hear of the river overflowing into the streets, causing floods every summer, which made the conditions even more unsanitary. The narrators also describe the city in terms of the overwhelming number of diseases they were exposed to, as well as the situation of the poorer Chinese people, many of whom died on the streets during winter time.

Along with descriptions of the conditions prevailing in Shanghai at the time, the narrators also recount their experiences with the Chinese. When asked to relate the conditions of the local Chinese population in Shanghai,[27] the narrators mention how both groups coexisted peacefully. Betty Grebenschikoff describes her family's relationship with their Chinese neighbors as one of "benign tolerance," remarks upon the absence of anti-Semitism, and considers the peaceful acceptance of the newly arrived refugees remarkable given the already scarce resources in the ghetto.[28] Almost all of the interviewees describe the Chinese population in terms of their respective economic hardships. Many comment on how the local population fared much worse economically than did the central European refugees, who were at least guaranteed a daily meal at the food kitchens run by the Jewish community in Shanghai. Although many of them lost a number of relatives and friends in European concentration camps, as well as in the struggle for survival in Shanghai, it is evident from their accounts that they are still haunted by images of yet another series of deaths they encountered – those of the local Chinese. Their accounts repeatedly describe images of seeing dead children wrapped in straw mats and newspapers on the streets in the morning, waiting to be picked up by the garbage truck, since their parents

68 *Shambhavi Prakash*

could not afford anything else. In one such difficult scene, described movingly by Harald Janklowicz, a close-up of his interview is interspersed with black and white photos showing a Jewish boy among a crowd of Chinese children and a poor Chinese woman leaning against a wall. While the film does not show images corresponding to this time, the haunting memory of deaths in Shanghai, not of those in the Jewish community but of their Chinese hosts, reveals again how memory transcends the boundaries of a fixed cultural identity and renders it impossible to exclude other histories of exclusion and trauma.

Another interesting aspect of these descriptions, however, is that the poverty of the Chinese population is often depicted by the interviewees in ahistorical terms. During this time period, China was the site of intense military conflict, with the Chinese and the Japanese fighting for military control. In the Yangtze delta alone, 300,000 Chinese civilians are said to have been massacred. It is also worth noting that the population of Shanghai, which had already witnessed multiple waves of migration from Europe, had more than doubled in the decades just prior to the Second World War. This happened because of the influx of local Chinese immigrants from surrounding areas (such as Ningbo, located in the south of Shanghai, which experienced major flooding of its two rivers during this time). As Bryna Goodman notes: "The stream of new immigrants, including peasants seeking factory employment and refugees from natural disasters or warlord-torn areas, meant that Shanghai continued to be a predominantly immigrant city and that native-place ties continued to be called upon in the service of settling and accommodating the problems of the newcomers."[29] By the early 1930s, Shanghai's population of 1.2 million inhabitants had increased to 2.6 million, and, according to some other accounts, to 3.5 million.[30] Although during this period Shanghai saw a heavy influx of refugees from other parts of China, these Chinese populations are not described as refugees in the oral accounts of the Jewish survivors in the film. Instead, they seem to be statically portrayed as if outside of history, rather than also directly affected by historical events and political power structures. (Exceptions are the references to the mistreatment of both communities at the hands of the Japanese occupiers.)

Although *Shanghai Ghetto* relies heavily on interviews of survivors, it frames their recollections of Shanghai through the extensive use of personal and public archival material. Almost every sequence in the film consists, apart from the interviews, of archival images and footage of interviewees, standing in queues for food at the lodgings (*Heime*) and hospitals run by the Jewish communities, as well as visuals of the more prosperous areas of the city like the Bund and the Nanking Road.[31] Narratives by the survivors are supported and expanded further with accounts provided by Sinologist Irene Eber, historians David Kranzler and Xu Buzeng, as well as with background commentary by Martin Landau. Together they serve to lay out the larger historical background and present a chronological description of historical events as they unfolded from the 1930s and 40s.

Jewish exile and models of memory 69

The film thus employs different kinds of historiography: a univocal official narrative (through Landau's commentary) carrying forward accounts based on individual memories of survivors, which work together to present a cultural memory of this history. Both kinds of historiography (one focused on presenting history as a single arc, the other on multiple individual memories), however, remain within the bounds of a narrow group identity, also bound by nationality, since the film retains its focus on German and Austrian Jews in its choice of interviewees. As we shall see later in this chapter, Ottinger's film adopts a substantially different approach.

In the commentary accompanying the DVD version of the film, the directors describe the necessity of mapping out the broader historical context before focusing upon the Jewish refugees in Shanghai. They therefore chose to begin the film with a brief overview of the rise of National Socialism in Germany, since it shaped the refugees' experience of exile in Shanghai, and since they found it important to present it as a caution for the future given the contemporary political context. This focus is also evident in their extensive use of archival material and historians' accounts, as well as the closely followed historical chronology in the presentation and background narration by Landau. As mentioned previously, the film does not present an overview of the colonial context of Shanghai, apart from a brief remark in the directors' commentary included with the DVD. In addition to this, the directors also seem focused in their efforts to capture contemporary shots for the film from exactly the same point of view as found in archival images employed in the film (this is also mentioned in the directors' commentary). They describe the difficulty of getting the same shots due to changes in the cityscape and their wish to capture images that mirror the old Shanghai and that are absent of the disruptions of contemporary Shanghai such as the constant traffic and advertising billboards on old colonial buildings. This view is also echoed in how the film uses contemporary footage of Shanghai but in sepia tones that aim to mirror the archival images of the lanes of the Hongkew district.

This approach, fairly traditional for a historical documentary attempting to recreate episodes from history, is especially interesting when seen in conjunction with the next documentary, whose approach to contemporary footage of Shanghai is entirely different. Apart from their statements in the commentary, the cinematic strategies in *Shanghai Ghetto* point toward a view of the past as uncontaminated by the present, even as the film simultaneously relies on later historical works to weave the story together. They also show a specific understanding of the function of this film and its relation to collective memory and history. For instance, the directors mention the decision to exclude the interviews of some people who came from Poland through Russia and Japan to Shanghai, since they decided to "only keep what would serve the story the best." The film thus also seems to depict memory within the frame of a nation-state.

70 *Shambhavi Prakash*

In an attempt to preserve the history of this Jewish exile (as the directors also emphasize in the commentary to the film), the interviews mostly focus on aspects of life in Shanghai that directly affected the community of central European refugees. The interviews do not go into detail regarding the other histories of violence that intersected in this multicultural city, and which the refugees might have encountered along with other intercultural experiences. However, despite this focus and understanding of collective memory as limited to a group identity, one comes across other instances (both in the interviewees' as well as in the directors' accounts) that display an openness to multidirectional memory and, echoing Rothberg, show memory as an associative process where solidarity and empathy can reach across group identities.

One such example of collective memory interconnecting different histories of violence occurs during the directors' commentary included in the DVD version of the film. The interviewees as well as the directors draw parallels between the racism experienced by the Jewish community and by the local Chinese population. They describe the terrible conditions that the refugees as well as the locals had to face under Japanese occupation. In 1942, after the Japanese attack on Pearl Harbor and the entry of the United States into the Second World War, the Japanese forces occupying Shanghai ordered all "stateless" refugees who had arrived in Shanghai after 1937 (which were primarily the European Jewish refugees) into what was euphemistically called the "Restricted Sector for Stateless Refugees" in the Hongkew district of Shanghai, and which the refugees came to describe as "the ghetto." The final years of the Second World War were the most difficult ones for the refugees, and many died due to the terrible living conditions in the ghetto during this time. Although they were dependent upon the arbitrary mercy of Kanoh Ghoya,[32] some historians point out that the Japanese occupiers treated the Jewish population with more circumspection than they treated the Chinese.[33] Japanese soldiers killing Chinese civilians on the streets of Shanghai was commonplace, and many Chinese lost their lives at the hands of the Japanese Imperial Army. In the accompanying commentary, both directors draw direct parallels between the racism experienced by Jews at the hands of National Socialists and that experienced by the Chinese under the Japanese. For instance, one of the directors, Dana Janklowicz-Mann, remarks in the filmmakers' commentary, "The Japanese treated the Chinese horribly; they looked at them as racially inferior – kind of like the Nazis looked at the Jews – there's a parallel there." The other director, Amir Mann, adds, "Or the other racism in Europe like the Slavs or whatever – the Nazis looked at them as a race of slaves that'll serve us; that's how the Japanese looked at the Chinese." Racism faced by the local Chinese population at the hands of their Japanese occupiers is thus invoked in connection with the history of National Socialism in Europe. This twin recollection of the two traumas, to use Rothberg's phrase, rearticulates the memory of Jewish exile in Shanghai in ways that "construct solidarity out of the specificities, overlaps, and echoes of different historical experiences."[34]

Palimpsestic memory in *Exil Shanghai*

Ulrike Ottinger's *Exil Shanghai* is composed of interviews with six people who spent the war years in Shanghai. Some of them were born in Shanghai after their families had fled there during the time of the Russian Revolution, while the others arrived in the city from Europe by ship between 1937 and 1941. All the interviews conducted by Ottinger in the film took place in 1995 in California, where the interviewees had eventually settled after leaving Shanghai at the end of the Second World War. The extensive footage of contemporary Shanghai we see in the film was shot by Ottinger in 1996, and the film was released in 1997.

In their accounts of the time spent in Shanghai, all six interviewees focus on the background of their families, the arrival in Shanghai, and the cosmopolitan milieu of the city with separate legally protected zones for the colonial powers. As in the previous film, *Exil Shanghai* depicts the attempts of the central European refugees to survive in the new city with the help of the Committee for Assistance of European Jewish Refugees in Shanghai, their struggles to rebuild their lives through initiative and hard work, as well as their forced settlement and precarious existence in the Hongkew section, where their movements were restricted by curfews. While there are passing references to the impoverished conditions of the local people who shared these spaces with them and also struggled to survive there, the accounts are largely devoid of references to other aspects of Chinese culture that they may have encountered in Shanghai. The emphasis in their accounts also remains largely on the life of the European community in this city.

Through her research for the film, Ottinger, like the directors of *Shanghai Ghetto*, had access to extensive archival material from this time period. She chooses, however, to use very little of it in the film. The four-and-a-half-hour-long film includes instead long extended footage of Shanghai from the 1990s, interspersed with the interviews, sometimes with the voiceover of the interviewees, at other times with diegetic sounds from the streets unaccompanied by commentary, and at yet other times with a variety of musical scores from Chinese and Yiddish traditions. There is a frequent crosscutting of scenes, spatially as well as temporally. The interviews from 1995, wherein witnesses narrate their memories of a 1930s and 1940s Shanghai, are interspersed with contemporary street scenes from Shanghai. As the historical narration continues, there is often a spatial jump across continents. We continue to hear accounts of the interviewees' memories of Shanghai, but the narrations are accompanied by visuals of contemporary Shanghai. The choice of these edits has the effect of a collage/montage, and the combination of the narrated theme and the visuals (often disconnected on the surface) generates rich, evocative connections.

72 Shambhavi Prakash

Although the broader theme of her documentary is similar to *Shanghai Ghetto*, Ottinger's approach to documenting this aspect of the history of the Holocaust differs in several ways from the previous collection of interviews discussed above. Unlike *Shanghai Ghetto*, Ottinger does not restrict the focus of interviews to only central European refugees fleeing National Socialism. Of the six people interviewed, half are of Russian or Viennese backgrounds, some of whose families had migrated from Russia to Shanghai many decades prior and had flourished in the city. The other three had fled Germany and Austria soon after *Kristallnacht*, or the German annexation of Austria, or via the *Kindertransport* to London before their families arranged for them to travel to Shanghai. The choice to include these interviews not only highlights stories of Jewish refugees who fled from National Socialism, but also incorporates other histories of migration, exile, and exclusion. The stories of persecution under National Socialism in Germany and Austria are juxtaposed with those of anti-Jewish pogroms of the nineteenth and early twentieth centuries in Russia. Ottinger does not provide, therefore, a single authoritative historical account within which individual narratives are to be understood and which connects these narratives for the viewer. Instead, with the narrators each tracing their own historical backgrounds, we are provided with multiple histories.[35] Some of these accounts overlap, while others vary according to the different historical periods of migration and the individual family histories of the narrators. Yet together, they provide a rich tapestry of the various historical movements that formed the Jewish community in Shanghai, while at the same time leaving room for the viewers to connect the intersecting histories for themselves.

Although Ottinger had access to plenty of archival material, she uses it sparingly. For most of the film, as the narrators recall their experiences, we see neither archival material validating, authenticating, or supporting these accounts (as in the previous film), nor are these experiences presented within a thematic grouping introduced by guiding explanations.[36] Instead of maintaining the focus solely on the past (as the previous film does through its extensive use of archival material), this film does the opposite. As the narrators continue to relate their memories of colonial Shanghai, the visuals often lead away from medium close-up shots of the narrators and focus instead on contemporary Shanghai. Long sequences that provide no commentary to guide the viewer, and which at times are unaccompanied by interviewees' narration, also appear often. Such sequences usually include only diegetic sounds or different genres of music without any translation. By calling attention to the intimate witness accounts as much as to long sequences of scenes from contemporary Shanghai without accompanying commentary, the film heightens the gaps and silences about other intersecting histories of violence and exclusion that existed in the highly stratified, war-torn, colonial Shanghai of this period. Through these immersive scenes of unending activity and myriad little aspects of everyday life on the streets,

Jewish exile and models of memory 73

in hotels, and in the Hongkew lanes of Shanghai in the 1990s, the film manages to make the presence of this absence linger.

In their article on this film, Kristen Harjes and Tanja Nusser insightfully point out that, rather than validating the narratives of interviewees with authentic footage from the location, Ottinger repeatedly distracts the viewer.[37] I would add that Ottinger not only distracts the viewer but also creates a depth to the narrative of the interviewees by adding multiple layers (in time and space), revealing what Max Silverman refers to as "palimpsestic memory." While we listen to the street sounds of Shanghai as intently as to the memories of the interviewees, the past and present, the old Jewish communities, and the contemporary Chinese city are repeatedly juxtaposed until one starts to resonate through the other.

Such immersive scenes play multiple functions in the film. Since the accounts by the narrators only reveal the cultural life of various Jewish communities inhabiting the city, these scenes often provide glimpses of the broader culture that existed alongside these communities, which we rarely glimpse in the narratives' portrayal of cultural life in Shanghai. For instance, as one of the interviewees describes the excellent Viennese cafes of wartime Shanghai, the camera does not show archival images of these cafes. Instead, it juxtaposes this story with a contemporary Shanghai street, bustling with customers, by slowly panning across the varieties of street food being cooked in the open. The commentary by directors of the *Shanghai Ghetto* emphasized that it was important for them to capture shots of contemporary Shanghai in a manner that mirrored the old Shanghai being narrated. A city bustling with traffic and with billboards on a lot of the old buildings therefore presented an obstacle for them. For Ottinger, presenting an "authentic" cityscape of the old Shanghai through visuals does not seem to be the primary objective. Therefore, she does not rely on archival material to convey the atmosphere or the culture of the version of Shanghai that the refugees experienced. Instead, contemporary Shanghai is allowed to resonate with the stories being narrated, and "[o]ne buried memory turns out to be an investigation into another."[38] Amy Villarejo's excellent reading of the film helps in understanding the significance of these Shanghai scenes: "Ottinger's orchestration of Jewish exiles' recollections with extended glimpses into the life of Shanghai as it is now provides a critical apparatus with which to displace or dislodge the authority of the archive as dead repository and to effect a mode of direct translation from the past to the present, from Europe to Asia, from memory to a kind of documentary presence. [. . .] Ottinger, in other words, refuses the authority of the past as convention (old photographs, maps) but similarly refuses the continuity of the present as identity (we, Jews, then and now)."[39]

The juxtaposition of the narratives of former Jewish residents about the old Shanghai with visuals of contemporary Shanghai creates a palimpsest that enables the viewer to draw new connections, and allows for a collective

74 *Shambhavi Prakash*

memory that is open rather than confined within the boundaries of a specific group identity or a time period. A sequence from the section on George Spunt exemplifies this. Spunt, who died just a year after the interview, presents a narrative that is memorable in its vivid description of his and his family's colorful life in Shanghai. He describes his parents' Russian and Viennese Jewish background and how their families came to Shanghai at the turn of the century. His parents met in 1904 in Shanghai as teenagers, and his father became the most successful cotton broker in the city. Although he died in 1925 (when he was just 45 years old), he left his family an estate that secured them a lavish lifestyle till the end of the war, after which they migrated to California. During this narration, the camera stays in a fixed position and, as with all of the other interviewees in the film, we see Spunt in a medium close-up shot. He then starts to describe the penthouse in the International Settlement that his parents moved into in 1918, and at this point Ottinger introduces an interesting crosscutting sequence in the film. When Spunt describes elegant penthouse living in the first two decades of the century, the camera cuts to contemporary footage of a few buildings through a low angle shot of the top floors. Ottinger chooses to crosscut to this scene again from a medium close-up of Spunt as his description moves from the family to an enumeration of their many Chinese servants. As he starts to mention the cooks, "coolies," gardeners, and other Chinese domestics, his voiceover continues over a slow-moving tilt of the camera, which traverses the building from the top and comes to rest down at street level, revealing a group of people reclining on benches with their mattresses spread out over what seems to be their packed belongings. From the way they are dressed (they do not appear destitute), it is hard to tell if the group on the pavement of the Nanking avenue are tourists, immigrants, or refugees, and this scene seems to underscore our inability to know these stories fully.

As Spunt continues to describe the servants and especially the death of the Chinese cook whom he loved dearly, the camera cuts between a medium close-up of him and back again to the street scene. This time we see two of the Chinese in the group sipping tea next to their belongings on the street. Soon thereafter, as we hear Spunt's voiceover narrative move from a discussion of the servants to one of his family, the camera slowly tilts up from the street scene to the top floors of the building on Nanking Road. The edit leads us back from the street to the elegant life in the penthouse. The camera movement from top to bottom and then back up to the top as it traverses the façade of the imposing historical buildings in the International Settlement, as well as the edits between Spunt's evocative recollections, black and white family photos, and the footage of contemporary Shanghai create a tension between the narrative we hear through the voiceover of Spunt and what we see on screen. It juxtaposes the life upstairs with the street downstairs, while also connecting the Shanghai of the 1920s to that of 1990s, implicitly connecting the lives we hear about with those we do not, and dwelling upon the silences and gaps in these stories.

At the same time, the immersive scenes of contemporary Shanghai also play against another kind of silence. It is the silence that entails the lack of varied visible signs of this community – whose stories we are hearing from the narrators – in contemporary Shanghai. Ten years after the release of this film, the Shanghai Jewish Refugees Museum was established in the Hongkou district at the site of what used to be the Moishe Synagogue. While the museum serves to preserve this aspect of Shanghai's history, which took so long to come to light, this memorialization shows at the same time their absence from the everyday life of the city and echoes Pierre Nora's oft acknowledged insight: "There are *lieux de mémoire*, sites of memory, because there are no more *milieux de mémoire*, real environments of memory."[40]

Other sequences in the film reveal as well a palimpsestic approach to memory that connects different temporal traces. One relevant sequence, which illustrates this approach to memory, appears in the section on Inna Mink. Like Spunt's story, Mink's too involves her grandparents, how they fled Siberia during the Russian Revolution and started a flourishing bathhouse business in Harbin, and how her father eventually came to Shanghai. Inna's narrative in the beginning involves detailed reminiscing about the glamorous life in Shanghai. As she later comes to describe the other side of life in the city, she says, "On the other hand, the poverty was unbelievable. The beggars on the street were horrendous. You would get up in the morning and you would see a black van driving up and down the streets collecting the dead little girls that were thrown out in the garbage can by the Chinese."

At this point, Ottinger does something she does not do often in this film and which is in sharp contrast to the crosscutting strategy she used in the George Spunt sequence discussed earlier. The camera cuts to close-ups of archival documents that authenticate what Inna has just described to us about the plight of the poorer classes in Shanghai. The camera rests on a newspaper article in German titled "Kinder der Strasse" [Street Children], which contains black and white pictures of Chinese street children beaming at the photographer.[41] It then slowly tilts down the length of the article to reveal another photograph – that of the body of a dead child lying on the side of a Shanghai street, wrapped in a mattress. However, this crosscutting does something more than the usual documentary technique of validating a witness account with authentic archival material. This becomes evident in the next cut, as we see a second newspaper article titled "Der Kindersarg" [Children's Coffin] by the Berlin art historian Lothar Brieger, who had fled to Shanghai during this period. As the camera again tilts down slowly through this article, it comes to rest on more black and white photographs of Chinese street children, one of them of a toddler holding a baby with the caption underneath in German: "Flüchtlingskinder" [Refugee Children]. And so as we listen to Inna's memories as a child of refugees from Europe, their poverty, and how it appeared to her as a never-ending horrendous crisis, what we see on the screen is another kind of a refugee child and another

76 Shambhavi Prakash

continuing horror in 1940s Shanghai. Ottinger's juxtaposition here again also brings into sharp focus Michael Rothberg's understanding of memory as "subject to ongoing negotiation, cross-referencing, and borrowing: [memory] as productive and not privative."[42]

All in all, the camera stays on the three pages for almost half a minute, most of it without any narration or non-diegetic sound. Toward the end of this sequence, however, with a close-up of the last page of the article, Inna's narration resumes as she exclaims, "I can't really fathom what the heck was going on with my brains, why I never saw any of it that way, then, that I see today. It's just absolutely amazing." She adds, "But I was a little kid, and all I had to worry about was how to get to school, and how to go to a birthday party, and how to wear the right dress, and fight my mother because of the ruffles; those ruffles just never ended!"[43] As the voiceover narrative is juxtaposed with images of newspaper articles, both kinds of words together form a palimpsest. The trauma of the witnesses who spent their childhood in Shanghai, who also had to flee the country after the war, and who are speaking to us today overlaps with that of Chinese refugee children who were very much a part of that history too, and whose history intersects with the history of Jewish refugees' exile in Shanghai during the war.

Let us consider for a moment the "disparate spaces and times" that Ottinger brings together in this sequence by juxtaposing Inna's voiceover narrative with images from the migrant newspaper *Gelbe Post*. On the one hand, in Inna's voiceover narrative we have the stories of her grandparents' migration from Russia and her own childhood in Shanghai which ended with her migration after the war, while on the other hand, through visual juxtaposition the same scene brings together stories of central European refugees fleeing National Socialism with stories of a war-torn China and Chinese refugee children struggling for survival in Shanghai. All these moments are held together in one sequence in a palimpsest that reveals the filmmaker's "anti-identitarian 'take' on cross-cultural exchange and affective alignment."[44]

Conclusion

We have seen that the choice of cinematic strategies in *Shanghai Ghetto* demonstrates a particular approach to memory. The film grasps collective memory as though it were primarily grounded in group identity. The filmmakers also favored a chronological approach in their framing of historical events. *Exil Shanghai* does not strive for a chronology. Instead, disparate spaces and times are drawn together as palimpsests that reveal the co-existence of moments, events, and historical processes in the present. This approach is more alive to the possibilities of solidarities across group identities.

The two films differ considerably in their aesthetic strategies and their approach to memories of this history. This can be better understood by comparing a scene from each of the two films. In their attempt to mirror the past, the directors of *Shanghai Ghetto* retrace the steps of former refugees by accompanying two of them to Shanghai, to their former living spaces in Hongkew. As one of them visits the tiny, cramped apartment her family used to live in, the camera focuses on her in a medium close-up shot. As she narrates anecdotes from her childhood in that apartment, we can see all the belongings of the current residents. The residents themselves are kept out of the frame, one of them appearing for a brief moment in the frame, only to hurriedly step out of the frame again. Throughout, the camera stays focused on the narrator and her recollections.

The current residents of Hongkew, left outside the neat frame of *Shanghai Ghetto*'s "main story," appear differently in a scene in *Exil Shanghai*. The sequence takes us from views of Hongkew's lanes to a medium close-up shot of a Chinese woman. The woman, a longtime resident of Hongkew, recalls days from her childhood, when her father worked as a carpenter during the years that saw an influx of Jewish refugees. Hers remains the sole Chinese voice in a fairly lengthy film. It is safe to conclude that Ottinger's primary interest was not to present a comprehensive account of this history. One Chinese voice in the film does not allow for multiple "authentic" perspectives to emerge. What it does do, however, is to hint at the multiple histories intersecting within the history of the Jewish exiles in Shanghai; it stands in contrast to the fleeting and voiceless presence of the current Hongkew resident in *Shanghai Ghetto*.

The seamlessness resulting from *Shanghai Ghetto*'s editorial choices enables identification. At the same time, it also misses or elides other connections that might emerge from a view of collective memory that goes beyond group identities and draws upon intersecting histories. *Exil Shanghai* works with a more fluid frame. While the narrators all share a connection with the Jewish community of Shanghai, the long immersive scenes from contemporary Shanghai allow for the film to transcend the theme of Jewish exile in Shanghai. By juxtaposing contemporary Shanghai with this history, the film offers a different "relation between histories and their memorial legacies."[45]

Although both films are different in their overall approach to individual and cultural memories of the Jewish exile in Shanghai, both offer valuable examples of memory's multidirectionality. Both films also hint at memory's ability to transcend group identities. In the directors' commentary of *Shanghai Ghetto*, Janklowicz-Mann notes the parallels between the experiences of European and Chinese refugees. She follows this by remarking on the resilience of the Chinese and connects this to her choice of the film's poster. The poster, a black and white image of a Chinese rickshaw puller wading through flooded streets reflects a transnational solidarity. For Janklowicz-Mann, this black and white image became emblematic of the situation of the Chinese. Thus, the poster of a documentary film about the exile of European Jews evokes the misery of a Chinese rickshaw puller and underscores the

78 Shambhavi Prakash

daily struggle for survival of both groups, a struggle that cut across ethnic lines.

Ottinger's *Exil Shanghai* also achieves this, but through a different approach to history and memory, as well as their relationship to the present. In *Exil Shanghai*, the drawing together of disparate spaces and times happens slowly and subtly over many scenes, and the long duration of the film plays into this as well. As we are overwhelmed by the stories of survivors, their struggles, near-death escapes from Europe, and the immeasurable losses of their families and friends who did not manage to escape, the visuals insistently dwell on seemingly unconnected footage from 1990s Shanghai. However, through the apparent lack of coherence of the Shanghai scenes, there slowly emerge many stories and silences that add to the witness accounts. We become increasingly aware therefore of the everyday minutiae of the immediate context that may not have been articulated in witness accounts, while also being confronted by the noises as well as the silences of contemporary Shanghai. The voiceovers and visuals come together to form palimpsests in this film and present a non-competitive and non-essentialist model of memory. The film, to paraphrase Silverman, offers a poetics of memory that holds the possibility of an inclusive politics of memory.

Notes

1 For a concise overview of the history of Jewish migration to Shanghai, see the introductory chapter of *Voices from Shanghai: Jewish Exiles in Wartime China*, ed. Irene Eber (Chicago: University of Chicago Press, 2008).
2 At the Evian Conference held in 1938 in France to discuss a solution to the German and Austrian Jewish refugee problem, all of the thirty-two participating countries (with the exception of the Dominican Republic) refused to ease their restrictions to allow the immigration of Jewish refugees.
3 An exception to this trend was David Kranzler's *Japanese, Nazis & Jews: The Jewish Refugee Community of Shanghai, 1938–1945* (New York: Yeshiva University Press, 1976), which appeared much earlier and is regarded as an authoritative account.
4 For a detailed bibliography of biographical and other literary works focusing on this period of Shanghai, see Wei Zhuang, *Erinnerungskulturen des jüdischen Exils in Shanghai (1933–1950): Plurimedialität und Transkulturalität* (Berlin: LIT Verlag, 2015).
5 *Exil Shanghai*, directed by Ulrike Ottinger (Tranfax Film Productions/Shanghai Film Studio, 1997), DVD; *Shanghai Ghetto*, directed by Dana Janklowicz-Mann and Amir Mann (Rebel Child Productions, 2002), DVD. For interview compilations, see Steven Hochstadt, *Exodus to Shanghai. Stories of Escape from the Third Reich* (New York: Palgrave Macmillan, 2012), and Berl Falbaum, ed., *Shanghai Remembered. . . : Stories of Jews Who Escaped to Shanghai from Nazi Europe* (Troy, MI: Momentum Books, 2005).
6 Michael Rothberg, *Multidirectional Memory: Remembering the Holocaust in the Age of Decolonization* (Stanford, CA: Stanford University Press, 2009), 11.
7 "Culture Shock" is the title given by Steven Hochstadt to a chapter in his book *Exodus to Shanghai*; the chapter documents accounts by Jewish refugees of their

arrival in Shanghai. Other memoirs which deal with this history of Jewish exile in China also bear titles that underscore the deprivation or strangeness of their new city. See, for instance, Sigmund Tobias, *Strange Haven: A Jewish Childhood in Wartime Shanghai* (Champaign: University of Illinois Press, 2009) and Evelyn Pike Rubin, *Shanghai Ghetto* (New York: Shengold, 1993).

8 See Bruche M. Staves and Linda Shopes, "Series Editors' Foreword," in Steven Hochstadt, *Exodus to Shanghai, Stories of Escape from the Third Reich* (New York: Palgrave Macmillan, 2012), xv.

9 Maurice Halbwachs, *On Collective Memory*, trans. and ed. Lewis Coser (Chicago: University of Chicago Press, 1992).

10 Robert A. Rosenstone, *History on Film, Film on History* (London; New York: Routledge, 2012), 14.

11 Astrid Erll, "Literature, Film, and the Mediality of Cultural Memory," in *Cultural Memory Studies: An International and Interdisciplinary Handbook*, ed. Astrid Erll and Ansgar Nünning (Berlin: Walter de Gruyter, 2008), 389.

12 Rothberg, *Multidirectional Memory*; Max Silverman, *Palimpsestic Memory: The Holocaust and Colonialism in French and Francophone Fiction and Film* (New York; Oxford: Berghahn Books, 2013).

13 Silverman, *Palimpsestic Memory*, 12.

14 Rothberg, *Multidirectional Memory*, 5.

15 Ibid.

16 Ibid., 11.

17 Silverman, *Palimpsestic Memory*, 11.

18 Ibid., 11, 12.

19 Rothberg, *Multidirectional Memory*, 6.

20 Ibid., 19.

21 One of the Jewish survivors of exile in Shanghai explains in a newspaper interview why the term "survivor" defines their refugee community too: " 'We lived in a utopia compared with the Jews who stayed in Europe,' said author Rubin. 'We never looked over our shoulders; we didn't have to worry about being put in gas chambers [. . .] [But] we had to flee our homeland and lived under bad conditions, under the Japanese occupation, so we're survivors too.' " Henry Chu, "Shanghai's Jews Live to Tell Story at Last," *Los Angeles Times*, July 15, 1997, accessed May 15, 2017, http://articles.latimes.com/1997/jul/15/news/mn-12725/3.

22 See, for instance, the memoirs by Betty Grebenschikoff, Sigmund Tobias, and Evelyn Pike Rubin, who were all featured in the film. The other survivors interviewed in the film include Alfred Kohn and Harald Janklowicz.

23 A recent work to follow this thematic grouping is Hochstadt, *Exodus to Shanghai*.

24 Since the narrations by interviewees were edited to fit together into thematic sections dealing with different stages of this exile thus highlighting their collective experiences, my treatment of this film too focuses on the group as a whole instead of on individual accounts.

25 In the filmmakers' commentary, one of the directors makes a brief reference to the colonial context of Shanghai as being similar to "what the British did in India."

26 In his memoir, Ernest Heppner describes the way colonial hierarchies affected the newly arrived European refugees in Shanghai. Finding employment was particularly difficult due to the "loss of face" suffered by the white community in "a society where Europeans were respected for their power or wealth, where manual labor on their part was unheard of." Ernest G. Heppner, *Shanghai Refuge: A Memoir of the World War II Jewish Ghetto* (Lincoln, NE; London: University of Nebraska Press, 1995), 43.

80 *Shambhavi Prakash*

27 The directors point out in the filmmakers' commentary that their questions guiding the interviews were deliberately left out of the film, since they wanted the words of the narrators to dominate the story.

28 In the film Betty Grebenschikoff remarks, "We were 20,000 in their territory, pushing them out, living really in poverty," and she emphasizes that they "never once saw a sign of anti-Semitism, disgust, or criticism" from the Chinese.

29 Bryna Goodman, *Native Place, City, and Nation: Regional Networks & Identities in Shanghai 1853–1937* (Berkeley: University of California Press, 1995), 224.

30 Eber, *Voices from Shanghai*, 6.

31 The Committee for the Assistance of European Jewish Refugees in Shanghai, run by the Jewish communities in Shanghai and aided by the American Joint Distribution Committee, was crucial to the survival of the refugees in Shanghai. It led the effort to provide food, shelter (through community homes called *Heime*), and medical facilities to central European refugees who were arriving by the thousands in Shanghai in the late 1930s and early 1940s.

32 Kanoh Ghoya was the Japanese official in charge of granting passes that allowed the "stateless" Jewish refugees to leave the ghetto for work, procuring food, etc. He is mentioned in most witness accounts as having been notorious for his cruelty, short temper, and the arbitrariness with which he refused passes.

33 Historians David Kranzler and Irene Eber, interviewed in *Shanghai Ghetto*, maintain that this was largely because the Japanese bought into the National Socialist myth of the power and economic importance of the Jews, and, therefore, did not want to antagonize them.

34 Rothberg, *Multidirectional Memory*, 16.

35 The first interview in the film is that of Rena Kresno, who deftly and vividly traces the various waves of Jewish migration to Shanghai in the last two centuries and thus provides a sort of historical context for the theme of the film right at the beginning, especially since the opening credits of the film (and the rest of her interview) begin right after this narration. However, despite this, it differs from *Shanghai Ghetto* because the historical context is set here through an individual recounting her community's history rather than through an authoritative anonymous narrator.

36 Hochstadt, *Exodus to Shanghai*, provides short introductions to guide the reader through the various phases of exile described by former refugees.

37 Kirsten Harjes and Tanja Nusser, "An Authentic Experience of History: Tourism in Ulrike Ottinger's 'Exil Shanghai,'" *Women in German Yearbook*, no. 15 (2000): 247–63.

38 Silverman, *Palimpsestic Memory*, 12.

39 Amy Villarejo, "Archiving the Diaspora: A Lesbian Impression of/in Ulrike Ottinger's 'Exile Shanghai,'" *New German Critique*, no. 87, Special Issue on Postwall Cinema (2002): 181, 183.

40 Pierre Nora, "Between Memory and History: Les Lieux de Mémoire," *Representations*, no. 26, Special Issue: *Memory and Counter-Memory* (Spring 1989): 7.

41 The two newspaper articles in this sequence are from *Die Gelbe Post*, an important German-Jewish monthly of the time in Shanghai. It was run by the journalist Adolf J. Storfer. For more on the small but thriving German Jewish newspapers in Shanghai at the time, see Wilfried Seywald, *Journalisten im Shanghaier Exil 1939–1949* (Salzburg: Neugebauer, 1987).

42 Rothberg, *Multidirectional Memory*, 14.

43 Amy Villarejo has an insightful reading of this scene: "These are moments of self-incrimination, of the adult indicting the excesses and privileges not only of colonial power but of adolescent naiveté or blindness. [. . .] The question the film

poses, however, is how are we to counter the impressions of age/race/ethnicity/religion/gender/class/sexuality as they are recoded as Jewishness itself in the archive of victimage? Testimony refuses the certainty of such codings." Villarejo, "Archiving the Diaspora," 186.
44 Ibid., 184.
45 Rothberg, *Multidirectional Memory*, 11.

Part II

Japanese images of Germany and transnational flow between Germany and East Asia

4 A close country in the distance

Japanese images of Germany in the twentieth century[1]

Toru Takenaka

It is safe to say that the images we form of other countries emanate from both the head and the heart. Objective assessment, reflecting the former (head), is determined by the rational calculation of interest determined by profit or loss. The latter subjective view (heart) is based on seemingly spontaneous feelings that are shaped unconsciously by broad cultural representations. This is aptly illustrated through a comparison of Japanese attitudes toward the United States and Germany. The Americans, together with the English, were branded "bestial Anglo-Saxon devils" and enemy number one during World War II. This pernicious stereotype was inculcated in the Japanese population with wartime propaganda. Despite this violent imagery, the Japanese fascination with American pop culture never weakened. Soon after the war's end, Hollywood movies again became box-office hits, and jazz, boogie-woogie, and other pop numbers conquered the Japanese music scene. The objective wartime designation of America as foe could not overcome the subjective Japanese attachment to American popular culture.

A similar yet opposite disconnect can be observed in the Japanese images of Germany, which glorified German social, industrial, and scientific achievements yet maintained a subjective aloofness to all things German. Even as Germany became a model of modernization following the Meiji Restoration, Japanese sentiment remained remote and stiff. Unlike their effusive embrace of American culture, the Japanese never really warmed to the German achievements in philosophy, literature, music, and science that they otherwise praised and admired. Perhaps the geographical distance between East Asia and Europe played a role. Yet even Britain and France were reflected more amiably in Japanese views, due perhaps to the perceived casualness of French and English manners. In any case, Germany fell short in being able to arouse a personal fondness among most Japanese.

This chapter focuses on how Japanese images of Germany have changed throughout the twentieth century and considers how this bifurcated view of Germany – both appreciative and aloof – emerged and developed. The methodological point of departure is the assumption that our perception of others is less an objective view and instead is primarily a reflection of our own values and self-awareness. We see in an object only the things we want

86   Toru Takenaka

to see and take them to mean what we want them to mean. We tend to not recognize things that do not address our own interest. Or we ignore things that do not fit into our personal frame of reference. Accordingly, Japanese images of Germany are first of all mirror images of the Japanese themselves. They changed when the attitude of the Japanese public changed, even if little had actually changed in German society. By the same token, even a revolutionary change in Germany may have had little if any influence on the Japanese perception of Germany. The primary focus of this article, therefore, is how Japan understood itself at a given point in time and how this influenced Japanese views of Europe and particularly of Germany.[2]

Over the course of some 150 years, Japanese views of Germany went through roughly five stages. From the mid-nineteenth century until World War I, the Japanese perspective on Germany might be characterized as a "cool" admiration. This was followed by a second stage ending in 1945, during which Japan enjoyed a heightened self-confidence and consequently sought to be treated as an equal. In the postwar period, Japan's reserved "coolness" toward Germany diminished and by the 1970s, Germany had become a more familiar country. In a fourth phase beginning in the 1980s, Japanese familiarization with Germany included a new admiration for the German organization of everyday life culture. As the importance of Germany's high-cultural achievements receded, the new German-inspired motto became "quality of life." Consistent throughout these four stages was the Japanese belief that Germany provided a model worthy of emulation. This has become questioned in recent years, and Germany, in the Japanese view, may finally be attaining the status of a normal country.[3]

Cool admiration of Germany, 1871–1918

The Japanese first began to look to Germany as a possible model for building a nation-state quite early on. The Iwakura Mission, a delegation of leading policymakers in the Meiji government sent on a long tour through America and Europe in 1871–73, was quite impressed by Germany. In its report the delegation recommended that "it will be of more benefit to make inquiries into this country's politics and its people's affairs than into those of Britain and France."[4] Their judgment is understandable. Germany's historical trajectory of having overcome centuries of disarray and finally achieving national unification appealed to the leaders of the newly born Meiji nation-state. Their attention was equally attracted by Germany's success in building up its national power within a short time and its rapid assumption of a position as a major European power. Furthermore, Germany's achievements as a frontrunner in science and technology gave them another reason to look to the country as a model. The delegation's positive attitude toward Germany was apparently widely shared among the Japanese political class. For example, Aoki Shūzō advocated learning from Germany, which he described as "full of energy just like the rising sun . . . and fares brilliantly in cultural and

A *close country in the distance* 87

academic fields."[5] It is not surprising that such flattering praise came from the one-time foreign minister, who was a central figure of the pro-German connections in Japanese political circles. Still, Aoki was not alone in this unqualified admiration. Ugaki Kazushige, who later served as army minister, also revered Germany and emphasized the allegedly excellent quality of its people. Germany's success, according to Ugaki, could be attributed to the three merits of the German national character, namely "integrity, honesty, and loyalty."[6] Needless to say, there were also Japanese views of Germany that were far less positive. Notably, Germany seldom fared well among the political opposition which succeeded the liberal People's Rights movement, on account of its authoritarian regime.[7] Yet, taken as a whole, a positive image of Germany was prevalent in the Meiji public sphere.

Toward the end of the century, this fondness for Germany, particularly in academic circles, gained more ground as public awareness of Germany's prominence in scientific research grew ever more widespread. In many disciplines, ranging from science and technology to humanities and social sciences, scholars turned to Germany for state-of-the-art research. This was evident by the number of German instructors at the Imperial University in Tokyo, which tended to hire Germans rather than their Anglo-American colleagues.[8] In addition, the emergence of *kyōyōshugi* is worth mentioning in this context. This was a new cultural trend, translated literally as "cultivation-ism," which appealed particularly to the younger elite after the turn of the century. This trend was inspired mainly by the German idea of *Bildung*, that is, the perfection of the individual personality achieved cultivating oneself through reading the Western classics. Its adherents indulged themselves in reading and self-reflection in a manner quite unlike the preceding generation, which had a decidedly more career-oriented mindset.[9]

As strong as the inclination for Germany might have been in Meiji Japan, we should be cautious to not overestimate its impact. It did not overshadow the influence of English elements in Japanese cultural life. In fact, it was at the time a general objective, as the multitalented scholar Ueda Bin once said, "to get knowledge mainly through English, not only in literature, but in politics, economy, diplomacy, religion, and others."[10] Beyond the realm of science and art, moreover, Anglo-American cultural hegemony reached deep into the worlds of the elite. Highly telling in this context is the fact that at the First High School, the cradle of Japan's rising elite in politics, business, and officialdom, baseball was one of the most popular sports.[11] This stands in stark contrast to the nature of Germany's influence, which was effectively confined to the world of high culture. We might summarize as follows: the Japanese image of Germany was indeed admiring, but it was a gaze strongly coupled with a sense of stiffness. Simply put, it was "cool admiration."

There were incidents, however, that damaged Japanese feelings toward Germany. The first was the Triple Intervention (1895), a coordinated diplomatic action by Russia, Germany, and France. The European powers joined forces in order to pressure Japan to return the Liaotong Peninsula to China,

88 *Toru Takenaka*

which Tokyo had forced Beijing to cede after the Sino-Japanese War (1894–95). The intervention threw cold water on the Japanese elation at their victory, and quickly aroused general indignation. The national outrage was so great that, as one journalist recollected, even "elementary school pupils almost cried at the insult" by the Europeans.[12] Unfortunately for Germany, Japanese media mistook Berlin for the ringleader, although it was actually Russia that had initiated the intervention. Japanese sentiments were further injured by the Kiautschou Bay concession (1898). The lease of the naval base, which Germany had pressured out of China, provoked the Japanese, who saw Berlin as trespassing in the contest for power in East Asia. German emperor Wilhelm II added further fuel to the fire. With his racist remarks on the alleged imminent threat from Asia, the Kaiser incensed the Japanese, who blamed the German monarch for having supposedly originated the rhetoric of the "Yellow Peril."[13] In the end, Germany emerged as the source of all the obstacles that stood in the way of Japanese national interests.[14] Not surprisingly, Japan immediately declared war on the German empire at the outbreak of World War I.

Anti-German discourse spread. Yoshino Sakuzō, a professor of political science at Tokyo Imperial University and standard-bearer of democratic thought, vehemently denounced Germany's behavior during the world war. He contended that "the country [Germany] does not shy away from any means in order to achieve its war aims. . . . The country's extremely arrogant actions, which ignore every rule of friendship common to the international community, are far from those of a civilized nation."[15] In the same vein, career diplomat Mushanokōji Kintomo, who had once served in the Berlin embassy and who would later become the president of the Japanese-German Friendship Association, described Germans as egotistical and supercilious by nature, and claimed that they "have highly unpleasant sentiments . . . and are apparently not warm people to keep friendly company with."[16]

This pejorative discourse, however, did not obliterate admiration for the country altogether. Ozaki Yukio, the mayor of Tokyo, expressed this ambivalence when he said, "Even though the Germans are an inferior one of the European races, their civilization offers [us] much [from which we can] learn."[17]

Japan's heightened self-confidence and its desire for equal footing with Germany, 1919–1945

After 1918 the aversion and exasperation that had characterized Japanese attitudes toward Germany before the war dissipated following Germany's defeat. In a reversal from the antipathy of the immediate prewar years, the earlier stance of "cool admiration" continued and even deepened. The academic interest in Germany gained more strength during the interwar period. This is revealed, for example, by observing the destination of students studying abroad. This period saw a remarkable growth in the number of

A close country in the distance 89

students headed abroad, triggered by the expansion of higher education and the ensuing demand for teaching staff.[18] It is striking that the vast majority, almost 80 percent, of these prospective professors selected for study abroad went to Germany.[19]

In addition, *kyōyōshugi* intensified on campuses. Through this trend, the devotion to "German culture, philosophy, literature, and the ideal of German *Bildung* as its basis" became firmly rooted in the student subculture.[20] The German orientation of Japanese academia was further reinforced by Marxism, which succeeded *kyōyōshugi* as a significant intellectual trend on campuses. It was above all through the conduit of literature in German that European socialist thought was introduced.[21] At this point Germany's influence was no longer confined to the realm of high culture. Students' worldviews were now strongly colored by German elements. This was visible in various jargon words derived from German, such as "Arubaito (*Arbeit*)" and "Metchen (*Mädchen*)," which became indispensable linguistic elements of prewar student subculture.[22] This phenomenon is worth stressing as here we may observe arguably the first group of Japanese, if still only a handful, who felt a sense of personal familiarity with Germany.

At the same time, a dramatic shift was taking place in Japan's general intellectual mood that revised the view of Germany based on Japan's strengthened sense of self-confidence. Japanese now looked at themselves and their relations with the outside world in a more affirmative light. This shift was caused by Japan's modernization, under way since the mid-nineteenth century, which had finally borne fruit in the unparalleled industrial boom during the world war. Japanese felt that their decades-long toil in catching up with the West had been suitably rewarded. In particular, they were pleased by the fact that Japan's contributions during World War I were recognized with membership in the League of Nations' Council. It was widely taken for granted that "today's Japan is one of the main pillars of the League of Nations and therefore a main actor in world affairs," as Konoe Fumimaro, a prime minister shortly before World War II, claimed in a high-spirited mood in 1920.[23]

This increased self-confidence did not leave the cultural realm untouched. While the Japanese had been eager since the Meiji Restoration to simply learn from the advanced West, this new assurance signaled that it was now time for the Japanese to assume an equal footing with Europe. Fujishiro Teisuke, a professor of German literature at Kyoto Imperial University, declared his country's new cultural mission (echoing Konoe's remark above): "There is no question whatsoever that our Japanese Empire has been among the world powers for these few years . . . we should stop being subservient and accepting the schooling one-sidedly of Westerners. Instead, we should make as much of our culture as possible known to them. After all, our culture is so rich in excellent things to teach them."[24] It goes without saying that this claim for equal footing was pointedly aimed at Germany because of the role German teachers had previously played in Japan's own modernization.

90   *Toru Takenaka*

The heightened Japanese self-esteem represented another strand of continuity from the preceding period which remained unbroken into the 1930s. An eloquent example of this is a journal entry from 1938: "Japan, once a backward country, has quickly advanced through inexorable hard work to [become] a strong power comparable to Europe and America. In the fields of the military, the legal system, science and others we are now self-reliant. Consequently it is safe to say that we can dispense with the advisory role that Germany has played for Japan."[25]

What impact did the Nazis' seizure of power have on the Japanese image of Germany? Interestingly, its basic shape remained unaffected despite the growing political rapprochement between the two countries. To be sure, the coverage of Germany in the Japanese media skyrocketed in quantitative terms. The number of hits in the database of the largest daily newspaper, *Yomiuri*, for the keyword "Doitsu (Germany)," grew from 1180 (in the period 1925–30) to 2946 (1930–35) and then again to 10,144 (1935–40).[26] Qualitatively, too, Germany seemed to arouse avid interest among the Japanese. In fact, a delegation from the Hitler Jugend, the Nazi youth organization, who visited Japan in 1938 was met with a broadly popular reception.[27] Yet all this was nothing but a propaganda show staged by the authorities and the cooperative news media. It is questionable how much of the emotional ambiguity that had previously distanced Germany from Japan was actually resolved.

Iwamura Masashi, who has analyzed Japanese public opinion of Nazi Germany, did not find a consistent attitude within the press. Instead, the media's outlook varied considerably, explicitly reflecting various political, diplomatic and military interests.[28] Japanese journalists, for example, first attacked Hitler as a dictator and denounced the persecution of the Jews. As soon as it became clear, however, that Nazi foreign policy aligned with that of Japan's in challenging British hegemony, the *Führer* was hailed as a pioneer in the pursuit of a new world order. When Germany acknowledged the Japanese puppet country Manchukuo, the pro-German tenor in the Japanese press grew even stronger. Berlin's decision was taken as a friendly diplomatic action to rescue Japan from its international isolation after its expansion into China.

Yet this goodwill did not last long. The press was exasperated when the Hitler-Stalin Pact was concluded. The Japanese could not forgive its ally, who had abruptly and without considering Japan's national interests taken the side of an arch-enemy, the Soviet Union. Furthermore, beyond the official acclamation for Nazi Germany critical voices could also be heard. A newspaper article concerning German rearmament, for example, described economic life as strained in spite of the boom triggered by military spending.[29] While many intellectuals extolled the Nazis in accordance with the authorities' propaganda, there were also some like Takeyama Michio who condemned them for their repressive state machinery.[30]

A close country in the distance 91

Birth of a "familiar" Germany, 1945–1970s

The year 1945 was the biggest watershed not only in the modern history of Japan and Germany but also in relations between the two. It ended the period of close cooperation during the Axis alliance. Interestingly, this significant juncture hardly seemed to affect the Japanese view of Germany. Although it may appear odd at first glance, this was actually not surprising given the challenges shared by both countries. Reconstruction from the devastation of war demanded that both countries muster all of their available resources, and in foreign affairs alignment in the USA-led alliance system in the Cold War emerged as a top priority for both countries. Neither nation was in a position to deal materially or mentally with its distant former ally. Under these conditions, contact between the two grew rare, and as a result very little occurred that would have altered one's image of the other.

We should not overlook, however, that a significant shift was under way beneath the surface. The Japanese image of Germany, while it retained its highbrow associations, extended its social basis substantially. Put another way, elements of German high culture began appealing to a wider segment of the population. This can be attributed mainly to the explosive growth of higher education. After the prewar school system was demolished in favor of an American-type educational structure, the government launched an ambitious program to establish new universities and colleges. As a result, the number of students exploded. The ratio of those enrolled in tertiary sector institutions rose to 38.9 percent in 1975, a fourfold increase from 1955 and a thirteen-fold increase from before the war.[31] It should be noted that, despite this explosive expansion, it was the elite student subculture of the prewar era that managed to survive the transformation and eventually dominate the new campuses. It was magnified through the mass university, as it were, before finding entry into the general public. *Kyōyōshugi*, essentially unchanged in its substance, turned into "popular modernism," which shaped the intellectual climate in the postwar decades.[32] With it, the German orientation immanent in *kyōyōshugi*, which was commonly associated with names such as Kant and Schopenhauer, was widely diffused. It is in this context that we can talk about the birth of the popular image of Germany as a familiar country.

Many of the depictions of Germany drawn at the time were characterized by adoring phrases, which, purged of the feudal and military elements of the prewar perspective, exalted Germany as a lofty paragon of culture. Maeda Keisaku, a professor of German literature, for example, spoke admiringly of a row of massive brick houses in a German town, "how the temporal continuity of life is maintained and well-being and culture steadily accumulated and consolidated." In his eyes, it was this urban landscape that embodied the long tradition of German indigenous culture. In contrast, Japanese houses, notoriously constructed out of paper and wood, represented, according to his view, the shallowness of his country's culture, to

92   *Toru Takenaka*

say nothing of the "concrete apartment houses of American design, which represent discontinuity and negation of time and are nothing but existential nothingness."[33] It is, by the way, not hard for us to recognize in his discourse the traditional German dichotomy of culture versus civilization. To the educator Etō Kyōji, "the Germans . . . as a reflective nation pervaded with a longing for the mystical, nurture dynamic, simple but ample emotions in their innermost bosom."[34] In his book Etō attempted to trace this allegedly ever-present "German soul" in history from Germanic antiquity by drawing from his own experiences of living in Germany in the late 1960s. It is worth noting that he focuses, as his book's subtitle reveals, on the "spirit of Weimar." This obviously highlights his intention to break with the prewar affinity for the martial Prussian-German tradition. In precisely the same vein, Ezawa Kennosuke, a Japanese professor working for a German university for over two decades, confessed his almost pious dedication to the allegedly sublime German nature, when he claimed to recognize in countless Germans' eyes "a certain cool shininess drifting, namely sparkles of pure eyes that transcend the worldly in an intellectual manner and reveal their devotion to eternity."[35]

Germany as a model for the quality of life around the 1980s

The first significant shift in postwar Japanese attitudes toward Germany occurred around 1980. A prime example of this new trend is the professor of economics Teruoka Itsuko, who, after having lived for a year in Germany in the mid-1980s, described her experiences in a book titled *What Is Well-Being*. In Germany, according to Teruoka, towns are full of green spaces and well regulated by careful city planning, thus offering an "aesthetically harmonized ambient beauty." They also displayed "vivid humane aspects" because of the rich interactions among citizens through a number of clubs and cultural events. The younger generations are provided with high-quality education. At school, children enjoy learning, free from the stress of cramming, in the intimate air of small classes. Students develop a mature awareness of political and social issues like peace and the environment. The elderly have no worries thanks to well-equipped old age care and nursing. Housing is spacious and yet inexpensive. A highly developed transportation network enables "people's free mobility, which, not hampered by traffic expenses, contributes to the stability of life as well as the equality among them," she says.[36]

The author contrasts what she sees as the exemplary civil society of Germany with the bleak reality of contemporary Japan. Teruoka deplored how her countrymen, obsessed with materialist values, pursued only superficial affluence. Admittedly, the Japanese were much better-off as a result of their efforts during the postwar reconstruction. At the same time, however, pressured incessantly by constant overtime at work and busy daily schedules, they could not afford to reflect on what they have unwittingly sacrificed for that success. Now they are paying the price: an impoverished social life, poisoned by "the spirit of the worship of money and efficiency." In short, Teruoka concluded: "Japan has taken a wrong turn in search of well-being."[37]

It is easy to see in Teruoka's discourse a considerably different thrust from the old clichés about German high culture. And she was not alone. From the 1980s onward, many publications paid tribute to Germany's supposedly mature society with its excellent quality of life. The quality-of-life discourse addressed various aspects of German social life but took up two issues in particular: leisure and the environment. A trade union, for example, once sent a delegation to Germany to inspect the current state of work-and-life balance there. Indeed, Germany was often dubbed in the media the "*jitan senshinkoku* [the forerunner nation of working hour reduction]." The delegation's report revealed that the members were all but stunned in admiration when they observed how employees "are treated humanely at work" as a result of the superb working conditions. Interestingly, the delegation did not stop at simply praising the merits of the advanced German workplace. Rather, they ascribed them to higher civic virtues in German society. Consequently, according to the delegation, the shorter working hours were not merely an outcome of well-managed industrial relations; rather, they were the natural result of a "liberty and democracy that has matured in social life."[38] Representative of the second issue, the environment, was the active media attention paid to the "eco city" Freiburg i.B. There were detailed reports about the ecological programs implemented in the southwestern German city, such as the tram-centered public transportation system.[39] Major dailies hailed Freiburg as a model for realizing eco-friendly urban life in the future.[40] It is striking that here too, discussion was often linked, well beyond merely elaborating on specific ecological measures, to an argument regarding the civic awareness of the population. That is why, for example, a newspaper article concerning a project for the preservation of the Schwarzwald forest, not far from Freiburg, paid particular attention to the commitment of the community.[41] In the same vein, another writer stressed that ecological practices in Freiburg "are not given by the authorities through subsidies, but are born and maintained by the self-rule of the locals."[42]

What caused this shift of perspective since the 1980s? We may safely guess that one major cause was the transformation of Japanese society in the preceding decade. The oil shocks had brought a halt to the high-growth boom era that had existed since the war's end. As in the sobered mood that might follow an orgy, it became clear just how high a price the Japanese had to pay. An alarming number of *karoshi* (death from overwork) cases, for example, showed how seriously family life was strained to the point that individual lives were put at risk. Furthermore, grave ecological crises were reported across the country, among which Minamata disease, a syndrome caused by widespread mercury poisoning, was one of the most dire. Serious soul-searching could not be avoided. Yet what would be an alternative way

94   *Toru Takenaka*

of life? It was in this context that Germany seemed to offer an answer to Japan.

The Japanese believed that it was not piecemeal remedial actions that were required. Their entire conventional life style was now fundamentally in question and their values put under interrogation. That was presumably why the quality-of-life discourse, beyond merely showcasing good practices in Germany, specifically addressed the social virtues that were assumed to reinforce them. In fact, Germany's civil society (something that by tacit implication Japan lacked) was one of the favorite topics in this new image of Germany. The writer Inukai Michiko was impressed, while staying in Bonn, by the orderly behavior of German passengers at the railway station. She observed how people, unlike in Japan, bought tickets without the direction of railway personnel and made their way to their train independently, without being guided by annoying announcements looped on loudspeakers. From this, Inukai concluded, "Such is the citizen!"[43]

With this change of perspective, a paradigm shift occurred in the 150-year-old image of Germany in Japan. Since the mid-nineteenth century the Japanese had been continuously preoccupied by the thought of catching up with the West by setting modernization as a national goal. This mindset remained unchanged even after 1945. Regardless of whether a new constitution was promulgated or the Anglo-American world order was replaced by the US-Soviet standoff in the Cold War, the Japanese remained fixated on the notion of "catching up." It is worth noting that the old image of Germany was embedded in this mindset. Not surprisingly, the allegedly German virtues of diligence, punctuality, and discipline corresponded well to the value system most conducive to industrialism and modernism. However, all of this changed dramatically in the 1980s when post-materialism displaced modernism as the new popular frame of reference. In accordance with this change, Germany took on a new profile in a post-materialist light.

"German rationality" in everyday life since the 1980s

Another aspect of the turnaround since the 1980s is the way in which the mundane sphere of everyday life becamed increasingly foregrounded as a setting for images of Germany. Among the most conspicuous examples were the books and magazine articles that began to appear detailing the "housekeeping techniques of German housewives." These publications depicted how thoroughly the "rational German style" was practiced in the German household and recommended its techniques for coping with busy daily life. One such author, Oki Yukiko, itemized the German "rational wisdom of living," which she believed to be "practical and yet warm, impressive and comfortable."[44] Similarly, Morita Hiroko insisted that there was much for Japan to learn from the German way of life, "which is rational, efficient, thrifty, and sound." According to her, German know-how comes into its own when answering the dilemma of how to put away household utensils in a cramped Japanese home.[45] Another writer, Klein Takako, similarly highlighting the German virtues of practical housekeeping, stressed the thrifty way the Germans treat goods. At German homes, says Klein, "diapers that the parents themselves once used as babies are put aside for their babies."[46]

This connection to the everyday signified another distinct departure from the old stereotype. The pure pragmatism left few traces of the affected highbrow *kyōyōshugi*, which had extolled Germany as a "country of poets and thinkers." Admittedly, we still encounter some motifs of this past cliché resonating in the new paradigm, such as rationality, simplicity, and sturdiness. Yet the difference is obvious. These values were cleansed of the militarist or industrialist implications of the past and redefined along the logic of a better quality of life, often applied, by extension, to the agenda of environmentalism as well.

This paradigm shift, nevertheless, should not obscure the fact that it never called into question the normative connotations that had adhered all along to the image of Germany. Germany continued to be a model, regardless of context, for the Japanese to learn from. In fact, we easily see how strongly the authors after the turnaround, just like their predecessors, were laboring under pro-German preoccupations. Some of them were quite hasty to generalize one facet of German life into a laudable characteristic of the whole society. Indeed, it is not at all difficult to refute Teruoka's idealized descriptions with contrary empirical facts. Likewise, we may wonder how many of Oki's "German housewives" in late twentieth century society had an advanced level of gender empowerment. Others, although unanimous in acclaiming the same German virtues, were actually drawing on completely opposite perceptions. Morita, for example, praised German family life because it reinforced traditional gender roles. Yoshinaga Ise, on the other hand, affirmed German domesticity as evidence of women's liberation.[47] Still others, building on the same facts, did not hesitate to draw thoroughly contrary conclusions. In their praise for German-style housekeeping, Morita emphasized "throwing away" as its core tenet, while Klein insisted that its philosophy revolved around "not throwing away" (as revealed by their books' respective subtitles). Such conflicting arguments were possible due to the *a priori* fixation with Germany as model.

That being said, the reversal since the 1980s did substantially reduce Japan's psychological distance from Germany. For the first time in history, Germany became a familiar country for ordinary Japanese. Before the turnaround, in spite of the expansion of its social profile, the dignified air of high culture had remained part of Germany's image since the prewar era. Now this long-standing stereotype has been at last torn down. "Cool admiration" was replaced with associations of leisure and vacation, high-quality civic life, ecology, and – to name other "soft" components, which are not mentioned in this article – beer, sausage, cars, and soccer. At first glance, softening a country's image is likely to enhance its attractiveness. Did the

96 Toru Takenaka

popularization of Germany's new profile help to stoke Japanese interest in the country?

Conclusion: Germany, a normal country in the present?

In contemporary society, with its extreme diversification and the unprecedented flood of information enabled by technology, it is hard to discern certain trends. Nonetheless, Japanese interest in Germany, by all accounts, does not seem to be on the rise. This is not surprising. By descending, as it were, to the mundane, everyday level, the image of Germany suffered a decline in its original appeal as a state with an elevated culture, which could only be partly offset by new attributes. Taken together, this has meant that there was less need for the Japanese to turn to Germany for guidance.

Indeed, we cannot ignore the sober observations that appeared in parallel to the old images of Germany. Fukuda Naoko, for example, addresses topics such as Germans' fondness for companion dogs or do it-yourself work at home. She treats them in a cool, distanced style and also acknowledges their shortcomings. Regarding the do-it-yourself ethos, which was applauded in the quality-of-life discourse as a symbol of Germans' good sense of family, she discusses the broader context by noting that this is just an example of consumers' defensive actions. Germans just want, she says, to dispense with hired workers in their house maintenance because their fees are quite expensive.[48]

Kawaguchi Mahn Emi breaks with the old stereotypes even more decisively. Her position is expressed clearly in a number of books on various subjects related to Germany, including working habits, vacation, education, consumption, and nuclear energy. For example, on the issue of education Kawaguchi's position stands in marked contrast to that expressed by Teruoka. Whereas Teruoka identified constructive German school practices that nurtured children's creativity by replacing rote learning with interactive approaches, Kawaguchi Mahn sees nothing here but the unjustifiable neglect of basic knowledge cultivation. While, from Teruoka's viewpoint, the half-day of school in Germany is exemplary for avoiding students' overwork, Kawaguchi Mahn sees in it an irresponsible renunciation of children's education. After all, as Kawaguchi Mahn contends, countering Teruoka's critical stance on current Japanese education, "I think we should not shrink from saying: The Japanese school system is far from bad."[49]

We should be reminded that the Japanese view of Germany has all along been suffused with admiration, whether for the sake of modernization or for improving quality of life. In this regard, Kawaguchi Mahn is surely a novelty because of her clear lack of humility toward Germany. Nothing reveals her standpoint more clearly than a sales tag attached to one of her books, which says: "70 Years after the War's End: There Is Next to Nothing for Japan to Learn from Germany!"[50]

A *close country in the distance* 97

Certainly one of the reasons for the emergence of this more sober and critical view of Germany has been the growth in the amount of information available in Japan. It has become widely known that European countries, which had been previously presented in an idealized light, are actually not free from problems. But this alone does not suffice as explanation. More crucial is the fact that the Japanese have gradually come to make more affirmative judgments about themselves. With a world-class living standard, decades-long political stability, and maturation in social life, Japan in the twenty-first century has gained confidence that its own social systems function as well as, and perhaps better than, those of most European countries.

To be sure, praise for Germany has not been altogether replaced by a sober or critical tone. The old images still persist alongside this new standpoint. That makes it difficult for us to predict the direction in which the Japanese view of Germany will develop in the future. We may, on the one hand, assume that the level of interest in Germany among the Japanese public will continue to decline. Since Germany has become less of a model for the Japanese, there is less reason to engage deeply with the country. In addition, even in the age of globalization, geographic distance still considerably influences not only the actual interactions between the two nations but also their mutual perceptions. Moreover, we should take into account the specific problem that the coverage of Germany in the Japanese media is conflated to a certain extent with that of the European Union, which makes Germany less visible. On the other hand, it is certainly imaginable that Germany, the hegemonic power in Europe and one of the major actors in the international community, is unlikely to shrink in the Japanese worldview. In fact, one of the favorite themes in the media recently is a "German Empire," which is said to dominate Europe and determine the fate of the whole world.[51] Either way, future images of Germany will depend primarily on how the Japanese perceive themselves and the outside world, just as they have done to this point. After all, the images we make of others never cease to be mirror images of ourselves.

Notes

1 Concerning the Romanization of Japanese names in this article, the Japanese convention of giving the surname first, followed by the given name, is adhered to, except in the bibliographical data in the notes.

2 I have previously tried to survey the Japanese view of Germany over the past 150 years. Cf. Toru Takenaka, "The Japanese Image of Germany over the Past 150 Years," in *Begegnungen in Vergangenheit und Gegenwart: Beiträge dialogischer Existenz*, ed. Claudia Rammelt, Cornelia Schlarb, and Egbert Schlarb (Münster: LIT, 2015), 257–66. In this survey, however, there is considerable room for improvement from a contemporary perspective, not in the least because developments in recent years were not addressed on account of limitations of space.

3 Historical research on Germany in the twentieth century is an enormous field, and this chapter will focus primarily on accounts of travel and sojourns in

98 *Toru Takenaka*

Germany provided by Japanese authors. One topic handled in many Japanese publications, which will not be addressed in this article, however, is Germany's struggle to overcome the legacy of its past (*Vergangenheitsbewältigung*).

4 Kunitake Kume, *Beiō kairan jikki* [Accounts of the Journey to America and Europe] (Tokyo: Iwanami, 1979), vol. 3: 298.

5 Shūzō Aoki, *Aoki Shūzō jiden* [Autobiography of Aoki Shūzō] (Tokyo: Heibon, 1970), 13, 26.

6 Kazusige Ugaki, *Ungaki Kazushige nikki* [Diary of Ugaki Kazushige] (Tokyo: Misuzu, 1968–71), vol. 1: 3.

7 *Chōya Shinbun*, "Doitsu naikaku wo ronzu" [About the German Cabinet], May 17, 1884.

8 Tokyō Daigaku, ed., *Tokyō Daigaku hyakunen shi* [One Hundred Years of Tokyo University] (Tokyo: Tokyō Daigaku Shuppankai, 1984–87), vol. 1: 161, 478.

9 Kayoko Watanabe, *Kingendai Nihon no kyōyō ron: 1930 nendai wo chūshin ni* [Discourses on Cultivation: Centering on the 1930s] (Tokyo: Kōro, 1997), 14.

10 Bin Ueda, "Taiō shokan" [Impressions of Europe], in *Teihon Ueda Bin zenshū* [Complete Works of Ueda Bin] (Tokyo: Kyōiku Shuppan Sentā, 1978–81), vol. 6: 221.

11 Yoshishige Abe, *Iwanami Shigeo den* [Biography of Iwanami Shigeo] (Tokyo: Iwanami, 1957), 47.

12 Toshirō Ubukata, *Meiji Taishō kenbunki* [Memories of the Meiji and Taisho Periods] (Tokyo: Chūō Kōron, 1978), 45.

13 *Tokyō Asahi Shinbun*, "Doitsu tei no Nihon hyō" [Comments on Japan by the German Emperor], August 4, 1906.

14 Reikichi Kita, "Doitsu kokuminsei to sono seijiteki kekkan" [German National Character and Its Political Problems], *Gaikō Jihō* 438 (1923): 453.

15 Sakuzō Yoshino, *Gendai no Seiji Daini* [Contemporary Politics, Part 2] (Tokyo: Jitsugyō no Nihon, 1916), 227.

16 Kintomo Mushanokōji, "Doitsu kokuminsei no chōsho to tansho" [Merits and Demerits of the German National Character], *Chūō Kōron* 30, no. 9 (1915): 84.

17 Yukio Ozaki, *Gendai no seinen* [Today's Youth] (Tokyo: Kōbundo, 1915), 264.

18 The number of higher education institutions grew from 12 in 1915 to 106 twenty years later. Cf. Ikuo Amano, *Kōtō kyoikuno jidai* [The Age of Higher Education] (Tokyo: Chūō Kōron, 2013), vol. 1: 358.

19 Tetsurō Katō, *Waimāru-ki Berurin no Nihonjin: Yōkō chishikijin no hantei nettowāku* [Japanese in Weimar Berlin: An Anti-Imperialist Network of Intellectuals Abroad] (Tokyo: Iwanami, 2008), 28.

20 Rieko Takada, *Bungakubu wo meguru yamai: kyōyōshugi, Nachisu, kyūsei kōkō* [Disease Around the Faculty of Letters: Cultivation-ism, Nazis and High Schools] (Kyoto: Shōrai, 2001), 18.

21 Henry D. Smith, *Japan's First Student Radicals* (Cambridge, MA: Harvard University Press, 1972), 73.

22 Donald Roden, *Schooldays in Imperial Japan: A Study in the Culture of a Student Elite* (Berkeley: University of California Press, 1980).

23 Fumimaro Konoe, *Sengo Ōbei kenbunroku* [Travel Accounts on Postwar America and Europe] (Tokyo: Chūō Kōron, 1981), 49.

24 Teisuke Fujishiro, "Nihon no bunkateki shimei" [Japan's Cultural Mission], *Taiyō* 28, no. 1 (1922): 145, 148.

25 Tokyōshi, "Nihon ni okeru Doitsu ongaku" [German Music in Japan], *Ongaku Kenkyū* 3 (1938): 79.

26 *Yomidasu Rekishikan* (Yomiuri's Online Database), accessed March 1, 2017, www.yomiuri.co.jp/database/rekishikan.

27 Hisakazu Nakamichi, *Kimi ha Hitorā Yūgento wo mitaka? Kiritsu to nekkyō, aruiha mekanikaru na bi* [Did You Look at the Hitler Jugend? Discipline, Enthusiasm or Mechanical Aesthetics] (Tokyo: Nansō, 1999).

A *close country in the distance* 99

28 Masashi Iwamura, *Senzen Nihonjin no tai-Doitsu ishiki* [Images of Germany in Prewar Japan] (Tokyo: Keiō Gijuku Daigaku Shuppankai, 2005).

29 *Tokyō Asahi Shinbun*, "Gunbi saiken no kage ni kizamu kokumin no aegi" [People's Groan in the Shadow of Rearmament], September 12, 1936, morning ed.

30 Michio Takeyama, *Doitsu, atarashiki Chūsei?* [Germany, a New Middle Age?], vol. 1 of *Takeyama Michio Chosakushū* [Works of Takeyama Michio] (Tokyo: Fukutake, 1983).

31 Keiichi Yoshimoto, "Sengo kōtō kyōiku no taishūka katei [Popularization Process of Higher Education in the Postwar Period]," in *Daigaku to kokka: seido to seisaku* [University and State: System and Policy], ed. Masataka Murasawa (Tokyo: Tamagawa Daigaku Shuppanbu, 2010), 24; Amano, *Kōtō kyōiku no jidai*, vol. 1: 356.

32 Yō Takeuchi, *Kakushin gensō no sengoshi* [History of the Illusion of Progressivism in Postwar Japan] (Tokyo: Chūō Kōron, 2015), vol. 2: 271–77.

33 Keisaku Maeda, "Yōroppa de mita rekishi no renzokusei" [Historical Continuity I Observed in Europe], *Yomiuri Shinbun*, May 2, 1971, morning ed.

34 Kyōji Etō, *Doitsu no kokoro: Waimāru seishin no tankyū* [German Soul: In Search of the Weimar Spirit] (Tokyo: Kōdansha, 1980), 23f.

35 Kennosuke Ezawa, "Richi ni yoru ikikata to ningen no kokoro: Nijūyo nen no Doitsu seikatsu kara" [A Rational Way of Living and the Human Soul: From Experiences of Living in Germany for Over Twenty Years], in *Doitsu bunka no kitei: Shiben to shinjō no orinasu sekai* [Foundation of German Culture: An Inner World Woven with Reflections and Sentiments], ed. Kanji Nishio (Tokyo: Yūhikaku, 1982), 163.

36 Itsuko Teruoka, *Yutakasa toha nanika* [What Is Well-Being?] (Tokyo: Iwanami, 1989), 23, 27, 61.

37 Ibid., 10, 16.

38 Aichi Rōdō Mondai Kenkyūshoet al., ed., *Jitan senshinkoku Doitsu* [Germany as a Forerunner Nation in the Reduction of Working Hours] (Tokyo: Gakushū no Tomo, 1992), 50f. This is a rather curious booklet, which was obviously hastily compiled as a makeshift report. That is why I cannot determine precisely how the team of authors was organized. I would therefore like to suggest crossing out "et al." and using instead: Aichi Rōdō Mondai Kenkyūsho, ed., *Jitan. . .*

39 Mineko Imaizumi, *Fraiburuku kankyō repōto* [Reports on Ecology in Freiburg i.B.] (Tokyo: Chūō Hōki, 2001); Yoshio Fuchigami, *Gaikoku no machikado de Nihon wo furikaeru: Watashi no Doitsu kikō* [Looking Back to Japan from Towns Abroad: My Travel Record in Germany] (Osaka: Fūei, 2014).

40 *Mainichi Shinbun*, "Waga machi wo 'Ekoporisu' ni" [Let Us Make Our Towns "Eco-Polis"], October 30, 1992, morning ed.; *Yomiuri Shinbun*, "Kamakura to Doku Furaiburuku ga kankyō taisaku de jichitai kōryū" [City-Level Cooperation in Eco-Programs between Kamakura and Freiburg in Germany], September 5, 1996, morning ed.

41 Toshihiro Sasaki, "Mamorō midori, hirogaru wa: Nishi Doitsu [A Widening Circle of the Movement "Let's Protect Green": A Report from West Germany]," *Asahi Shinbun*, December 26, 1983, morning ed.

42 Fuchigami, *Gaikoku no machikado*, 49.

43 Michiko Inukai, *Rain no kawabe: Doitsu dayori* [On the Rhine: Letters from Germany] (Tokyo: Chūō Kōron, 1973), 50.

44 Yukiko Oki, *Doitsu ryū shinpuru seikatsu: Saishōgen no tema to mono de saikō wo te ni ireru rūru 125* [The German Way for a Simple Life: 125 Rules to Get the Best with Minimum Effort and Goods] (Tokyo: Daiwa, 2003), 2f.

45 Hiroko Morita, *Doitsu shiki shinpuru ni seikatsu suru shūnō seiri sōji jutsu: Ie no naka no "suteru" gijutsu* [How to Pack, Tidy Up and Clean for a German-Style Simple Life: Techniques of "Throwing Away" at Home] (Tokyo: Shōgakukan, 2001), 3f.

100 Toru Takenaka

46 Takako Klein, *Sutenai seikatsu: Kaitekina Doitsu ryū raifu sutairu* [A Life Without Throwing Away: The Comfortable German Lifestyle] (Tokyo: Popura, 2001), 12f.

47 Ise Yoshinaga, *Shufu no mita mōhitotsu no Doitsu* [Another Germany in the Eyes of a Housewife] (Tokyo: Sanshū, 1979), 79, 98.

48 Naoko Fukuda, *Doitsu no inu ha naze hoenai* [Why Do German Dogs Not Bark]? (Tokyo: Heibon, 2007); Naoko Fukuda, *Yasumu tame ni hataraku Doitsujin, hataraku tame ni yasumu Nihonjin* [Germans Work to Have Holidays, Japanese Have Holidays to Work] (Tokyo: PHP, 2004), esp. 37.

49 Emi Kawaguchi Mahn, *Doitsu ha kunō suru: Nihon to amarinimo nikayotta mondaiten ni tuite no kōsatu* [Germany in Agony: Reflections on Problems Fairly Common to Japan] (Tokyo: Sōshi, 2004), 122–41, esp. 137.

50 Emi Kawaguchi Mahn, *Nihon to Doitsu, rekishi no tsumi to batsu: 20 seiki no senso wo do kokufuku subekika* [Japan and Germany, the Crime and Punishment of History: How to Overcome the Wars of 20th Century] (Tokyo: Tokuma, 2015). The above-mentioned Takako Klein sometimes sides with the critics of Germany. Cf. Mahn, *Ohitoyoshi no Nihonjin, shitatakaya Doitsujin* [Naïve Japanese, Tough Germans] (Tokyo: Kairyū, 2001).

51 Cf. Kōetsu Aizawa, *Yomigaeru Nihon, teikoku ka suru Doitsu: Haisenkoku Nichi-Doku no sengo to mirai* [Reviving Japan, a Nascent Empire Germany: The Postwar and the Future for a Defeated Japan and Germany] (Tokyo: Suiyō, 2015). In this context it is worth mentioning the following book, a Japanese translation of essays by a French scholar, which found wide resonance in the reading public. Cf. Emmanuel Todd, *"Doitsu Teikoku" ga sekai wo hametsu saseru: Nihonjin heno keikoku* ["German Empire" Will Ruin the World: A Warning for Japanese] (Tokyo: Bungei Shunjū, 2015).

5 The Lex Adickes in its East Asian contexts

The introduction of land readjustment and its spatio-political effects

Jin-Sung Chun

Introduction

"Lex Adickes" is the common name of a planning law drafted by a Lord Mayor of Frankfurt am Main named Franz Adickes (1846–1915). The 1902 law, officially named the "Prussian Law concerning the Land Readjustment in Frankfurt am Main" was a milestone in the history of urban planning, not least as the inspiration for the concept of land readjustment, which subsequently spread rapidly beyond the European continent.

Land Readjustment (hereafter called LR) is a land development technique utilized to reorganize an irregular pattern of agricultural land holdings into regular building plots, and then subsequently to construct the supporting roads and public facilities. It is an efficient method of dealing with worldwide urbanization and the subsequent demand for urban lots: LR projects are usually initiated by taxpaying landowners who set up a legal association and pool their individual resources. The landowners, who contribute a certain percentage of their holdings without prior compensation, expect to share in the profits resulting from substantial increases in property values. The advantage of using this method is the promotion of urban development without the need for public financial input. On the basis of economic partnership between the private and public sectors, LR projects aim to provide a high level of basic urban infrastructure and, ultimately, to prevent urban sprawl. It is a modern planning strategy used in many countries around the world.[1]

LR was originally developed as an adaptation of a method of agrarian land management to the project of urban development. It is no wonder that this technique was developed in Germany, where impractical earlier land reforms had resulted in numerous agricultural plots. This shortcoming subsequently hindered urban development in the era of industrialization. LR provided an effective means of promoting urban growth by guaranteeing the initiative of landowners and their cooperation. But the full-scale rearrangements of existing property structures could not entirely avoid relying

102 *Jin-Sung Chun*

on the coercive power of higher authorities.[2] With the goal of national prosperity through modernization at stake, public authorities hoped to compel private land contribution and control subsequent development, and thus to recapture a certain amount of profit from the land developed. Generally speaking, governments tend to privilege national interests over those of their citizens.

The dominance of public interests in LR projects is relevant not only to Germany but also to Japan, which is often referred to as the Prussia of Asia. It is well known that Meiji Japan's rapid Westernization was modeled after the Prussian model of reform, that is, "reform from above." Despite the numerous arguments to the contrary, this thesis helps account for the transfer of particular ideas and technologies across continents. The fragmentation of land ownership in both countries, caused by previous incomplete land reforms, prevented both Germany and Japan from responding effectively to rampant urban development and therefore motivated them to create and adopt a new method of land management.[3] It should be noted, however, that this transfer did not reproduce an identical effect. This line of transmission is, at best, superficial if the differences are not taken into consideration, especially the involvement of a third country which had been forcibly occupied by Imperial Japan, namely Korea.

Japanese colonial rule in Korea divested civilian interests from LR projects and made them thoroughly instruments of state power. The authoritarian character of LR under Japanese colonial rule continued without major alterations in post-liberation South Korea. Under the sway of the Park Jŏng-Hee military regime, LR facilitated development under the dictatorship and had a sizable impact on South Korean society. All the same, the Korean case should not be seen as a significant departure, given that LR served the public management of urban space and shaped socio-structural transformation in Germany, Japan, and elsewhere.

This chapter aims to offer neither expertise on a particular planning technology nor details on the process of transfer, but rather the historical features and meaning of this kind of transfer, which leads us to rethink a general problem of modernity. Land readjustment is modern not just in the sense that it is a rational rearrangement of urban space, but also as an example of public encroachment on private life. By radically transforming inherited, autochthonic environments into standardized modern conditions, LR has been a vehicle for creating transnational urbanism.

This is most evident in the cases of Imperial Germany, Imperial Japan, and post-colonial Korea. Under these authoritarian regimes, LR was invented, adopted, and imposed under charismatic leaders, including a mayor, a governor-general, and a military dictator. The central question regarding these historical figures is whether their administrative paternalism was a feature of municipal communalism or state monopoly capitalism. At issue here is the historical meaning of the Lex Adickes and its various legacies.

Land readjustment in the German context

The Prussian Building Line Act as a springboard to the Lex Adickes

LR was a peculiarly German technique of urban planning, triggered by historically fragmented land ownership and the financial deficits arising out of an arrested state formation. The German term "Umlegung" refers to all activities of modern land conversion, including the acquisition and expropriation of land, the relocation of residents, the clearance of properties, and the construction or alteration of roads, water supply, sewage systems, and other public facilities. This term was firmly established in the German legal system with the draft code from Frankfurt am Main, submitted by Frankfurt's mayor Franz Adickes to the Prussian State Parliament (*Landtag*) in December 1899. The law was ultimately enacted in 1902. The Lex Adickes was designed to readjust scattered residential lands in order to create more favorable market conditions for construction. This pioneering law provided a legal regulation for orderly, planned urban growth, as well as an effective means for coping with the impecuniousness of many municipalities.[4]

The Lex Adickes was not itself full-scale urban planning legislation, but focused instead on the transformation of existing rural structure into urban space. This law was deeply related to the prevailing Prussian Building Line Act, "Fluchtliniengesetz," which collated the individual laws that had been prepared to cope with the inevitability of urbanization.[5] Even before German unification in 1871, the population of major cities had sharply increased. Especially in Berlin, the capital of the Kingdom of Prussia and later of the German Empire, the 1855 population of 430,000 increased by 20,000 to 30,000 every subsequent year. By 1871 it had reached 825,000 people, and by 1880 it exceeded 1 million. In the early 1890s, this figure approached 2 million people, including the city's outskirts. This rapid population growth forced Berlin to incorporate the northwestern districts of Moabit and Wedding in 1816, mainly as a residence for workers from the countryside, especially from East Prussia.[6]

The Architectural and Police Act for Berlin, enacted in April 1853, was the first step toward urban planning legislation. Of particular note here is Article 10, which placed the building lines (*Fluchtlinien*) under the full supervision of police officials.[7] The policy of delegating control over construction projects to police forces was deeply rooted in the General State Law for Prussia, the civil code of 1794.[8] Although authoritarian, the Prussian legal tradition encouraged reckless urban development, because developers only needed to comply with formal building codes. A turning point was the Prussian Building Line Act of 1875. Consisting of 20 articles, this act regulated the height limits, site layouts, and locations of industrial centers. It is recorded as one of the first planning acts in Europe that legalized the development of master plans.[9]

104 *Jin-Sung Chun*

Despite this progress, the Prussian Building Line Act was inadequate in mitigating the overcrowded, slum-like, disease-ridden conditions in cities. In fact, the act gave the local communities more discretion by stipulating that the building line would be decided by the head of the municipal executive board, with the consent of the landowners' associations and the approval of the local police authority. There is no doubt that the act was intended to address local communities' financial difficulties; as long as the construction projects were carried out independently and autonomously according to local conditions, the private associations were willing to relinquish a portion of their land with the expectation that land values would increase as a result of overheated speculation. Furthermore, construction and maintenance costs were imposed on the proprietors who purchased the land.

The impact of the Prussian Building Line Act on actual urban space is most clearly seen in the imperial capital Berlin. Once a neoclassical city, with the splendid legacies of Prussian architect Karl Friedrich Schinkel and landscape architect Peter-Joseph Lenné on public display, Berlin was increasingly stigmatized by the end of the nineteenth century as the city of "barrack-like tenement-houses" (*Mietskaserne*). This unfortunate development cannot, however, be attributed entirely to the Prussian Building Line Act. For Berlin, the impact of a specific local ordinance, the Hobrecht Plan of 1862, was far more significant. Proposed by drainage and canal specialist James Hobrecht and authorized by Berlin authorities, the Hobrecht Plan was designed to keep intact the preexisting neoclassical cityscape of the downtown area while also organically integrating it into the surrounding environs through modern infrastructures.[10] This plan, although aimed at rationalizing urban space, has been criticized for its lack of building regulations, which likely contributed to the birth of "the world's largest tenement-house city."[11]

The Hobrecht Plan failed to codify building types and entrance patterns, resulting in an unprecedented expansion of high-density rental housing with narrow backyard gardens. All the same, this initial plan was epoch-making, because it protected rotaries, squares, and urban green spaces as much as possible, which contributed to the elimination of social barriers in urban spaces. In short, the Hobrecht Plan changed the overall urban spatial structure for the expansion of existing cities.

An array of planning methods conceived in the Hobrecht Plan were largely incorporated into the Prussian Building Line Act, which became an important source of modern urban planning through subsequent legislation. Most significantly, the zoning system provided a new mode of regulating land use: It determined the use of each district based on its size and area and dictated building height and occupation density accordingly. This gave municipal authorities legal control over building types. These planning regulations served as a model for similar legislation in other German states.[12]

The distinctive features of the Lex Adickes

The historical significance of the Lex Adickes is that it was the first attempt to legalize land readjustment or land consolidation. After the annexation of the Free City of Frankfurt by Prussia in 1866, the city's population increased sharply within a few decades, caused in part by industrial employment. Soaring land costs and housing shortages became the most pressing issues related to city governance. It was necessary to enact an alternative law to replace the existing Prussian Building Line Act, which had failed to readjust irregular patterns of land division, hindering in turn the fair market valuation of land. Under the administration of Lord Mayor Franz Adickes, who took office in 1891, a draft code of urban extensions and zonal expropriations was introduced in 1892. This was a coercive as well as a protective law: It required the compulsory readjustment of lands, owned by different owners, as well as the assertion of eminent domain for housing needs in order to hinder speculative land transactions and a consequent price increase for building land. In favor of a more rational use of land, this bill was intended to accelerate the development of new construction sites.[13]

The path to the enactment of the Lex Adickes, however, was anything but straightforward. Franz Adickes' first draft was adopted in the Prussian Upper Chamber with amendments but failed in the Prussian House of Representatives, because the option of zonal expropriations was regarded as too much of a violation of private property. For many years Adickes requested approval for his legal provisions in the Prussian *Landtag*. In the end, he received permission to apply his late-1899 draft within his own city, and the Lex Adickes was passed on July 28, 1902.[14]

According to a historical report from the Civil Engineering Bureau in Frankfurt, the core of the Lex Adickes was the expropriation of private property for housing needs. This is unsurprising, since the city's population had tripled from 91,040 in 1871 to 288,989 in 1900. Numerous related urban planning policies were subsumed under the Lex Adickes, including building regulations, zoning, detailed planning (*Bebauungsplan*), and the rehabilitation of insalubrious neighborhoods. A lack of cultivable terrain, whether due to unprofitable estates on the suburban fringe or to fragmented land ownership, could be redressed by the subdivision of agricultural lands on the suburban fringe and then by the transformation of them into an orderly urban building site. Although the right of eminent domain allowed municipalities to expropriate private property for public facilities, many small plots still remained which were unsuitable for consolidation due to their size, shape, and oblique position to the new road line. Therefore, public authority had the obligation to enact LR in the interest of "the public welfare" (*das öffentliche Wohl*).[15]

LR projects could be carried out at the request either of the municipalities or of the landowners when a majority of them controlled at least half of the area to be readjusted. In one scenario, up to 30 percent of the project areas

106   Jin-Sung Chun

would be pre-emptied and transferred to the municipality free of charge. The municipality would then use this reserved vacant land for the purpose of either park or street constructions. The costs incurred for this purpose would be collected by estimating the profit from the completed construction, rather than through public spending. Alternatively, financial compensation to landowners could be achieved by rapidly allocating new, replotted lots as substitution for the original plots. The proportion of building and road area would be calculated for each block according to newly engineered road axes, and the built-up areas would be redistributed to the landowners based on the original rate of ownership. The particular advantage of the Lex Adickes was its ability to combine private and public interests. Without a doubt, it was a pioneering form of land reform.

Before launching the first draft of the Lex Adickes, Frankfurt mayor Franz Adickes created a municipal zoning act. The 1891 zoning act, drafted with the assistance of Reinhard Baumeister, a pioneering German city planner, divided the city into two subsections, the inner and outer city, [each of] which was divided again into subdivisions. This system of multilayered zones was designed to maintain the unique character of the urban topography and thereby control its growth pattern.[16]

In the first draft of the Lex Adickes, the section on "zonal expropriations" comprised the main part of the bill, and this was submitted to the Prussian House of Representatives on January 30, 1892. According to a contemporary report from C. Merlo, the Frankfurt district court judge, the first draft had already proposed a master plan based on thorough calculations. For example, the costs of building the necessary infrastructure in a particular area was compared against the estimated total value of all lots. This ratio determined the cost-equivalent rate, which dictated the percentage of the lot areas to be sold. In these administrative procedures, private interests were merely a factor in motivating participation and were ultimately subject to public interest. It is therefore not surprising that the author was worried about "the protests against this unprecedented infringement of private property."[17]

The first draft of Lex Adickes was completed without significant modification, barring slight changes in the methods used to purchase lands and the designation of building lines. The Lex Adickes succeeded in creating the basic prerequisites for the stable expansion and development of Frankfurt, and thereby gained importance as the basis for standardized land-planning procedures throughout Germany and later the world. Its influence was derived from a specific rationality, which did not merely involve technological efficiency. Measures for more adequately controlled profit allocation, for instance, suggest that the modesty of the "unprecedented" law was strategically intended as a reasonable way to win as much consent as possible. Its leading advocate, Lord Mayor Franz Adickes, shared the national-liberal orientation dominant in the intellectual milieu of Germany at that time. Having already led urban planning and land reform in Dortmund and

Altona, beginning in 1873, he relished the opportunity to realize his ideals in Frankfurt am Main after 1891.[18]

The Lex Adickes was based on the idea that the city is an organic whole and that the municipal administration has the right to shape the city and to promote its further development. To this end, Mayor Adickes distanced himself from the more radical implementation and enforcement of the principle of self-administration, which would have served the selfish interests of private groups. The governing principle was the public welfare, for which independent, properly trained municipal civil servants were responsible. Despite this paternalistic orientation, Adickes opposed any form of bureaucratic obstinacy and tried to address the issue of housing for the broader population. Given the political reality, wherein the majority of the city council seats were held by conservative property owners, Adickes' orientation was rather liberal. Mayor Adickes himself regarded his planning proposal as part of his new economic and social policies. In fact, his administrative endeavors were situated between a communalism – "municipal socialism," as it was often referred to at that time[19] – and liberal rationalism. His position also echoed the then prevailing romantic conceit of depicting any political entity as a living organism. It was because of the utility of the various features of the Lex Adickes that the seeds of German experience could be so easily transplanted to heterogeneous milieus.

From Franz Adickes to Gotō Shinpei

The path to the enactment of the Japanese urban planning law

Land readjustment, or "Kukaku-Seiri" in Japanese, has been a key part of the Japanese urban planning system since it was first introduced as an effective means of preventing urban sprawl. In Japan, this project was preceded by the indigenous tradition of land consolidation, "Kochi-Seiri," which dates back to the Shogunate period. The tradition of communal land management, which had originated under feudalism, was heavily undermined by the Land Tax Act of 1873. By monetizing land as a commodity without altering the old landowning patterns, this act created significant obstacles to orderly urban growth. In 1899 the Agricultural Land Consolidation Law was passed to readjust scattered landholdings into larger plots and to build irrigation facilities. When it was first implemented in the early twentieth century, LR applied the method of land consolidation to urban development.[20]

In Meiji Japan, the laws concerning urban development enacted by the government consisted of the Tokyo Municipal Improvement Ordinance of 1888 and the subsidiary Regulations on the Disposal of the Lands and Buildings of 1889. "Shiku-Kaisei," the keyword of this ordinance, literally meaning "reforming the municipal districts," aimed at promoting urban revitalization of the new imperial capital Tokyo in order to enhance national prestige. In fact, the Meiji oligarchy envisioned a project similar to

108   Jin-Sung Chun

Haussmann's reconstruction of Paris under Napoleon III but did not similarly prioritize features such as boulevards. The focus of the project was placed rather on a series of practical works such as sanitizing, widening, and straightening preexisting traffic arteries or improving water supply facilities. The most visible achievement of the Tokyo *Shiku-Kaisei* was a grid system of streets connected by a series of rotaries.[21]

The reconstruction of the imperial capital during the Meiji period was based on the official idea of Tokyo as a showcase, rather than on a full-scale planning concept. The city of Tokyo, which was abruptly transformed from the medieval shogun city of Edo into a modern imperial capital, experienced turmoil from this transition, including a sharp decline in population, and therefore needed to be revitalized ahead of any other city.[22] As a result of this urgency, the projects enabled by the Tokyo Municipal Improvement Ordinance foreshadowed some distinctive features of modern urban planning in Japan.

First of all, direct government involvement in municipal improvement reflected some of the general characteristics of Imperial Japan. The political impotence of municipalities and of civil society continued to hamper Japanese urban planning. It is, therefore, no accident that Japanese planners, beyond the Meiji era, continued to focus on improving the built-up areas of major cities, rather than on expanding urban areas. The main purpose of Japanese urban planning was, in fact, establishing a suitable infrastructure in the inner city rather than providing housing for the broader population on the urban fringe.[23]

In this regard, the situation in Japan was quite different from that in Germany, although the latter provided the former with a source of inspiration for the future. Indeed, the Tokyo Municipal Improvement Ordinance of 1888 was adopted as the most viable alternative to a rival plan, a series of draft plans for a new government district in the heart of Tokyo, officially named the "Project for Concentrating Government Offices in Hibiya." This neo-Baroque-style urban planning reflects the so-called German turn in the Westernization of Japan in the 1880s: It was proposed by the pro-German foreign minister Inoue Kaoru, designed by a representative architectural firm in Berlin, Ende & Böckmann, and later supervised by James Hobrecht, the technical designer of modern Berlin.[24] The Ordinance of 1888, which superseded this project, was too practically oriented to establish a German preponderance in Japanese urban planning, although it was gradually supplemented by the introduction of the German methods of modern urban planning. An important piece of this development was the translation of German building codes by the Germanophile medical doctor and novelist Mori Ōgai, who served as a member of the Tokyo Municipal Improvement Committee.[25]

It was considered urgently necessary to expand nationwide the projects initially limited to the improvement of Tokyo's infrastructure. This approach was further developed with the modern-level planning methods

The population of Tokyo, in particular, grew from 1,120,000 in 1900 to 2,170,000 by 1920 and the consequent urban sprawl was unavoidable.[26] After a longstanding controversy and many reservations, a proposal was finally completed in 1918 to expand the existing Tokyo Municipal Improvement Ordinance to five other major cities. However, this was immediately superceded by new legislation. In April 1919, the Urban Planning and Urban Building Laws were passed. Unlike the Ordinance of 1888, this legislation encompassed all major cities and their outer districts, and thereby strived to channel the economic dynamism from the suburban fringe into urban growth. These codes lasted for almost half a century until the introduction of the new Urban Planning Law of 1968.[27]

There was certainly a substantial gap between the 1888 Ordinance and the 1919 Planning Laws. The latter involved all the plots and buildings within a given number of roadblocks, and thereby attempted to reorganize the overall urban space. Most of all, the adoption of the German zoning system produced a carefully balanced division of land into residential, commercial, and industrial areas and the corresponding designation of the building height, materials, coverage ratio, and windows. In line with the zoning system, the German building line system as well as land readjustment could be firmly integrated into the Japanese legal code.[28]

Land readjustment in the spirit of colonial management

LR was legalized in Japan by the Urban Planning Law of 1919. The methods of executing this kind of project, however, needed to conform to the Agricultural Land Consolidation Law of 1899.[29] The proper implementation of LR presupposed a clear-cut and viable concept of urban planning which could counter the resistance of the privileged classes. Indeed, the 1919 laws originally proposed some radical measures such as a betterment levy, namely a tax on increases in land values, as well as a sort of "excess condemnation," which forced the landlords to sell their lands at a lower price and repurchase at a higher one. These provisions, which ran counter to the vested interests of the landlord, were eventually deleted in the final draft. An example of a more expedient solution was the dispute over roadway width: The requirement for a minimum road width of 2.7 meters, established by the German building line system, could be avoided by excluding certain roadways from the strictures of the building code.[30] It was not until around the 1910s that the term "toshi keikaku," the Japanese rendering of the British concept of "town planning," was recognized in Japan. In fact, the 1907 Japanese translation of Ebenezer Howard's prominent book *Garden Cities of To-morrow* (1902) found great resonance.[31]

The real breakthrough, however, came with the Great Kantō earthquake in 1923. The earthquake devastated large swaths of the Tokyo metropolitan area, including the older wooden settlements. Quite suddenly, the disaster provided an unprecedented opportunity to realize the ambitious ideas of urban planning, which were included in the original draft of the 1919 laws. The "Imperial Capital Revival Plan" led to the enactment of the Special Urban Planning Act on December 24, 1924, which began a genuine agenda of urban planning that attempted to improve and modernize the traditional structure of Japanese cities. It was also the starting point of the full Japanization of the German Lex Adickes.

At the heart of this huge project was the former Tokyo Mayor Gotō Shinpei, who played a major role in drafting the planning laws of 1919. On the day after the earthquake, he was reappointed home minister for the second time and took charge of a large-scale rehabilitation project over the next six years. His original plan had an enormous projected cost exceeding 700 million yen, although even this was the result of a drastic reduction following a protracted dispute. The plan entailed regulations for a minimum road width of 50 meters throughout the Tokyo metropolitan area. It also required a 10 percent land contribution from all landowners for the LR-related projects. Although these radical measures could not avoid provoking opposition from vested interests and were only implemented on a limited basis, Gotō's Revival Plan proved to be a decisive moment for the implementation of the LR in Japan, which was later extended to postwar reconstruction projects and established as "the mother of urban planning."[32]

One of the main features of Japanese LR projects was the reallocation of land holdings and the provision of infrastructure along the main arteries of existing cities, not least in the Tokyo metropolitan area.[33] This was in contrast to the German LR projects, which focused mainly on the preparation for residential development in suburban fringe areas, although intensive land use usually required a revision of land boundaries. In fact, the LR projects in Japan were largely initiated by the central government and driven by its needs.

Gotō Shinpei, a man with a wealth of administrative experience who had trained originally as a medical doctor before becoming director of the Sanitary Bureau of the Home Ministry, was a key figure in respect to these specific policies. His talent for outstanding administration enabled him to climb to the top of Civilian Affairs in the Japanese Government-General of Taiwan in 1898. Thanks to his experience with colonial rule in Taiwan, including a series of local research projects and the *Shiku-Kaisei* practices, Gotō became the first director of the South Manchuria Railway Company in 1906, often abbreviated as "Mantetsu," which was effectively responsible for the colonial management of the attached lands (*fuzokuchi*). After pursuing several other careers, he became mayor of Tokyo in 1920. As noted, he was home minister in 1919 while drafting the Urban Planning Law. Despite

The Lex Adickes in its East Asian contexts 111

their original radical framing, the 1919 laws were moderated considerably by Gotō's basic pragmatism, the product of his experience as an imperial administrator. A doctor by training, Gotō always emphasized a scientific approach. His local research projects in Taiwan were actually intended to govern indigenous people according to the principles of biology.[34] It would not seem far-fetched to claim that this attitude of privileging science over political logic had pronounced colonial implications.

Nevertheless, Japanese urban planning was not limited to colonial management. Seki Hajime, who served as mayor of Osaka for fourteen years beginning in 1923, represented another lineage of Japanese urban planning. Seki attempted to approach the city as a structural whole beyond the confines of the existing developed built-up areas, and even pioneered the construction of the satellite city in order to solve ongoing housing problems. Seki's municipal enterprise in Osaka was actually based on the idea of municipal political autonomy.[35] It was, however, connected to Gotō's highly statist projects via personal networks. As vice mayor of Osaka City in 1917, Seki established a commission of inquiry on a city improvement plan in cooperation with Kataoka Yasushi, the president of the Kansai Architectural Association. In the spring of 1918 Kataoka began a campaign for urban planning legislation together with Sano Toshikata, the vice president of the association and a pioneer in the study of earthquake resistant architecture. Their goal was easily accomplished. Gotō Shinpei immediately accepted their proposals and set up relevant organizations attached to the Home Ministry. Gotō had already established the Urban Research Association in 1917 and he himself was actively involved in research and campaigning for the planning legislation. As a result, Gotō's Home Ministry personnel played a major role in enacting the 1919 laws, included by the future home minister Mizuno Rentarō and by Ikeda Hiroshi, who headed the Urban Planning Department in the Home Ministry and drafted the Urban Planning Law in conjunction with Sano Toshikata and other experts.[36]

Gotō Shinpei, in his role as a key figure in regard to Japanese urban planning, functioned as a conduit for the implementation of the German Lex Adickes. The facts that Gotō had received a governmental scholarship to study in Germany, and that his mentee Ikeda Hiroshi was known to have been strongly impressed by the German planning techniques during his long-term official visit to Europe, were rather trivial in themselves. More crucial was a rigorous legal formalism: In the procedures related to the actual LR, private agreements were bound to observe certain preemptory rules and official sanctions, so that legal grounds were essential for the implementation of the projects. LR was an administrative measure, rather than a voluntary act, tout court. In both Germany and Japan, the democratic ideals of "self-financing" and of fairly distributed benefits could not prevent the accelerated bureaucratization of the actual decision-making process.[37]

112 Jin-Sung Chun

Land readjustment in Seoul

Urban planning in colonial Seoul

The implementation of LR was restricted in the Japanese mainland itself, until after it had proven its utility in the Japanese overseas colonies. Visionary urban planning projects were usually applied experimentally in the colonies, before being introduced into the mainland. From the perspective of Japanese bureaucrats, the colonies were no more than an empty space, a sort of *tabula rasa* upon which they could test their acquired knowledge and technical capacities. This is why the forms of urban planning introduced into the colonies made constant destruction and ruthless domination seem natural. But not to be overlooked here is that the Japanese officials' accounts of the colonies as empty spaces were not that different from their attitudes toward the mainland. The only difference was that they were able to do what they wanted in the colonies, unlike on the mainland.[38] It would not be unduly tendentious to claim that urban planning, including LR, exposes the cardinal traits of modernity.

It is well known LR methods similar to those of the Japanese were implemented in a number of developing countries, including Indonesia and Nepal as well as Turkey.[39] Taiwan and Korea differed, however, from these cases in that they were directly under Japanese rule. In these neighboring colonies, which had cultural and racial affinities with the mainland, Japan's authoritarian imposition of newly developed techniques involved not just technological transfer. As demonstrated in the case of Gotō Shinpei, who applied his experience of colonial management in Taiwan and Manchuria to the imperial capital of Tokyo, urban planning and LR were recognized and represented as the embodiment of East Asian modernity.

The Lex Adickes in East Asia was highly modern in terms of the efficiency of its legal formalism. The leading role of the central governments was, indeed, much more prominent in the colonies, where a small number of officials focused on the efficient provision of the infrastructure essential for economic and military growth. It was thus not surprising that public support for managing this urban development and improving the living conditions of residents was virtually absent in the colonies.

The Japanese colonial enterprise in the city of Seoul was not much different from other cases in this respect. It emerged later than in Taipei, but almost simultaneously with Mukden and Dalian, and much earlier than in Shinkyō, the grandiose capital of the puppet state of Manchukuo. Colonial Seoul, however, was too complex to be treated as merely an empty space by a small number of colonial officials. It was known as Hansŏng, the five-century-old capital of the old Korean kingdom, Chosŏn (1392–1910), and it was reborn as the Japanese colonial city Keijō, or Kyŏngsŏng in Korean. In 1897, just a few years prior to the Japanese occupation of the Korean peninsula, the Chosŏn dynasty declared the establishment of the Korean empire,

The Lex Adickes in its East Asian contexts 113

the "Great Han Empire." This refashioning of the antiquated dynasty, however, was doomed to failure. The fragile monarchy was soon demoted to the position of a protectorate of Imperial Japan and then, eventually, its official colony. Despite its political vulnerability, the capital of the Great Han Empire was already on its way to becoming an imperial city, with a radial and circular road system. It was actually the first city in East Asia to be simultaneously equipped with electricity, trams, waterworks, telephones, and telegraphs. In the defunct imperial capital, therefore, the Japanese colonial government was forced to proceed from the urban reconstruction that was already under way, rather than from some imaginary *tabula rasa*.[40]

After the Japanese annexation of Korea, Seoul, as the primate city on the Korean peninsula, became the subject of special attention from the colonial government. The Japanese Government-General of Chosŏn introduced a host of Western-style buildings, as well as the Japanese technique of the *Shiku-Kaisei*, into the space of colonial Seoul. The specific plan for the Keijō Municipal Improvement, "Kyŏngsŏng Shigu-Gaesu" in Korean, was first announced in 1912, and after many modifications, its final amendment was officially promulgated in 1919.[41] The amended plan was distinguished by a north-south axis in the form of a thoroughfare between the former site of the Kyŏngbok Royal Palace, the site designated for a soon-to-be-built General Government Building, and a monumental Shinto shrine already under construction. Although the plans for the *Kyŏngsŏng Shigu-Gaesu* promoted the transformation of the old monarchical castle town into a colonial primate city, this shift was not so much a renovation as it was a colonially charged building project. The construction of modern infrastructure, especially a grid pattern of widened, straightened, and sanitized roads, reflected the impact of the Japanese *Shiku-Kaisei*, and this lineage can be traced to the first director of the Engineering Bureau of the Japanese Government-General of Chosŏn, Mochiji Rokusaburō, who had been in charge of the *Shiku-Kaisei* projects at the Japanese Government-General of Taiwan before being sent to Chosŏn to lead the 1912 plan.

The *Kyŏngsŏng Shigu-Gaesu* project was typical of Japanese military rule during the first phase of the colonial occupation of Korea. Unlike the Tokyo Municipal Improvement Ordinance, which had been enacted twenty-four years earlier, its Korean equivalent did not consider the need for public facilities for residents, such as water supply and sewage, terribly important, with the exception of certain road improvements. This one-sided project was intended to symbolize the superiority of modern Japanese civilization and to establish the legitimacy of its rule. However, the Japanese governors had to subsequently bear the political costs of this kind of military rule.[42]

The March 1 Independence Movement of 1919 marked a shift toward the so-called cultural rule of the 1920s, which refrained from overtly oppressive military rule and supported instead the cultural assimilation of the Korean people under the political hegemony of the Japanese empire. This new policy was adopted by the Japanese Government-General as a more "rational"

114   *Jin-Sung Chun*

way to reinforce colonial domination over the Koreans, and thereby created favorable conditions for the introduction of full-scale urban planning in Seoul. At that time the colonial primate city was in urgent need of rational solutions to emerging urban problems, especially the rapid population growth stemming from rural-urban migration and the consequent urban sprawl. In fact, the modern problem of (sub)urbanization in colonial Seoul developed coterminously with other big cities globally.[43]

Meanwhile, Japan also entered the era of urban planning in the 1920s with the advent of the Imperial Capital Revival Plan. The fact that Japanese urban planning was directly linked to its Korean counterpart in the colonial primate city Keijō is evidenced by figures like Mizuno Rentarō, who played a major role in the enactment of the Japanese Urban Planning law of 1919 and then immediately took office as the director-general of political affairs in colonial Korea. He was a founding member of the Keijō Urban Planning Research Association, which was composed mainly of young Japanese engineering bureaucrats and entrepreneurs living in Seoul. Also noteworthy is the request made by the Keijō Prefectural Government to Okazaki Shōtarō, a public servant in Osaka City, to draft an urban planning law in the late 1920s. He was known as one of the best city planning legislators, due to his wealth of practical experience in Nagoya and Osaka. Nonetheless, the urban planning endeavors of the 1920s ultimately proved unsuccessful. Although Mizuno Rentarō, in his capacity as an adviser to the Keijō Urban Planning Research Association, inducted as honorary members such prominent figures as Kataoka Yasushi and Sano Toshikata, the association did little more than serve as a civilian advisory board, a position incomparably lower than that of the Urban Research Association under Gotō Shinpei.[44]

The 1920s debates over urban planning legislation remained at the level of theory, and even that was confined to the Seoul metropolitan area. It was only after the Manchurian Incident of 1931 that full-scale national urban planning suddenly became part of the agenda. In 1931, the newly appointed governor-general, Ugaki Kazushige, embarked on the task of building up the industrial base on the Korean peninsula in coordination with the Japanese invasion policy of the continent. It thus became necessary to develop a stronghold city on the Korean peninsula, and Najin, a fishing village facing the northeast border, was selected as the best route from Korea to Manchuria. In keeping with the urgent goal of developing Najin, the Chosŏn City District Planning Ordinance was promulgated on June 20, 1934, and its enforcement regulations were announced the following month.[45]

This ordinance consisted of three chapters and fifty articles. Chapter 1, the General Rules, defined the objects and enforcement bodies of the plan, and Chapter 2 prescribed building regulations and the zoning areas as four categories: industrial, commercial, residential, and unspecified. Chapter 3 prescribed the regulations for land readjustment. The historical significance of this ordinance lies in the fact that not only did it parallel existing urban planning laws on the Japanese mainland, but that it actually extended further in scope. As the term "City District Planning" suggests, it focused on providing basic infrastructure for urban extension areas throughout the country. Unlike Japan, it did not allow landowners to voluntarily enforce LR projects. Otherwise, landowners would have had to meet the impossible condition that all of them in a district agreed on the project. The limitation of private participation resulted partly from the lessons learned from mainland Japan's trial-and-error. In the early 1930s the Japanese government enacted the Provisional Urban Planning Act and its amendments, which were intended to strengthen public control. It was an irresistible trend across the entire Japanese empire to control land prices and population through the power of the state, which, for its part, did not hesitate to deploy the rhetoric of "for the national benefit."[46]

Modernization of the capital Seoul before and after 1945

The Chosŏn City District Planning Ordinance of 1934 was actually a government-centered plan, enacted and enforced solely by the governor-general. This ordinance focused on the expansion of existing cities or the creation of new cities, such as the port city Najin, rather than the improvement of older downtown districts. It was a new form of colonial rule, rather than just the introduction of urban planning techniques, which usually stemmed from the voluntary requests of urban proprietors, as in Osaka and Seoul in the 1920s. The predominance of imperial control was most explicitly revealed in the LR projects; the opinions of residents directly impacted by these measures were completely ignored.

Article 42 of Chapter 3 of the Chosŏn City District Planning Ordinance clearly states that the purpose of LR was to "use" existing land in accordance with national priorities. LR projects, which variously enabled the "exchange, subdivision or combination of land, alternation of its category, additional change of its qualities, and creation, modification, removal of roads, squares, rivers, parks" could be seen as a pursuit of modern capitalist rationality, which understands land as a use value to be maximized for efficiency. However, the dark side of this rationality is revealed in a provision of Article 44: Landowners were granted only a one-month voluntary application period, after which the government was entitled to issue an administrative order and confiscate the land. The areas planned for development were never announced in advance, and the process remained secretive and confidential. Moreover, betterment levies were introduced unilaterally in a manner not allowed on the Japanese mainland. The pretext of preventing land speculation or correcting the evil of absentee landlordism was not enough to legitimize this kind of a coercive measure.[47] LR became firmly established in the Korean legal code by the Japanese Government-General's announcement of an amendment to the enforcement regulations on City District Planning in September 1938.[48]

LR soon spread beyond the port of Najin to major cities throughout Korea, expanding to twenty-two cities by the collapse of the Japanese empire. The most representative case was, of course, the Keijō City District Planning Project. Launched in 1936, it projected the expansion of Seoul and the development of its outskirts through LR methods. This project was initiated in the same year by the Chosŏn Government-General, which announced the Keijō City District Planning Area, the amended administrative jurisdiction of the Keijō Prefecture, and the LR project districts consecutively.[49] The debate over the extension of Seoul's administrative districts had been centered around the Keijō Urban Planning Research Association since the early 1920s, but it gained momentum under the auspices of the 1934 ordinance. The Keijō Prefectural Government primarily focused on the Yŏngdŭngp'o and Donam districts.[50]

The Yŏngdŭngp'o district, located on the south bank of the Han River, was designated a factory site, and its original landowners were forced to organize an association to negotiate land values with the prefectural government and then to vacate the land. Donam district in northeastern Seoul was designated as a purely residential district, which aimed at developing a self-sufficient residential community for the urban middle class. Of the two districts, the latter is particularly noteworthy, because it is the only case from the colonial period in which an entire LR project was completed, including land development, allotment, and housing construction. Under the influence of Ebenezer Howard's theory of the garden city, Donam district was designed to be independent from the downtown and was equipped with housing, transportation networks, schools, markets, parks, and other infrastructure. It was also notable in that it targeted mostly Korean residents. Although this plan for a "cultural residence" was intended to create a luxurious residential area surrounded by greenery in a secluded suburban area, its actual result was the so-called modified Korean-style house, based on a standardized large-scale housing complex. Although it was an outcome of Japanese colonial rule, it also established the character of the subsequent development of the Korean capital.[51]

Despite this attempt to plan a suburban "cultural residence," LR projects in colonial Korea were focused mainly on the construction of new development capable of absorbing the overcrowded urban population connected with industrial areas. These basic trends continued in post-liberation Seoul. In the capital of a new state in which municipal organization was weak and resources were limited, LR methods guaranteed considerable savings. The devastating consequences of the Korean War (1950–1953) following the nation's division, stimulated a reintroduction of LR during the postwar reconstruction. The first LR project in postcolonial Seoul was begun in the midst of the war with the Seoul Rehabilitation Plan of March 2, 1952. This plan, which was to deal with the imperfect LR districts designated by the Japanese Government-General, remained however little more than a makeshift plan that failed to designate parks and school grounds.[52]

The Lex Adickes in its East Asian contexts 117

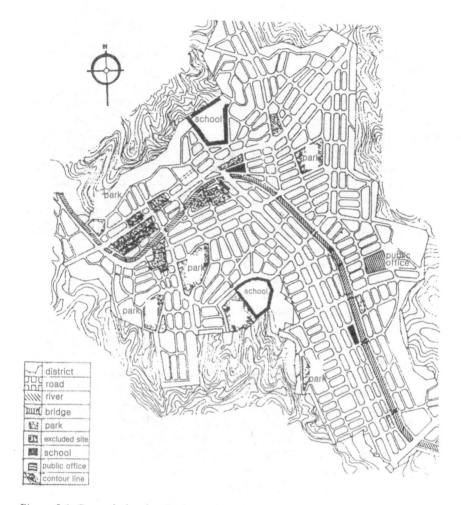

Figure 5.1 Ground plan for the Donam District Readjustment (1939)
Source: Son Jŏng-Mok, "Ilche ha ŭi dosikyehoek e kwanhan yŏn'gu (IV)," *Gukto Kyehoek* 21, no. 2 (1986), 52.

A full-fledged LR project in the Republic of Korea began in the early 1960s, when the Park Jŏng-Hee regime seized power in a military coup and embarked on the task of economic development. With the beginning of the first five-year economic development plan, the Urban Planning Law and the Building Law were promulgated successively in January 1962. Although these laws succeeded the LR projects from the end of the colonial period, they also reflected more recent changes in the social conditions of Seoul. The population of Seoul in 1945 of 900,000 had declined sharply during the Korean War but soon recovered and had reached 2.5 million by 1960.

118 Jin-Sung Chun

As the economic development policies of the military regime promoted land expropriation, the average land value increased by 55 percent per year from the early 1960s to the 1980s.[53]

During this period, the Park Jŏng-Hee government started to advocate for a land policy in support of its industrial policy, beginning with the enactment of the Comprehensive National Territory Planning Act of 1963. There had emerged by this time a need to construct a new development zone on Seoul's urban fringe to address housing problems and to provide sites for public infrastructure. Fortunately, there was a huge swath of undeveloped land south of the Han River. Because public finances at that time could not support compensation for eminent domain, the Land Readjustment Project Act of August 1966 diverged from the Urban Planning Law of 1962. The 1966 act reintroduced the betterment levy of the Japanese colonial period to cover almost all of the project's costs, and this coercive policy was easily enforced in Korea under authoritarian rule. According to the 1977 statistics of the Ministry of Construction, the Seoul City Government controlled 38 of 43 LR projects in Seoul, under the approval of the Ministry of Construction. Until the Urban Development Act superseding the LR was enacted at the very beginning of the new millennium, LR was clearly the most important land policy in Korea. During the 1960s and 1970s, 44 percent of Seoul's total urbanization area was in LR districts, and by the end of the 1980s, approximately 130 km² of the land in Seoul had been developed through LR projects.[54]

The military government's land policies focused on supporting efficient economic development rather than equitable land distribution. Unlike in the Japanese colonial period, LR guaranteed huge development benefits for landowners. However, the increase in land and housing prices resulted in hardships for ordinary people, who could no longer afford homes. The effect of this developmental dictatorship on the social structure of the city is a question still under debate. What is clear is that the policy failed dramatically as a form of social justice. As a result of the overreliance on land price increases through the sale of reserve land, landowners and developers gained significantly while government tax revenues also grew. When the government tried to minimize the amount of land used for public utilities, its obvious intent was to maintain an upper limit of land-reduction rates in favor of landowners. Actually, the government seemed more obsessed with land speculation than with the LR itself, even while implementing a new social policy of cross-subsidization for low-income housing. It is no surprise, therefore, that the LR projects in Korea contributed to rather than curtailed the disorderly expansion of the city area.[55]

Conclusion: municipal communalism or capitalist modernization?

The transfer of the LR, both in theory and in practice, halfway around the globe is significant in that it has led to changes in the social configuration

The Lex Adickes in its East Asian contexts   119

of land, the most basic measure of human space. The surgical intervention upon Mother Earth has had a profound impact on the mode of spatial perceptions and representations, as well as on social structures and political behaviors, giving rise thereby to a transnational urbanism. Under the unique conditions of East Asia, where a colonial relationship was established between neighboring countries, an authoritarian system of Prussian provenance was imposed upon colonial Seoul through Japanese colonial rule.

The LR techniques implemented in Germany, Japan, and Korea differed from each other, but they had an inherent common denominator. Namely, LR provided an effective means to reduce the inconveniences of land fragmentation and to construct urban infrastructure without the expensive acquisition of land, as well as to control profit allocation. In Germany, the LR projects promoted legislation for publicly supported housing against vested interests. In the cases of Imperial Japan and postcolonial Korea, by contrast, the use of LR was predominantly adopted as national policy for the purpose of modernization and colonial rule. The historical and political assessment of the outcomes of these long-term transfer processes is still open to debate. At least in the case of the postcolonial city of Seoul, the stranglehold imposed on the housing market is hard to see as a policy enacted for the benefit of residents, because the government itself has often encouraged land speculation in order to cover the construction costs. This has concurrently resulted in a failure to prevent urban sprawl.

The ambivalence of land readjustment, between coercion by higher authorities and the voluntary requests made of urban proprietors, between a mildly conservative form of municipal communalism and a purely capitalist modernization, is most clearly revealed in (post)colonial Seoul. But it is also a broader legacy as well that extends around the globe. In terms of its coercive and developmental rationality, the history of LR gives some indication as to the ambivalence of modernity per se.

Notes

1 William A. Doebele, "Introduction," in *Land Readjustment: A Different Approach to Financing Urbanization*, ed. William Doebele (Lexington, MA: Lexington Books, 1983), 1–28.
2 Gerhard Larsson, *Land Readjustment: A Modern Approach to Urbanization* (Aldershot: Avebury, 1993), 11, 15.
3 André Sorensen, *The Making of Urban Japan: Cities and Planning from Edo to the Twentieth-First Century* (London: Routledge, 2002), 58.
4 Dorothea Berger-Thimme, *Wohnungsfrage und Sozialstaat: Untersuchungen zu den Anfängen staatlicher Wohnungspolitik in Deutschland 1873–1918* (Frankfurt a. M.: Peter Lang, 1976), 213–20.
5 Helmuth Croon, "Staat und Städte in den westlichen Provinzen Preußens 1817–1875: Ein Beitrag zum Entstehen des Preußischen Bau-und Fluchtliniengesetzes von 1875," in *Stadterweiterungen 1800–1875: Von den Anfängen des modernen Städtebaues in Deutschland*, ed. Erhard Fehl and Juan Rodriguez-Lores (Hamburg: Hans Christians, 1983), 72–74.

120   *Jin-Sung Chun*

6 Peter Ring, "Bevölkerung," in *Berlin Handbuch* (Berlin: FAB, 1992), 237; Horst Matzerath, "Berlin, 1890–1940," in *Metropolis 1890–1940*, ed. Anthony Sutcliff (Chicago: University of Chicago Press, 1984), 293–94.

7 Walter Kieß, *Urbanismus im Industriezeitalter: Von der klassizistischen Stadt zur Garden City* (Berlin: Ernst & Sohn, 1991), 227 ff.

8 Reinhart Koselleck, *Preußen zwischen Reform und Revolution: Allgemeines Landrecht, Verwaltung und soziale Bewegung von 1791 bis 1848* (1975: Munich: dtv, 1989), 23–51.

9 The full title was "Law on the Creation and Modification of Streets and Squares in Cities and Rural Areas," and the original text can be found at the following website: www.berlin.de/imperia/md/content/dienstleistungsdatenbank/verm/preussisches_fluchtliniengesetz_1875_gs.pdf?start&ts=1329464810&file=preussisches_fluchtliniengesetz_1875_gs.pdf.

10 Daniel Ehebrecht, *Der Hobrechtplan von 1862 und seine Einflüsse auf das Stadtbild von Berlin* (Munich: Grin Verlag, 2008).

11 One of the main critics is Werner Hegemann, *Das steinerne Berlin, Geschichte der größten Mietkasernenstadt der Welt* (Berlin: Ulstein, 1930), 207 ff.

12 Harald Bodenschatz, *Berlin Urban Design: A Brief History of a European City* (Berlin: DOM Publishers, 2013), 18–26; Thomas Hall, *Planning Europe's Capital Cities. Aspects of Nineteenth Century Urban Development* (London: Routledge, 2010), 192–99.

13 Anthony Sutcliffe, *Towards the Planned City: Germany, Britain, and the United States and France, 1780–1914* (Oxford: Basil Blackwell, 1981), 32, 37.

14 Berger-Thimme, *Wohnungsfrage und Sozialstaat*, 213–20.

15 Städtisches Tiefbauamt, ed., *Umlegung von Grundstücken in Frankfurt am Main* (Frankfurt am Main: Schirmer & Mahlau, 1903), accessed January 12, 2017, https://archive.org/stream/umlegungvongrun00tiefgoog#page/n4/mode/2up.

16 John Robert Mullin, "American Perceptions of German City Planning at the Turn of the Century," *Landscape Architecture & Regional Planning Faculty Publication Series* 35 (1976): 9–10.

17 C. Merlo, *Der Gesetzentwurf Betreffend Stadterweiterungen und Zonenenteignungen: Lex Adickes* (Cologne: Kölner Verlags-Anstalt, 1894; Whitefish: Kessinger Legacy Reprints, 2010), 3.

18 Lothar Gall, *Franz Adickes: Oberbürgermeister und Universitätsgründer* (Frankfurt a. M.: Societäts Verlag, 2013).

19 Ibid., esp. 17–18.

20 André Sorensen, *The Making of Urban Japan*, 57 ff.; Yasuo Nishiyama, "Western Influence on Urban Planning Administration in Japan: Focus on Land Management," in *Urban Development Policies and Programmes, Focus on Land Management*, ed. Nagamine Haruo (Nagoya: United Nations Centre for Regional Development, 1986), 331.

21 Fujimori Terunobu, *Meiji no Tōkyō keikaku* (Tokyo: Iwanami Shoten, 2012), 247–55; Sorensen, *The Making of Urban Japan*, 71 ff.

22 Henry D. Smith II, "Tokyo as an Idea: An Exploration of Japanese Urban Thought Until 1945," *Journal of Japanese Studies* 4, no. 1 (1978): 45–80; Shun-Ichi J. Watanabe, "Metropolitanism as a Way of Life: In Case of Tokyo, 1868–1930," in *Metropolis 1890–1940*, ed. Anthony Sutcliffe (Chicago: University of Chicago Press, 1984), 406–8.

23 Nishiyama, "Western Influence on Urban Planning Administration in Japan," 315–55.

24 Fujimori, *Meiji no Tōkyō keikaku*, 277–326.

25 Sorensen, *The Making of Urban Japan*, 69–71.

26 Ishida Yorifusa, *Nihon kindai toshi keikaku no hyakunen* (Tokyo: Jichitai kenkyūsha, 1987), 110–12.

The Lex Adickes in its East Asian contexts 121

27 Koshizawa Akira, *Tōkyō no toshi keikaku* (Tokyo: Iwanami shinsho, 1991), 13–15.

28 David B. Stewart, *The Making of a Modern Japanese Architecture: 1868 to the Present* (Tokyo and New York: Kodansha International, 1987), 119–21.

29 Ishida Yorifusa, "Nihon ni okeru tochi kukaku seiri seidoshi gaisetsu 1870–1980," *Sōgō toshi kenkyū* 28 (1986): 54–55.

30 Koshizawa, *Tōkyō no toshi keikaku*, 19–21; Stewart, *The Making of a Modern Japanese Architecture*, 110.

31 Watanabe, "Metropolitanism as a Way of Life," 417.

32 Koshizawa, *Tōkyō no toshi keikaku*, 34–86; Sorensen, *The Making of Urban Japan*, 69–71; André Sorensen, "Urban Planning and Urban Sprawl in the in the Tokyo Metropolitan Area," *Urban Studies* 36, no. 13 (1999): 2333–5.

33 Yorifusa, "Nihon ni okeru tochi kukaku seiri seidoshi gaisetsu 1870–1980," 60 ff.

34 Koshizawa, *Tōkyō no toshi keikaku*, 11–12, 31 ff.; William Shaw Sewell, *Japanese Imperialism and Civic Construction in Manchuria: Changchun, 1905–1945* (Vancouver: University of British Columbia Press, 2000), 65–67.

35 Sorensen, *The Making of Urban Japan*, 133 ff.

36 Koshizawa Akira, *Tōkyō no toshi keikaku*, 13–23; Stewart, *The Making of a Modern Japanese Architecture*, 133–36.

37 Peter Nakamura, "A Legislative History of Land Readjustment," in *Land Readjustment: The Japanese System*, ed. Luciano Minerbi et al. (Boston, MA: Oelgeschlager, Gunn & Hain, 1986), 17–32; Larsson, *Land Readjustment*, 11, 15, 32.

38 Mark R. Peattie, "The Japanese Colonial Empire, 1895–1945," in *The Cambridge History of Japan*, ed. Peter Duus (Cambridge: Cambridge University Press, 1988), 264; Carola Hein, "The Transformation of Planning Ideas in Japan and Its Colonies," in *Urbanism: Imported or Exported?* ed. Joe Nasr and Mercedes Volait (Chichester: Wiley-Academy, 2003), 54, 67 ff.

39 André Sorensen, "Conflict, Consensus or Consent: Implications of Japanese Land Readjustment Practice for Developing Countries," *Habitat International* 24, no. 1 (2000): 51–73.

40 Todd Henry, "Respatializing Chŏson's Royal Capital," in *Sitings: Critical Approaches to Korean Geography*, ed. Timothy R. Tangherlini and Sallie Yea (Honolulu, HI: University of Hawaii Press, 2008), 18–22; Andre Schmid, *Korea Between Empires, 1895–1919* (New York: Columbia University Press, 2002), 72–80; Bruce Cumings, *Korea's Place in the Sun: A Modern History* (New York: Norton, 1997), 132–33.

41 *Chōsen sōtokufu kanpō* 56 (October 7, 1912), Chōsen sōtokufu kūnre, no. 9, 1.

42 Son Jŏng-Mok, *Ilche gangjŏmgi dosikyehoek yŏn'gu* (Seoul: Iljisa, 1990), 98–114.

43 Todd A. Henry, *Assimilating Seoul: Japanese Rule and the Politics of Public Space in Colonial Korea, 1910–1945* (Oakland: University of California Press, 2014), 22–61.

44 Park Se-Hun, "1920 nyŏndae Kyŏngsŏng ŭi dosi kyehyŏk kwa dosi kyehoek undong," in *Cheguk Ilbon kwa singminji Chosŏn ŭi kŭndae dosi hyŏngsŏng*, Park Jin-Han et al. (Seoul: Simsan, 2013), 90, 96–101; Son, *Ilche gangjŏmgi dosikyehoek yŏn'gu*, 115, 170–76.

45 "Chōsenshigaiji keikakure," *Chōsen sōtokufu kanpō* 2232 (June 20, 1934), Chōsen sōtokufu seire no. 18, 1–3; "Chōsenshigaiji keikakure chikōkisoku," *Chōsen sōtokufu kanpō* 2264 (July 27, 1934), Chōsen sōtokufu re, no. 78, 1–4. On the *Chosŏn Shigajigehoek'ryŏng*, see Son Jŏng-Mok, *Ilche gangjŏmgi dosikyehoek yŏn'gu*, 151–57, 184–87, 195–200.

46 Lee Myŏng-Kyu, "Ilbon bonguk kwa Chŏson Chongdokbu dosikyehoek bigyo yŏn'gu: Dosi kyehoek bŏpryŏng ŭl jungsimŭro," in *Chŏson Chongdokbu dosikyehoek gongmunsŏ wa girokpyŏnggaron*, ed. Han'guk gukga girok yŏn'guwŏn

122　Jin-Sung Chun

(Seoul: Jinritamgu, 2008), 291–95; Yŏm Bok-Kyu, *Sŏul ŭi kiwŏn, Kyŏngsŏng ŭi tansaeng 1910–1945* (Seoul: Idea, 2016), 161–75.

47　Son, *Ilche gangjŏmgi dosikyehoek yŏn'gu*, 253–81, 383.

48　"Chōsensh igaiji keikakure chikōkisoku naka kaisei," *Chōsen sōtokufu kanpō* 3506 (September 21, 1938), Chōsen sōtokufu re, no. 193, 1–14.

49　"Keijō shigaiji keikaku kuiki," *Chōsen sōtokufu kanpō* 2758 (March 26, 1936), Chōsen sōtokufu gokuji, no. 180, 2; Sŏul tŭkbyŏlsi, *Tojiguhoekjŏngri baeksŏ* (1990), 36.

50　Yŏm, *Sŏul ŭi kiwŏn, Kyŏngsŏng ŭi tansaeng 1910–1945*, 119–32.

51　Sŏul tŭkbyŏlsi, *Tojiguhoekjŏnri yŏnhyŏkji* (1984), 73–76; Yŏm, *Sŏul ŭi kiwŏn, Kyŏngsŏng ŭi tansaeng 1910–1945*, 192–216, 247–82.

52　Son Jŏng-Mok, *Sŏul dosikyehoek iyagi*, vol. 4 (Seoul: Hanul, 2003), 289; Kim Ŭi-Wŏn, "Urinara Tojiguhoekjŏngrisaŏb ŭi doib kwa jŏn'gae," *Tosimunje* 18, no. 2 (1983): 20.

53　Kwŏn Yong-Uh, *Sudokwŏn ŭi ihe* (Seoul: Bosŏng'gak, 1999), 73; Park Minkyu, Kang Myounggu, and Jung Sanghoon, "Land Readjustment of Seoul and Tokyo Metropolitan Area in the 1960s and 1970s from the Perspective of the New Institutionalism: Its Implications on the International Transfer of Urban Planning System," *Gukto yŏn'gu* 86 (2015): 168.

54　Jung Hee Nam, "The Evolution of Korean Land Policies Since Independence, 1948–2008," *Budongsan yŏn'gu* 20, no. 1 (2010): 281–306; I. J. Kim, M. C. Hwang, and W. Doebele, "Land Readjustment in South Korea," in *Land Readjustment*, ed. William Doebele, 132–33; Kim, "Urinara Tojiguhoekjŏngrisaŏb ŭi doib kwa jŏn'gae," 20.

55　Kim, "Urinara Tojiguhoekjŏngrisaŏb ŭi doib kwa jŏn'gae," 22–24; Yang Sang-Wook, "Sŏul guhoekjŏngrisaŏb ŭi gonggan gusŏng e kwanhan yŏn'gu," *Honam daehakkyo nonmunjip* 17 (1996): 562–63.

6 A nuclear fall-out turning political

The German-Japanese relationship and the consequences of the Fukushima nuclear incident

Volker Stanzel

The relationship between Germany and Japan may not be the most significant of their respective international relationships, but for more than a century, for various reasons, this connection has been defined by a superficial appraisal as being somehow special. This pervasive societal understanding, shared by both countries, has experienced unexpected "twists" as a result of the Fukushima nuclear incident in March 2011. These changes are noteworthy because they may compound bilateral problems already developing in both countries regarding both attitudes toward China and divergent approaches to macro-economic policy. One result of these developments may therefore be that the relationship between the two countries increasingly corresponds to a more sober reality. This article, written against the backdrop of the prevalent view of the special character of German-Japanese relations, tries to identify these "twists" and to evaluate the consequences they engender. Given that until now only particular aspects of the impact of the Fukushima catastrophe on the bilateral German-Japanese relationship have been examined, this paper is based mainly on statements and postulates taken from the public sphere and the media.

The Fukushima nuclear incident

"Fukushima" has become an internationally and instantly recognized code word for the greatest nuclear accident in the world since Chernobyl in 1986. On March 11, 2011, an earthquake measuring 9.0 on the Richter scale occurred off the coast of the eastern Tohoku region of northern Japan. While the direct damage caused by the quake alone was limited – relative to its magnitude – the tsunami following the quake wreaked havoc on 561 square kilometers of the coastal region; about 550 people were killed by the quake, and almost 20,000 by the tsunami. Six years after the quake, the damage caused by the tsunami is far from repaired. Most dangerously devastated by the tsunami was the Fukushima Daiichi nuclear power station. Located on

124 *Volker Stanzel*

a hill close to the coast, the power station's emergency generator was insufficiently protected against the tsunami – the quay wall being only 5.2 meters high with the tsunami wave reaching 13.1 meters. When the quake halted the normal flow of electricity, the emergency generator provided electricity only until the tsunami waves struck. Without sufficient cooling, the fuel rods began to melt three hours after the quake. On March 12 a hydrogen explosion occurred in the building of reactor Block 1, in Block 3 on March 14, and in Block 4 on March 15; Block 2 was vented twice on March 13 and 15. The greatest amount of radioactivity was released on March 15. Neither this information nor the fact that radioactivity had escaped was released to the public at the time, many of whom doubted whether the scenario that had caused the explosions or even potentially a meltdown was even possible.[1]

The triple disaster impacted Germans in Japan in much the same way as it did nationals of other countries. At the time of the quake there were about 5,000 German nationals in Japan (about 3,000 in the larger Tokyo region, fewer than 100 in Tohoku).[2] The first question to be clarified by German officials therefore was whether any German nationals had been injured by the quake or the tsunami, a concern that was quickly alleviated with the help of Germany's honorary consul in Tohoku's capital Sendai and the head of the German cultural center there. As news of the nuclear accident spread, concern for quake and tsunami victims was quickly replaced by fears that Germans in Japan, as well as Japanese, would suffer physical harm similar to that caused by Chernobyl. Calls and emails from Germany inundated the embassy, the consulate general in Osaka and the foreign office in Berlin reflecting early media reports: "Tokyo Gripped by Deadly Fear"[3] was a typical headline of a serious daily. Early on in the crisis, the foreign office dispatched a government aid team (THW) with dogs trained to search for quake victims, and sent a nuclear radiation expert to the embassy. Whereas the latter was increasingly in demand (he and his replacements worked at the embassy until late 2013), the former soon discovered that no surviving quake victims were to be found because of the tsunami.

In the meantime, Germans from the wider Tokyo region left either on their own or with embassy support; the embassy sent a bus from the German school in Yokohama to Tohoku to pick up the Germans there who wanted to leave. Finally, confronted with the danger of further explosions and possibly a meltdown, the German foreign minister, along with a number of other governments, decided on March 16 that the embassy staff would evacuate to the German Consulate General in Osaka for about one month. Like the German embassy, other diplomatic missions also dispatched their radiation experts. These professionals were in constant contact with one another to evaluate what was happening in Fukushima on the basis of the government information provided through daily information sheets and at a meeting of the Japanese-speaking ambassadors in Tokyo with the Secretary General of the governing Democratic Progress Party (DPJ), Katsuya Okada, on March 15. Uncertain how quickly vital information would be provided, the

US had already deployed an aircraft carrier to the vicinity of Japan in order to pick up American nationals if necessary. Based on announcements by the International Atomic Energy Agency (IAEA) in Vienna, official press communication, and news extracted from the media, experts in Germany also tried to evaluate what was going on. While the German media were already speculating in reports that Japan was thoroughly irradiated,[4] experts still believed that a meltdown could not have taken place because such a catastrophe would have caused much greater damage than the explosions had done so far; however, it still might happen. If so, the consensus was that taking iodine tablets and staying indoors would be sufficient protection. At that point the French embassy required that its nationals only leave their houses if wearing protective gear. France, Britain, and other countries prepared air flights to evacuate their nationals. When these arrived, it turned out that there weren't enough nationals left to fill the planes (the German government had already decided against sending a plane for that very reason).

The first statements by the German government were not dramatically different from those issued by other Western governments in that they only warned to avoid travel to Greater Tokyo and Tohoku.[5] There was, however, an obvious difference in the way Japanese media reported on the situation, emphasizing mostly how people victimized by the tsunami dealt bravely with their fate.[6] They were, however, also critical of how the Japanese government was handling the situation, and when it turned out that Prime Minister Kan Naoto – nicknamed "Raging Kan" (ira-Kan) – was impatient and angry at the obfuscation strategy of Tepco, the company that owned the Fukushima power station, the media criticized him for overriding the authority of Tepco managers. No one at that point had any idea how serious the situation actually was. Later, Kan would explain: "Fukushima had six reactors at the No. 1 site, and four at the No. 2 site. It had 11 pools for storing used nuclear fuel. If all those had become uncontrollable, then there could have been many times more nuclear fallout than from Chernobyl. Radiation would have fallen over a very large area, including Tokyo – possibly requiring the evacuation of 50 million people."[7]

German-Japanese relations

One hundred fifty years ago, on January 24, 1861, the first treaty between a German state – Prussia – and Japan was concluded, constituting the official beginning of German-Japanese relations. Extensive planning had therefore been devoted to commemorating the anniversary throughout 2011. Various activities had already taken place, the crown prince was scheduled to visit Germany in May, and the German federal president was to visit Japan in October. On January 26 the German Bundestag unanimously passed a resolution on German-Japanese relations, emphasizing the "natural partnership" between the two countries.[8] On March 30, the Japanese Lower House passed a similar resolution.[9]

126   *Volker Stanzel*

Politically, Japan and Germany had never played crucial roles toward one another. From the nineteenth century on, the United States had played a dominant role in the Asia Pacific. Only the United Kingdom had ever achieved a comparable influence on East Asian affairs. As for Germany, its decisive relations had always been with other European states, with the United States playing an increasing role since its entry into the First World War. For both Germany and Japan this had remained the case since the end of World War II. However, almost from the outset of their relationship in 1861, a mutual regard had arisen between the two countries that would prove resilient and lasting. This attitude consisted of two components.[10] To begin, there was the popular notion that the "character" of both peoples is similar; both the Germans and the Japanese regard themselves as given to hard work, diligence, punctuality, seriousness, and efficiency, and each attributes the same virtues to the other. While this aspect of their mutual impressions might be considered emotional, the second component is more political – and more important. Each regards the other as struggling under the same burden: both fated to play "catch up" against stronger nations in working toward modernization, which often was used to justify an imperialist-aggressive or even colonialist foreign policy. That idea was articulated forcefully in a speech by German chancellor Otto von Bismarck on March 15, 1873 to the members of the so-called Iwakura mission, the most significant mission of Japanese leaders to the US and Europe after the Meiji restoration of 1868: "Our wars were unavoidable to protect German interests. . . . Born in a small country myself, I can understand your situation well, as we fight for our own rights without caring for the opinion of the world. . . . Japan is similar to Germany in that it seeks to maintain its rightful interests."[11]

With the rise of Germany's economy after its victory over France in 1871, economic relations between the countries flourished, mainly in the field of arms exports. But even more significant was the Japanese decision to have German experts play a major role in Japan's modernization through official training (with US and British experts more in demand by civil society), e.g. in medicine, law, military training, architecture, and music. At the same time, the Japanese government sent its state-sponsored students mainly to Germany (again, privately funded students preferred the US).[12] Even though the two countries were opponents during World War I – Japan having set its ambitions on the German colonies in China and the South Pacific – this situation did not change noticeably after the war. Elite contacts became even closer with former students in Germany now occupying elevated positions in Japan, economic relations gradually improving, and both countries, for reasons of their own, becoming political outcasts of international society,[13] until both went to war against the Allies.

Despite official propaganda, and even postwar perceptions, actual cooperation between the two wartime allies was minimal, both because of the lack of trust between the leaders of the two countries and due to the geographical

A nuclear fall-out turning political 127

difficulties of implementing military cooperation. Both countries, however, shared a similar sense of rebirth as nations. Japan's infrastructure and industry was destroyed, compounded by the suffering brought on by two atomic bombs; its society subsequently underwent an America-led purge of its militarist wartime leaders, the revelations of the Tokyo War Crime Trials, and democratic "reeducation" and democratization. Germany similarly suffered far-reaching destruction domestically. Reconstruction efforts were made even more difficult by the partition and reallocation of nearly one third of its territory to Poland and the Soviet Union; an influx of 12 million German refugees; denazification; the confrontation with revelations about the Holocaust; and the transition into a democratic nation in the West and a communist one in the East. Yet the new democracies in Japan and West Germany rebuilt themselves as economic powers during their respective postwar "economic miracles," with both soon becoming the strongest economic powers in the world after the United States. Over the course of the postwar era, Germany was one of the leaders of European integration, and Japan pursued its dream as "Japan as No. 1" (Ezra Vogel) until, in 1990, the economic "bubble" burst.

For more than a hundred years both countries have pursued similar goals of modernization and of "catching up" with the earlier industrialized powers. Steered by increasingly destructive governments, both brought immense suffering on other peoples, as well as to their own, through trying to imitate nineteenth century imperialism at a time when, after the First World War, international society was developing different strategies of competition and resolving conflicts, and had condemned war as a means of policy. In the second half of the twentieth century both embarked on a course of export-led growth, based on liberal market economies and the development of pluralist modern democratic societies. They never formally coordinated their strategies or politics but cooperated economically and in science and culture. This has resulted in a popular image of the two countries as sharing similar fates, and even similar "national characteristics." It was only with the end of the Cold War, together with the acceleration of globalization, that the parameters of the relationship changed significantly.[14] Both remain export-dependent second-tier powers with similar agendas. But for Germany, the expansion of the EU and NATO eastward, as well as the dissolution of political order in the Middle East, has brought new tasks that are peripheral to Japanese concerns. For Japan, the emergence of China as a new world power is a challenge for which it is still seeking an effective strategic response. China, meanwhile, has become an increasingly key economic partner for Germany. The consciousness of the parallels between Germany's and Japan's development has therefore weakened over the last decades, and the relationship may therefore be assumed to be more vulnerable to conflicts arising out of concerns fundamental to both countries' future courses. One potential trigger of such a conflict may be the question of the civilian use of nuclear energy.

128 *Volker Stanzel*

Dealing with "Fukushima": Germany

In October 2010, not even half a year prior to the Fukushima disaster, the Conservative/Liberal governing coalition of CDU/CSU/FDP had altered Germany's nuclear policy. Under an earlier Social-democrat/Green government, Germany's parliament had passed a law in 2002 which ratified a compromise with Germany's nuclear industry on the question of how long the process of phasing out Germany's nuclear power stations would last, with the last one slated to close in the early 2030s. Chancellor Angela Merkel's government, in consultation with Germany's nuclear industry, now decided to prolong the operational lifespan of the country's nuclear reactors, which meant that the last would shut down in 2036 at the earliest. In parallel with this decision, the government now described nuclear energy as a "bridge technology" between traditional energy technologies and renewable energies. After the accident in Fukushima, Germany effectively made a 180-degree turn. With her background as a trained physicist, Merkel managed to remain credible when she shifted abruptly from being a supporter of the continued use of nuclear energy to a proponent for its immediate phase-out. As she said in a speech to parliament on March 12, "the incredible events in Japan teach us that what had been deemed impossible according to scientific criteria could become possible nevertheless."[15] In a situation where previously held convictions thought to be scientifically proven were rapidly losing the trust of the public, Merkel's role became that of a hinge between the traditional conservative supporters of nuclear energy and those professionals who, having previously warned of the risks of an obviously unreliable technology, were now increasingly trusted.[16] Only two days after the nuclear meltdown in Fukushima, the German government temporarily suspended the prolongation of reactor running time that had been decided upon in October 2010. The seven oldest reactors were taken off the grid immediately. On March 14, 2011 the federal government decided to implement a three-month moratorium in order to examine the safety of all of the country's reactors. The findings, which were published in May, reported that not one of Germany's nuclear power stations was completely safe. The government appointed an "ethics commission"[17] charged with presenting proposals on how to deal with the post-Fukushima situation and ideas for a "prudent exit" from the civilian use of nuclear power. Their proposals resulted in a new law affirming that Germany would phase out the civilian use of nuclear energy by 2022. This decision was supported by 44 percent of the population, whereas 31 percent considered 2022 to be too late. The law passed the Bundestag with a majority of 85 percent. There were no similar categorical reactions undertaken by any other government globally.[18]

This law was not the only consequence of the Fukushima catastrophe in Germany. It also led to an unprecedented political upheaval. In March, after the accident, about 250,000 people participated in demonstrations demanding an end to the use of nuclear energy. The Greens, the party which had

A *nuclear fall-out turning political* 129

been formed partially in response to growing demands to ban nuclear energy in the late 1970s, were supported in polls by 24 percent of the population, an increase of 9 percent since before Fukushima.[19] Then, in the election in the federal state of Baden-Wurttemberg on March 27 a political earthquake occurred: the conservative Christian Democratic Union, which had been in power in that state since the foundation of the Federal Republic, lost to the Greens, who now, for the first time in German history, won the position of prime minister in a federal state.[20] This momentum did not weaken with the passage of time; for the next several years tens of thousands of people continued to march in order to demand an immediate decommissioning of nuclear reactors. German politics during the period from the Fukushima catastrophe to the elections on March 27 have to be seen, therefore, as steered partly by fear of the wrath of an increasingly anti-nuclear public. Compared with other European countries, it was only in Germany that the impact of Fukushima was a lasting one. While the nuclear disaster made it harder to ignore the vulnerabilities of the technology elsewhere, only in Germany did it spell the complete and almost immediate end of nuclear power. Only politicians unaffected by electoral considerations dared to speak out against the trend. Former chancellor Helmut Kohl said: "Using nuclear energy in Germany has not become more dangerous than before because of the disaster in Japan."[21] After Fukushima, however, such statements accepting an inherent degree of risk led directly to mounting distrust in nuclear energy.[22] Even the head of the IAEA, Yukiya Amano, said one year after the incident that Fukushima had been a "wake up call": "I cannot guarantee that there will be never again such an accident." He claimed to understand that this consideration had made Germany decide to ban the use of nuclear power.[23] The substantive claim spread across the political spectrum that an accident in a highly developed country such as Japan proved that nuclear power could never be handled safely. Chancellor Merkel said as much during her visit to Japan on March 9, 2015: "For me Fukushima was a crucial event because it happened in a country with an extraordinarily high technological level."[24]

In Germany Merkel's new nuclear energy policy confirmed the German public's widespread suspicion of atomic energy. Nuclear energy had enjoyed a positive image in Germany in the 1950s and 1960s. It was only in the 1970s, when the nascent environmentalist movements discovered the risks involved in depositing nuclear waste over centuries or millennia, that an anti-nuclear movement emerged. It gained strength with the disaster at Chernobyl, which affected large areas of Germany; the law of 2002 to phase out the use of nuclear energy can be seen as a result of the subsequent change in the public's attitude. After Chernobyl, representatives of both industry and government continued to argue that such a worst case scenario was statistically extremely rare. But not even twenty-five years had passed when Fukushima occurred. After Chernobyl, nuclear energy had become the object of public suspicion; Fukushima represented the tipping point in

130 *Volker Stanzel*

the consciousness of the German public. The result was a "German nuclear ban made in Japan."[25] Germany went ahead with what seemed to be great determination to push the consequences by promoting renewable energies that would provide Germany with about 80 percent of its energy by the year 2050.[26]

Dealing with "Fukushima": Japan

Much later than in Germany, but with similar decisiveness once the extent of the disaster and where it could lead became clear, the Japanese public experienced a similar process of consensus-building as Germany and a similar loss of citizens' trust.[27] In its editorial of June 7, 2011 the *Yomiuri Shimbun* argued that Germany's decision to phase out nuclear energy was "a monumental policy shift that might threaten the competitiveness of German industry."[28] Tens of thousands of citizens participated in anti-nuclear demonstrations in Tokyo and elsewhere. Polls indicated a gradual decline in support for the use of nuclear energy. In 2011, right after the disaster struck, 50 percent of Japanese were still in favor of continuing the use of nuclear power. By May that figure had decreased to 40 percent, while 55 percent wanted to decrease or terminate its use. Two years later the former figure had risen to 73 percent, with 22 percent wanting continued use.[29] For a year, it seemed that Germany might even become a model for Japan, pursuing the idea that a rapid switch to renewable energy would enable the industry to become a world leader in fields such as solar, wind, or geothermal power. All the same, an analysis of media reaction to the earthquake compared reports in Germany, Japan, Switzerland, France, and Great Britain[30] and came to the conclusion that the German media had very early on focused mainly on the nuclear catastrophe.[31] In both Great Britain and Japan expressions of fear and sadness related to the suffering of the tsunami victims dominated, while in German (and Swiss) media anger and fury were the dominant emotions, connected to questions of responsibility for the accident, risks, and demands for political consequences. In Japan the national media continued to support the established logic of the mechanisms of energy supply, and these conceptual schemata did not fundamentally change.[32] In Germany, doubts concerning the safety of nuclear energy were additionally framed by a narrative concerning the opportunity for more employment and technological progress through the development of renewables. The alternative of renewable energy could therefore provide extra proof of trustworthiness, besides its safety. This process did not occur in Japan for a number of reasons.

One reason for the lack of discussion in Japan was the widely accepted knowledge that Japan's power supply depended to an unavoidably high degree on nuclear energy (in 2010, fifty-four nuclear power stations contributed more than one quarter of Japan's energy consumption). Even if 70 percent of the population criticized the use of nuclear energy, Japan's economic and political elite did not think it possible to forgo nuclear energy

A nuclear fall-out turning political 131

and to rely on imported oil and gas for decades until renewable energy could present a viable alternative. Three commissions worked on the question of how "Fukushima" could have happened, one governmental, one established by the Japanese parliament, and one by an independent think tank (Rebuild Japan Initiative Foundation).[33] All came to the conclusion that the catastrophe had been "man-made" – the uncritical reliance on insufficiently tested technologies, a lack of technical and mental crisis preparation, and unclear responsibility structures – all problems that could neither be blamed on the earthquake nor easily remedied. Yet none of these findings, which were comparable to those made in Germany, led to drastic conclusions concerning the future of nuclear energy in Japan. This resulted in an obvious stand-off between what is called Japan's "nuclear village" and the general public.

The expression "nuclear village"[34] refers to the traditionally close relationship between the nuclear industry, politics, media, and academics. It is the result of decades-long efforts by politicians and industry to mitigate any suspicion that the civilian use of nuclear energy might lead to the eventual building of bombs – a natural association in the only country attacked with atomic weapons. The industry thus began early on funding campaigns to educate the public and financing university chairs in nuclear physics – these professors, with their logical bias in favor of nuclear energy, often appear in the media – as well as supporting the election campaigns of parties friendly to the use of nuclear energy, and offering employment opportunities to friendly politicians after retirement. As a result of such structural incentives, there was considerable pressure from many sides to avoid sustained scrutiny of the causes of the Fukushima accident. This was necessary in order to allow Japan's reactors to continue to run, helping to prevent the higher energy costs associated with importing more gas and oil. At the same time, there emerged a strong opposition to nuclear energy. Politicians from the prefectures where the reactors were located did not support the trend. Strong anti-nuclear movements sprang up mainly in these prefectures; elsewhere their support came primarily, maybe not surprisingly, from young mothers.[35] Several anti-nuclear parties were founded, with the participation of former prime ministers such as Kan Naoto from the DPJ and Koizumi Junichirō and Hosokawa Morihirō from the Liberal Democratic Party (LDP); a new committee in the Japanese Diet was formed, the Genpatsu-zero no Kai ("Association for Zero Nuclear Reactors/Energy Shift Japan") propelled by an extremely active former pediatrician, Abe Tomoko.[36] Noda Yoshihiko, the successor to Prime Minister Kan, was sufficiently influenced by the findings of the three commissions and public pressure to finally order safety inspections for all reactors in Japan beginning in October 2011, which led to their complete standstill. Although the measures were implemented slowly, the DPJ government at the time did decide to follow Germany's example in subsidizing the production of renewable energy. Noda, taking into account Japan's dependence on nuclear energy and the concerns of the nuclear industry, presented an "Energy Development Plan" in September 2012, which set the year 2039 as the target year to completely phase out the civilian use of nuclear energy. This decision was so controversial, however, that the government ultimately relented. At the end of 2012 the conservative LDP won the general election. Abe Shinzo, who had avoided the nuclear issue during the election campaign, became prime minister, focusing on his promise to get Japan's economy back on track. It took until spring 2014 for his government to present its proposed Energy Guidelines.[37] They stated only in very general terms that dependence on nuclear energy was to be decreased and renewables were to be supported for the next three years. However, in order to minimize the use of pollution-causing energies such as coal, the guidelines proposed to restart the idle reactors once their safety had been assured, and even intensify work on an integrated fuel cycle, which included completing the construction of a reprocessing plant and the construction of a new fuel rod production facility. Convinced of the safety of reactors made in Japan, the Abe government also initiated new negotiations to export its technology and sell reactors to countries such as Turkey.

A striking dichotomy, however, has since appeared in Japan's society. The majority of the people, when voting in local elections, vote for politicians who promise to keep the reactors idle (and safe).[38] The majority, however, does not vote for anti-nuclear parties in national elections but rather for the LDP because of its assumed economic competence. As a result, the anti-nuclear parties have more or less dropped out of the national electoral races. Over the years, the Abe government has made various efforts to restart the reactors but was successful in only four cases. Even its proposed new energy policy aimed at moving from nuclear to renewable energy by 2040 failed to sway the electorate in the prefectures. The result: Japan, a country that previously relied on nuclear energy for one quarter of its electricity consumption, controlled by a government working hard to restart reactors, has managed de facto since the end of 2011 without nuclear energy.

Dealing with "Fukushima," in controversy: Germany and Japan

The first high-ranking foreign official to visit Japan after the catastrophe was German federal foreign minister Guido Westerwelle. On April 2, 2011 (the same day a new crack was discovered at the Fukushima power plant), he was received by Japanese foreign minister Matsumoto Takeaki. Matsumoto tearfully promised "greater transparency" in investigating what had occurred at Fukushima, while Westerwelle promised German support for the people of Tohoku.[39] Federal president Christian Wulff would make the same statement to the Japanese emperor in October. If there was indeed ever something special about the German-Japanese relationship, it must have been manifest during that period.

Even when the German exit policy encountered problems, such as the delayed growth of a new electrical grid supplied by windmills in the North

A nuclear fall-out turning political 133

Sea, the popular consensus on phasing out nuclear energy held. Examination of German popular opinion about efforts to increase renewable energy production reveals strong positive feelings about everything related to the energy shift in Germany. According to a 2015 survey, 92 percent polled were in favor of the energy turnaround.[40] By 2015 Germany's energy turnaround was far ahead of schedule: Renewable energy already accounted for 33 percent of the gross electricity consumption in Germany (instead of 22 percent as planned); wind energy had become the single most significant energy resource for generating electricity. The demands made by energy companies such as EnBW, Eon, RWE, and Vattenfall for compensation in sums exceeding a hundred million euros were denied in court.

For some in Japan, Germany became a model for the dismantling of reactors and for promoting renewables.[41] Already in October 2011, at the time of Federal President Christian Wulff's visit to Japan, the German Chamber of Commerce in Japan was organizing trips by Japanese companies to Germany to explore the possibility of joint efforts in the field of renewable energy production. In January 2016 Nukem Technologies received an order for four feasibility studies on decommissioning the Fukushima nuclear plant.[42] At the same time, cooperation between experienced anti-nuclear activists in Germany with their Japanese counterparts intensified. Beginning in 2011, the vanguard of the decades-long German fight against nuclear energy came to Japan, visited sites close to Fukushima, established consultation platforms with Japanese activists, and supported the anti-nuclear parties in their election campaigns as well as in their legal battles against government plans to restart reactors.[43]

But what was actually happening was that "Germany" and its energy policy was becoming a tool for domestic infighting within Japan. The divide in Japan's society between the "nuclear village" and its supporters on the one hand, and the anti-nuclear majority on the other was reflected in the attitudes of both sides toward Germany. On one side were the activists protesting both nuclear energy and, to a more limited extent, Japanese industry, and trying to compel the development of new alternative energy technologies. They used "Germany" as proof of how things could work and to document by contrast how dangerously the Japanese government and established energy industries were acting. On the other side were the proponents of nuclear energy, as well as those who may have shared the sentiment that Japan risked losing "face" as a high-tech nation (because of a disaster resembling what had occurred thirty years earlier in the underdeveloped Soviet Union), who resented the criticism directed against Japan by Germany. Neither Japan nor Germany had previously been this critical of the other, despite the acknowledgement of the Japanese media that, in the first months after the accident, there was not even one party in Japan, compared with Germany, willing to adopt the cause of a phase-out of nuclear energy.[44] Until details regarding how dire the catastrophe could have been became accessible to the wider Japanese public after the summer

134 *Volker Stanzel*

of 2011 and the mood of the public in Japan shifted, it did not seem necessary to draw drastic conclusions. The Japanese media observed with more or less detached curiosity what was happening in Germany (compared with the less dramatic reactions in other European countries). Costs were one major argument against a quick phase-out of nuclear energy, along with the fact that Europe's continent-wide electricity grid enabled states to draw on energy reserves from neighboring countries if necessary. A widely repeated argument that put Germany's new policy into a critical perspective was – and still is – that Germany could easily close down its reactors and readily try to develop alternative energy sources because it could always rely on electricity imports from France, produced by French nuclear reactors. The *Yomiuri Shimbun*'s editorial "Germany's N-policy flip-flop may blunt its industrial edge" (June 7, 2011) argued that "Germany can turn off the switch on its nuclear power because it can import electricity from neighboring countries not separated by sea. In fact, Germany already imported electricity from France, which relies on nuclear power generation for 80 percent of its power supply, and on the Czech Republic, which still operates old Soviet-type nuclear reactors."[45] In 2013, *Mainichi*'s Berlin correspondent reported that because of the "panic" over Fukushima, no "free discussion had been possible," and it was doubtful that Germany's electorate would support the nuclear energy phase-out policy over a longer period.[46]

This critical view of Germany's new energy policy was expressed most forcefully at a now-famous conference held in Berlin on July 7, 2011 by influential Japanese journalist Miyoshi Norihide, one of Japan's foremost experts on Germany. Norihide leveled a scathing critique at Germany (later repeated in a book)[47]: (1) Because of the Germans' attitude toward nuclear energy in general, an accident in a nuclear facility by nature had to be a "catastrophe"; therefore the situation was regarded as out of control, leading to the suspicion that all Japanese now were infected by radiation. Contrary to the view generally taken by media in other countries, "Fukushima" for Germans equaled a "worst case." (2) Lacking knowledge of the facts on the ground and of Japan in general, German media, more so than that of other countries, fell back on old stereotypes of and prejudices against Japan. These stereotypes said, for example, that misinformation was a natural way of reporting in Japan, that Japanese society was so sclerotic that criticism of authorities was out of the question, and that the Japanese people had become victims of their government and of industry. (3) German media lacked any kind of empathy for the suffering of the people affected. The individuals brave enough to work in Fukushima in order to contain the damage were contemptuously dismissed by Germans as "homeless, minors, and foreign workers." Similarly, the well-known essayist Ken'ichi Mishima claimed in an interview that the widespread belief in Germany that Japanese could only learn the facts about Fukushima through foreign media was "pure ethnocentrism."[48]

A *nuclear fall-out turning political* 135

In Germany these arguments are seen as beside the point. There, "Fukushima" constitutes the point of departure for a domestic dispute, which developed almost independently from the reality of Fukushima into a "focusing event" for domestic politics. In much the same way that "Germany" has become an icon of anti-nuclear policies in the domestic discussion in Japan – and is thus regarded negatively or positively – "Fukushima" in Germany has become a powerful symbol in a political discourse, which, once invoked, suffices to justify an anti-nuclear position, exemplified by the rejection of the unpopular 2010 revision of the original law of 2002. What really had happened in Japan became almost irrelevant. When in May 2016 the German minister for the environment Barbara Hendricks paid the first ministerial-level visit to the Fukushima power plant, she accordingly made her expected statement: "The real challenges have not yet been met."[49] And when Kan Naoto visited Germany, he was sure to receive a hero's welcome.[50]

Conclusions

People who experience the exact same event display different reactions and attitudes, depending on the specific social environment in which they live. This results in a multivalent constructed complex of communication and action, which can lead to variable consequences in the real world. "Fukushima" is an extreme example of such an event which has shaped this communication/action construct in both Germany and Japan. For both Germans and Japanese it was nearly impossible to gain firsthand knowledge about the event itself or about its causes, regardless of proximity, or to discern how to most appropriately deal with it. Assumptions – which are different from "knowledge" – about the technical and economic preconditions for the use of nuclear energy as well as the cultural context (such as the memory of Hiroshima and Nagasaki in Japan, or of Chernobyl in Germany) exerted a considerable influence as well. People, therefore, even within the upper ranks of Japan's "nuclear village" or among nuclear experts in Germany, had to rely on media and on government- or company-provided "knowledge" of the "facts," which was unavoidably inadequate. With the involvement of civil society, the influence of "knowledge keepers" with varying degrees of expertise became manifold, even indirectly, and created emotional and "simple" ways for the general public to maintain their own (new) convictions. This goes a long way in explaining how Japanese society has become so divided since the event, and how in Germany a tsunami in Japan could topple one government and bring another to power. At the same time, it is obvious, but begs further exploration, why Germany in particular was so much more deeply affected by Fukushima than its neighbors (who also had suffered from Chernobyl), or neighbors of Japan which, after all, were in much greater danger of being exposed to radioactivity from Fukushima.[51]

In both countries these complicated gaps between elites and public, which are by their nature already rare, have drawn public attention because of their specific qualities. The question remains, however, whether they will have a serious impact on the more general relationship between the two countries, possibly even affecting the mutually held belief in a vague similarity or shared fate. Only time will tell. But the question will have to be answered in the context of the strains this relationship has experienced since the 1990s. Having belonged to the "West" and been positioned against and threatened by the Communist "East" during the Cold War, Germany and Japan are more similar in their interests, values, and strategies now than in the past. Depending on a liberal world order based on the ideal of the rule of law, both countries – internationally as much as domestically – are affected by shifts in international trade and economic exchange, by the impact of rising – and for the most part undemocratic – powers, by the instability of the international position of the US, by global crises such as terrorism, by health threats, migration, and climate change, and by questions of global governance in general. Yet in comparable situations, both countries, as members of the G7, now have many more partners sharing similar concerns; this enables more cooperation within the two countries' own regions and lessens the relative importance of the bilateral relationship for each side. Differences of opinion over mutual problems may therefore become more frequent. Two recent problems have affected both countries significantly. One is the question of how to ensure future economic growth. Here, Japan has traditionally – and even more so since the Abe government assumed power in 2012 – relied on expansionary monetary policies, while Germany has opted for a more austerity-oriented policy. Both countries have therefore stood on opposite sides in related international negotiations, such as in the framework of the G7 or the G20.[52] China is the other potentially controversial issue. If China is a new world power today, its newly strengthened influence is still not considered a direct threat in Germany. For Germany it makes sense to maintain a close dialogue, for example through annual cabinet meetings. For Japan, on the other hand, the simple fact of China's growing strength means that there is much more potential risk for conflict in East Asia, relating not only to territorial claims but also to the control of the sea lanes leading to and from Japan, China's bargaining power, and relationships among Japan's close regional partners. Even Japan's relationship to the US is affected. It is only logical, therefore, that Germany and Japan do not always see eye to eye over questions concerning China.[53]

The political fall-out of the nuclear incident in Fukushima in March 2011 may prove to mark a fundamental shift in how the two countries view themselves as well as the world. Since Fukushima, this mutual scrutiny has become a critically important tool in domestic conflicts over the two countries' respective energy policies. This has affected the relationship in ways that may have an even greater impact once it intersects with other sources of friction between the two countries. The legend of the two countries' shared fates, which has endured almost a century and a half, may even, as a side effect of "Fukushima," gradually develop into a new and truer reality.

Notes

1 For the entire timeline of the incident see "Report of Japanese Government to the IAEA Ministerial Conference on Nuclear Safetey – The Accident at TEPCO's Fukushima Nuclear Power Stations," accessed May 6, 2016, http://japan.kantei.go.jp/kan/topics/201106/iaea_houkokusho_e.html; "Additional Report of Japanese Government to the IAEA Ministerial Conference on Nuclear Safetey – The Accident at TEPCO's Fukushima Nuclear Power Stations,"accessed May 6, 2016, www.iaea.org/newscenter/focus/fukushima/additional-japan-report; World Nuclear Association, "Fukushima Incident," accessed May 6, 2016, www.world-nuclear.org/focus/fukushima/fukushima-accident.aspx. See also German nuclear expert Hans-Jochen Luhmann, "Was war die Ursache des Reaktorunglücks in Fukushima: Zur Kontroverse Erdbeben oder Tsunami," *Proprium*, accessed June 22, 2016, www.sinn-schaffen.de/kolumnejl/was-war-die-ursache-des-reaktorangluecks-in-fukushima/.

2 See Volker Stanzel, "Japan, dreifach getroffen," in *Japan an jenem Tag: Augenzeugenberichte zum 11. März 2011*, ed. Albrecht Rothacher (Munich: iudicium, 2014).

3 See "Tokyo in Todesangst" (Tokyo Gripped by Deadly Fear), a 10-page special supplement in *Die Welt*, accessed March 16, 2016, www.welt.de/print/die_welt/politik/article12841234/Tokio-in-Todesangst.html; see also "Atom-Gipfel im Kanzleramt" (Nuclear Summit at the Chancery), accessed June 15, 2016, www.bild.de/politik/2011/atomkraftwerk/im-kanzleramt-16755974.bild.html.

4 The empathy felt by Germans for suffering Japanese, reflected in the number of donations and offers to accept children in "safe havens" in Germany, was therefore not just a response to reports about the tsunami catastrophe, but also arguably at least as much about the Fukushima incident.

5 See "Auswärtiges Amt rät von Japans Nordosten ab" (Foreign Office advices against traveling to Japan's Northeast), accessed March 30, 2016, www.spiegel.de/politik/deutschland/reisewarnung-auswaertiges-amt-raet-von-japans-nordosten-ab-a-750520.html.

6 See "Sender beginnen Evakuierung" [Networks Begin Evacuation], accessed March 30, 2016, www.tagesspiegel.de/medien/radioaktive-wolke-sender-beginnen-evakuierung/3950214.html.

7 Naoto Kan in "Naoto Kan Speaks Out," *The Japan Times*, August 31, 2013, accessed May 15, 2016, www.japantimes.co.jp/life/2013/08/31/people/naoto-kan-speaks-out/#.V2gBfVfg8_U. On May 29, 2012, Kan explained while speaking to Japan's parliament: "I was frightened and felt helpless. . . . You can't expect a nuclear expert to be prime minister or a cabinet minister, so we need top regulatory officials to provide expertise and help us. We didn't have those people." See Fukushima inquiry: "I Felt Helpless, Says Former PM," accessed May 15, 2016, www.theguardian.com/world/2012/may/29/fukushima-inquiry-naoto-kan.

8 See Bundestag document 17/4545, January 26, 2011, "Antrag der Fraktionen CDU/CSU, SPD, FDP und BÜNDNIS 90/DIE GRÜNEN: 150 Jahre diplomatische Beziehungen zwischen Deutschland und Japan," accessed June 22, 2016, http://dip21.bundestag.de/dip21/btd/17/045/1704545.pdf.

9 See Japanese Diet document "Nichidoku kōryū hyakugojushūnen ni atari nichidoku yūkō kankei no zōshin ni kansuru ketsugi-an" [Draft Resolution on Promoting Friendship Between Japan and Germany on the Occasion of the Hundred and Fiftieth Anniversary of the Exchange Between Japan and Germany], accessed June 22, 2016, www.shugiin.go.jp/internet/itdb_gian.nsf/html/gian/honbun/ketsugian/g17713005.htm.

10 Both elements constitute an important backdrop to this article. In both cases, the literature is substantial, ranging from the most astoundingly weird assumptions

138 *Volker Stanzel*

on a relationship between two far-away peoples to erudite analyses on various aspects of this relationship. The author can only encourage the reader to venture for herself into the wide field of speculation as well as well-founded conceptualizations about the relationship between Germans and Japanese throughout their 150-plus year long relationship. He would, however, specifically mention as notable Kume Kunitake's report on Germany, Austria, and Switzerland written during the Japanese mission to Europe for his logbook in 1873. Peter Pantzer, ed., *Die Iwakura-Mission* (Munich: iudicium, 2002), or the contributions – starting with Foreign Minister Walter Steinmeier's, in Ruprecht Vondran, ed., *Gelebte Partnerschaft: Deutschland und Japan* (Düsseldorf: Droste Verlag, 2014).

11 Speech excerpts translated by the author from the German; see Otto von Bismarck, *Die gesammelten Werke*, vol. 8, chap. 51, 64–65 (Berlin: Otto Stollberg & Co, 1926). Interestingly, there is no German document confirming the notes recorded by a member of the Japanese delegation, who additionally remarked upon the general appreciation for Bismarck's words among the Japanese statesmen.

12 See Volker Stanzel, "Die Beziehungen zwischen Deutschland und Japan," in *Länderbericht Japan: Die Erarbeitung der Zukunft*, ed. Raimund Wördemann and Karin Yamaguchi (Bonn: Bundeszentrale für Politische Bildung, 2014), 184–200, esp. footnote 6.

13 Both left the League of Nations in 1933, Germany because it felt discriminated against for its rearmament ambitions, Japan because of international criticism over its conduct in Japan-occupied Manchuria.

14 Cf. e.g. Hanns W. Maull, "Germany and Japan: The New Civilian Powers," 1990/91 (Winter), accessed May 15, 2016, www.foreignaffairs.org/articles/asia/1990-12-01/germany-and-japan-new-civilian-powers.

15 See "Merkel: 'Ein Einschnitt für die Welt'" [Merkel: "A Decisive Moment for the World"], accessed May 15, 2016, www.tagesspiegel.de/politik/atomunfall-merkel-ein-einschnitt-fuer-die-welt/3945068.html.

16 On the question of the loss of trust, see Jens Seiffert und Birte Fähnrich, "Vertrauensverlust in die Kernenergie. Eine historische Frageanalyse," in *Fukushima und die Folgen. Medienberichterstattung, öffentliche Meinung, politische Konsequenzen*, ed. Jens Wolling and Dorothee Arlt (Ilmenau: Universitätsverlag Ilmenau, 2014). Also cf. "Fukushima ga kimeta datsu-genpatsu" [Fukushima Decided the Exit from Nuclear Energy], "Ronsetsu-shiryohan II" (Material for Editorial Comments II: The Situation of Nuclear Energy in Europe), *Kyodo News Agency*, June 15, 2011, 12:38:24.

17 See the recommendations of the Ethics Commission on a Safe Energy Supply: "Germany's Energy Transition – a Collective Project for the Future," accessed June 6, 2016, www.bundesregierung.de/ContentArchiv/DE/Archiv17/_Anlagen/2011/05/2011-05-30-abschlussbericht-ethikkommission_en.pdf?__blob=publicationFile&v=2.

18 See e.g. Laka Foundation, ed., *Responses after Chernobyl and Fukushima. Comparative Analysis of Germany and the Netherlands as Amplified Examples*, accessed June 20, 2016, www.laka.org/info/publicaties/2012-chernobyl-fukushima.pdf.

19 Deutsche Welle, "Fukushima und die Folgen für Deutschland" [Fukushima and the Consequences for Germany], December 27, 2011, accessed April 7, 2016, www.dw.com/de/fukushima-und-die-folgen-in-deutschland/a-15562222.

20 This was former teacher Winfried Kretschmann, who built his campaign around the anti-nuclear issue.

21 Quoted in *Die Welt* on March 25, 2011, "Altkanzler Kohl kritisiert Merkels Atom-Wende" [Former Chancellor Kohl Criticise Merkel's Nuclear

A *nuclear fall-out turning political* 139

Turn-Around], accessed June 22, 2016, www.welt.de/politik/deutschland/article12951656/Altkanzler-Kohl-kritisiert-Merkels-Atom-Wende.html.

22 See Jens Seiffert und Birte Fähnrich, "Vertrauensverlust in die Kernenergie: Eine historische Frageanalyse," in *Fukushima und die Folgen: Medienberichterstattung, öffentliche Meinung, politische Konsequenzen*, ed. Jens Wolling and Dorothee Arlt (Ilmenau: Universitätsverlag Ilmenau, 2014), 62–63.

23 Quoted in *Der Spiegel* on March 10, 2012, "Japans dunkelster Tag" [Japan's Darkest Day], accessed June 20, 2016, www.spiegel.de/panorama/gesellschaft/fukushima-katastrophe-japans-dunkelster-tag-a-820581.html.

24 See *Die Welt*, "Merkel wirbt für den Atomausstieg" [Merkel Promotes Exiting Nuclear Power], accessed May 30, 2016, www.welt.de/politik/ausland/article138202369/Merkel-wirbt-in-Japan-fuer-Atomausstieg.html and Merkel's speech, accessed May 30, 2016, www.japan.diplo.de/Vertretung/japan/ja/05-politik/055-politik-in-deutschland/bk-reden/20150309-asahi-rede.html.

25 See Hans-Jürgen Weiß, Sabrina Markutzyk and Bertil Schwotzer, "Deutscher Atomausstieg made in Japan? Zur Rolle von Fukushima als Schlüsselereignis in der Medienberichterstattung über die deutsche Atomdebatte 2011," in *Fukushima und die Folgen. Medienberichterstattung, öffentliche Meinung, politische Konsequenzen*, ed. Jens Wolling and Dorothee Arlt (Ilmenau: Universitätsverlag Ilmenau, 2014), 79. See also Atomkatastrophe in Fukushima: "Wie sich Deutschland gegen Atomkraft entschied," *Focus*, March 9, 2012, accessed June 28, 2016, www.focus.de/panorama/welt/tsunami-in-japan/atomkatastrophe-von-fukushima-wie-deutschland-sich-gegen-die-atomkraft-entschied_aid_722373.html.

26 See Stefan Lechtenböhmer and Hans-Jochen Luhmann, "Decarbonization and Regulation of Germany's Electricity System After Fukushima," *Climate Policy*, vol. 13, Special Issue: *Low Carbon Drivers for a Sustainable World*, sup 01 (2013): 146–54.

27 These were the findings of an Energy White Book compiled by the Japanese government in October 2011. Cf. also "Tachidomaru kikai ni shiyō" [Let Us Make It an Opportunity to Stop!], ronsetsu-memo (Comment-Memo), *Kyodo News Agency*, April 4, 2015, 14:53:02; Martin Fackler, "Japan's Nuclear Energy Industry Nears Shutdown, at Least for Now," *New York Times*, March 8, 2012, accessed March 20, 2016, www.nytimes.com/2012/03/09/world/asia/japan-shutting-down-its-nuclear-power-industry.html?ref=energyandpower&_r=0. For an early discussion of a switch to the use of renewables, see the editorial, "Saisei-kanō eneruji: Genpatsu-daiti wa jūbun kanō da" [Renewable Energy: Sufficient Possibility to Substitute Nuclear Reactors], *Mainichi Shimbun*, August 3, 2011, 5.

28 The editorial's title in the paper's own English translation: "Germany's N-policy flip-flop may blunt its industrial edge."

29 See the poll results overview by the World Nuclear Association, "Nuclear Power in Japan," accessed June 29, 2016, www.world-nuclear.org/information-library/country-profiles/countries-g-n/japan-nuclear-power.aspx.

30 See Hans Mathias Kepplinger and Richard Lemke, "Framing Fukushima. Zur Darstellung der Katastrophe in Deutschland im Vergleich zu Großbritannien, Frankreich und der Schweiz," in *Fukushima und die Folgen: Medienberichterstattung, öffentliche Meinung, politische Konsequenzen*, ed. Jens Wolling and Dorothee Arlt (Ilmenau: Universitätsverlag Ilmenau, 2014), 125–52.

31 Indeed, it was often difficult to differentiate between victims of the tsunami and those of the nuclear accidents. There were no deaths yet due to radiation, compared with the almost 20,000 killed by the tsunami and the quake.

32 The *Yomiuri Shimbun* realized early on what was coming: "Japan's crisis will affect N-power worldwide," and argued that Japan should make an effort to resolve the Fukushima crisis: "The future of the peaceful use of nuclear energy

140 *Volker Stanzel*

around the world rests with how effectively this country can cope with the situation," editorial, *Yomiuri Shimbun* (English version), March 29, 2011.

33 See the National Diet of Japan, "The Official Report of the Fukushima Nuclear Accident Independent Investigation Commission" (2012), accessed March 17, 2016, www.nirs.org/wp-content/uploads/fukushima/naiic_report. pdf; "Report of Japanese Government to the IAEA Ministerial Conference on Nuclear Safety – the Accident at TEPCO's Fukushima Nuclear Power Stations," accessed March 17, 2016, http://japan.kantei.go.jp/kan/topics/201106/iaea_houkokusho_e.html; Rebuild Japan Initiative Foundation, "Investigation on the Fukushima Daiichi Nuclear Accident" (2011), accessed March 17, 2016, https://ratical.org/radiation/Fukushima/IotFDNArpt.html.

34 See Jeff Kingston, "Japan's Nuclear Village," *The Asia-Pacific Journal* 10, issue 37, no. 1 (September 9, 2012), accessed June 29, 2016, http://apjjf.org/2012/10/37/Jeff-Kingston/3822/article.html. Cf. the report by Waseda University professor Segawa Shiro on the efforts to suppress findings concerning the dangers of radiation from the Fukushima plant in *The Japan News*, "The Nuclear Power Plant Accident and the Media: Did They Overcome the Imperial General Headquarters' Announcement?" accessed May 20, 2016, www.yomiuri.co.jp/adv/wol/dy/opinion/earthquake_110523.html. Also Nicole Takeda in *Truman* on the institution of the "press clubs" at ministries: "Self-Censorship and Saving Face: Japanese Media and the Aftermath of Fukushima," accessed May 20, 2016, http://trumanfactor.com/2011/japanese-media-and-the-aftermath-of-fukushima-3389.html. The fact that Tepco, the company responsible for the crucial failures in constructing Fukushima Daichi, did not shy away from asking for compensation from the government not long after the accident speaks for itself. See *Mainichi Daily News*, October 24, 2011, 1: "Edano tells TEPCO to cut 'at least' 2.5 tril. yen in costs."

35 See the observations in "In Japan, a Mothers' Movement Against Nuclear Power," *Yes! Magazine* (undated), accessed June 20, 2016, www.yesmagazine.org/peace-justice/in-japan-a-mothers-movement-against-nuclear-power. See also the reports of the Genshiryoku-shimin-i'inkai (Citizens' Commission on Nuclear Energy), accessed June 9, 2016, www.ccnejapan.com (accessed June 9, 2016).

36 For various activities of this association and of others see the website of Kankyō-enerugi- Kenkyūjo (Institute for Sustainable Energy Policies), accessed June 9, 2016, www.isep.or.jp/library/5024.

37 For Abe's energy policy and Japan's energy situation in general see the World Nuclear Association, "Nuclear Power in Japan." See also Detlef Rehn, "Energiepolitik Japans: Abschied von der Kernkraft?" in *Länderbericht Japan: Die Erarbeitung der Zukunft*, ed. Raimund Wördemann and Karin Yamaguchi (Bonn: Bundeszentrale für Politische Bildung, 2014), 297–313.

38 See Hiroshi Onitsuka, "Hooked on Nuclear Power: Japanese State-Local Relations and the Vicious Cycle of Nuclear Dependence," accessed March 16, 2016, www.japanfocus.org/-Hiroshi-Onitsuka/3676. German researcher Florian Meissner of the German Institute for Japan Studies, Tokyo, discovered that local media diverged significantly from the national media in their reporting about nuclear energy, in that they gave more prominence to doubts and dangers. On new movements springing up in the prefectures, see *The Asia-Pacific Journal* 14, issue 13, no. 1 (July 1, 2016): "A New Wave Against the Rock: New Social Movements in Japan Since the Fukushima Nuclear Meltdown," accessed July 4, 2016, http://apjjf.org/2016/13/Oguma.html. A wealth of information on activities against Japan's use of nuclear energy is available in the Genshiryoku-shiryō-jōhō-shitsu (Citizens' Nuclear Information Center), accessed June 9, 2016, www.cnic.jp.

A nuclear fall-out turning political 141

39 See *Der Spiegel*, "Westerwelle sagt Japan Hilfe bei Wiederaufbau zu" [Wester-welle Promises Reconstruction Support], April 2, 2011, accessed May 5, 2016, www.spiegel.de/politik/deutschland/solidaritaetsbesuch-westerwelle-sagt-japan-hilfe-bei-wiederaufbau-zu-a-754672.html.

40 See the analysis of emotions and rational judgements concerning nuclear and other energy sources in Germany and how they changed after Fukushima, in Michael Nippa und Roh Pin Lee, "Zum Einfluss der Nuklearkatastrophe von Fukushima auf die Bewertung unterschiedlicher Energiequellen in Deutschland: Erkenntnisse aus einer empirischen Untersuchung," in *Fukushima und die Folgen: Medienberichterstattung, öffentliche Meinung, politische Konsequenzen*, ed. Jens Wolling and Dorothee Arlt (Ilmenau: Universitätsverlag Ilmenau, 2014), 341–59.

41 See Minori Takao, "Renewables Unite Locals," *NHK World*, March 10, 2016, accessed May 25, 2016, http://www3.nhk.or.jp/nhkworld/newsroomtokyo/aired/20160310.html. See also "Kagaku no keikoku wo uketome yo" [Accept the Warnings of Science!], in Ronsetsu-memo ["Comment Memo"], *Kyodo News Agency*, September 27, 2013, 14:13:49.

42 See *Japan Times*, "Germany Looks to Export Reactor Decommissioning Technologies," May 1, 2016, accessed May 25, 2016, www.japantimes.co.jp/news/2016/05/01/business/germany-looks-to-export-reactor-decommissioning-technologies/#.V1v12Ffg-8V. See also Sylvia Kotting-Uhl's analysis for Boell Foundation, "Fukushima: Es ist noch lange nicht vorbei" [Fukushima: It Is Far from Over], October 28, 2013, accessed March 15, 2016, www.boell.de/de/2013/10/28/fukushima-es-ist-noch-lange-nicht-vorbei.

43 Participants of the German anti-nuclear movement went to Japan soon after the Fukushima incident, and members of Japanese anti-nuclear groups joined German groups protesting against areas identified as possible nuclear waste deposit sites in Northern Germany. Greenpeace Germany concluded a cooperative agreement with Greenpeace Japan to support the development and use of renewables. The most active Green member of the German parliament, Sylvia Kotting-Uhl, who has visited Japan almost annually to coordinate activities (see her "Travel Diary," accessed May 30, 2016, https://ratical.org/radiation/Fukushima/IotFDNArpt.html), however, conceded that "in Germany it took 30 years until the country decided to exit nuclear energy."

44 See the report in *Mainichi Shimbun*'s evening edition of May 16, 2011, 4: " 'Datsugenpatsu' no min'i wo meguru sō'i: Doitsu ni 'Midori no Tō' shūshushō-tanjō, Nihon ni wa uke-sara seitō nashi" [Differences in Popular Will over Phase-Out of Nuclear Energy: In Germany the First Prime Minister of the Green Party in a Federal State, in Japan no Party to Take that Path].

45 The editorial, "Germany's N-Policy Flip-Flop May Blunt Its Industrial Edge," *Yomiuri Shimbun* (English version), June 7, 2011; Cf. also the editorial, "Fukushima no kōgeki wa omoi" [The Severe Shock of Fukushima], The *Mainichi Shimbun*, June 15, 2011, 5. In fact, the reliance on French nuclear energy is a myth, as Germany exports more electricity than it imports, depending on the availability of wind in Germany and demand elsewhere. See the Fraunhofer Insitute's charts, accessed June 29, 2016, www.energy-charts.de/exchange.htm. The question of the consequences of these differences of opinion over Germany's phase-out of nuclear energy has been well discussed in Germany, as elsewhere in Europe. See, for example, a contribution by the former federal minister for the environment of the Green Party, Jürgen Trittin, to the Heinrich Böll Foundation, "Erneuerbare sind schon heute günstiger als Kohle und Atom" [Renewables Even Today Are More Economical than Coal and Nuclear], March 8, 2012,

142 Volker Stanzel

accessed May 20, 2016, www.boell.de/de/oekologie/klima-energie-interview-trittin-jahrestag-fukushima-14125.html).

46 See *Mainichi Shimbun*, October 18, 2013, 10.

47 The script of the lecture was made available to the author by Mr. Miyoshi. The book is *Doitsu risuku: "yume miru seisaku" ga hikiokosu konran* [German Risk: The Policy of Dreams Causes Chaos] (Tokyo: Shinsho, 2015). For a critical view of the Japanese media's reporting see Lars Nicolaysen, "Japans Massenmedien," in *Länderbericht Japan: Die Erarbeitung der Zukunft*, ed. Raimund Wördemann and Karin Yamaguchi (Bonn: Bundeszentrale für Politische Bildung, 2014), 201–12. For a deeper analysis see Reinhard Zöllner, *Japan. Fukushima. Und wir. Zelebranten einer nuklearen Erdbebenkatastrophe* (Munich: iudicium, 2011). For a different perspective, see the observations by Swiss novelist and essayist Adolf Muschg, "Japan und die Katastrophe," in *Länderbericht Japan: Die Erarbeitung der Zukunft*, ed. Raimund Wördemann and Karin Yamaguchi (Bonn: Bundeszentrale für Politische Bildung, 2014), 25–37.

48 Quoted by Miyoshi, *Doitsu risuku*. See also done by Jochen Leggewie, "Guroobaru-jidai no kaigai-kōhō ni okeru seikō-yōin" [Elements of Success of Information in the Age of Globalism], in 2011 for CNC Communications (Munich/London).

49 See "Aufgeräumter als in Tschernobyl" [Tidier than Chernobyl], *Tageszeitung*, May 20, 2016, accessed May 25, 2016, www.taz.de/Deutsche-Umweltministerin-in-Fukushima/%215302971/.

50 This happened on October 13, 2015 in Berlin at an event hosted by the Böll Foundation and the Japan-German Center Berlin, as reported by Stefan Schaaf from the Böll Foundation in Berlin on October 23, 2015: "Fukushima: 'Die Götter haben Beistand geleistet'" [Fukushima: "The Gods Have Helped"], accessed June 29, 2016, www.boell.de/de/2015/10/23/fukushima-die-goetter-haben-beistand-geleistet.

51 The author would venture to speculate that it was due to the prior existence of an anti-nuclear movement in Germany, which found a way to express itself politically through the Greens. This movement consisted of a coalition of anti-militarist, human rights, environmentalist, and lifestyle groups. This politically strong force possibly accounts for the effectiveness of the German anti-nuclear movement compared with that of other countries. Daniel Blackmore, "Abandoning Nuclear Power: A Social Constructivist Analysis of Germany's Response to Fukushima," *Journal of Politics & International Studies* 9 (Summer 2013): 44–54.

52 See *Japan Markt* online on June 6, 2016, "Merkel und Abe wollen 'Dreiklang' für Wachstum" [Merkel and Abe Want "Triangle" "for Growth], accessed June 20, 2016, www.japanmarkt.de/2016/05/06/wirtschaft/merkel-und-abe-wollen-dreiklang-fuer-wachstum/.

53 See the *Japan Times* on April 16, 2015, "Germany's Merkel Urged Japan to Join AIIB: Sources," accessed June 20, 2016, www.japantimes.co.jp/news/2015/04/16/business/germanys-merkel-urged-japan-join-aiib-sources/#.V3QAe1fg86g.

Part III

German and Austrian intellectuals/writers and East Asia

7 Max Weber and East Asian development

Keumjae Park

Max Weber (1864–1920) is inarguably one of the most important sociologists of all time. Though not an expert on East Asia, he was one of the rare social theorists who attempted to integrate analyses of East Asian societies into his general sociological theorizing during the early days of the discipline. Weber's theory of East Asia, presented mainly in his essays on world religions, focused on the relationship between culture and economic systems. Although there are multiple interpretations of Weber's stance on Asia, his general argument that only Protestantism in the West had provided fertile ground for the development of modern capitalism has been much criticized throughout the second half of the twentieth century.[1] Some of the commonly debated points have included Weber's ethnocentric perspectives on East Asian societies, his misunderstanding of Confucianism and other Asian religions, and his cultural determinism. These have been particularly relevant points of debate in light of the spectacular economic rise of East Asia after 1945. Indeed, while Weber acknowledged the rational orientations of East Asian religions, his conclusions on Confucianism and Buddhism provided little indication of East Asia's future as a major player in global capitalism. Ironically, contemporary research on East Asia's economic development has often emphasized the positive effects of Confucian culture on its booming economies.[2]

How do we read Weber in light of this paradoxical historical development? What does a Weberian encounter with East Asia's contemporary prosperity reveal about the interplay between culture and economic systems? This essay explores these questions in three parts. The first will briefly review Weber's thoughts on East Asia, focusing on his work on Confucianism. The main Weberian texts discussed in this paper are *The Protestant Ethic and the Spirit of Capitalism* and his essays published in the volume *The Religion of China*.[3] The second section will consider contemporary economic development in East Asia while engaging in a critical dialogue with the concept of "Asian values" as a key formula of economic success. This discussion will include a conceptual consideration of culture as a dynamic and shifting set of values which are put into practice by individuals and institutions. The paper will focus on the ways in which "Asian values" have

146 *Keumjae Park*

been strategically appropriated and mobilized by state and economic entities for their economic agendas during East Asia's rapid development. The third section will explore the ways in which Weber's methodology enjoins us to interrogate the relationship between culture, institutional structures, and economic systems within East Asian contexts.

World religion and modern capitalism

Weber's study of Asian societies – India, China, and Japan – sits at the juncture of his three most significant theoretical interests: rationality as a paramount force shaping modern society[4]; capitalism as a driving force, as well as a manifestation, of rationalization; and finally, the influence of culture on economic structures. Throughout his work, Weber showed a particular interest in studying systems of ideas and the meaning of human action. For this reason, he is often compared to Karl Marx. Yet, unlike Marx, who argued that society's material base dictates society's system of ideas and beliefs, Weber maintained that economic systems cannot evolve without a parallel transformation in values and ideas. Thus, the affinity between capitalist material systems and cultural systems of ideas became a central intellectual inquiry in Weber's most influential book, *The Protestant Ethic and the Spirit of Capitalism* (hereafter, *The Protestant Ethic*).

In this book, Weber first established a statistical correlation between the presence of a Protestant population and the development of wealth and ownership in capitalist enterprises. He then analyzed the similarities between the Protestant religious ethic and the economic mindset underlying capitalism. According to Weber, modern rational capitalism is supported by an array of positive attitudes toward wealth, capital accumulation, and the encouragement of technological innovations. Promoted as elements of a personal work ethic, frugality, discipline, and self-control are the dominant values constituting Weber's notion of "the spirit" of capitalism. At the same time, he held that the tenets of certain forms of Protestantism, Calvinism in Europe and New England Puritanism in particular, closely resembled the spirit of capitalism. For instance, Calvinist teachings encouraged its followers to conduct an ascetic life and dedicate themselves to a vocational "calling" as a way of following God's commands. Material enrichment through professional success was not viewed with suspicion by these reformist Protestant sects, but instead as a likely sign of divine blessing. Furthermore, the inability of humans to know whether they were destined for salvation motivated followers to redirect anxiety about their spiritual status into the secular world of actions, providing a particularly strong impetus for social change.[5] In this sense, the Protestant ethic gave a new religious significance to the rational pursuit of profitability and entrepreneurial success, thereby inadvertently supporting the emergence of a modern capitalist economic system. Weber's emphasis here was to demonstrate the convergence, or "elective affinity," of these two systems of ideas.[6] In short, what he demonstrated were the

Max Weber and East Asian development   147

consistent similarities in the religious teachings of early Protestantism and the value orientation of capitalism.

There has been much debate about how to interpret Weber's thesis in this work. While reviewing the full range of interpretation of *The Protestant Ethic* is beyond the scope of this essay, it is worthwhile to consider two points that shape our discussion in the following section. The first is that his main thesis in this analysis is not a culturally determinist one. Not only do many Weberian experts interpret it in this way, but this is also consistent with Weber's own general approach to social science methods, which was to investigate "probabilistic associations," not deterministic ones, between historical and social processes.[7] Indeed, his interpretive methods of understanding, or *Verstehen*, called for understanding social actions in context, and complex and historically situated investigations rather than one-dimensional causal analyses.[8] The second point is that Weber's inquiry into the relationship between culture and economy was at an early stage of development in this book, and then was expanded in the comparative study of world religions and economic systems in Weber's later works. The thesis of *The Protestant Ethic* was therefore a preliminary hypothesis. As a way to figure out the cultural context for the emergence of the rationality that had been instrumental for the development of the modern capitalist system in the West, he turned to far more complex analyses of cultural ideas, group interests, and institutional contexts, including trade systems, the family, and political structures. These analytic goals would become much clearer only in his later analyses of world religions.

In short, Weber's intention was not to postulate that Protestantism propelled the development of a capitalist set of values, but to emphasize that Protestant values were an important piece of the puzzle in explaining the historical emergence of a modern capitalist system in European society. Moreover, these religious and secular streams of ideas intersected with each other at a particular historical period to provide an optimal context in which rational bourgeois capitalism emerged. Weberian sociology of economic development thus calls for a comprehensive examination of the dialectic interplay between ideas, people, material interests, and institutional specificity. Such a contextualized analysis would inform the practice of the Weberian method of *Verstehen*. However, whether Weber himself was fully engaged in *Verstehen*, as defined here, in his body of work on East Asian societies is open to debate. We will revisit this point in a later section.

While much of *The Protestant Ethic* is dedicated to describing the "elective affinity" between religion and an economic ethic, Weber's subsequent historical analyses of world religions took a broader institutional approach through the inclusion of discussions of market, legal, and political structures, and, of course, religion. The essays in *The Religion of China*, for example, encompass a wide range of topics about Chinese society, such as the monetary system, deities, urban structure, government administration, law, and the literati class, in addition to Confucian values. These discussions of

148 *Keumjae Park*

various aspects of Chinese society allowed him to further refine his thoughts on the ways in which cultural ideas interact with other systems in society. In terms of core religious values, Weber argued that Confucianism had a similarly rational and outwardly directed orientation as Protestantism. For instance, Confucianism provided teachings on "sobriety and thriftiness" and an orientation toward the "acquisition of wealth."[9] However, it was distinct from Protestantism in an important way: Confucianism, unlike the Calvinist and Puritan variants of Protestantism, lacked any anxiety about the uncertainty of salvation. Weber argued that it was this tension and anxiety over salvation within Protestantism that gave followers an impetus to turn to the secular world and transform it. On the other hand, he claimed, as the ethic of men with education and status in Imperial China, Confucianism encouraged the privileged class to use knowledge in order to participate in the governance of society rather than to change it. In other words, Confucianism represented an affirmation of the existing world, and not a rejection of it, and therefore became a religion of "world adjustment."[10]

It is also noteworthy that Weber's explanation for the absence of self-generated rational capitalism in China was grounded as much in institutional analysis as it was in cultural analysis, although embedded religious values were a central focus of his study. Weber examined five institutional conditions that he understood to be functional requirements for modern capitalism: a money system, cities and guilds, the patrimonial state, kinship organization, and law.[11] In Weber's view, Imperial China lacked an effective monetary and banking system. Cities, instrumental to European industrialization and capitalist development, could not fully establish themselves as independent and politically autonomous units in China because of the power of the imperial state.[12] In addition, the patrimonial state of China failed to develop a specialized system of administrative bureaucracy because Confucianism, with its central emphasis on the broad education considered necessary to become a "gentleman," discouraged technical professionalization. Strong kinship-based authority and family structure also undermined rational governance by law and bureaucratic administration.[13]

In the end, what the Weberian thesis of East Asia boils down to is the argument that despite some of the favorable material conditions capable of fostering a capitalist economy, the ethics of East Asian religions (e.g., Confucianism, Buddhism) did not generate, for these various reasons, the same kind of drive for capitalist transformation. Moreover, Weber argued that the overall traditionalist structures of Asia (e.g., the patrimonial state, the powerful influence of kinship and family) inhibited the development of a self-generated rational capitalist system.[14] In Weber's mind, the precise convergence of cultural climate, institutional conditions, and material interests conducive to a rational economic system had only occurred with European industrialization. East Asian societies were positioned in Weber's analysis as what sociologists refer to as "negative cases," defined by the absence of those enabling conditions. This did not mean that East Asia would never be an

Max Weber and East Asian development   149

adequate ground for any advanced capitalist development. In fact, according to Weberian scholars, Weber indicated the potential for the successful "assimilation" of East Asia to capitalism, although these Asian economies might assume forms different from the ideal type of Western capitalism.[15] For example, Weber predicted a potential capitalist development in China based on individual, family-based entrepreneurial models once opportunity structures opened up. Examples of this model can be found in the family-based system of entrepreneurship in pre-war China, and that of the Chinese diaspora in Southeast Asia.[16] Nevertheless, Weber's central conclusion in *The Religion of China* was that the orientation of East Asian societies (i.e., China and Japan) toward traditionalist culture and institutional social order inhibited an indigenous rational capitalism at the dawn of modernity.

Given this conclusion, Weber might have been surprised by the explosive economic development of East Asia in the post-1945 era, and especially by the ways in which Confucian values have been credited for East Asia's remarkable success. Was Weber wrong about East Asia? Weber's views have naturally invited criticism among contemporary scholars of Asian development. Some critiqued Weber's view of East Asia as a region composed of fundamentally "traditionalist societies" and of Confucianism as a cultural system lacking transformative energy due to its compliance with the existing social order. Many agree that this was a critical misunderstanding of Confucianism and an Orientalist misrepresentation of the East from the perspective of the West.[17] Weber was certainly limited by the scholarly resources on China available at his time. Among them, one can count significant works by Ferdinand von Richthofen and Ernst Faber in the late nineteenth century, and by Jan Jakob Maria de Groot, Otto Franke, Richard Wilhelm, and Heinrich Hackmann in the early twentieth century. Yet, while most of his liberal contemporaries, particularly Richard Wilhelm, were more inclined toward Sinophilic interpretations, Weber pursued a Sinophobic line by relying chiefly on works by the Dutch Sinologist de Groot at the University of Berlin.[18] Ethnocentric biases in Weber's generalizations have been discussed in a recent work by George Steinmetz, who stresses that Weber's thesis was predetermined on a presumption of China's economic stagnation and traditionalism. Steinmetz points out, for instance, that Weber was unaware of Chinese regional capitalism, and that he completely dismissed the destructive impact of Western imperialism on Chinese society during the nineteenth century.[19]

On the other hand, defenders of Weber argue that he had never intended to write a comprehensive theory of China. Instead, Weber was fundamentally interested in categorizing different religious systems in order to establish a theoretical explanation about why only certain kinds of embryonic values matured into a rational capitalist ethic, such as that found in the West. This interpretation emphasizes that Weber never intended to posit Asian cultures as irrational or inferior to those of Europe. In writing about other "negative cases" around the world, Weber's goal was to simply highlight the optimal

150 *Keumjae Park*

historical conditions that had existed in Europe, which was his focus all along. Andrea Buss refers to this Weberian approach as a case of "heuristic ethnocentrism"[20]; while he did not posit Europe as the superior normative model that other countries would follow, Weber's studies of other cultures were simply, in Weber's own words, "oriented to the problems which seem important for the understanding of Western civilization."[21] This may explain Weber's short-sightedness about East Asia and his less than fair discussions of Confucianism.

Weber and East Asian development

The rise of East Asia is arguably one of the defining features of the world economy since the 1960s. The region has advanced, in only a few decades, from colonial occupation, poverty, and obscurity into the center of global capitalism. Asia is a large continent, whose economic development has been admittedly uneven. The western and central regions have not grown any quicker than the rest of the world, while much of the eastern part (primarily ten countries, including China, Hong Kong, Indonesia, Japan, Malaysia, the Philippines, Singapore, South Korea, Taiwan, and Thailand) has performed better than the rest of the world in terms of economic growth. The prosperity of Japan, Hong Kong, and Singapore now places them among the richest countries in the world. South Korea and Taiwan are closing the gap with the most prosperous countries in Europe and North America. The remarkable pace at which different economies in East Asia have grown is well documented. The countries of Northeast Asia (Japan, South Korea, Taiwan, and China) and of Southeast Asia (Hong Kong and Singapore) have become prominent economic players in the world, in terms of both actual wealth and the size of their economies.

According to Dwight Perkins' recent overview of East Asian development, the developmental models of East Asian countries are diverse, and yet there are some common characteristics.[22] Japan, a latecomer to modern capitalism compared with Europe and North America, has nevertheless seen its economy grow faster than its Western counterparts since the Meiji Restoration in 1868. By 1930, Japan was fully industrialized and had grown into a regional colonial power expanding its influence to Korea, China, and Taiwan. Japan suffered severe destruction during World War II but rebuilt its economy at a remarkably fast pace after 1945. By the early 1970s, Japan had already joined the ranks of first-world industrialized nations. The next group of East Asian countries that entered the global spotlight were the "Four Dragons," namely, Hong Kong, Singapore, South Korea, and Taiwan. Beginning in the early 1960s, these four countries mobilized development projects, and achieved economic growth rates that surpassed that of Japan during its era of postwar growth. Between 1960 and 1994, for example, Singapore, South Korea, and Taiwan had annual average GDP growth rates of 8.3 percent, 8.5 percent, and 8.7 percent, respectively. These were more

Max Weber and East Asian development   151

than double the typical GDP growth rates of industrialized countries in the West during the same period.[23] Today, these four countries rank among the most industrialized nations in the world. China is still a developing country. However, since its policy shifted toward a market economy in 1978, China has averaged about 9.6 percent GDP growth per year between 1978 and 2005, and per-capita income has grown seventeen-fold in a little over three decades.[24] In 2012, China became the world's second largest economy, and is now positioned to become the world's largest economy in the next decade or so.

The rapid growth of these six East Asian countries has often been described as "explosive" and "miraculous" because they outperformed so significantly the previously established trajectories of economic development globally. For that reason, there has been a lot of scholarship attempting to explain "the secret" of the Asian economic miracles. A full review of the development literature on East Asia is beyond the scope of this chapter. However, we will discuss two characteristics of what is known as the East Asian model, which are particularly relevant to the Weberian discussion of East Asian capitalism.

The role of the state

While the developmental models adopted by these countries are not uniform, one common characteristic of East Asian development is the active role of the state.[25] Few economies in the West had a model of industrialization wherein the state took control over the planning and execution of development projects to the extent that it did in East Asia. The governments of these countries intervened actively in development through various means, including policy initiatives, control of banking (i.e., state ownership of banks), foreign exchange licenses, import restrictions, and generally close ties with industries via regular meetings, personal networks, and "parachute" employment of former government officials in the private sector. Control of the economy by the government was more significant in South Korea and Taiwan, where land reforms, the protection of agriculture, and the growth of selective sectors were carried out under state directives. Hong Kong and Singapore, both former British colonies, had relatively laissez-faire economic models with more active use of private investment. However, the government in Hong Kong was still involved in land ownership, housing construction, and investment in public universities. Similarly, Singapore's left-leaning government controlled home ownership policies, implemented forced mandatory savings policies, and ran several significant national flagship businesses such as airlines and telecommunication. State control was more significant in the 1960s and 1970s in all of the Four Dragon countries but shifted toward more market-driven systems by the 1980s. Even after adopting a more open market system, these governments have continued to emphasize public investment in education and human capital in order

152 Keumjae Park

to stimulate high tech industries and to build a competitive edge in those sectors.[26]

The state-led model of East Asian development provides an interesting contrast to Western capitalism, which was developed based on individualism and an economic ethic supportive of free market competition. The surprising success of the state-led model offers a sharp counterpoint to the Weberian view, which considers individualism a necessary component of the ethos of capitalism and competition, a critical dynamic that encourages innovation and technological development. Individualism, for instance, helped to undermine the Old Regime in Europe and promote the development of rational economic and political systems. By contrast, Weber considered the strong patrimonial state of Imperial China to be a deterrent to the development of vibrant and competitive cities, a condition he deemed crucial for the emergence of modern capitalism in Europe.[27] The achievement of East Asia's state-led economies might have surprised Weber. But there are external variables, unforeseen by Weber, which could explain this paradoxical outcome. East Asian development in the twentieth century went hand-in-hand with broader global economic trends that provided the context for their development projects. For example, East Asia jump-started development projects through access to large consumer markets of already industrialized countries. Hsin-Huang Michael Hsiao has especially emphasized the post-1945 economic boom and market expansion in the United States as a significant external condition for East Asia's rapid growth.[28] While differing in their specific approaches, East Asia's developing countries commonly adopted export-oriented policies that took full advantage of these external environments. Furthermore, the global economy has taken an accelerated turn toward the globalization of production and free trade since the late 1970s, creating expanded opportunities for newly industrialized economies in manufacturing and export. While China's economic shifts are still unfolding, its earliest growth spurts between 1978 and 1984 undoubtedly benefited from foreign trade – especially the export of light industrial goods – along with the implementation of household farming policies. The Chinese government has since gradually released its control over to market forces, especially since joining the World Trade Organization in the 1990s. Export and trade, riding on the tide of the global integration of markets, undoubtedly remain the most critical segments of China's booming economy.

Another external factor which may have affected East Asian economic development in a way not predicted by Weber was foreign investments. For example, government-mediated foreign loans allowed countries like South Korea to secure the initial capital to establish developmental projects and expedited the process of capital accumulation. This is not always a constructive opportunity, however, because it can also help to strengthen the influence and power of an authoritarian government over economic entities dependent on their ties to the political regime in negotiating favorable terms of business. This was particularly true in the case of South Korea, whose

Max Weber and East Asian development   153

developmental model focused on the growth of large business conglomerates. These export-oriented developmental models, shaped by the demands of global division of labor in production, also caused exploitative working conditions for workers in several of these countries and gave rise to class inequality and tension, although the level of inequality varied widely by country.[29]

Weber's original analysis of Asian societies discussed several institutional conditions such as kinship and family structure, the power of government, and class structure, but it largely focused on domestic conditions. To these, we may add the external contingencies of the contemporary global economic system, which has taken a different shape since Weber's time of Western imperial expansion. In other words, the particular forms of contemporary global trade could have been an influential factor that converged with other conditions to create optimal contexts in propelling the East Asian economic "miracles." But it appears that Weber did not foresee East Asian countries' expansion in the global market, and their emergence as the benefactors of global capitalism. Weber's short-sighted prediction for East Asia may be due in part to this new historical development, unforeseen in his time.

Another important way in which the state has led developmental projects in East Asia is through cultural movements intended to encourage a particular mindset toward economic development. There probably was a need for a different imperative and ethos of capitalism among the latecomers who had to play "catch up" within the already established global hierarchy of economies. Some empirical research has documented examples of government-led mobilization of particular attitudes and values for economic benefits. For example, Keedon Kwon's study examines what he calls the "moral economic campaigns for cultural transformation" during the Meiji period in Japan and during the 1970s in South Korea.[30] Kwon argues that in these two cases, the state strategically denounced some elements of traditional culture as old and obsolete while selectively promoting other Confucian values (e.g., activism, hard work, thrift) for the purpose of economic mobilization. In other words, the state mobilized its considerable power by engaging in cultural engineering for the purpose of modernization projects. Although following a different pattern, Singapore's political leaders also promoted "Asian values" beginning in the early 1980s as a functional surrogate to the West's Protestant ethic.[31] These analyses reveal that there was a keen understanding of the power of culture among East Asian political leaders. We now turn to the question of culture, which is central to Weberian discussions of East Asia's development.

The question of Asian values

One of the most important legacies of Weberian historical sociology is the premise that cultural values and systems of thought are an important impetus capable of shaping economic development. In the midst of the East Asian

154 *Keumjae Park*

rise in the global economy, especially when the Newly Industrialized Countries of South Korea, Taiwan, Hong Kong, and Singapore dazzled Western observers with their rapid economic ascent, one of the more popular explanations of this phenomenon was the "Asian values" thesis. This directly challenged the Weberian predictions for Asia, since Weber had cast East Asian cultures as an inhibiting factor to the rise of capitalism. According to Michael Hill, in the earlier period of East Asian development Weberian scholars tried to explain the empirical reality of Asia's rise by searching for the worldly asceticism – a functional equivalent of the Protestant ethic – in Asian cultural values.[32] This was essentially an attempt to discover elements of Confucianism conducive to the development of capitalism that Weber may have misinterpreted or missed altogether. Hard work, thrift, respect for education, loyalty to authority, and emphasis on harmony were among the cultural traits often discussed in these works as uniquely Asian values amenable to economic development. Into the late 1970s and 1980s, a variation of this idea even contended that modern versions of Confucianism were more advantageous for the purpose of modern-day industrialization than the individualistic Protestant values of the West. For example, Herman Kahn's book on Asian development made the argument that modern Confucian values like loyalty, responsibility, and collectivism were more conducive for the organizational efficiency required in modern capitalism.[33] Similarly, Ezra Vogel praised the "communitarian vision" of Japanese enterprise as a key to its success.[34] Hofheinz and Calder presented Singapore's strict, austere, and disciplined rules of public life as a model example of modern Confucian "virtues" which bolstered the Singaporean economy.[35] Sociologist Peter Berger described post-Confucian culture as the "comparative advantage" of East Asian economies.[36]

Given Weber's emphasis on culture, these are all important considerations. However, this approach comes with a few problems that need to be addressed. To begin, the Confucian/Asian values thesis displaces diverse religious and non-religious cultural constructs within East Asia into a reified and homogenized notion of the "Confucian" ethic. While largely observable in the everyday practice of people in East Asia, whether the aforementioned "virtues" originate specifically from Confucian tradition is debatable, since diverse religions, including Buddhism, folk religions, and Christianity are all practiced and influence the collective value systems in contemporary East Asia. Especially in the case of Singapore, despite the fact that almost three-quarter of its population is ethnic Chinese, Buddhism, Christianity (including Catholicism), and Islam are practiced among more than two thirds of the population.[37] Moreover, culture and value systems are not static. It could be disputed that there is an invariable Asian "tradition" that is frozen in time, free from the influence of constant flows and mixing of cultures. In fact, countries in East Asia have experienced rapid social changes on all fronts, and traditions have been displaced and redefined constantly. For example, in China, the Cultural Revolution (1966–1976) attacked many of the old traditions and Confucian ways. Though this kind of an aggressive assault on tradition has receded in China since the 1980s, it would be erroneous to assume that traditional Confucian values are the main spiritual support of China's modernization projects. Similarly, Confucianism is often treated as an old archaic way of life in contemporary South Korean society, which has become much more Westernized and globalized.

In fact, overemphasizing Asian cultural values and attitudes as the "secret" force of Asian style success of capitalism may miss one important point of the Weberian thesis; culture is only one part of multiple interlocking forces affecting the development and transformation of an economic system. As reviewed at the beginning of this essay, the Weberian thesis of religion and economy was not a theory of cultural determinism. Nor did the Weberian idea of culture claim to identify a system insulated from material conditions. Such a static and reified view of culture would misrepresent the massive social changes in East Asia, which have included not only economic development, but also significant political, social, and cultural transformations. In this regard, Keedon Kwon's "dynamic and agentic" conceptualization of culture makes a convincing theoretical case for understanding how culture interacted with other institutional factors to create a fertile ground for East Asia's economic growth since the 1960s.[38]

Whether there exists a static core of East Asian values is a question that needs to be approached with considerable caution. There is evidence, however, that political and economic institutions have appropriated and promoted certain cultural attitudes for their economic benefit in the name of "Asian values." For example, loyalty and patriotism were frequently invoked to foster toleration for collective hardships and external threats, as shown through the postwar reconstruction periods in Japan and South Korea. Another example of a state's cultural engineering project can be found in Singapore, a country with mixed cultural traditions and Western influence, due to its geopolitical history. In 1982, Lee Kuan Yew's government revitalized Confucian education in public schools' moral education programs, because state leaders believed that they needed to promote particular values in order to economically compete with "the Confucian block" (i.e., Hong Kong, Taiwan, and South Korea). Kahn provides a good summary of the ways in which East Asian states took advantage of certain aspects of Asian values. They include (1) a personal ethic of hard work and responsibility, (2) group loyalty, and (3) cooperation and identification with the organization.[39] It is also noteworthy that these values were encouraged not only for their economic benefits, but also for stable nation-state building in the aftermath of conflict and political turmoil in these countries, as well as during periods of potential moral disorganization due to rapid social changes.[40]

While this paper critiques the tendency to evoke Asian values as the paramount explanation for East Asia's success, one cannot completely dismiss the influence of culture. There are a few specific ways in which cultural traditions may have affected contemporary East Asian development. For example, education had been commonly valued under Confucianism as a means of achieving the status of a Confucian "gentleman" and thus being able to follow a path of service to the country. In my observation, this cultural tradition has remained strong in the region, creating a work force with high-quality human capital. Access to education had been uneven before 1945 and patterns of educational inequality have varied by country. However, active investment in education, both by individuals and by the government, has been widespread in East Asia since the 1960s. An abundant and well-educated work force has been an asset for East Asia's first labor-intensive export economy and later technology-focused development. High population density and the intensely competitive labor market have also encouraged a strong and sustained emphasis on human capital, a trend that continues today. But at the same time, one should not posit that the pursuit of education was simply a generic influence of Confucian tradition. For instance, the technology-oriented professions and STEM-related skills for which East Asia is now known are not the kind of education typically valued within a Confucian context. In other words, cultural priorities have changed with time and, more importantly, in relation to material needs. It is highly likely that it was the labor market environments which contributed to the intense emphasis on education and credentialism as a key mechanism for upward social mobility in the rapidly transforming economic structures of East Asia. Similarly, the popular assumption that the corporate culture of East Asia, with its emphasis on lifetime employment, loyalty to the group, and self-sacrifice, is due to traditional culture needs to be reexamined within historical contexts. Indeed, recent scholarship suggests that this system was established precisely because it served economic rationality.[41]

Conclusions

Weber's study of China had an implicit Eurocentric bias which prevented him from fully anticipating the future capitalist potential and prosperity of East Asia. As discussed above, his misjudgment is reflected through his overestimation of the traditional characteristic of East Asian societies and his underestimation of capitalist potentials embedded in their culture and institutions. One of the pioneering sociologists of his time, Weber may have been aware that he did not draw upon a sufficient range of data. He may also have been aware that he did not pay enough attention to the specificity of Asian history and culture. Nevertheless, he seems to have taken the risk of misrepresenting East Asia, largely because of his "heuristic ethnocentrism."[42] He was far less interested in producing accurate knowledge about East Asian societies; instead, he sought to establish a general theory of culture and economic change in European society, contrasting it against Asia, which served as a "negative case." In other words, his sociology of East Asia was meant to highlight its difference from, and deficits in comparison to, the European capitalist model. This is the irony of this brilliant sociologist's

Max Weber and East Asian development 157

career; his heuristic ethnocentrism prevented him from fully practicing *Verstehen*, his own interpretive method of understanding, in producing a theory of East Asia grounded in the specificity of its cultural, structural, and historical contexts.

Nevertheless, there are still lessons to be gleaned from the Weberian methodology of the cultural and institutional study of economic systems. The Weberian method of interpretive understanding cautions us against the one-dimensional "culture thesis" of East Asia. It is an interesting twist that contemporary scholars of Asian development often resorted to "Asian" values in responding to Weber's underappreciation of East Asia's economic and entrepreneurial potential. Despite the paradox in this, one could argue that revisiting the Weberian methodology of *Verstehen*, if practiced carefully, could provide us with a useful tool with which to evaluate the storied economic rise of East Asia in the twentieth century and its continuing success into the twenty-first century. For example, his attention to the complexity of social phenomena, especially his emphasis on historical context, promotes multifaceted institutional analyses that cannot be reduced to a simple cultural determinism. To the extent that culture is an important force of social transformation, it still has to be considered in its complex interplay with the material system, political interests, and various power dynamics at multiple levels. All of these factors must be considered simultaneously. Some of the research cited in this essay demonstrates that culture is a dynamic construct that not only shapes material systems but also is practiced, mobilized, and reinvented by people. Moreover, economic and political institutions have played a significant role in East Asia's development.

Because Weberian methods of historical sociology, in principle at least, reject one-directional and one-dimensional causal determinism, historical change must be considered in any study on the twentieth century economic development of East Asia. This essay discussed, for example, what new external conditions could be considered. Weber's ideal type rational-bourgeois capitalism was based on late nineteenth and early twentieth century European industrial capitalism. His ideas were based on the classical economic model of a free market mobilized by a rising bourgeois class in democratic political regimes. On the other hand, the most spectacular growth of East Asian capitalism occurred only in the second half of the twentieth century, well after the Keynesian model of state involvement and safety net policies had become standard practice in many places. East Asia's state-led economic projects, while different from the classical model of European capitalism, offer a different rational model that makes sense in the contemporary global context. An important element for their success was the East Asian economies' ability to take advantage of the thriving markets in the United States and Europe, which opened up timely opportunities for export-focused development strategies. It was in this changing environment that East Asia was integrated into the world system of capitalism, thereby achieving prosperity in the process. Perhaps the success of post-1945 East Asian capitalism

158 *Keumjae Park*

developed from the convergence of these historically specific material and cultural conditions that were both external and internal: a "perfect storm" of opportunity structures in the global economy; strong states with urgent nation-building projects; an actively mobilized and reconstructed "Asian" ethic of hard work and compliance with collective goals; and investment in education. East Asian states were active and efficient agents, taking advantage of the convergence of these conditions and strategically appropriating elements of cultural tradition for economic benefit.

Applying Weber to Asian development today may require asking a new set of questions about culture and economy. Some questions inspired by the proposal of Hamilton and Kao should be considered in future inquiries.[43] First, while religious values remain important to many people, they seem less decisive in guiding individual behavior today than they were in the early twentieth century. Weber himself had sensed a rising force of secularization during his own lifetime.[44] Indeed, the new twenty-first century "spirit" of capitalism may demand not methodical asceticism but a new ethos of creativity and innovation. Future analysis may ask what the new spirit of capitalism in the twenty-first century will be, and how it can interact with the rapidly increasing global cultural mixing. Second, many scholars have discussed East Asia's economic development as uniformly successful, focusing on the quantifiable indices of economic growth, such as GDP and per capita income. However, the negative changes caused by such rapid growth have been subjected to far less scrutiny. For instance, would a different kind of dehumanizing trend emerge if indigenous values and institutions were displaced within such a short period by institutions and values driven by capitalist economic machinery? Weberian perspectives inspire us today to investigate these new questions with careful cultural, institutional, and historical analysis.

Notes

1 Jack Barbalet, "Weber's Daoism: A Failure of Orthodoxy," *Journal of Classical Sociology* 14, no. 3 (2014): 284–301; Peter Berger, "An East Asian Development Model," *The Economic News*, September 1984, 17–23; Thomas A. Metzger, *Escape from Predicament: Neoconfucianism and China's Evolving Political Culture* (New York: Columbia University Press, 1977); Johannes Han-Yin Chang, "Culture, State, and Economic Development in Singapore," *Journal of Contemporary Asia* 33, no. 1 (2003): 85–105; Frank Parkin, *Max Weber*, 2nd ed. (London: Routledge, 2002), 23–27; Yusheng Peng, "Lineage Networks, Rural Entrepreneurs and Max Weber," *Research in the Sociology of Work* 15 (2005): 327–55; Tu Wei-Ming, ed., *The Triadic Chord: Confucian Ethics, Industrial East Asia and Max Weber* (Singapore: The Institute of East Asian Philosophy, 1991).

2 Fang Deng, "Is Max Weber Wrong? The Confucian Ethic, Migrant Workers, and China's Rise," *Bridgewater Review* 35, no. 2 (2016): 28–32. In addition, Liu Dong's essay also discusses the "Confucian ethic" made popular among Weberian scholars in China during the 1990s. Liu Dong, "The Weberian View

and Confucianism," trans. Gloria Davies, *East Asian History* 25/26 (2003): 191–217.

3 Max Weber, *The Protestant Ethic and the Spirit of Capitalism*, trans. Talcott Parsons (New York: Charles Scribner's Sons, 1958); Weber, *The Religion of China: Confucianism and Taoism*, trans. and ed. Hans H. Gerth (New York: The Free Press, 1964).

4 Weber variously used the terms, *Rationalismus*, *Rationalität*, and *Rationalisierung*. Rationalization is a term describing ongoing social change toward methodical and calculable practices based on rules of reason. Weberian theory scholars would agree that this is the central intellectual inquiry guiding Weber's historical sociology. See Stephen Kalberg, "Max Weber's Types of Rationality: Cornerstones for the Analysis of Rationalization Processes in History," *The American Journal of Sociology* 85, no. 5 (1980): 1145–79.

5 C. K. Yang, "Introduction," in Max Weber, *The Religion of China: Confucianism and Taoism*, trans. and ed. Hans H. Gerth (New York: The Free Press, 1964), xv–xvi.

6 Hans H. Gerth and C. Wright Mills, "Intellectual Orientations," in *From Max Weber: Essays in Sociology*, trans. and ed. Hans H. Gerth and C. Wright Mills (New York: Oxford University Press, 1958), 45–74.

7 Lewis Coser, *Masters of Sociological Thought: Ideas of Historical and Social Context* (New York: Harcourt Brace Jovanovich, 1977), 224–26.

8 Max Weber, *The Theory of Social and Economic Organization*, ed. Talcott Parsons, trans. A. M. Henderson and Talcott Parsons (New York: Oxford University Press, 1947), 88.

9 Weber, *The Religion of China*, 247.

10 Schluchter, " 'How Ideas Become Effective in History': Max Weber on Confucianism and Beyond," *Max Weber Studies* 14, no. 1 (2014): 11–31.

11 Yang, "Introduction," xx–xxvii.

12 Weber, *The Religion of China*, 13–30.

13 Yang, "Introduction," xxviii–xxxiv.

14 Max Weber, "The Social Psychology of the World Religions," in *From Max Weber: Essays in Sociology*, trans. and ed. Hans H. Gerth and C. Wright Mills (New York: Oxford University Press, 1958), 267–301.

15 Gary G. Hamilton and Cheng-Shu Kao, "Max Weber and the Analysis of East Asian Industrialization," *International Sociology* 2, no. 3 (1987): 289–300.

16 Ibid., 289–300.

17 Barbalet, "Weber's Daoism," 285, 297–98; Gary G. Hamilton, "Patriarchy, Patrimonialism and Filial Piety: A Comparison of China and Western Europe," *British Journal of Sociology* 41, no. 1 (1990): 77–104; Yang, "Introduction," xxxix; Tu Wei-Ming, *The Triadic Chord: Confucian Ethics, Industrial East Asia and Max Weber*. In addition, for a critique of Weber's Orientalist treatment of Islam, see Joseph Jon Kaminski, "Beyond Capitalism: A Critique of Max Weber's General Understanding of the Islamic Discourse," *Intellectual Discourse* 24, no. 1 (2016): 35–58; Edward Said, *Orientalism* (New York: Vintage Books, 1978), 259–60.

18 I am indebted to Joanne Miyang Cho for the information on various works by Sinologists during Weber's time.

19 George Steinmetz, *The Devil's Handwriting: Precoloniality and the German Colonial State in Qingdao, Samoa, and Southwest Africa* (Chicago: University of Chicago Press, 2007), 415–16. Earlier in this book, Steinmetz describes the divergent attitudes toward China among German intellectuals of the time. Steinmetz argues that there were generally more negative attitudes toward China, that is, Sinophobia, among the German military and business elites (pp. 51–52),

160 *Keumjae Park*

while the educated middle class (*Bildungsbuergertum*) held more positive views. Steinmetz provides as examples the conservative intellectual Hermann von Keyserling and the liberal intellectual Richard Wilhelm, who were both Sinophiles. I thank Joanne Miyang Cho for this insight.

20 Andreas Buss, "Max Weber's Heritage and Modern Southeast Asian Thinking on Development," *Southeast Asian Journal of Social Science* 12, no. 1 (1984): 1–15.

21 Weber, *The Protestant Ethic and the Spirit of Capitalism*, 27.

22 Dwight Perkins, *East Asian Development: Foundations and Strategies* (Cambridge, MA and London: Harvard University Press, 2013).

23 Susan M. Collins and Barry P. Bodsworth, "Economic Growth in East Asia: Accumulation versus Assimilation," *Brookings Papers on Economic Activity* 2 (1996): 136.

24 Carsten A. Holz, "China's Economic Growth 1978–2005: What We Know Today About China's Economic Growth Tomorrow," *World Development* 36, no. 10 (2008): 1665.

25 Peter L. Berger and Hsin-Huang Michael Hsiao, eds., *In Search of an East Asian Development Model* (New Brunswick, NJ: Transaction Books, 1988).

26 Perkins, *East Asian Development*.

27 Weber, *The Religion of China*, 13–32.

28 Hsin-Huang Michael Hsiao, "An East Asian Development Model: Empirical Explorations," *Bulletin of the Institute of Ethnology Academia Sinica*, no. 60 (1985): 149–64.

29 Perkins, *East Asian Development*. Also see Wang Feng, "The End of 'Growth with Equity'? Economic Growth and Income Inequality in East Asia," *Asia Pacific Issues* 101 (2011): 1–8; Ravi Kanbur, Anthony. J. Venables, and Guanghua Wan, "Introduction to the Special Issue: Spatial Inequality and Development in Asia," *Review of Development Economics* 9, no. 1 (2005): 1–4; Yehua Dennis Wei, "Geography of Inequality in Asia," *Geographical Review* 107 (2017), no. 2: 263–75.

30 Keedon Kwon, "Economic Development in East Asia and a Critique of the Post-Confucian Thesis," *Sociological Theory* 36 (2007): 55–83.

31 Michael Hill, "'Asian Values' as Reverse Orientalism: Singapore," *Asia Pacific Viewpoint* 41, no. 2 (2000): 177–90.

32 Hill, "Asian Values' as Reverse Orientalism: Singapore," 177–90. Examples of the works on Asian asceticism include Robert N. Bellah, *Tokugawa Religion: The Values of Pre-Industrial Japan* (Glencoe, IL: Free Press, 1957) and David C. McClelland, *The Achieving Society* (New York: Free Press, 1967).

33 Herman Kahn, *World Economic Development 1979 and Beyond* (Boulder, CO: Westview Press, 1979), 113–76.

34 Ezra Vogel, *Japan as Number One: Lessons for America* (Cambridge, MA: Harvard University Press, 1979). Also Lawrence Harrison, *Who Prospers? How Cultural Values Shape Economic and Political Success* (New York: Basic Books, 1992).

35 Roy Hofheinz, Jr. and Kent E. Calder, *The Eastasia Edge* (New York: Basic Books, 1982).

36 Peter Berger, "An East Asian Development Model," *The Economic News*, September 1984, 17–23.

37 Department of Statistics, Ministry of Trade & Industry, Republic of Singapore, *Census of Population 2010 Statistical Release 1: Demographic Characteristics, Education, Language and Religion*, 11, accessed August 4, 2017, www.singstat. gov.sg/docs/default-source/default-document-library/publications/publications_and_papers/cop2010/census_2010_release1/cop2010sr1.pdf.

Max Weber and East Asian development 161

38 Kwon, "Economic Development in East Asia," 55.
39 Kahn, *World Economic Development*, 121–23.
40 Hill, " 'Asian Values' as Reverse Orientalism: Singapore."
41 Kwon, "Economic Development in East Asia," 57.
42 Buss, "Max Weber's Heritage and Modern Southeast Asian Thinking on Development," 1.
43 Hamilton and Kao, "Max Weber and the Analysis of East Asian Industrialization," 289–300.
44 Weber wrote, "In the field of its highest development, in the United States, the pursuit of wealth, stripped of its religious and ethical meaning, tends to become associated with purely mundane passions, which often actually give it the character of sport." Weber, *The Protestant Ethic and the Spirit of Capitalism*, 182. Weber also maintained close relationships with several radical liberal Protestant theologians, including Ernst Troeltsch, who sought to understand Christianity through historical analysis and questioned the absoluteness of Christian dogmas. I thank Joanne Miyang Cho for this insight.

8 "History as a poet"

Stefan Zweig's historical and biographical writing in Maoist China

Arnhilt Johanna Hoefle

Between 1950 and 1954 Chinese publishers released several of Stefan Zweig's (1881–1942) historical and biographical works in Chinese transla- tion.[1] Works by the world-famous Austrian-Jewish author had been read in China since the 1920s.[2] During the Civil War between the Nationalists and the Communists in the 1930s and 1940s, left-wing critics had increasingly attacked Zweig as a writer of decadent bourgeois literature. The choice to publish Zweig only a few months after Mao proclaimed the founding of the People's Republic of China (PRC) thus seems rather unexpected. In order to explain this accumulation of translations at such a turning point in Chinese history, I address the question of genre, which has played a par- ticularly important role in the Chinese reception of Zweig. I will explore how Zweig's own poetology of historical and biographical literature and his concept of "history as a poet" ("Geschichte als Dichterin") not only reso- nated with traditional as well as Maoist approaches to life writing in China but also was purposefully employed by intellectuals during turbulent times. Remarkably, Chinese readers had at least temporary access to the works of a bourgeois Austrian writer during one of the most strictly controlled periods of modern Chinese history.

Zweig's poetology of life writing

Stefan Zweig's fame as a writer of biographical and historical fiction was closely linked to a boom of these genres in Europe in the early twentieth cen- tury.[3] As hybrid genres between historiography and literature they quickly triggered fierce controversies among writers as well as between writers and historians. Specifically, they fought over the problematic relationship of fact and fiction and contested historicity and literaricity as conflicting priori- ties. In 1918 the publication of Lytton Strachey's *Eminent Victorians*, which proposed a radical break with biographical conventions, had a tremendous impact on this debate. The British writer attacked Victorian-style biogra- phies and called for modern biographies that were more accurate and objec- tive. As much as some critics regarded Stefan Zweig as the exemplar of a modern biographer in this sense, others reproved the decidedly literary and

"History as a poet"   163

subjective style of his works. Very early in his career Zweig had portrayed contemporary as well as historical figures, philosophers, intellectuals, politicians, and in particular writers. His acclaimed first biographical study of the Belgian poet Emile Verhaeren (1910) was followed in the 1920s by the successful three-volume work *Master Builders* (*Die Baumeister der Welt*), which contained shorter biographical essays on Balzac, Dickens, Dostoyevsky, Hölderlin, Kleist, Nietzsche, Casanova, Stendhal, and Tolstoy. He dedicated book-length biographies to Joseph Fouché (1929), Marie Antoinette (1932), Erasmus of Rotterdam (1934), Magellan (1938), and several others. His "historical miniatures" collected in the volume *Shooting Stars* (*Sternstunden der Menschheit*) were and remain among his most popular historical writings. In his lecture "History as a Poet" ("Die Geschichte als Dichterin"), intended for the Seventeenth International PEN Congress in Stockholm in 1939, he elaborated on his poetological approach in more detail.[4] As Zweig's most significant commentary on his approach to historical and biographical writing it deserves closer attention.

Apart from extensively using the personal pronouns "we" and "us," Zweig's main literary device in this lecture is personification. He opened his text by taking his readers back to school, where "we" all first encountered history. As a "great teacher" ("große Lehrerin"), a "great governess" ("große Erzieherin"), history took us by the hand and guided us along the "tremendous pathway of humanity" ("ungeheuren Weg der Menschheit") from the caves of our prehistoric ancestors to the present era. But history soon revealed her other face to us; we recognized her as a merciless judge ("eine mitleidlose Richterin"), who without love or hate and absent any prejudice, took note of all the chaotic events of world history. Sometimes, however, history also appeared as a poet. History, according to Zweig, did not compose literary works all the time; most of the time she was just a chronicler, a mere reporter of facts. But every now and then she created perfect and complete, insurmountably dramatic and artistic works, which Zweig called "immaculate crystals" ("makellose Kristalle") or "stellar hours" ("Sternstunden").[5]

In the next section Zweig developed his allegory of "history as a poet" in more detail. First of all, as in most novels or plays, there had to be more than one single protagonist, at least one antagonist, or even better, a "pack of ingeniously contrasting figures" ("ein Rudel genial kontrastierender Gestalten"), who acted like cataracts in disturbing the often monotonous rhythm and peaceful flow of history. History as a poet could act as a narrator of clear and epic works but she never arrogantly scorned other genres. She was able to compose a suspenseful crime or detective novel just as flawlessly as she wrote a cheeky farce, a sentimental or martial ballad, a lyrical or dramatic poem, as well as an anecdote or even a joke. Yet she never produced a complete book. Rather, Zweig described her literary creation as a palimpsest, a conglomerate of fragmented manuscripts, where many hundreds of pages remained undecipherable or were lost.[6]

164   *Arnhilt Johanna Hoefle*

In the final part of the lecture Zweig claimed that it was ultimately the task of the poet to make sense of these mysterious fragments of history. Poets should fill in the blank spaces between the perfectly crafted "crystals" that history had composed. These materials needed to be treated respectfully, he warned, without unduly romanticizing, heroizing, or caricaturing them. Poets should avoid excising or simplifying any sections potentially too weighty for the audience's stomach to digest. Criticizing in particular recent developments in the biographical genre, Zweig warned that writers of the popular *biographie romancée* garnished biographies with literary elements and mixed truth with fiction. These novel-like biographies ignored the "small" moments of a life and amplified the heroic and more interesting ones. In this way they remained on the surface and created mere "posters" ("Plakate") rather than "portraits of the soul" ("seelische Porträts"). He himself preferred the historically faithful biography, which did not resort to fabrication but humbly and faithfully *served* the superior spirit of history ("*dient* demütig getreu dem überlegenen Geist der Historie"). Any strictly factual and historical biography did not necessarily need to turn into a sterile collection of documents, a cold report. Rather, poets had to be psychologists. They had to listen themselves "into" the event ("Tief-in-das-Geschehnis-Hineinhorchen") to be able to distinguish the many different historical truths. It was the task of poets to peel history like an artichoke to penetrate layer after layer of its many truths. Any period between the poetic *Sternstunden* of history that might appear dead or boring only did so, Zweig argued, because the writer had failed; there were no unimportant characters in history, there were just bad writers. Maybe history did not even exist independently, Zweig concluded. History was instead created by the art of narration, by the vision of a true poet who transformed facts into history.[7]

The collection *Shooting Stars* is one of the most important but also most controversial works in Zweig's oeuvre.[8] In the five episodes of its 1927 first edition, Zweig chose different historical moments that in his view exemplified the "stellar hours" or "immaculate crystals" of historical creation.[9] The first episode, "The World Minute of Waterloo" ("Die Weltminute von Waterloo"), relates General Grouchy's failed attempt to come to the rescue of Napoleon at the battle of Waterloo in 1815. In "The Elegy of Marienbad" ("Die Marienbader Elegie"), the old and heartbroken Goethe is depicted writing his famous poem of the same title after Ulrike von Levetzow's refusal of his proposal in Marienbad in 1823. "The Discovery of Eldorado" ("Die Entdeckung Eldorados") follows Johann August Suter's discovery of gold in California and his demise following the Gold Rush in 1848. "Heroic Moment" ("Heroischer Augenblick"), the only episode written in verse form, describes the last-minute reprieve of Fyodor Dostoyevsky from his execution in 1849. "The Fight for the South Pole" ("Der Kampf um den Südpol") portrays Robert F. Scott's fatal race to be the first to reach the South Pole before his Norwegian competitor Roald Amundsen in 1912.

"*History as a poet*" 165

To confirm the factuality of his writing, Zweig provided each of the five episodes with a specific title that indicated not only the historical personage but also the exact date and place of the event. By retelling such established historical events, however, Zweig exposed himself inevitably to critical scrutiny and has been subsequently accused of many inaccuracies, misunderstandings, and misrepresentations.[10] Indeed, Zweig might not have adhered strictly to one of the most central rules of historical writing set down in his lecture: to faithfully serve history and not to garnish, romanticize, or heroize it. In his *Shooting Stars* Zweig extensively employed metaphorical language, mythical analogies, parallelism, and narration in the present tense; these literary devices intensified the readers' experience of excitement and suspense and might have been aimed at creating an illusion of immediacy and authenticity. On the other hand, these techniques were also essential with respect to another crucial demand expressed in the lecture: poets must be psychologists. Rather than focusing on the actual, abstract, and impersonal historical events he chose to analyze the "psychological undercurrents" that propelled a particular incident.[11]

The conflict between internal and external worlds, fact and fiction, is also one of the pivotal ideas of Zweig's biography of Balzac. Zweig had been fascinated with the French writer for many decades.[12] He had started to plan a major biographical work in 1904. Beginning in 1906, he published several shorter and longer works on Balzac; the 1920 compilation *Master Builders* features his most famous essay "Balzac," which has received much more scholarly attention than his book project.[13] For his "Big Balzac," as he called it, he compiled a manuscript of 600 pages and an additional 2,000 pages of notes. As a collector of autographs, he acquired more than 700 pages of proofs with handwritten corrections by Balzac. Depression, war, and exile prevented him, however, from finishing the book. It was posthumously edited and published by Richard Friedenthal in 1946.[14] Some scholars have critically reviewed Zweig's "Big Balzac," most famously Theodor W. Adorno, who blisteringly attacked both Zweig's singular focus on the psychology of a creative man as well as the abstract ideas and clichés ingrained in his work.[15] Generating a discourse of the great and the exceptional, Zweig certainly did not stint with superlatives or references to the most famous and the most important places or figures, in particular Napoleon. Others, on the other hand, have declared *Balzac* to be the "most complete application" of his theories on biographical writing.[16] Although the historical accuracy of the work definitely did not comport with strictly applied scholarly standards, Zweig drew extensively from archival material. Zweig did not cover up Balzac's many weaknesses and failures and, to the contrary, actually discussed them at length. He thus at least partially fulfilled his own requirement for an objective and balanced biographical approach.

In his lecture "History as a Poet" Zweig developed a poetology of historical and biographical writing that he applied, more or less successfully, in his literary works. In his view history and literature were entangled in

166   Arnhilt Johanna Hoefle

a complex and, most importantly, inseparable and mutually constitutive relationship. Consequently, in his opinion the genre of literary biography was a legitimate form of historiography. Triggered and sustained by his biographical works, Zweig's successful reception in China first of all needs to be understood against this poetology, on the one hand, and the Chinese tradition of life writing, on the other. In fact, the translators of Zweig's work could rely on conventions of life writing that, for thousands of years, had connected not only literature and historiography but also the genre of biography with politics.

Zweig and the Chinese trajectories of life writing

Since its beginnings, biographical writing in China has been deeply rooted in historiography. Although historical works had already included portraits of individuals during the Spring and Autumn (*Chun qiu*) period (770–479 BCE), as well as that of the Warring States (*Zhan guo*) (476–221 BCE), the historian Sima Qian (145–90 BCE) is generally considered the first biographer in China.[17] In his *Historical Records* (*Shiji*) he delivered the first comprehensive history of China from the earliest times to his own era. In addition to genealogical tables (*biao*) and chapters on the state and culture (*shu*), the bulk of this work consisted of biographies: biographies of emperors (*benji*), of feudal lords and celebrated personages (*shijia*), as well as collected biographies of exemplary people and other figures in society (*liezhuan*). His technique of presenting history through a series of biographies became the model for all later dynastic histories (*zhengshi*). Despite an emphasis on historical facts, this traditional form of life writing was characterized by a strong didactic zeal, with the eulogies of public achievements intended to illustrate general principles.

Sima Qian's *Shiji* established strict generic conventions. Neither the style nor the format of life writing changed significantly until the late nineteenth century. After the failure of the Hundred Days' Reform (*Wuxu bianfa*) of 1898, Liang Qichao began to promote biography as an instrument of national reform. In exile in Japan, he helped introduce foreign theories and models of biographical writing, in particular Japanese, English, American, and French. He also wrote several Western-style biographies of Chinese and Western historical figures and formulated the first modern Chinese definitions of life writing in his theoretical writings.[18] He approached life writing partly as historiography and partly as literature, and believed it to have a strong social and political function. During the years leading up to the fall of the Chinese empire in 1911, newspapers and journals, following a clear anti-imperial and nationalistic agenda, featured numerous biographies of national heroes and revolutionaries.

In their attempt to uncouple biography from its long-standing connection to official historiography, intellectuals associated with the New Culture Movement (*Xin wenxue yundong*) in the late 1910s and 1920s translated

"History as a poet"   167

Western biographical works and theoretical literature on an unprecedented scale.[19] Following its success in Europe, Lytton Strachey's *Eminent Victorians* quickly proved to be similarly influential in China. Intellectuals and writers, such as Hu Shi in his essay "Biographical Literature" ("Zhuanji wenxue," 1914) and Yu Dafu in his essays "Biographical Literature" ("Zhuanji wenxue," 1933) and "What Is Biographical Literature" ("Shenme shi zhuanji wenxue," 1935), critiqued the stagnant conventions of life writing and argued that Chinese biographers needed to learn from their European counterparts. The main focus should be on the development of a person's character. Distancing themselves from stereotypical biographies that only glorified and flattered the portrayed figure, they argued that the subject's individual life story, thoughts, and personality, with both its positive and negative aspects, as well as the individual's intellectual and psychological development, must be at the center of the text. Modern Chinese biographies should demystify and expose rather than eulogize their subjects. The sizable volume of biographical writing published in the 1920s and 1930s also reflected new interest in humanism, individualism, and in particular psychology.[20] Freud's psychoanalysis was received with great enthusiasm after its introduction into China. The genre of life writing became a medium that allowed writers and intellectuals of the New Culture Movement to express their critique of the Confucian subordination of the individual, which had been viewed primarily in respect to its role in society. Not only did they redefine biography as a distinct art form independent from official historical writing, but they also developed different styles of biographical writing.

Stefan Zweig's works first received attention in China as part of this process of importing European literature and theory. Despite the great interest in his novellas, in particular *Letter from an Unknown Woman* (*Brief einer Unbekannten*), *Amok* (*Der Amokläufer*), and *The Governess* (*Die Gouvernante*), his biographical texts were among his most popular works in China. In recognition of Romain Rolland's sixtieth birthday, Zweig's biography of the French pacifist writer, intellectual, and Nobel Prize laureate was the first of his works to be translated into Chinese, in 1926. Between October 10 and December 25, a translation by Zhang Dinghuang was serialized in the journal *Wilderness* (*Mangyuan*) in six installments.[21] In 1928 the Commercial Press (*Shangwu yinshuguan*) in Shanghai published a translation by Yang Renpian in book form.[22] In his preface, Yang invited his readers to study the "great but difficult life" of the French writer, who was already well known in China at the time. Rolland persevered as a pacifist and idealist during the war and was thus a "lighthouse" that would guide the way for the discouraged and bewildered youth of China, who were standing at a crossroads and desperately trying to discern the right way to go. Rolland was a "comforter" to China, a nation suffering from its own serious injuries. Yang also acknowledged the friendship between Rolland and his biographer Zweig, who remained friends despite being on opposite sides during the war. In Yang's estimation, as both a literary work and as a piece

168　*Arnhilt Johanna Hoefle*

of research on Rolland, there were only two characters needed to describe Zweig's biography: it was "beautiful" (*meili*). In short and concise chapters, Zweig was able to engage and encourage his readers.[23]

Several of Zweig's biographical works on other celebrities followed the publication of *Romain Rolland*, including shorter essays on Leo Tolstoy, Fyodor Dostoyevsky, Johann Wolfgang von Goethe, Friedrich Hölderlin, Jakob Wassermann, and Auguste Rodin. Many of these translations were similarly connected to significant anniversaries, such as Tolstoy's centenary in 1928 and the 30th anniversary of his death in 1940 or the 120th anniversary of Dostoyevsky's birthday in 1941. As demonstrated by Yang's preface on Rolland, Zweig's biographies served a specific function during the 1920s. Through their introduction of European thought, they were selected as guides for "orientation" at a time when China as a nation was indeed at a turning point following the collapse of the empire. Zweig's work was commended for its scientific qualities on the one hand, and for its stylistic beauty on the other. However, the main interest in Zweig's work during the New Culture Movement was his psychological approach to biographical writing. Zweig was praised for allowing his Chinese readers insight into a person's struggles during difficult times. Zweig's biographies therefore enabled not just the first translations of his works into Chinese in the 1920s. They also played a major part in reconceptualizing life writing as a powerful tool in the ongoing fight for China's political and cultural modernization. In their depictions of individuals and their private emotions, these works were purposefully chosen for translation because of the contrast they provided to traditional Confucian imperatives and their focus on familial and social duties.

Zweig's biographies in communist China

The ideological radicalization which occurred over the course of the Civil War between the Nationalists and the Communists in the 1930s and 1940s significantly changed the selection and presentation of subjects in biographical works. Following the foundation of the PRC in October 1949, the production and reception of literature had to strictly follow the guidelines outlined by Mao in his speeches in Yan'an in May 1942: Literature was to serve the communist revolution, and socialist realism was its approved form. Biographical works became immensely popular during this period. Between 1949 and 1966 more than five hundred biographies were published in China (not including translated works).[24] They usually portrayed individuals from one of the following four groups: model workers and peasants; martyrs who devoted their lives to the communist revolution or anti-foreign invasion; historical figures who played an important role in traditional China; and thinkers, literati, and artists who made contributions to Chinese culture. Education again became the main purpose of the genre and many of these works' authors were in fact secondary school teachers,

"History as a poet"   169

scholars, or university professors who combined life writing with their teaching and scholarly research.

Biographical writing also played a particularly important role in the personality cult of Mao Zedong. Official biographies deified Mao's life and revolutionary achievements. One of the most influential biographies of the time not focusing on Mao was certainly Chen Guangsheng's portrait of Lei Feng, a soldier and young martyr of the People's Liberation Army.[25] This biography was reprinted several times between 1963 and 1964 with an eventual distribution of over 2 million copies.[26] Employed for a nationwide propaganda campaign, it caused a sensation. People were exhorted to follow Lei Feng's example and emulate his modesty, selflessness, and devotion to the revolution. The government soon ordered massive compilations of other model biographies of exemplary workers, peasants, and soldiers. In order to extol revolutionary virtues and to expose the flaws of past social systems, these works idealized and glorified their heroes, in particular their self-sacrifice and courage, sometimes even to the extent that it has become doubtful whether they ever actually lived, as in the case of Lei Feng.

The new political climate and the rules imposed on literary production under Mao also changed the reception of foreign literature.[27] The reception of German-language literature in Maoist China was soon restricted to classics and works from the newly founded German Democratic Republic. Stefan Zweig and other bourgeois European writers had been attacked by Chinese left-wing critics since the 1930s. According to them, Zweig's works promoted individualism; they portrayed empty and parasitical bourgeois lives and reduced human behavior to biological and sexual needs, while denying the significance of social responsibilities and class struggle.[28] Soviet and Marxist critics had fiercely attacked Zweig's biographical writing in Europe as well, declaring his focus on the individual to be reactionary pseudo-humanism.[29] It is therefore somewhat surprising that several of his biographical works appeared in China during the 1950s. As some of the most important historical materials related to Zweig's reception in China, the so-called paratexts, in particular the preface or afterword by the translator, provide some initial clues with respect to the motivation behind the selection, translation, and publication of these works.

In 1950 a translation by Lou Yishi of Stefan Zweig's *Shooting Stars* was published in Shanghai.[30] This translation was released just months after the founding of the PRC. It was based on the first German edition of 1927, which included the five essays on history's "stellar hours" discussed above. In a short postscript to the translation, Lou Yishi argued that Zweig's "beautifully written" work served as a model in studying the most important events and characters of world history. Lou thus introduced an argumentative pattern that, on the one hand, praised Zweig's writing but, on the other, explicitly acknowledged the scholarly quality of the work which was intended to serve as study material for readers.[31]

170 *Arnhilt Johanna Hoefle*

In 1951 a collection of Leo Tolstoy's texts, *The Living Thoughts of Tolstoy*, selected and introduced by Zweig, was issued in Shanghai in a translation by Xu Tianhong.[32] In a more detailed preface Xu explained that the translation had already been published in 1940 but was not available to readers for more than a decade due to the political climate in the "wrong, treacherous, and oppressive social system ruled by the reactionary and capitalist Nationalist Party." Before "the liberation" it had not been possible to publish a work on Tolstoy's idealism, his humanism, and his approach to resisting evil without using force. Tolstoy's ideas, Xu continued, had had a considerable impact on Russia's Bolshevik Revolution. However, Xu warned in the preface, there were contradictions even in Tolstoy's great thoughts and he hoped that his readers would "carefully, sharply, and objectively examine them." In his introduction and selection of the texts, Zweig, according to Xu, had not only "outlined the development of Tolstoy's thought." Indeed, one of his biggest achievements was pointing out the "shortcomings of Tolstoy's ideological system."[33]

In 1951 and 1954 Zweig's monumental literary biography of Balzac was published in Shanghai in a translation by Wu Xiaoru and Gao Mingkai.[34] The translation was based on the English translation of Richard Friedenthal's version by Dorothy and William Rose, released by Viking Press in New York in 1946. Gao Mingkai's substantial preface sheds significant light on the translation's publication history and the publisher's choice of this particular work. Marx and Engels had themselves, Gao clarified, approved and commended the works of Balzac; we thus "need to read his works carefully and learn more about the life of a great writer like Balzac," Gao argued. The French realist was one of the literary giants not only of nineteenth-century France but of the nineteenth century in general. Gao further explained that the initial plan had been to translate *The Human Comedy* (*La Comédie Humaine*) in celebration of the hundredth anniversary of the writer's death in 1950. This masterpiece depicted all of the various characters existing in society, which was why some critics regarded it as a history of the nineteenth century and even compared it to a so-called *guanshi* or "official history." Gao was not able to complete the translation of the *Comedy* in time, however, and was commissioned by the publishing house to translate Zweig's biography instead in order to commemorate the French writer's anniversary.[35]

In the next part of the preface, Gao introduced Zweig as a famous poet, novelist, and dramatist but, most importantly, as a biographer. Giving several examples from his works on Marie Antoinette, Maria Stuart, Magellan, and Erasmus, Gao argued that Zweig's biographies displayed his literary talent at its zenith. Moreover, Zweig was "not only a literary master but also a scholar." He had spent decades studying Balzac's more than a hundred literary works and collected materials, such as his letters and manuscripts, which he had carefully analyzed. Because of this wealth of materials, the biography was "unique," Gao claimed. While using "the precision of a

"*History as a poet*"   171

scholar" it also showcased Zweig's literary skills, almost even "reminding the reader of Balzac himself." In the final paragraphs of the preface, however, Gao critiqued Zweig, arguing that his point of view was "not entirely correct." His most important shortcoming was that he did not strongly enough consider and explain the "objective circumstances of the period of Balzac's life and work." In other words, he did not analyze Balzac's social context. Despite these flaws Gao concluded that the book could still serve as a reference for studying Balzac due to its wealth of material, its detailed analysis, and the beauty of its writing.[36]

These paratexts accompanying the translations show remarkable similarities in their argumentation. First of all, they emphasized two reasons for their publication: Zweig's beautiful style and his scholarly approach to life writing. In this way the translators justified the distribution of potentially problematic works under Maoist censorship. They also severely criticized Zweig for this reason, pointing out that his works did not pay enough attention to social circumstances. Furthermore, the Chinese translators did not mention Zweig's interest in the psychology of the figures he portrayed. While the psychological exploration of a subject had been one of the main reasons why Zweig's works were first chosen for publication in China, this aspect had to be denied, or at least concealed. Under Mao, psychology, with its focus on the individual, was considered counter-revolutionary. The translators successfully shifted the focus away from the psychological to the educational potential of Zweig's works. In this case, Zweig was introduced as a poet who, in accordance with his own poetology, was first and foremost a historian. They also avoided mentioning Zweig's own bourgeois class background. These postscripts and prefaces mostly restricted their discussion of his life to a brief account of his most important works and some basic biographical information. Apart from the dates and places of his birth and death, only Gao Mingkai mentioned that Zweig had been forced to flee from the National Socialists to London, the United States, and finally to Brazil, where he committed suicide.[37] Otherwise, the focus of the discussion remained on the biographical subjects. The particularity of the biographical genre allowed the translators to direct their attention away from the bourgeois Austrian writer and toward the great historical subjects of his biographies. By praising the beauty as well as the scholarly quality of Zweig's biographies, these translators were able to exploit Zweig's approach to life writing for their own purposes. Only in this way could his works be considered acceptable and publishable even after 1949, at least for a short time.

The only other translations of Zweig's works that were published in China during the Maoist period were three novellas that were featured in a literary journal between 1957 and 1963: *Twenty-Four Hours in the Life of a Woman* (*Vierundzwanzig Stunden aus dem Leben einer Frau*), *The Invisible Collection* (*Unsichtbare Sammlung*), and *The Governess* (*Die Gouvernante*).[38] In contrast to the biographies published in the early 1950s, the introductory texts to the novellas all explicitly commented on Zweig's bourgeois class

172 Arnhilt Johanna Hoefle

background. Unable to refer to the historiographic value of his writing or the importance of the portrayed historical characters, these translators and editors were in need of a different justification for their publications. They therefore developed a new way of reading Zweig as a bourgeois writer who had, in fact, created strictly anti-bourgeois works, a reading that has persisted in China until today.[39]

Despite all of these camouflage techniques which initially enabled the translations of Zweig to circumvent censorship, none of his works appeared in China from 1963 until the Mao era came to an end. The Maoist demands on life writing soon also suppressed the enthusiasm for Zweig's historical and biographical works of the early 1950s. As a result of the political persecution of writers and intellectuals during the Cultural Revolution (1966–1976), many writers were censored or arrested, among them several well-known biographers, such as Wu Han and Zhu Dongrun. Any promotion of feudal or bourgeois ideology was strictly punished, and the production and reception of literature nearly came to a standstill. But biographical writing was soon used again for political purposes. The Gang of Four (*Siren bang*) instrumentalized the genre as a powerful tool in their political campaigns, for example as part of the large-scale political propaganda campaign "Anti-Lin Biao, Anti-Confucius" (*Pi Lin pi Kong*) of 1973, during which they distributed several heavily distorted biographical pamphlets on historical figures, such as Confucius and Mencius.[40]

Only the newly gained freedom during the beginning of the reform era under Deng Xiaoping in the late 1970s enabled the reception of Zweig again. As part of a new boom of life writing, Zweig's biographies, together with portraits of modern and ancient, Chinese and foreign, and even politically sensitive figures, flooded the book market with great success.[41] In the 1980s and 1990s, Chinese textbooks featured Zweig's biographical writings. They were selected in order to educate Chinese readers and improve their historical knowledge.[42] But most importantly, Zweig's works were part of a large-scale rediscovery of subjectivism and psychology by Chinese writers and readers.

In his famous lecture "History as a Poet" Zweig developed his poetology of historical and life writing, claiming that the historian was just as much a poet as the poet was a historian and a psychologist. This simple formula enabled the initial reception of his works in China, where life writing and politics had been closely connected for millennia; and it largely withstood the twists and turns of Chinese history in the twentieth century. Turning against the imperial conventions of the genre, intellectuals in the verve of the New Culture Movement were eager to engage with new European theories and chose Zweig's works because of their applicability to contemporary political concerns in China. In its revised form, Zweig's poetology enabled a short-lived interlude in which his biographical and historical writing could still be published under Mao. Facing the new communist demands on life writing, which again declared education to be the main purpose of the

"History as a poet" 173

genre, Chinese translators eagerly engaged with Zweig's works. Carefully maneuvering around the bourgeois writer, they presented his biographical writing as an exemplary case of literature that could educate readers about important writers and events of world history. After 1979 and the beginning of the reform era, these works became part of a "Stefan Zweig fever" that still persists in present-day China. Taking the specific Chinese legacy of life writing and its modern adaptations into account, the genre of the biography, as a hybrid form between literary and historical work, has thus played a particularly crucial role in the Chinese reception of Stefan Zweig.

Notes

1 Chinese characters are given either in traditional or simplified script according to the original source. Pinyin is used to transcribe characters throughout except where a different spelling is established and conventionalized (e.g., Chiang Kai-shek). Wherever possible the translation of texts and book titles is based on published editions. All other translations are mine if not otherwise stated.
2 See Arnhilt Johanna Hoefle, *China's Stefan Zweig: Dynamics of Cross-Cultural Reception* (Honolulu: University of Hawai'i Press, 2017).
3 See for example Georg Huemer, "Stefan Zweig als Biograph von Balzac" (Diploma thesis, University of Vienna, 2010), 7–47.
4 Due to the outbreak of the Second World War, the Congress was canceled. The lecture was later published in Stefan Zweig, "Die Geschichte als Dichterin," in *Zeit und Welt: Gesammelte Aufsätze und Vorträge, 1904–1940*, ed. Richard Friedenthal (Stockholm: Bermann-Fischer, 1943), 363–88. Here quoted from: Stefan Zweig, "Die Geschichte als Dichterin," in *Theorie der Biographie: Grundlagentexte und Kommentar*, ed. Bernhard Fetz and Wilhelm Hemecker (Berlin: De Gruyter, 2011), 177–90. On the publication history of the text, see Georg Huemer, "Biographie als legitime Form der Geschichtsschreibung. Zweig, "Die Geschichte als Dichterin," 191–97.
5 Zweig, "Die Geschichte als Dichterin," 177–79.
6 Ibid., 180–84.
7 Ibid., 185–89.
8 Stefan Zweig, *Sternstunden der Menschheit: Fünf historische Miniaturen* (Leipzig: Insel, 1927).
9 Ibid., 3.
10 David Turner, "History as Popular Story: On the Rhetoric of Stefan Zweig's *Sternstunden der Menschheit*," *The Modern Language Review* 84, no. 2 (1989): 393–94.
11 Stephen Howard Garrin, "History as Literature: Stefan Zweig's *Sternstunden der Menschheit*," in *Stefan Zweig: The World of Yesterday's Humanist Today. Proceedings of the Stefan Zweig Symposium*, ed. Marion Sonnenfeld (Albany: State University of New York Press, 1983), 125.
12 Wilhelm Hemecker and Georg Huemer, "'Weltbildner': Stefan Zweigs Essay über Balzac," in *Die Biographie: Beiträge zu ihrer Geschichte*, ed. Wilhelm Hemecker and Wolfgang Kreutzer (Berlin: De Gruyter, 2009), 253–71.
13 Stefan Zweig, "Balzac," in *Die Baumeister der Welt: Versuch einer Typologie des Geistes*, vol. 1 (*Drei Meister: Balzac, Dickens, Dostojewski*) (Leipzig: Insel, 1920), 11–50.
14 Stefan Zweig, *Balzac*, ed. Richard Friedenthal (Stockholm: Bermann-Fischer, 1946).

174 Arnhilt Johanna Hoefle

15 Theodor W. Adorno, "Der Essay als Form," in *Gesammelte Schriften*, vol. 11 (*Noten zur Literatur*), ed. Rolf Tiedemann (Frankfurt am Main: Suhrkamp, 1974), 9–33.

16 For example Michel Reffet, "Stefan Zweigs unbewusste Auseinandersetzung mit der literarischen Vatergestalt in seiner Balzac-Biographie," in *Stefan Zweig: Exil und Suche nach dem Weltfrieden*, ed. Mark H. Gelber and Klaus Zelewitz (Riverside, CA: Ariadne Press, 1995), 253.

17 Pei-Yi Wu, "China: To the 19th Century," in *Encyclopedia of Life Writing: Autobiographical and Biographical Forms*, vol. I, ed. Margaretta Jolly (Chicago: Dearborn, 2001), 206–7.

18 Shao Dongfang, "Transformation, Diversification, Ideology: Twentieth-Century Chinese Biography," *Literary Studies East and West* 13 (*Life-Writing from the Pacific Rim: Essays from Japan, China, Indonesia, India, and Siam, with a Psychological Overview*) (1997): 19–21.

19 Wu, "China: To the 19th Century," 207.

20 Shao Dongfang, "China: 19th Century to 1949," in *Encyclopedia of Life Writing: Autobiographical and Biographical Forms*, vol. I, ed. Margaretta Jolly (Chicago: Dearborn, 2001), 209.

21 Stefan Zweig, "Luoman Luolan" 蘿曼羅蘭 [Romain Rolland], trans. Zhang Dinghuang 張定璜, *Mangyuan* 19–24 (1926).

22 Stefan Zweig, *Luoman Luolan* 蘿曼羅蘭 [Romain Rolland], trans. Yang Renpian 楊人梗 (Shanghai: Shangwu yinshuguan, 1928).

23 Yang Renpian 楊人梗, "Yizhe xuyan" 譯者序言 [Translator's Preface], in *Luoman Luolan* 蘿曼羅蘭 [Romain Rolland], trans. Yang Renpian 楊人梗 (Shanghai: Shangwu yinshuguan, 1928), 3–6.

24 Feng Di and Dongfang Shao, "Life Writing in Mainland China (1949–1993): A General Survey and Bibliographical Essay," *Biography* 17, no. 1 (1994): 34–35.

25 Chen Guangsheng 陈广生, *Mao Zhuxi de hao zhanshi – Lei Feng* 毛主席的好战士 – 雷锋 [Chairman Mao's Good Soldier – Lei Feng] (Beijing: Zhongguo qingnian chubanshe, 1963).

26 Di and Shao, "Life Writing in Mainland China," 35–36.

27 Zhang Yi, *Rezeptionsgeschichte der deutschsprachigen Literatur in China von den Anfängen bis zur Gegenwart* (Frankfurt am Main: Peter Lang, 2007), 153–204.

28 See for example the reviews published in Stefan Zweig, *Yi ge mosheng nüzi de laixin* 一個陌生女子的來信 [Brief einer Unbekannten], trans. Sun Hanbing 孫寒冰 (Shanghai: Shangwu yinshuguan, 1935).

29 Michel Reffet, "Stefan Zweigs historische Biographien und die Gegner der 'bürgerlichen Literatur,'" in *Stefan Zweig im Zeitgeschehen des 20. Jahrhunderts*, ed. Thomas Eicher (Oberhausen: Athena, 2003), 281–92. On the similarly ambivalent reception of Zweig and the role of his biographical writing in the Soviet Union, see Christian Nymphius, *Die Stefan-Zweig-Rezeption in der UdSSR* (Mainz: Liber, 1996).

30 Stefan Zweig, *Lishi de chanajian* 歷史的剎那間 [Sternstunden der Menschheit], trans. Lou Yishi 樓適夷 (Shanghai: Shanghai chuban gongsi, 1950).

31 Lou Yishi 樓適夷, "Yizhe houji" 譯者後記 [Translator's Postscript], in *Lishi de chanajian* 歷史的剎那間 [Sternstunden der Menschheit], by Stefan Zweig, trans. Lou Yishi 樓適夷 (Shanghai: Shanghai chuban gongsi, 1950), 80–82.

32 Stefan Zweig, ed., *Tuo'ersitai de sixiang* 托爾斯泰的思想 [The Living Thoughts of Tolstoy], trans. Xu Tianhong 許天虹 (Shanghai: Shanghai wenhua gongzuoshe, 1951).

33 Xu Tianhong 許天虹, "Qianji" 前記 [Preface], in *Tuo'ersitai de sixiang* 托爾斯泰的思想 [The Living Thoughts of Tolstoy], ed. Stefan Zweig, trans. Xu Tianhong 許天虹 (Shanghai: Shanghai wenhua gongzuoshe, 1951), 1–2.

34 Stefan Zweig, *Ba'erzhake zhuan* 巴爾扎克傳 (Balzac), trans. Wu Xiaoru 吳小如 and Gao Mingkai 高名凱 (Shanghai: Haiyan shudian, 1951); Stefan Zweig, *Ba'erzhake zhuan* 巴爾扎克傳 [Balzac], trans. Wu Xiaoru 吳小如 and Gao Mingkai 高名凱 (Shanghai: Xin wenyi chubanshe, 1954).

35 Gao Mingkai 高名凱, "Yi xu" 譯序 [Preface to the Translation], in *Ba'erzhake zhuan* 巴爾扎克傳 (Balzac), by Stefan Zweig, trans. Wu Xiaoru 吳小如 and Gao Mingkai 高名凱 (Shanghai: Haiyan shudian, 1951), 1–3.

36 Ibid.

37 Gao Mingkai, "Yi xu," 2.

38 Stefan Zweig, "Yi ge nüren yi sheng zhong de ershisi xiaoshi" 一个女人一生中的二十四小时 (Vierundzwanzig Stunden aus dem Leben einer Frau), trans. Ji Kun 紀琨, *Yiwen* 9 (1957): 3–45; Stefan Zweig, "Kan bu jian de shoucang – Zhanhou Deguo tonghuo pengzhang shiqi de yi ge chaqu" 看不见的收藏 – 战后德国通货膨胀时期的一个插曲 [Die unsichtbare Sammlung – Eine Episode aus der deutschen Inflation], trans. Jin Yan 金言, *Shijie wenxue* 3 (1963): 68–79; Stefan Zweig, "Jiating nü jiaoshi" 家庭女教师 (Die Gouvernante), trans. Mo Mo 墨默, ed. Peng Zhi 彭芝, *Shijie wenxue* 3 (1963): 80–94.

39 Arnhilt Johanna Hoefle, *China's Stefan Zweig*; see also Arnhilt Johanna Hoefle, "Habsburg Nostalgia and the Occidental Other: Chinese Perspectives on Stefan Zweig's Novellas," *Journal of Austrian Studies* 47, no. 2 (2014): 105–30.

40 Di and Shao, "Life Writing in Mainland China," 38–39.

41 Shao Dongfang, "China: 1949 to the Present," in *Encyclopedia of Life Writing: Autobiographical and Biographical Forms*, vol. I, ed. Margaretta Jolly (Chicago: Dearborn, 2001), 210–11.

42 Zhang Xiaoqing 张晓青, "Si Ciweige zai Zhongguo (1949 nian – 2005 nian)" 斯·茨威格在中国（1949年 – 2005年）[Stefan Zweig in China (1949–2005)] (PhD diss., Shanghai waiguoyu daxue, 2007), 100–102.

9 Ming Ying transreads women
Christa Wolf and Chen Ran

Robert Cowan

At the 2016 American Comparative Literature Association meeting at Harvard University, Huiwen Zhang defined what she termed "prompted transreading" as the practice of finding "prompts" in a text that cause the reader to pause and analyze. Zhang argued, "They present themselves in the form of twist, ambiguity, paradox, allegorical imagery, absent presence, suggestive architecture, palimpsestic trace, and historical-cultural allusion or controversy."[1] Zhang's intentional attention to that which grabs us as we read is compelling, for often it is difficult to ascertain what it is in a text that causes us to pause and reflect, to connect one point or moment to those in other texts or in one's own experience.

One of my students, Ming Ying, was prompted to analysis by certain points in her reading of the 1968 novella *Thinking about Christa T.* by Christa Wolf (1929–2011),[2] at which cracks in the repressive ideological social façade are perceived and a light of a more individualistic hue shines through. She found that her "transreading" of Wolf's view of the German Democratic Republic (GDR) prompted a parallel critical response to issues of conformity and individuality in her own People's Republic of China (PRC). She wondered how and in what ways interpersonal relationships are guarded in China, particularly between men and women; what the gendered relationships between the individual and the collective are in terms of agency, freedom, and fulfillment; and how we understand the pasts and futures of our countries – both native and adopted – and our own roles in those time-spaces.

Thus, the first section of this essay will address Ming Ying's "transreading" of Wolf's novella, which prompted her identification with both the narrator and protagonist, as women lost in the constant pressures of conformity from all sides. The next section will look at her comparison of Wolf's novella to the 1992 novella *Sunshine Between the Lips* by Chen Ran (b. 1962), another transgressive female writer,[3] for the example of how Ming Ying transreads women in the 1960s GDR and the 1990s PRC shows that the struggles of twenty-first-century women to self-define within repressive social strictures change as societies' relationship to capitalism itself changes.

Transreading Christa Wolf

After our explorations of a Chekhov play, some Italian futurist manifestoes, and a graphic novel about Paris' legendary Kiki de Montparnasse in my Spring 2015 *Modern European Literature* class, Franz Kafka's unfinished 1926 novel *The Castle* sparked Ming Ying's interest in German literature. She wrote of it in a response paper:

> This was my first Kafka's book and at first I can't really understand this novel but as pages are turned I find myself incapable to stop. Something is holding me to this story and I feel like I am not just a reader – but I am a part of the story. I feel like I am present in the story not merely watching and feel for him because what in a real life is something look the same as K's situation that a lot of the stuff you wish to get is not as easy as you thought it is. You will need to put your effort in order to achieve. After I finished it – I felt disappointed that Kafka is dead and he will never finish this novel and we will never find out how everything would end. So when I finished it I felt empty, because I already knew K. and Frida and was sad that our journey together is over.[4]

The situations of Kafka's characters K. and Frida had deep resonance for Ming Ying, for she was acutely aware of the erection of seemingly insurmountable obstacles in one's path. She was a 30-year-old immigrant with a bachelor's degree in computer science from Beijing University of Technology, who had recently arrived in Brooklyn, taken a menial job, and enrolled at Kingsborough Community College, part of the City University of New York (CUNY) system. Reading and writing in English was a challenge for her and she was finding that she had to devote a great deal of time to preparing for my course. Her own journey in America was just beginning and the challenges of making her way alone in a new country – working, going to school, meeting new people, understanding foreign ways of doing things – was alienating. Kafka spoke to her fears and anxieties as a solitary individual immersed in giant systems that often did not make sense.

Later in the course – after Aimé Césaire's Négritude epic poem *Notebook of a Return to the Native Land* and Marguerite Duras' screenplay *Hiroshima, Mon Amour* – Ming Ying once again found characters that spoke distinctly to her, this time in a work of East German literature. The narrator and title character in *Thinking about Christa T.* prompted her to transread Christa Wolf.

Wolf's work was influenced by socialist realism of the Soviet Union, which was the result of the Russian transition from Tsarism to communism. Similarly, the adoption of socialist realism in East Germany, the mode in which Wolf was required to work, was intended to facilitate the transition from fascism to socialism after the Second World War. Stalin had famously

178   Robert Cowan

conceptualized the writer as the "engineer of the soul," which was evident in the program of the Soviet Writer's Association, which not only set guidelines for how writers should write, but meted out reprisals for those who did not conform to party ideology. The German Writer's Union served the Socialist Unity Party, just as the Soviet Writer's Association served the Russian Communist Party, to carry out its cultural mandates and control its members' cultural creations.[5] These very restrictive policies were predicated on the idea that all branches of cultural production must have positive impacts on the character of the nation's citizens and thus on the nation as a whole. Culture, like other economic and socio-political forces, was seen as a tool of the federal government, not as something independent. Socialist realist art and literature was thus meant to appeal to all people in the republic, particularly the least educated workers, and thus relied on very simple styles and concepts. As Margit Resch points out, "to serve this agenda GDR culture bureaucrats devised a set of mandates to which every writer was expected to conform. These mandates specified the following criteria: objective reflection of reality, partiality [to socialism], national orientation (*Volkstümlichkeit*), portrayal of the typical [conveying universal truth] and of a positive hero [that is, exemplary prototypes of the new human being]."[6] Socialist realism was what Dieter Sevin calls "an ideologically fixed and limited literary theory,"[7] in which distinctions between the author's ideas, the character's ideas, and either's political relationship to the state were often unclear.

Christa Wolf's ability to navigate this restricted terrain and still produce work that was and remains compelling is what makes her such a thrilling author. Through conceptual and stylistic sophistication, despite the mandates of communist dictatorship, she managed to become a bestselling author while subverting socialist realist aesthetics, stepping completely outside its insistence on objective narration and characterization. Gail Finney argues,

> Whereas realist or socialist realist writers are confident of their ability to draw a convincing character and of their readers' ability to believe in that character's fictional existence, Wolf's narrator again and again emphasizes the difficulty of knowing and hence recreating another human being, of conveying another person to readers. [. . .] Flying directly in the face of the doctrine of socialist realism, Christa T. represented to the censors a character who is 'unfit for life' (*lebensuntüchtig*): although a valuable human being, she is too sensitive for life in a socialist society. As the authorities read it, *Nachdenken über Christa T.* implied that only those who conformed would survive in the GDR, and this implication disturbed them. They feared that the literary public was not yet ready, not mature enough, for such a message and such a character.[8]

Indeed, though revolutionary, Wolf was not completely alone in finding ways to circumvent the rules of socialist realism. Beginning in the late 1960s, she

Ming Ying transreads women   179

was in the company of writers like Hermann Kant and Stephen Hermlin, who were both advocates of theoretical socialism but critical of its praxis in the GDR. Thus, these new writers began to emphasize as their primary theme the individual in conflict with society. As Resch points out, "Christa Wolf, more than any other writer of her generation who remained in the East, was a pioneer of such reforms. Aware of the author's vital function in GDR society, she felt keenly and embraced sincerely her role as mother confessor and her responsibility as guidance counselor and reformer."[9] It is precisely this commitment to ideology that informed her decision to stay in the GDR and see the socialist experiment through, like Russian and Chinese dissident writers before and after her, such as Anna Akhmatova and Wei Jingsheng.

Choosing to remain in her homeland despite its upheaval may be evidence of Emmanuel Lévinas' argument that one affirms one's being by defending one's *right* to be, by actively responding to the intentional and unintentional encroachments upon one's rights, which manifest themselves fundamentally in the face-to-face encounter.[10] In Wolf's *Thinking about Christa T.*, it is the reconstruction of those face-to-face encounters between the narrator, the title character, and others that opens up Christa T.'s unusual way of asserting her identity in opposition to the limitations placed on her by the larger society. Wolf begins with the line: "The quest for her: in the thought of her. And of *the attempt to be oneself*," noting at the end of the first paragraph that "[m]emory puts a deceptive color on things."[11]

My student Ming Ying was trying to establish who she would be in this new place far from her country of origin – at the only community college in Brooklyn, with students from 142 countries – perhaps someone different from who she was before, her memory, in a totally new milieu, putting a deceptive color on things. Thirty can be a complicated age, when one has settled into oneself but that self is changing; responsibility is mounting but the road forward may be obscure. Ming Ying had not been in New York long and her displacement from the Middle Kingdom to the other side of the planet was causing her to reassess herself. Wolf's object of study, the semi-fictional Christa T., dies at the strikingly young age of thirty-five – an age that was not far off for Ming Ying, a fact that was not lost on her. Suddenly, her experience of China was not immediate, but the stuff of memory.

Too bashful to speak much in class in the company of some other outspoken students, Ming Ying came regularly to office hours to ask me to explain passages in the readings. She was drawn in by Wolf's simple vocabulary and conceptual sophistication, by the thoughts and actions of both the narrator and title character. She found Wolf's GDR familiar in ways that were eerie and confining, but somehow felt transcendent. She was struck by the means – both elegant and inelegant – that people try to establish and hold on to their ethically grounded identities within the tremendous limitations imposed upon them by political systems and social mores – not unlike Kafka's K. attempts to do. Ming Ying questioned how a person could find one's

180   *Robert Cowan*

authentic but fluid self when it is destabilized by shifting outside forces. She would tell me which passages struck her, which prompted her, such as this passage from early in the novel, when Wolf's narrator realizes that Christa T. is someone she wants to be like and be with: "We aroused envy, we were considered taboo, even before we exchanged a single word in confidence. Rapidly and regardlessly I had broken all other threads; suddenly I felt, with a sense of terror, that you'll come to a bad end if you suppress all the shouts prematurely; I had no time to lose, I wanted to share in a life that produced such shouts as her *hooohaahooo*, about which she must have knowledge."[12] Here the narrator emphasizes that the breaking out of constraints, of breaking taboos, of unlocking the knowledge that may lead to a kind of freedom, is a basic necessity of survival in a repressive society.

Ming Ying felt that Wolf's narrator was correct – that one can't suppress the shouts one has or it inhibits one's ability to speak at all, and perhaps eventually even to breathe. She felt, though, that America is a country in which the tendency is to suppress *none* of one's shouts, which doesn't work either. We discussed the fact that Wolf grew up in the most surveilled society in history, in which she had very little, where everyone was under suspicion – in some ways, worse than in China.[13] Ming Ying pointed out a section in Wolf's text on Christa T.'s place in such a society: "Child of a star, not a great gentleman's child. Without comment. She wrote it down among the certainties. She knew: it was true. But it wouldn't have been right to waste any words on it."[14] Ming Ying argued that this passage indicated that Christa T. recognizes that, although she does not come from a family that is powerful, she has her own power that is more important and more fundamental. She thought about it a second in the unflattering fluorescent light, shifting uncomfortably on the hard, wooden chairs on which students sit in my office, as I felt for a split-second like a Stasi interrogator. Then, she presented the insight that, in communism, you're supposed to think that *the whole society* is special. That that was what Wolf was afraid of, for she doubted that other people had enough imagination for the experiment of her country to work. Ming Ying read me the following passage:

> What she wished for more intensely than anything [. . .] was the coming of our world; and she had precisely the kind of imagination one needs for a real understanding of it. Whatever they may say, the new world of people without imagination gives me the shudders. Factual people. Up-and-doing people, as she called them. And in her dark moments she felt inferior to them. Also, she did try to accommodate herself to them, to acquire a profession that would have brought her into public life: with this aim she surprised and outsmarted even herself. And she compelled herself to be rational.[15]

I pointed out that the expression "up-and-doing people" is even better in the German – "Der Hopp-Hopp-Menschen" – and we both laughed, adding

Ming Ying transreads women   181

that, even though Wolf uses the term "Menschen" (meaning "humanity") and not "Männer" (meaning men in particular),[16] I read the conservative line of thinking that her narrator is talking about – the utter inability to think creatively – as gendered male in the text.

Ming Ying explained that the world that Christa T. hopes is coming is a world of imagination, not a world of facts, that these two women recognize that they need to make that world happen in a way that they seem to feel only women can. I added that the Soviet Union had shown the possibility of a kind of gender equality, and she responded that one can see in this book that Wolf believes in socialism as a compromise between too much suppression and having too much. She felt that some kind of socialism-democracy could work, but maybe only in a small society like East Germany, cut off from the world.

At the end of Wolf's novel, the narrator describes the year-long process of her "Krischan" dying from leukemia while she is pregnant with another child: "Since she has crossed the limit, other laws apply; in the country where she now is, people speak untruths in hushed voices [. . .]."[17] It is a country that Christa has never known how to embrace. And now her own physical self has begun to effervesce out of an emotional self that was already unfixed. "Outlines are blurred. One's own outlines seem to expand; but, as in certain dreams, one doesn't stand out clearly against one's background anymore."[18] Ming Ying explained to me that sometimes one has to cross over limits, go somewhere else, to try to find voices that sound more honest, adding noncommittally that that is one reason she left China. She felt she could just vanish into a boring life there. She was inspired that, even in the face of death, Christa T. does not just dissipate. Christa T. emphasizes: "We can do wonders sometimes, I've seen a few myself."[19] Trying to get the doctors to finally tell the patient what it is she is dying of, the narrator remarks, "If the truth does look as it seems to look, then one can get on without it,"[20] recognizing that both she and Christa have been suspicious of socially sanctioned truths from the outset. She writes, "Born equal. Outcome unsure,"[21] to drive home that, just because the society imposes a standardized form of equality on its subjects doesn't mean that they have to subscribe to it. Ming Ying thought that this is why the narrator concludes, "Oddly enough, we don't have to believe what we know."[22]

Later in the year that Christa T. is battling leukemia, after a healthy daughter is born, she relapses. "At last! she writes in the margin [of her notebook], and this is as much as to say: now there is no death. It's beginning, the thing she so painfully missed: we are beginning to see ourselves. Distinctly she feels that time is on her side, and yet she can't help saying: I was born too soon."[23] Finally, after her death, the novel ends with the narrator arguing that one day people will want to know who Christa T. was, to know who has been forgotten, and asks of our attempts to re-create people, "When, if not now?"[24]

182   Robert Cowan

Gesa Zinn and Maureen Tobin Stanley argue that European "woman's de-alienation is possible through the arduous, complicated, and individualized process of self-definition, of determining who she is, not a reflection of a group, not an incarnation of another's fears and desires, but rather someone she chooses to see herself and to give voice to, someone for all to hear."[25] Indeed, this is what Wolf's narrator and title character are trying to do in her GDR – to reverse their estrangement from their society and from other women by redefining terms of behavior, and by embracing actions that had once been taboo. Zinn and Stanley focus on forces that have displaced women and *Christa T.* begins with the title character's displacement, as a new girl in a new school, with a funny accent (even though she's not actually from that far away). Displacement is one of the overarching metaphors of the book, and her behavior will invite the narrator to displace herself. The narrator feels out of place so, by actively displacing herself, she will create a sort of double negative that will help her self-locate and thus self-define.

Transreading Chen Ran

Ming Ying wanted to write a comparison for her final project – between Christa Wolf's GDR and a representation of the PRC by a female Chinese author, thinking such a comparison might reveal similarities in authors' and characters' feelings about living within such limitations *as women*. She herself was born in 1984, at the time when Deng Xiaoping was changing a lot in China; the country was moving toward Western-style capitalism, and the view of the individual was shifting, lightening. "The burden of a nation is truly not as light as that of a singular 'I,'" wrote critic He Xianyang in a 1992 essay.[26] Chinese literature's concern for the nation had burdened writers since 1919 and the avant-garde movement that emerged in the wake of Chairman Mao Zedong's death in 1976 wanted the weight no longer. His remark encapsulates the rebellious flight of young people from oppressive duty to the collective, but it does not acknowledge that those writers would show that the isolating burden of being caught between conflicting ideologies and identity roles can be more terrible than anything that can be shared. In the country that, at the time, had the world's highest suicide rate for women – five times the world average[27] – this was especially true of female writers. Contrary to the Western stereotype of the inscrutable, submissive Chinese woman, these writings depict worlds positively rife with violent outbursts of emotion and action that had too long been stifled by family roles, traditional values, and the Communist Party. Yet, at the same time, the erosion of these sources of normativity made for a destabilization of identity roles based on gender and political ideology. Work opportunities in 1990s China separated many women from their families and home regions, so they moved away from the reliance on the collective and toward more individual forms of realization.

Ming Ying transreads women 183

Rey Chow notes in a 1991 article that cultural reproduction has always fostered a masculine, intellectual national identity or subjectivity,[28] which she identifies in writings on contemporary Chinese film and literature and in both Chinese and Western theory. Female writers such as Ai Bei, Can Xue, and Chen Ran illustrate that while the relaxation of political-intellectual strictures had given Chinese writers more freedom of expression, the erosion of hardline party policies and the emergence of China into an ill-defined ideological space had caused women to move from identity roles that were very limited but clearly defined, into those that offered more possibility but were also more destabilized and chaotic.

In *Chinese Modernism in the Era of Reforms*, Zhang Xudong notes that beginning in the "Xin Shiqi," the "New Era" of Deng Xiaoping's Reforms decade (1979–1989), Chinese writers, filmmakers, and intellectuals had become increasingly acquainted with and reliant upon the work of twentieth-century French, German, and American theorists. Just as Chow addresses issues of identity politics within the sphere of literary and film criticism, the purpose of Zhang's book is to look at the historical and cultural dimensions of what is called Chinese modernism in literature and film in post-Mao China. His Western theoretical points of departure are more social than textual, though – Althusser, Heidegger, Benjamin, Bourdieu – for, as Zhang notes, in China at this time, unlike in the West, art and theory could not be dissociated from political context. Zhang examines the emergence, for the first time in the history of the People's Republic, of the allowance for a discursive space for intellectual-political discussion outside of the state apparatus of ideology, and the so-called experimental fiction that came out of that. "This fiction," he writes, "is characterized by three basic elements: (1) its self-reflexive interplay with language and narrative possibility, (2) its quiet constitution of social individuality through the language game (rather than proposing a dissident collectivity by waging lofty 'aesthetic innovation'), and (3) the potential adaptability of this supposedly 'purely fictional' style to an emergent consumer society, despite the radicalism in literary experimentation that has become the hallmark of this style."[29] While the theoretical impact of the West is felt in the conscious relationship of Chinese modernist writers to Western forms, particularly among male writers, the adaptation of this fiction to the economic changes in China is more deeply inherent in the female writers, perhaps because their own situation has changed so much.

In the late 1970s and early '80s, "scar literature" that recounted the sufferings of the Great Leap Forward and the Cultural Revolution gave way to the "introspective writing" and the "root-seeking literature." Both of these later literary developments, however, as Howard Goldblatt notes, still fit into a Maoist system that made it impossible to ignore the political dimension altogether.[30] There was, beginning in 1987, however, an actual "Avant-Garde School," whose male authors are more well known than the

184   Robert Cowan

women. The Avant-Gardists felt the need to illustrate the violence of recent Chinese history, but attempted to make it into art, dissociating it from politics, through the formal changes Zhang outlines. Outside the Avant-Garde School, though, some female writers addressed the issues of the day in more elaborate and subtle ways, as capitalism became more fully established. Chinese literature of the 1990s is one of tremendous violence, confusion, emotion, and ambivalence. Zhang Xudong concentrates on the most famous of the male avant-garde writers: Ge Fei, Su Tong, and Yu Hua. But issues of difference in perception, representation, and identity surface more compellingly in female writers, like Ai Bei, Can Xue, Chen Ran, Chi Li, and Hong Ying. Despite the fact that these writers do not discuss the world outside China, the influence of that outside world is more implicitly present than ever before in Chinese literature since the 1949 revolution. Goldblatt states, "In fact, these young writers speak to the rest of the world precisely because they no longer care to speak *for* China. The common thread of misanthropy running through much of their work and the emphasis on skewed, anti-Confucian family relations, including incest, rape, murder, voyeurism, and more, underscore a belief that they are no more responsible for social instability in their own country than are entrepreneurs who want only to get rich, students who only want to leave, or petty bureaucrats who want only to get by."[31] Further on, Goldblatt refers to the need on the part of Chinese modernists to "experience as much decadence" as possible, now that at least some restrictions have been lifted.[32]

The irreconcilability of such past and present social dichotomies, and the confusion and ambivalence that they create, is a hallmark of Chen Ran's fiction, in which women are caught between traditional roles and rebellious impulses that do not conform to them. "She was one of the writers I read in high school," says Ming Ying, returning to my office the following week, happy because she had chosen a story to juxtapose to Wolf. "She wrote shocking stories, but maybe just right for a teenager."[33]

The novella she chose, *Sunshine Between the Lips*, tells of a love affair between Dai Er, a woman in her early twenties who is a proofreader, and Kong Sen, a male dentist a few years older, through whom Dai Er is able to overcome past traumas involving men and sex. "This story was my favorite from that time," said Ming Ying. I replied that I was familiar with that story, pulling Goldblatt's anthology off my shelf, finding the novella, and handing the book to her. The story is divided into eight brief sections whose chronological order has been shuffled. We sat there in silence for a few minutes while Ming Ying read the beginning of it in English. She read out loud the passage in which Dai Er explains her own view of the world, about whether she has any possibility of fulfillment:

> My problematic views and a tendency toward aberrant thinking are enough to deprive me of the chance to become a doctor or lawyer. They say that to be a writer, you must follow even more rules. I know only

too well that my deviant thinking and convoluted logic keep me at odds with those rules. Fortunately, I am aware of these flaws and have never expected or hoped to become much of anything. Yet there may be another possibility. You might happen to share my way of thinking, which means you could interpret my unorthodoxy as a rule in its own right. Anything is possible.[34]

Ming Ying felt that this passage sounded like Christa T. speaking. Chen Ran's heroine does not intimate that any gender difference will keep her from being a doctor or lawyer for, according to party ideology, men and women can do the same jobs; rather, her "deviant thinking and convoluted logic" may limit her. She intimates later that this convoluted logic is associated with stereotypes of women as irrational. Like Christa T., Dai Er may be *lebensuntüchtig*, "unfit for life," because her behaviors won't lead to the attainment of normative, socially acceptable goals. The freedom to openly think in a "deviant" way was a relatively new phenomenon in '90s China, for both men and women, and the fact that Dai Er says that "anything is possible" indicates that shift. The same was not true for Christa T. in '60s East Germany, however. But Ming Ying thought such new thinking was something Christa Wolf seemed to be arguing should be allowed.

In the second section, "Fear of Hypodermics," the narration shifts from first to third person and the narrator recounts a fear of needles on the part of "Miss Dai Er," shifting in time from a present-day dentist's office back to another doctor's office in the same hospital where Dai Er experienced a childhood trauma. She had come out of a meningitis-induced coma and didn't recognize her mother until the doctor – behind a white mask, just like the present-day dentist – advanced on her with a needle and she cried out loud, "Mommy, I don't want a shot."[35] The mother embraced her in tears, until the doctor insisted she leave: "She knew that her mother, too, was afraid of the man. Her leaving was testimony to this. She could not protect Dai Er. Now Dai Er was alone. She stopped crying, for she knew she had to face the cold needle by herself. The dentist told her: 'Lie on your stomach, and pull down your pants.' The long needle entered her buttock and stabbed at her heart. She grew up with that needle."[36] Dai Er screams as the present-day dentist tries to give her Novocain and finally decides to postpone her wisdom tooth extraction, the needle symbolizing untrustworthy men, the piercing phallus, and the imposition of unreasonable social demands and expectations. Here her "deviant thinking" is merely that she is unwilling to passively accept a man physically hurting her.

In *Sunshine Between the Lips*, as in *Thinking about Christa T.*, much of the action takes place in hospitals and doctors' offices. There is a lot of fear and mistrust of male doctors and, as Ming Ying points out to me, many indications that the men are not as emotionally intelligent as the female characters. But, while they are non-intuitive and gruff, they are also not as tough as the women, who continually endure both more physical pain

186 *Robert Cowan*

and more social estrangement. Prior to this, but in the same section, Dai Er remarks on the metaphor that the reader has presumably already associated with the title:

> Once you lean back in the chair and the lamp lights up the area around your lips, you clench your fists nervously and lay them in your lap. The young dentist presses up close to your face from the right. You open your mouth wide and let him work on your teeth with probes, forceps, and scalpel. His large, strong fingers move ceaselessly in the cramped space of your mouth. Because of the narrowness of the oral cavity, there is tremendous cohesive force as he pulls your tooth. He exerts all his strength, and you exert all yours. If you are a young woman like Miss Dai Er and have a vivid imagination, it will be easy to associate this with another activity.[37]

Dai Er is a traditional girl who has yet to even kiss a man, and yet, like Wolf's narrator, she recognizes her own sense of displacement within gender constraints and her overwhelming impulses to burst forth with strong emotion and physical force.

She then runs into the dentist five years later at the theater. His date hasn't shown up and he has better tickets than Dai Er does, so they sit together. She doesn't want him to walk her home, although she likes him, to which he replies, "You really are a little girl. You need me, but you're also afraid of me."[38] But a few lines later she decides she can trust him. The reader knows that the time that she screamed in his office is the only time they met and the following section returns to the moment before Dai Er screams and the short exchange of words in which she indicates that she finds the hypodermic phallic. Then they fall in love in the winter after the theater evening, and she revels in the ecstasy of touch but is reluctant to have intercourse because of another earlier trauma. She describes a girlhood game she played by herself in which she made mines by digging holes, placing paper balls in them and covering them up, and one time, while she was immersed in her game, an older male neighbor exposed himself to her and was later taken off to an asylum. The man eventually committed suicide by setting fire to his own house when his wife and children were not there. Ming Ying points out that these examples of irrational behavior by traumatized people in Chen Ran's novella are more extreme than in Christa Wolf's, but they are similar. In both novellas, people are traumatized by the inhumanity of the political system they live in. "Like a couple that jumped off the roof of my building when their son disappeared after starting a pro-democracy group," Ming Ying adds. Dai Er can never bring herself to commit violence. Her "convoluted logic" doesn't quite lead her there, but violence surrounds her, especially in the seemingly inescapable past.

In the last two sections of *Sunshine Between the Lips*, Dai Er and the dentist are married privately and she lets him extract her two impacted teeth:

Ming Ying transreads women **187**

"She opens her mouth wide, calmly accepting the highly symbolic hypodermic as it stabs her soft palate. Following a momentary sting, her mouth is suffused with a warm, sweet numbness. Sunshine enters her mouth, penetrates her jaw, permeates her tongue; it dances trippingly and sings gracefully in her mouth. A pink smile spills out over her lips."[39] The experience reminds her of their wedding night and "when the young Dr. Kong Sen noisily drops the two bloody wisdom teeth onto the milky tray, the secret anguish deeply buried in Miss Dai Er's remote past is finally uprooted."[40] This is a story about getting over the scars of past traumas but, although there is an acknowledgement of the problems of the centrality of male constructions of the female, Dai Er is still "saved" by the dentist. "This is similar to many people who feel that Western culture can save China. But this is not true of Christa T.," notes Ming Ying. "The men in the novel can't 'save' the women in East Germany, and America can't 'save' China." Christa T. still dies young, after rejecting both the men and the children in her life. "Both China and America have to save themselves separately, just like women and men have to."[41]

Both Christa Wolf's and Chen Ran's stories seem to indicate that as traditional familial roles have eroded and the social role of women has been destabilized by shifts to and from communism, some women – despite incredible frustration, anger, and the need to evade the roles in which they grew up – allow themselves to fall back on the idea of being saved by men. Though they may even feel repulsion from the tremendous metaphorical myopia of masculine consciousness, they need something familiar to cling to. A no-longer-repressed impulse for self-recognition attempts to lay its claim upon a world that has changed most fundamentally by problematizing social identity roles, forcing men and women to rely more heavily on the gender-based distinctions that communist ideology tried to do away with.

What Wolf's and Chen Ran's stories prompted for Ming Ying was the heroines' senses that they are actually sane if they are seen as deviant in societies that are insane and oppressive. Christa Wolf grew up under Nazism and then was confronted with communist dictatorship. Chen Ran grew up during the Cultural Revolution and was confronted with the deracinating transition to capitalism. In her final project on the PRC and the GDR, though, Ming Ying took neither a pro-Western nor pro-Chinese approach to feminism, not seeing either as clearly utopian or dystopian, but critiquing the globalization of each, unsure how it all affected her personally. "I have migrated to the United States and I am starting to feel like there was *the old Chinese me*, but I don't know what *the new American me* will be like. I don't know how the process of leaving everything and starting over . . . will re-make me," she said. Conservative British critic Roger Scruton argues, "In the conflict between the optimists and the dystopians we [. . .] encounter a deeper dispute concerning the place of the future in our thinking."[42] And this is what seems to most preoccupy Ming Ying as a twenty-first-century émigré woman – the future, for, as she said about Kafka, "a lot of the stuff

188 Robert Cowan

you wish to get is not as easy as you" thought it would be. In the end, Ming Ying could not decide whether workable forms of democratic socialism were still to come in China, or the US, or both, or neither, but that concern was almost immaterial. Her focus was on how to establish an authentic self regardless of any perceived or real limitations imposed upon her as a female immigrant. She strove to find out how many shouts is the right number.

Notes

1　Huiwen Zhang, "Prompted Transreading: A Critical Theory and/for a Present Phenomenon," 2016 annual meeting of the American Comparative Literature Association at Harvard University in Cambridge, MA.

2　In this class, we read Christopher Middleton's 1970 English translation, which is titled *The Quest for Christa T* [Christa Wolf, *The Quest for Christa T.*, trans. Christopher Middleton (New York: Farrar, Straus & Giroux, 1970)]. Like Margit Resch, however, I find the use of the word "quest" is a slight mischaracterization of Wolf's attempts to remember, and thus favor a literal translation of Wolf's title, *Nachdenken über Christa T.* (Frankfurt am Main: Suhrkamp Verlag, 2007). Margit Resch, *Understanding Christa Wolf: Returning Home to a Foreign Land* (Columbia: University of South Carolina Press, 1997), 55.

3　Howard Goldblatt, ed., *Chairman Mao Would Not Be Amused: Fiction from Today's China*, trans. Shelly Wing Chan (New York: Grove Press, 1995), 112–29. The original title of Chen Ran's novella is 嘴唇里的阳光 [Zuichun li de yangguang].

4　Ming Ying, a response paper in the author's "Modern European Literature" class, Spring Semester, 2015.

5　George Buehler, *The Death of Socialist Realism in the Novels of Christa Wolf* (Frankfurt am Main: Peter Lang, 1984), 42.

6　Resch, *Understanding Christian Wolf*, 19.

7　Dieter Sevin, *Christa Wolf: Der geteilte Himmel/Nachdenken über Christa T.* (Munich: Oldenbourg Verlag, 1988), 10.

8　Gail Finney, *Christa Wolf* (New York: Twayne, 1999), 32.

9　Resch, *Understanding Christa Wolf*, 21–22.

10　Emmanuel Lévinas, "Ethics as First Philosophy," in *The Levinas Reader*, ed. Seán Hand, trans. Michael Temple (Oxford: Blackwell, 1996), 82.

11　Wolf, *Quest*, 3.

12　Ibid., 11.

13　In the GDR, there was an agent or informant for every eight citizens, as opposed to 1:61 in the USSR. But, in the PRC, as of 2013, over 20 million surveillance cameras had been installed. Frank Langfitt, "In China, Beware: A Camera May Be Watching You," National Public Radio, 29 January 2013, accessed August 2, 2017, www.npr.org/2013/01/29/170469038/in-china-beware-a-camera-may-be-watching-you.

14　Wolf, *Quest*, 17.

15　Ibid., 51.

16　Ibid.; Wolf, *Nachdenken*, 64.

17　Wolf, *Quest*, 177.

18　Ibid.

19　Ibid., 178.

20　Ibid.

21　Ibid., 181.

22　Ibid.

Ming Ying transreads women 189

23 Ibid., 182.
24 Ibid., 185.
25 Gesa Zinn and Maureen Tobin Stanley, *Exile through a Gendered Lens: Women's Displacement in Recent European History, Literature, and Cinema* (New York: Palgrave Macmillan, 2012), 4.
26 " 'Shenfu' yu 'lianzu': Jianping xungen hou wenxue wenhua zhuti de liubian" [On 'Examination of the Father' and 'Attachment to the Ancestors': Comments on the Development of Post-Root-Searching Literature and Cultural Themes], *Wenxue pinglun* [Literary Review] 5, no. 41 (1992).
27 Peter Hessler, "Boomtown Girl: Finding a New Life in the Golden City," *The New Yorker*, May 28, 2001, accessed December 14, 2016, www.newyorker.com/magazine/2001/05/28/boomtown-girl.
28 Rey Chow, "Male Narcissism and National Culture: Subjectivity in Chen Kaige's *King of the Children*," *Cinema Obscura*, nos. 25–26 (1991): 9–41.
29 Zhang Xudong, *Chinese Modernism in the Era of Reforms: Cultural Fever, Avant-Garde Fiction, and the New Chinese Cinema* (Durham, NC: Duke University Press, 1997), 5.
30 Goldblatt, *Chairman Mao Would Not Be Amused*, viii.
31 Ibid., xi–xii.
32 Ibid., xii.
33 Ming Ying, in discussion with the author, March 2015.
34 Wolf, *Quest*, 113.
35 Ibid., 115.
36 Ibid., 116.
37 Ibid., 114.
38 Ibid., 119.
39 Ibid., 129.
40 Ibid.
41 Ming Ying, in discussion with the author, March 2015.
42 Roger Scruton, *The Uses of Pessimism and the Dangers of False Hope* (Oxford: Oxford University Press, 2010), 15.

Part IV

Politics and sports during the Cold War era

10 From war to peace
The Allied occupation of Germany and Japan

David M. Crowe

The State Department's Division of Special Research began planning for the defeat and occupation of Germany and Japan in early 1941. After Pearl Harbor and the German declaration of war on the US, it created an Advisory Committee that studied this question further, followed by separate studies by the State, Navy, and Treasury Departments as well as the White House, the OSS, and other agencies. In late 1944, the White House created the State, War, Navy Coordinating Committee (SWNCC) to oversee interdepartmental analyses about postwar Japan and Germany.[1]

In his "Four Freedoms" speech before Congress on January 6, 1941, President Franklin Roosevelt called for a world based upon "freedom of speech and expression . . . freedom of every person to worship God in his own way . . . freedom from want. . . [and] freedom from fear."[2] Later that summer, he and Winston Churchill issued the Atlantic Charter, which promised the "final destruction of the Nazi tyranny," followed by international peace that would assure that people could live their "lives in freedom from fear and want." It also called for the "abandonment of the use of force" internationally and global disarmament.[3] At the Casablanca Conference in early 1943, Churchill and Roosevelt pledged to defeat Germany first, followed by Japan. Equally important, the president declared, with Churchill's belated assent, the Allies would only accept the "unconditional surrender" of the Axis. This policy did not mean the destruction of the populations of these countries, but the "philosophies . . . which are based on the conquest or the subjugation of other people."[4]

That fall, the US, the UK, the Soviet Union (the Big Three), and China issued the Moscow Declaration, which laid out the basic parameters of the future occupations of Germany and Japan. It would be based on unconditional surrender, their disarmament, the creation of an international organization to "maintain international peace and security," and justice for those charged with committing wartime atrocities.[5] A month later, the Big Three, plus China, issued the Cairo Declaration, which stated that they had agreed on future "military operations against Japan" that would strip Japan of all of the territories that it had seized since 1914, and would do whatever was necessary to "procure the unconditional surrender of Japan."[6]

194 *David M. Crowe*

The defeat of Japan was a major topic at the Quebec Conference in the fall of 1944. The Joint Chiefs of Staff (JCS) prepared a detailed memorandum for President Roosevelt about military progress against the Japanese in the Pacific, which included plans for the transfer of US and British troops to the Asian front following the defeat of Germany. A joint memorandum from the British and US Combined Chiefs of Staff reconfirmed the unconditional surrender of Japan by striking hard against its military and seizing the "industrial heart of Japan." It was estimated that it would take 18 months to defeat Japan after the end of the war against Germany.[7] After the conference, Roosevelt entertained Churchill at Hyde Park, where they discussed the development of the atomic bomb.[8] At Yalta in February 1945, Stalin agreed to join in the invasion of Japan two to three months after the defeat of Germany in return for various territorial and other concessions.[9]

Germany: occupation, denazification, and war crimes trials

The Yalta Conference represented the high water mark in the Big Three's planning for the defeat of Germany and Japan. In 1943, they created the European Advisory Commission (EAC) to plan for the surrender and occupation of Germany. Over the next year and a half, it played a key role in determining the terms of surrender for Germany, its zones of occupation, and the "inter-Allied control machinery in those countries." At the Potsdam Conference in July and August 1945, it was replaced by a five-nation (China, France, the UK, the US, and the USSR) Council of Foreign Ministers that would deal with general questions about the "peace settlement" and an Allied Control Council for Germany.[10]

A year earlier, serious discussions began in Washington about the nature of the American occupation. In August, the State Department prepared a memorandum, *General Objectives of the United States Economic Policy with Respect to Germany*, which argued that the Allies should learn from the lessons of Versailles and avoid the breakup of Germany because it would have a negative impact on Europe's economy as a whole, and might lead to the resurgence of German nationalism. It also suggested that German industry should be restored to ensure "a minimum prescribed standard of living." This would also enhance Germany's ability to pay reparations and restitutions.[11]

Simultaneously, the War Department prepared a handbook to guide field commanders who were about to move into Germany. It dealt with three aspects of the initial military occupation of Germany:

(1) possible conditions in Germany and the essentials of US military government;
(2) the 12 functions of an occupation, including "food, financial, education, and religion";

From war to peace 195

(3) various ordinances and laws that would "constitute the legal bond between the Germans and military government."[12]

Henry Morgenthau, Roosevelt's treasury secretary and one of his most trusted advisers, got a copy of the handbook before it was released. He was stunned by what he read, particularly when it came to the question of liberal German "economic rehabilitation."[13] He wrote the president about his concerns, and in late August the president told Henry Stimson, the secretary of war, not to release it because "[i]t gives me the impression that Germany is to be restored just as much as the Netherlands or Belgium, and the people in Germany brought back as quickly as possible to their pre-war estate."[14]

Morgenthau followed this up with his own occupation plan – *Suggested Post-Surrender Program for Germany*[15] – for Roosevelt and Churchill to consider at the Quebec Conference in mid-September. If implemented, it would have transformed Germany into "'a primarily pastoral community' too weak to threaten Europe and the world."[16] The War and State Departments objected to many of Morgenthau's ideas, particularly when it came to the "forcible partition of Germany," control over the economy, and the appointment of an American High Commissioner for Germany.[17] Stimson added that the Morgenthau Plan would do nothing to "prevent war" but might "tend to breed" it.[18] Regardless, Roosevelt decided to discuss it with Churchill in Quebec, unaware that the British Cabinet had belatedly sent Churchill a wire urging him not to accept the plan before carefully studying it. Unfortunately, Churchill agreed to accept it before the cable arrived, though once news of the plan was reported in the press, both leaders backed away from it.[19]

Morgenthau's plan also suggested that a "list of the arch-criminals whose obvious guilt has generally been recognized by the United Nations" should be drawn up, and those on it arrested by the "appropriate military authorities." Once they were properly identified, he added, they should be executed by "firing squads." Lesser German criminals should be tried before Allied military commissions, while all former members of the SS, the Gestapo, "high officials of the police, SA, the security organizations, top government and Nazi Party officials" as well as any other "leading public figures closely identified with Nazism" should also be detained until their guilt could be determined.[20]

Later that fall, Churchill and Stalin discussed the trial of German war criminals in Moscow. Stalin supported the idea but insisted that there must be "no executions with[out a] trial" because their critics would argue that the Allies were afraid to hold trials of German war criminals. He was driven by the certainty of victory and wanted to use public trials of major Nazi war criminals to highlight the dreadful sacrifices made by the Soviet people during the war, and underscore the important role that his military made in defeating the Third Reich.[21]

196 David M. Crowe

Over the next few months, the Soviets, who had conducted highly publicized war crimes trials throughout the war, now mounted an extremely aggressive press campaign against German war criminals. At the Yalta Conference in February 1945, not much was said about this question, though Churchill insisted that they "agree on a list of Nazi war criminals who would be shot upon capture and identification."[22]

Several months earlier, Col. Murray C. Bernays, a member of the US Army General Staff, wrote a series of legal reports about the prosecution of German war criminals. He argued against the summary executions of Nazi leaders, since this would violate the very principles that had driven the United Nations to take up arms. This could also lead to the "martyrdom of Nazi leaders like Hitler."[23] He thought that the German people should be forced to face the guilt of their leaders as well as "their responsibility for the crimes committed by their government." He also proposed that an international court charge various Nazi party, government, and other groups like the SS, SA, and the Gestapo "with conspiracy to commit murder, terrorism, and the destruction of peaceful populations in violation of the laws of war."[24]

Evidence in such trials, he went on, should be sufficient to prove the criminal intent of these organizations so that individual members could be held accountable for "criminal acts other than conspiracy." Bernays was aware that conspiracy was an Anglo-American domestic legal concept, but pointed to a recent study by a prominent Soviet legal specialist, Aron Trainin, who argued in *The Criminal Responsibility of the Hitlerites* (1944) for the use of the charge of complicity, a concept similar to conspiracy, in war crimes indictments.[25] Bernays' ideas met with some opposition from specialists in the State and Justice Departments, but after revisions of his initial proposal,[26] it was approved by the White House and released as *Trial and Punishment of European War Criminals* in early 1945. It became the basis of US efforts to convince its other allies to move forward with plans to conduct trials of major German war criminals.[27]

On April 26, 1945, the War Department issued the *Directive to Commander-in-Chief of United States Forces of Occupation Regarding the Military Government of Germany* (JCS 1067), a document some considered as the "Morgenthau Plan lightly disguised."[28] It was meant to guide General Eisenhower, Supreme Commander of the Allied Expeditionary Forces in Europe, as he set up his military government in the US sector of Germany, and, hopefully, for military governance in the British, French, and Soviet zones. Its principal foci were the unconditional surrender of Germany, the joint military governance of Germany through the Allied Control Council, the treatment of Germany as a "defeated enemy nation," strict economic controls to ensure the payment of reparations and restitution, denazification, demilitarization, disarmament, the creation of a new German educational system, and other matters dealing with societal health and labor,

Figure 10.1 Allied occupation zones of Germany after World War II

Source: Earl Ziemke, *The U.S. Army in the Occupation of Germany, 1944–1946* (Washington, DC: Center of Military History. US Army, 1975), back cover

198   *David M. Crowe*

the alleviation of widespread disease and hunger, communications, and transportation.[29]

No policy directive could have prepared Allied forces for what John J. McCloy, the assistant secretary for war and later the American high commissioner for Germany, called destruction so widespread that he doubted the country would ever fully recover from it.[30] Adam Tooze added that the "destruction and human misery in Germany in 1945" was "barely describable in its scale." Large parts of the country were reduced to "a rubble strewn wasteland in which the living often envied the dead."[31] The war had decimated the population, with total losses of about 7 million, half of them civilians. In addition to the 65 million Germans who survived the war in Germany proper, the Allies also had to deal with the millions of ethnic Germans who were forced to flee the countries in central and eastern Europe under Soviet control, a figure estimated to be 13–14 million.[32] In addition, there were large numbers of refugees from other countries such as Holocaust survivors who had been driven westward by advancing Soviet forces now in makeshift displaced persons camps. Another 11 million former members of the Wehrmacht were placed in temporary POW camps though many of them were quickly released.[33]

In a letter to McCloy in mid-June, Gen. Lucius Clay, the deputy US military governor in Germany, warned that the forthcoming winter was going to be harsh with much hunger. While he thought suffering through such conditions "[was] necessary to make the German people realize the consequences of a war which they caused," he pledged to try to do what he could to alleviate it.[34] Directive 1067 stated that the US would provide the Germans in their zone with enough food to "prevent 'disease and unrest,'" an approach reconfirmed in IPCOG1, which superseded Directive 1067.[35]

Authorities in the other zones had their own serious postwar economic problems, which meant that the US was going to have to ship food to all of Germany to deal with these problems, though this was not sufficient to provide the average German with even 1,000 calories a day. According to General Clay, this seriously affected economic recovery because there simply was not enough food to "maintain the productive capacity of the worker."[36] Efforts to convince the French and the Soviets to create a single economic zone to deal with this matter fell on deaf ears, since both countries were using their zones to exact forced reparations, which complicated the shortage of food and economic recovery. Consequently, on January 1, 1947, the US and the UK created Bizonia, a common economic zone that would help lay the foundations of what became West Germany's dramatic economic recovery in the years ahead.[37]

Several months after the creation of Bizonia, the four occupying powers met in Moscow to discuss "a common policy for Germany."[38]According to Clay, the Soviets had no intention of reaching any serious agreements at the conference, and used it to criticize the US, the UK, and France for the pace of demilitarization, denazification, various economic issues, and the creation of a "centralized government" for Germany, an idea that Gen. George C. Marshall, the US Army Chief of Staff, said could lead to "the [Soviet] seizure of absolute control."[39]

Statistically, the Soviet denazification program proved to be far more aggressive than what took place in the other Allied zones. Soon after the war ended, the Soviets mounted a major purge of suspected "fascists" and created 262 denazification commissions overseen by the zone's communist Socialist Unity Party. By 1948, the Soviets claimed that it had completed the denazification process and had dismissed 520,000 former Nazis from their jobs. They also imprisoned another 240,000 Germans suspected of being dangers to the occupation. In addition, they tried 12,500 Germans for war crimes in special courts and tried another 18,000 Germans in secret military tribunals. In 1950, they turned over 14,000 suspected Nazi war criminals to the new East German government and sent an additional 20,000 alleged criminals to the Soviet Union.[40]

The Soviets argued that Allied Control Council (ACC) Law No. 10 gave them the right to try and punish alleged German war criminals as they saw fit, while ACC Directive No. 38 gave them similar authority to denazify their zone.[41] Directive No. 38 listed five categories of Nazis: (1) major offenders, (2) offenders, (3) lesser offenders, (4) followers, and (5) exonerated persons. By 1949, the Allied and German denazification courts dealt with the cases of over 3.6 million Germans, and found 1,667 major offenders, over 23,000 offenders, 150,425 lesser offenders, and more than a million followers. The Allied courts exonerated 1.2 million of any crimes. Another 1.26 million Germans were either amnestied or not charged with any offenses.[42]

The trials in the US and British zones were particularly important because they prosecuted many of those Nazis directly responsible for some of the Third Reich's most heinous German war crimes. The twelve American "subsequent" Nuremberg trials, for example, targeted those involved in medical experiments, the *Einsatzgruppen* mass killing squads, as well as principal industrial, military, and government leaders. The US also conducted 6 major and 250 minor trials at Dachau that dealt with personnel from some of the most infamous concentration camps, such as Dachau, Mauthausen, and Buchenwald, and their subcamps. One of the most dramatic trials at Dachau dealt with the Malmedy massacre of 84 Americans by the SS during the Battle of the Bulge in 1944.[43]

The British, using the *Royal Warrant* of June 18, 1945, tried SS personnel for crimes committed at Auschwitz, Bergen Belsen, and other camps, as well as civilians involved in the manufacture of Zyklon B gas that was used to mass murder Jews and others at Auschwitz, Gross Rosen, Majdanek, and other SS camps. The British also tried a number of senior military leaders for various war crimes. There were few trials in the French zone and they focused on the mistreatment of civilians, illegal deportations, the theft of property, the murder of guerillas, and other crimes.[44]

200   David M. Crowe

But the most significant trial took place in Nuremberg – the International Military Tribunal (IMT) – in 1945–46. In many ways, this trial represented the high point of Allied cooperation during the occupation of Germany. Serious Allied planning for the trial began at the London Conference from June 26 to August 8, 1945 and represented a sincere effort by the British, the French, the Soviets, and the US delegates to find common ground on the core legal and operational principles necessary for the successful conduct of the trial. This was no small task given that the Soviets had no experience with open, fair trials. This created problems for US Supreme Court justice Robert Jackson, a key player in the trial's planning, who thought that the Soviets were incapable of playing a reliable, non-obstructive role in the trial. At one point, he even suggested that the delegates drop the idea of a single Allied trial and pursue other legal options. In the end, at British instigation, a compromise was reached, and on August 8, the delegates signed the Nuremberg IMT Trial Agreement and Charter or constitution.[45]

The trial itself, which took place in Nuremberg's Palace of Justice, lasted from November 20, 1945 until October 1, 1946. Prosecutors charged twenty-four defendants (later twenty-one) with crimes against peace, war crimes, crimes against humanity, and involvement in a common plan or conspiracy to commit such crimes. The tribunal was made up of four judges from each of the occupying nations and four alternates. Each of the prosecution teams were given specific crimes to deal with. The US, for example, handled the crimes of aggressive war and joined with the British to handle charges of crimes against peace. The French dealt with war crimes and crimes against peace, followed by the Soviets, who dealt with crimes against humanity. For the most part, the trial went very well, though it lasted far longer than anyone initially thought, which frustrated the prosecutors and the judges. In addition to the prosecution of individual Nazi leaders, the court also tried various Nazi Party, government, and military organizations. The prosecutors argued that if the organizations were found guilty of crimes, then individual members of such organizations could later be tried for them as well. In the end, the tribunal found eighteen of the twenty-one defendants guilty and sentenced twelve to death. Those not acquitted were sentenced to prison terms ranging from life to ten years.[46]

By the time the trial ended, the rift between the Soviets and the other Allied powers had grown considerably. At the end of 1947, the foreign ministers of the four occupying powers met in London to discuss the plight of Germany. When the conference ended, the US concluded that "no Allied program for Germany could be expected"[47] because, as Secretary of State Marshall wrote, the Soviets refused to "relax in any way [their] hold on eastern Germany" and demanded reparations from the other zones.[48] Marshall, who had already alluded to the dangers Europe faced in the midst of its ongoing economic recovery crisis in a speech at Harvard University earlier in the year,[49] underscored what had always been the key to US policy in Germany – its coordination with Europe's recovery. This ultimately led

From war to peace 201

the US to create the Marshall Plan or European Recovery Program, which went into effect in the spring of 1948. Stalin refused to participate because he feared that it would give the US control over the Russian economy and lead to the "enslavement of Europe."[50] In June 1948, Britain, France, and the US agreed to create a single economic zone and open West Germany to the Marshall Plan. Stalin responded a few weeks later with a blockade of the Allied zones in Berlin, which led to the Berlin Airlift, the creation of the North Atlantic Treaty Organization (NATO), and the creation of the Federal Republic of Germany (FRG) in September 1949. The following month, Stalin created the German Democratic Republic (GDR).[51] Over the next decade, the FRG experienced "an amazing period of growth" while the GDR suffered through stilted, unimaginative Soviet-style planning that left a stagnant economy that continued to "slide toward its ineluctable final crisis" at the end of the communist era.[52]

Japan: the American occupation and the Tokyo IMT Trial

The defeat and occupation of Japan proved to be very different from what took place in Germany, in large part because the US had played a singular role in the defeat of Japan. Consequently, the US government gave Gen. Douglas MacArthur, the Supreme Commander for the Allied Powers (SCAP), the power to enact unilaterally any reforms he deemed necessary to ensure the revival of Japan's economy and its transformation along American lines. The US did create an eleven-nation Far Eastern Commission— based in Washington, that was essentially an advisory body that played a "minor role in the occupation."[53]

According to MacArthur:

> From the moment of my appointment as supreme commander, I had formulated the policies I intended to follow, implementing them through the Emperor and the machinery of the imperial government. I was thoroughly familiar with Japanese administration, its weaknesses and its strengths, and felt the reforms I contemplated were those which would bring Japan abreast of modern progressive thought and action. First destroy the military power. *Punish war criminals.* Build the structure of representative government.[54]

Gen. Courtney Whitney, MacArthur's major domo and chief apologist, wrote in his hagiographic *MacArthur: His Rendezvous with History*, that on the flight from the Philippines to Japan on August 30, 1945, he was already dictating his thoughts on the details of the occupation.[55] In reality, most of the policies that MacArthur adopted were dictated by Washington, particularly the SWNCC and the JCS.

202   David M. Crowe

With the impending defeat of Germany on the horizon in the spring of 1945, the State Department drew up a post-defeat proposal for Japan. On March 15, Henry Stimson, the secretary of state, gave President Roosevelt an update on the development of the atomic bomb, and a few days after Roosevelt's death informed President Truman of the nuclear program. Just after VE Day, a special committee made up of scientists and the military began a series of meetings to discuss "action that may turn the course of civilization" and concluded with the decision that the new weapon would be used against Japan "without warning."[56] Stimson told Truman that he thought it would take an invasion force of 5 million to take the Japanese home islands, with as many as a million US casualties. He also thought it would take nine to ten months to conquer Japan based on the "last ditch [Japanese] defense" of Iwo Jima and Okinawa. This would leave Japan "more thoroughly destroyed" than Germany. He also argued

> that the attempt to exterminate her armies and her population by gunfire or other means will tend to produce a fusion of race solidarity and antipathy which has no analogy in the case of Germany. We have a national interest in creating, if possible, a condition wherein the Japanese nation may live as a peaceful and useful member of the future Pacific community.[57]

Stimson never mentioned the atomic bomb but did talk about the need to give the Japanese government a "carefully timed warning" that underscored the Allied determination to use "overwhelming . . . force" to "destroy . . . all authority and influence of those who have decided and misled the country into embarking on world conquest." At the same time, the warning should promise the Japanese that once the Allies had purged Japan of its "militaristic influence," they were dedicated to the creation of a postwar economy that could provide the Japanese people with "a reasonable standard of living."[58]

As discussions continued on the use of the atomic bomb against Japan, the principal consideration was shortening the war. Consequently, by the time that Truman learned of the successful testing of the atomic bomb in the early days of the Potsdam Conference, the only decision to be made was when to drop it. On July 24, 1945, just a few days after he and his top staff had received a detailed briefing on the bomb's destructive power, he ordered it dropped between August 1 and 10.[59] Two days later, the US, China, and the UK released the Potsdam Declaration, which stated that they were ready to unleash their "prodigious land, sea, and air forces . . . to strike the final blows upon Japan . . . to prosecute the war against Japan until she ceases to resist." It called for the removal of those responsible for the war, the occupation of Japan, the loss of territory laid out in the Cairo Declaration, the complete disarmament of Japan, justice "for all war criminals," the restoration of basic civil and religious rights, the rebuilding of a peacefully oriented economy, and "in accordance with the freely expressed will of the Japanese people" the creation of "a peacefully inclined and responsible government."[60]

It would take two bombs – one on August 6 over Hiroshima and another three days later over Nagasaki – to convince Japanese leaders to accept the terms of the Potsdam Declaration. The uranium bomb destroyed 90 percent of Hiroshima and killed 130,000 people. The plutonium bomb dropped on Nagasaki missed the target yet still killed 70,000 people. According to Takemae Eiji, the use of "history's most hideous weapons against noncombatants . . . represented America's moral nadir" and "negated the very values the US claimed to be fighting for."[61]

On September 2, the Japanese government signed the Instrument of Surrender in Tokyo Bay. Three weeks later, the SWNCC issued policy document 150/4 – "Politico-Military Problems in the Far East: United States Initial Post-defeat Policy Relating to Japan." It stated that the emperor and his government were subject to the authority of Gen. MacArthur, who would "exercise his authority through Japanese governmental machinery and agencies," which he could change, and "act directly if the Emperor or other Japanese authority" did not meet his requirements for the effectuation of "the surrender terms." Like Germany, the US intended fully to disarm and demilitarize Japan and bring its war criminals to justice. SWNCC 150/4 also underscored the importance of the transformation of its government, economy, and media, and set the stage for questions of reparations and restitution.[62]

The most controversial part of 150/4 was the role of the emperor and the "emperor institution." Earlier drafts of SWNCC 150 had discussed the suspension of the "constitutional powers of the Emperor,"[63] though by the time MacArthur arrived in Japan attitudes had changed considerably about the importance of the emperor to the occupation. Initially, MacArthur was not totally convinced of the wisdom of keeping the emperor on the throne. However, on September 22, SWNCC told him in its directive "Identification, Apprehension and Trial of Persons Suspected of War Crimes" to "take no action against the Emperor as a War Criminal pending receipt of a special directive concerning his treatment." On the other hand, it gave him full authority to take actions against other alleged Japanese war criminals, including the creation of international military tribunals.[64]

During the war, the American public viewed the emperor as the "villainous symbol of Japan's fanatical military clique," and many thought he should be removed from power or executed.[65] MacArthur, however, established a strong rapport with the emperor, and later called him "the First Gentleman of Japan in his own right."[66]

On November 3, 1945, the JCS issued the "Basic Directive for Post-Surrender Military Government in Japan Proper" (J.C.S. 1380/15) that laid out the policies that MacArthur was to follow as SCAP. The principal US objective was the transformation of Japan in such a way that it would never again "become a menace to the peace and security of the world." It also

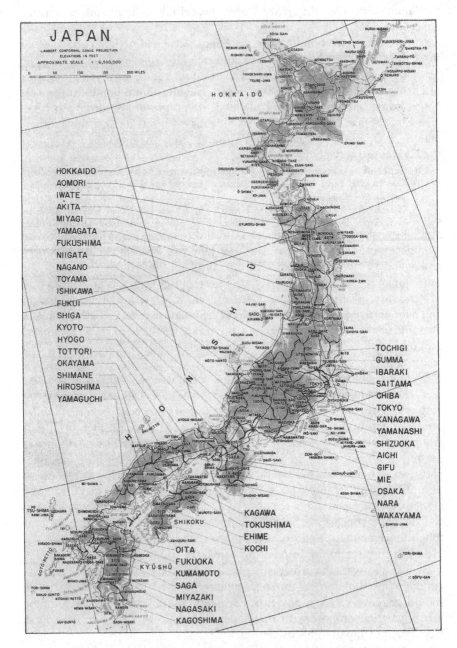

Figure 10.2 The principal political subdivisions of Japan after WWII

Source: Reports of General MacArthur, *MacArthur in Japan. The Occupation: Military Phase*, Vol. I Supplement. Prepared by his general staff (Washington, DC: US Government Printing Office, 1966), p. 43.

gave him vast authority to carry out these goals but not through a "direct military government." Instead, the JCS preferred that he achieve these goals "through the Emperor of Japan or the Japanese Government."[67]

Yet what was about to take place in Japan was quite different than what happened in Germany because of the singular nature of American rule and what John Dower calls "MacArthuresque control." The Supreme Commander gathered around him a staff driven by a "messianic fervor that had no real counterpart in Germany" and, for better or worse, changed the course of Japanese and world history.[68] Two documents, the JCS's "Basic Directive" and MacArthur's October 4, 1945 memorandum, the "Removal of Restrictions on Political, Civil, and Religious Liberties,"[69] and his statement a week later about the need to change the "traditional social order under which the Japanese people for centuries had been subjugated will be corrected," laid the basis for the transformation of Japan. He ordered the emancipation of women, encouraged the creation of labor unions, liberal educational reforms, the abolition of "secret inquisition and abuse," and the "democratization of Japanese economic institutions" with the goal of ending the monopolistic control of industry. Such changes, he added, would probably require "a liberalization of the Constitution."[70]

The disarming and demobilization of the Japanese Armed Forces were the first order of business for SCAP, and on September 24, he ordered United States Occupation Force Commanders (USOFC) "wherever they may be located" to destroy all materiel that could be used in "war or war-like exercises," while the rest would be turned over to the Japanese government for use for "civilian relief" or for the "restoration of [the] Japanese civil economy." Three weeks later, he stated that this process had been completed in Japan, though it would take three more years to achieve this in other parts of Asia and the Pacific.[71]

The idea that some of the seized goods could be used for economic relief underscored the most serious problem facing SCAP in the early days of the occupation – food shortages and malnutrition. One of Japan's top newspapers, the *Nihon Sangyo Keizai Shimbun* [Japanese Economics Newspaper] stated that "if we can be fed we don't care who has political power."[72] On May 6, 1946, SCAP released a report on the food situation that warned that if something dramatic were not done to address it, it would "make it impossible to achieve the major objectives of the occupation with an incalculable effect on the Allies not only in the Far East but the world over." Noting Japan's traditional dependence on food imports because of limited arable land, SCAP feared that it would mean "an annual consumption level of below 700 calories per day" for some Japanese. He explained that the original SCAP plan was to supply the urban population with 3.7 million tons of food (principally grain), enough for 1,550 calories a day for each Japanese citizen. Unfortunately, by mid-1946, MacArthur had been able to procure only 600,000 tons of grain from the Philippines, which provided many Japanese with only 900 calories a day. For now, SCAP concluded,

206   David M. Crowe

Japan was just "a vast concentration camp under the control of the Allies and foreclosed from all avenues of commerce and trade."[73] Though Washington ultimately did step in and begin to supply the Japanese with much needed foodstuffs, it would take several years before it was sufficient "to sustain a healthy lifestyle."[74]

Through all of this, Emperor Hirohito played an important role by encouraging "cooperation and goodwill" toward MacArthur and his reform program. Initially, many Japanese openly embraced the reforms.[75] One of the most important was the constitution of 1946, an amendment to the Meiji Constitution of 1889. Though MacArthur and his staff gave lip service to allowing Japanese politicians a hand in drafting it, the reality was that it was an American-written document. Chapter I (Articles 1–8) declared the emperor to be "the symbol of the State and of the unity of the people," whose powers depended on the approval of the cabinet or as designated in the constitution. Chapter II (Article 9) stated that the "Japanese people forever renounce war as a sovereign right of the nation," while Chapter III (Articles 10–33) laid out the rights and duties of the Japanese people. Chapter IV (Articles 41–64) dealt with the powers of the Diet, Chapter V (Articles 65–75) the cabinet, Chapter VI (Articles 76–82) the judiciary, and Chapters VII–XI (Articles 83–103) questions of finance, local self-government, amendments to the constitution, rights of the people and the constitution, and supplementary provisions.[76]

> In his January 1, 1948 message to the Japanese people, MacArthur told them that "[y]our new constitution is now in full effect, and there is increasing evidence of a growing understanding of the great human ideals which it is designed to serve. Implementing laws have reoriented the entire fabric of your way of life to give emphasis to the increased responsibility, dignity and opportunity which the individual now holds and enjoys."[77]

By early 1948, the tide of public opinion was beginning to turn against the strictures of US rule. Perhaps nothing more represented this shift in the dynamics of American governance than the Tokyo IMT trial and the Purge. In many but differing ways they reflected US frustration with the lengthy occupation but also, like Germany, the impact of the Cold War on its policies. The Purge, which began on January 4, 1946, was based on two documents – SCAPIN 548 and SCAPIN 550. The former ordered the Japanese government to "prohibit the formation of any political party, association, society or other organization or member of such organizations" that opposed the occupation, supported Japanese military aggression and related militarism, promoted terroristic ideals, or in any way hindered Japan's international relations. It also ordered the dissolution of 27 Japanese organizations with ties to Japan's militaristic past.[78]

SCAPIN 550 was more extensive and provided details on the "removal and exclusion of undesirable personnel from public office." Gen. Whitney told the press that the two directives were meant to "[b]last from their entrenched positions in the command posts of the government all those who planned, started and directed the war, and those who enslaved and beat the Japanese people into abject submission and who hoped to do the same with all the world."[79] The guidelines for those to be removed or excluded from public office were similar to those stated in SCAPIN 548. This matter was to be handled by the Japanese government using a three-page questionnaire prepared by SCAP. Unlike the *Fragebogen* in Germany, which required a person to give details about membership in fifty-six Nazi and Nazi-related organizations, the Japanese questionnaire had twenty-three questions asking for details about military or related service and memberships in organizations that had ties to Japan's wartime past. Separately, SCAPIN 550 listed eight categories that would be used to remove and exclude individuals from government service – war criminals; career military and others with ties to the military; influential members of various patriotic, nationalistic, and terroristic societies; prominent business leaders involved in Japanese overseas expansion efforts; governors of occupied territories; and additional "militarists and ultranationalists." By the spring of 1948, the government had screened 623,456 people and removed only 6,394 from public or appointive office. It also screened 9,293 people in the economic field and removed 3,096 from their posts.[80]

At SCAP's insistence, the government also broke up a number of giant *zaibatsu* holding companies, which in 1945 controlled "49 percent of capital investment in mining, machinery, and heavy industry," 50 percent of Japan's banks, and 61 percent of its shipping. A year later, the government began to dissolve most of the *zaibatsu* and purged many of their top leaders.[81] But by mid-1947, US policymakers began to adopt a "reverse course" on economic matters, driven by the realities of the Cold War and growing Japanese disillusionment with the occupation. They were also concerned by the stultifying impact the Purge had on prominent Japanese businessmen and their "will to produce." In 1950, the *US News and World Report* wrote that Japan was "on the verge of an economic depression." The new emphasis in US and Japanese policy was no longer demilitarization and democracy but "stabilization, economic recovery, [and] self-sufficiency."[82]

Such disillusionment also haunted the only major war crimes trial in Japan – the International Military Tribunal for the Far East (IMFTE; June 4, 1946–November 12, 1948), or the Tokyo trial. Like the Nuremberg IMT trial, it was meant to bring to justice those Japanese leaders responsible for the war. The US also wanted to showcase for the Japanese people the merits of democratic institutions in action through a fair trial process, and reveal the horrors of illegal aggressive war. On September 22, 1945, SWNCC issued its directive on the war crimes question and ordered MacArthur to wait for further instructions on the fate of the emperor. On the other hand

208   David M. Crowe

it gave him fairly broad authority to create military tribunals to deal with other Japanese war criminals in areas under US control.[83]

MacArthur responded by asking for permission to try Japan's wartime prime minister, Hideki Tōjō, which Washington rejected.[84] Undeterred, he decided to try two Japanese generals, Tomoyuki Yamashita and Masaharu Homma in the Philippines for what we now call "command responsibility" for war crimes committed by their troops. The results were two "show trials" in Manila in late 1945 and early 1946 that were widely criticized for what two US Supreme Court justices called the failure of the US military tribunals to afford the defendants the most elemental rights of due process guaranteed by the Fifth Amendment of the US constitution.[85]

In the meantime, President Truman appointed Joseph Keenan to be the Tokyo trial's chief prosecutor. Keenan, who built his reputation in the Roosevelt administration as an aggressive prosecutor of some of the most famous federal criminal cases in the 1930s, seemed perfect for the job. Over time, he and MacArthur became quite close, particularly as controversy enveloped the Tokyo trial.[86] Unfortunately, though modeled on the Nuremberg IMT trial, the Tokyo trial was plagued by difficulties from the outset, many of them caused by Keenan. These problems were compounded by MacArthur's efforts to try to dictate the course of the trial, which the Allied prosecutors successfully challenged.[87]

Yet these problems were just the tip of the iceberg when it came to the trial's myriad problems. The decision by the US not to indict Hirohito created serious challenges for the prosecution, since it was more difficult to prove the charge of conspiracy without him being indicted for his central role in the overarching crime of aggressive war. Moreover, instead of Nuremberg's 4 principal charges, the indictment was weighted down by 55 charges, which the judges later reduced to 10. In addition, eleven nations sat in judgment of the twenty-eight defendants, and each of them viewed the charges against those in the dock quite differently. There were also serious questions about the fairness of the trial, since the defense was handicapped, like Nuremberg, by not having timely access to prosecution documents. There were also serious differences over the translation of these documents and court testimony. The defense also lacked adequate Japanese legal counsel and had to rely upon US JAG military officers for most of their defense. Interestingly, these young American lawyers mounted an aggressive defense of their clients that surprised the prosecution. In the end, this did not really help the defendants, all of whom were found guilty of various charges. Six of them were sentenced to death, and the rest, except for one declared mentally unfit to stand trial and another who died during the trial, received lesser sentences (which were later reduced).

MacArthur had planned to hold a second trial of major war criminals but became so discouraged by criticism of the trial that he decided to drop such plans. He was particularly hurt by the dissenting opinions by several of the judges, and the separate judgment to Radhabinod Pal of India, who

From war to peace 209

found all of the defendants not guilty. He questioned the legal right of the eleven Allied countries to hold such a trial because it was based on *de facto* law. He also challenged the charge of aggressive war, because, he argued, it had no precedence in international criminal law before World War II. He also noted the hypocrisy of the Allied victors, who themselves had violated international law through policies of colonial domination, boycotts, and the use of weapons such as the atomic bombs.[88]

By the time the trial ended, Japan was in a bit of a wilderness, caught as it was in an economic and political quagmire brought on, in part, by the shifting dynamics of waning American interest in the occupation and a struggle to find its own way in an ever changing world. The outbreak of the Korean War in the summer of 1950 changed all of this, and, as one Japanese economist noted, "the tragedy of war in a neighbouring country turned out to be a windfall boon for the Japanese economy." Prime Minister Shigeru Yoshia called it a "gift of the gods."[89] A year later, 51 countries concluded a peace treaty with Japan, and in 1952 the US and Japan signed it as well as an Administrative Agreement and Security treaty that ended the occupation.[90]

Thus ended the most ambitious military occupation of a defeated country in modern history. Though the Allied occupation of Germany and Japan are justifiably controversial, given the context in which they took place, they were quite remarkable in what they achieved. The Allies had learned a hard lesson after World War I, and that was the price that the international community paid for its harsh treatment of Germany and its allies. This was a doubly remarkable lesson given that the Allies had far more substantial reasons to despise the Germans and the Japanese in 1945, given the untold horrors they committed in Europe and Asia. Yet the determination of Britain, France, and the US in Germany, and the latter in Japan, to use their occupations to try to rebuild both countries in such a way that would hopefully ensure they would never again be a threat to international peace was successful. Today, Germany and Japan are democratic and economic bastions of strength and stability internationally.

This was no small achievement given the distinct differences in the occupation policies in both countries. From the outset, the Allied occupation of Germany was handicapped by the division of the country into four zones and the fact that the Soviets, and to a lesser degree the French, were determined to follow a path quite different from that of the British and the Americans, who sought to coordinate occupation policies as much as possible. This included similar ideas about denazification, economic development, and efforts to bring to justice Nazi Germany's most prominent war criminals. Such efforts ran counter to Stalin's policies in the Soviet zone, which were designed to create an East German satellite loyal only to Moscow. In Japan, the US, the dominant occupying force in Japan, adopted a somewhat different course that was designed to rebuild Japan politically, economically, and socially along American lines. There was really nothing comparable in Japan to the aggressive denazification programs in occupied Germany,

210 David M. Crowe

and only one major war crimes trial. Moreover, the fact that China was in the midst of a civil war that prevented it from drawing greater attention to the massive war crimes committed by the Japanese in 1937–1945, and the growing importance of Japan as a barrier against the growing Sino-Soviet threat in East Asia, further diminished any possibility that Japan would be held accountable in East Asia and the Pacific during World War II for such crimes. This, coupled with collective horror in Japan over Hiroshima and Nagasaki, saw Japan and its people follow a different pathway when it came to the question of war guilt and responsibility for the vast crimes of the Japanese military in East Asia in 1937–1945.

Notes

1 Marlene Mayo, "American Wartime Planning for Occupied Japan: The Role of the Experts," in *Americans as Proconsuls: United States Military Government in Germany and Japan, 1944–1952*, ed. Robert Wolfe (Carbondale: Southern Illinois University Press, 1984), 3–9.

2 Franklin Delano Roosevelt, *The Four Freedoms*, January 6, 1941, 8, accessed February 1, 2017, www.americanrhetoric.com/speeches/PDFFiles/FDR%20 -%20Four%20Freedoms.pdf.

3 *Atlantic Charter*, August 14, 1941, Yale Law School, The Avalon Project, 1, accessed February 1, 2017, http://avalon.law.yale.edu/wwii/atlantic.asp.

4 Roger Daniels, *Franklin D. Roosevelt: The War Years, 1939–1945* (Urbana, IL: University of Illinois Press, 2016), 310; Martin Gilbert, *Churchill: A Life* (New York: Henry Holt, 1991), 737–38.

5 Joint Four-Nation Declaration (October 1943), Yale Law School, The Avalon Project, 1–3, accessed February 22, 2017, http://avalon.law.yale.edu/wwii/moscow.asp.

6 *Cairo Communique*, December 1, 1943, 1, accessed February 1, 2017, www.ndl.go.jp/constitution/e/shiryo/01/002_46tx.html.

7 United States Department of State, *Foreign Relations of the United States: Conference at Quebec, 1944* (Washington, DC: U.S. Government Printing Office, 1944), 442–66.

8 B.J.C. McKercher, "Toward the Postwar Settlement: Winston Churchill and the Second Quebec Conference," in *The Second Quebec Conference Revisited*, ed. David B. Wolner (New York: St. Martin's Press, 1998), 36; Roy Jenkins, *Churchill: A Biography* (New York: Farrar, Straus, and Giroux, 2001), 691; Gilbert, *Churchill*, 722–23.

9 *Protocol of Proceedings of Crimean Conference*, February 1945, Yale Law School, The Avalon Project, 2; S.M. Plokhy, *Yalta: The Price of Peace* (New York: Penguin Books, 2010), 216–28.

10 Report on the Tripartite Conference of Berlin (Potsdam), 17 July–2 August 1945, in *Documents on Germany Under Occupation, 1945–1954*, ed. Beate Ruhm von Oppen (London: Oxford University Press, 1955), 40–42; Termination of European Advisory Commission and Delegation of Authority to National Commanders in Chief, No. 320, June 26, 1945, United States Department of State, *Foreign Relations of the United States, Diplomatic Papers: The Conference of Berlin (the Potsdam Conference), 1945* (Washington, DC: U.S. Government Printing Office, 1945), 288–89.

11 United States Department of State, *Foreign Relations of the United States Diplomatic Papers, 1944. General*, vol. I (Washington, DC: U.S. Government Printing Office, 1944), 284, 285–87, 288, 291, 295.

From *war to peace* 211

12 Earl Ziemke, *The U.S. Army in the Occupation of Germany, 1944–1946* (Washington, DC: Center of Military History. US Army, 1975), 83–85; for the most part at this time, SHAEF was "'genuinely Anglo-American.'" Edward R. Flint, "The Development of British Civil Affairs and Its Employment in the British Sector of Allied Military Operations During the Battle of Normandy, June to August 1944" (PhD Diss, Cranfield Defence and Security School, Cranfield University, 2008), 197–98; *United States Army and Navy Manual of Military Government and Civil Affairs*, 22 December 1943 (FM27–5) (Washington, DC: War Department), 6–7.

13 Ziemke, *The U.S. Army*, 87–88.

14 Roger Daniels, *Franklin D. Roosevelt: The War Years, 1939–1945* (Urbana: University of Illinois Press, 2016), 421.

15 Herbert Levy, *Henry Morgenthau, Jr.: The Remarkable Life of FDR's Secretary of the Treasury* (New York: Skyhorse, 2010), 381–94.

16 Jenkins, *Churchill*, 754. A copy of the Morgenthau Plan can be found in *FRUS, Quebec, 1944*, 101–8.

17 Ibid., 94–95; Morgenthau, who was Jewish, was inspired by his father, Henry, Sr., the U.S. ambassador to the Ottoman Empire during World War I, who was among the first diplomats to speak out against the Armenian Genocide and provide the world with details of the Turkish massacres of Armenians. David M. Crowe, *War Crimes, Genocide, and Justice: A Global History* (New York: Palgrave Macmillan, 2014), 107.

18 Ibid., 100.

19 David B. Woolner, "Coming to Grips with the 'German Problem': Roosevelt, Churchill and the Morgenthau Plan at the Second Quebec Conference," in *The Second Quebec Conference Revisited: Waging War, Formulating Peace: Canada, Great Britain, and the United States in 1944–1945*, ed. David B. Woolner (New York; St. Martin's Press, 1998), 85–89.

20 *FRUS, Quebec, 1944*, 105–6.

21 Ibid., 92, 466–67; Crowe, *War Crimes*, 155–56.

22 Crowe, *War* Crimes, 157.

23 Telford Taylor, *The Anatomy of the Nuremberg Trials* (Boston, MA: Little, Brown, 1992), 35.

24 Ibid., 36.

25 A.N. Trainin, *Criminal Responsibility of the Hitlerites*, Part 2 (Moscow: Legal Publishing House, NKU, 1944), 109–17.

26 *Memorandum from Murray C. Bernays and D.W. Brown*, January 4, 1945. Rosenman Papers, War Crimes Files, October 1944–November 1945. Harry S. Truman Presidential Museum & Library, 1–6.

27 Crowe, *War Crimes*, 158–59; *Memorandum for the President: Trial and Punishment of Nazi War Criminals*, January 22, 1945, Yale Law School, The Avalon Project, 1–12, accessed March 1, 2017, http://avalon.law.yale.edu/imt/jack01.asp.

28 Earl Ziemke, "Improvising Stability and Change in Postwar Germany," in *Americans as Proconsuls: United States Military Government in Germany and Japan, 1944–1952*, ed. Robert Wolfe (Carbondale: Southern Illinois University Press, 1984), 58.

29 *Directive to the Commander-in-Chief of the United States Forces of Occupation Regarding the Military Government of Germany* (JCS 1067), April 1945.

30 Thomas Alan Schwartz, *America's Germany: John J. McCloy and the Federal Republic of Germany* (Cambridge, MA: Harvard University Press, 1991), 22.

31 Adam Tooze, *The Wages of Destructive: The Making and Breaking of the Nazi Economy* (New York: Viking, 2006), 672.

32 Ibid., 672; Michael Neiberg, *Potsdam: The End of World War II and the Remaking of Europe* (New York: Basic Books, 2015).

212 *David M. Crowe*

33 Mark Wyman, *DPs: Europe's Displaced Persons, 1945–1951* (Ithaca, NY: Cornell University Press, 1998), 17–18, 247–48; Tooze, *Wages of Destruction*, 672.
34 *The Papers of General Lucius D. Clay: Germany, 1945–1949*, ed. Jean Edward Smith, vol. I (Bloomington: Indiana University Press, 1974), 24.
35 *Directive of the United States Joint Chiefs of Staff to the Commander-in-Chief of the United States Forces of Occupation Regarding the Military Government of Germany* (JCS 1067), April 1945, in *Documents on Germany under Occupation, 1945–1954*, ed. Beate Ruhm von Oppen (Oxford: Oxford University Press, 1955), 16; *Directive to Commander in Chief of United States Forces of Occupation Regarding the Military Government of Germany* (IPCOG 1), April 25, 1945, in United States Department of State, *Foreign Relations of the United States, Diplomatic Papers 1945*, vol. III (Washington, DC: U.S. Government Printing Office, 1945), 494.
36 Lucius D. Clay, *Decision in Germany* (Westport, CT: Greenwood, 1970), 163.
37 John H. Backer, *Priming the German Economy: American Occupation Policies, 1945–1948* (Durham, NC: Duke University Press, 1971), 183–87.
38 Clay, *Decision in Germany*, 150.
39 Ibid., 152–53; Filip Slaveski, *The Soviet Occupation of Germany: Hunger, Mass Violence, and the Struggle for Peace, 1945–1947* (Cambridge: Cambridge University Press, 2013), 145–46.
40 United Nations War Crimes Commission, *Law Reports of Trials of War Criminals*, vol. III (Buffalo: Williams S. Hein, 1997), 24–49, 72; Jeffrey Herf, *Divided Memory: The Nazi Past in the Two Germanies* (Cambridge, MA: Harvard University Press, 1997), 72–73; Dick de Mildt, *In the Name of the People: Perpetrators of Genocide in the Reflection of the Post-War Prosecution in West Germany* (The Hague: Martinus Nijhhoff, 1996), 18–19.
41 *Control Council Law No. 10: Punishment of Persons Guilty of War Crimes, Crimes Against Peace and Against Humanity*, 20 December 1945, in *Documents on Germany Under Occupation, 1945–1954*, 97–101; *Control Council Directive No. 38: The Arrest and Punishment of War Criminals, Nazis and Militarists and the Internment, Control and Surveillance of Potentially Dangerous Germans*, in Office of Military Government for Germany (US), *Denazification Report of the Military Governor (1 April 1947–30 April 1948)*, No. 34, 14–26.
42 Konrad H. Jarausch, *After Hitler: Recivlizing Germans, 1945–1995*, trans. Brandon Hunziker (Oxford: Oxford University Press, 2006), 54.
43 Institute of Criminal Law, University of Amsterdam, *The Dachau Trials: Trials by U.S. Army Courts in Europe, 1945–1948*, 1, accessed March 6, 2017, http://www1.jur.uva.nl/junsvJUNSVEng/DTRR/Dachau%20trials%20intro.htm.
44 *Royal Warrant*, June 18, 1945, UNWCC, *Law Reports*, vol. I, 95, 97, 101, 102–3, 105, 107; United Nations War Crimes Commission, *History of the United Nations War Crimes Commission and the Development of the Laws of War* (Buffalo: William S. Hein, 2006), 518; UNWCC, *Law Reports*, vol. II, 1–3, 35, 4, 14, 62–63, 101, 121–25, 407–8; David M. Crowe, *The Holocaust: Roots, History, and Aftermath* (Boulder, CO: Westview Press, 2008), 407, 415; Wilhelm Lindsey, "Zyklon B, Auschwitz und der Prozeß gegen Dr. Bruno Tesch," *Vierteljahreshelfe für freie Geschichtsfforschung* I, no. 2 (2001): 169–88; UNWCC, *Law Reports*, vol. XI, 18–29; UNWCC, vol. VIII, 9–14; Henry Russo, "Did the Purge Achieve Its Goals," in *Memory, the Holocaust, and French Justice; the Bousquet and Touvier Affairs*, ed. Richard J. Goslan (Hanover: University Press of New England, 1996), 24, 101; UNWCC, *Law Reports*, vol. III, 23–49, 93–99.
45 The full transcript of the London Conference can be found in *Report of Robert H. Jackson, United States Representative to the International Conference*

From war to peace 213

on Military Trials, London, 1945 (Washington, DC: U.S. Government Printing Office, 1949), 1–441 *passim*.

46 Crowe, *War Crimes*, 151–93.

47 Michael Wala, "'Ripping Holes in the Iron Curtain': The Council on Foreign Relations and Germany, 1945–1950," in *American Policy and the Reconstruction of West Germany, 1945–1955*, ed. Jeffrey M. Diefendorf, Axel Frohn, and Hermann-Josef Rupieper (Cambridge: Cambridge University Press, 1993), 15.

48 Fifth Meeting of the Council of Foreign Ministers, London, November 25–December 16, 1947. *Report by Secretary Marshall*, December 19, 1947, 3–4. Yale Law School, The Avalon Project, accessed March 6, 2017, http://avalon.law.yale.edu/20th_century/decade24.asp.

49 Press Release, No. 455, June 4, 1947, GCMRL/G. George C. Marshall Papers [Secretary of State, Speeches and Statements], 3; the impetus for the Marshall Plan came first from President Truman, who, in a speech to Congress on March 12, 1947, noted that the peoples of a number of countries in the world had fallen under "totalitarian regimes," and that it was the responsibility of the US to support those who opposed such subjugations." He added that the best aid the US could provide was "economic and financial." Thus was born the Truman Doctrine. *President Harry S. Truman's Address Before a Joint Session of Congress, March 12, 1947*, Yale Law School, The Avalon Project, 1–3, accessed March 6, 2017, http://avalon.law.yale.edu/20th_century/trudoc.asp

50 Dmitri Volkogonov, *Stalin: Triumph & Tragedy*, trans. Harold Shukman (New York: Weidenfeld, 1991), 531, 534.

51 Jarausch, *After Hitler*, 86.

52 Ibid., 90–92.

53 The members of the Far Eastern Commission were Australia, Canada, France, India, the Netherlands, New Zealand, the Republic of China, the Soviet Union, the U.K., and the U.S. Burma and Pakistan were added in 1949. Takemae Eiji, *Inside GHQ: The Allied Occupation of Japan and Its Legacy*, trans. Robert Ricketts and Sebastian Swann (New York: Continuum, 2002), 96–99.

54 Douglas MacArthur, *Reminisces* (New York: McGraw-Hill, 1964), 282–83; though MacArthur has several tours of duty in Asia before World War II and served as the Field Marshal of the Philippine army from 1935 to 1941, "he had no serious first-hand experience with Japan, apart from war." John W. Dower, *Embracing Defeat: Japan in the Wake of World War II* (New York: W.W. Norton, 1999), 223.

55 Courtney Whitney, *MacArthur: His Rendevous with History* (New York: Alfred A. Knopf, 1956), 213.

56 David McCullough, *Truman* (New York: Simon and Schuster, 1992), 390–91.

57 Henry L. Stimson, "The Decision to Use the Atomic Bomb," *Harper's Magazine* 194, no. 1161 (February 1947): 102 [97–107]; in June 1945, the U.S. Joint Planning Committee estimated that the Allies could expect 220,000 casualties during the invasion of Kyushu and the Tokyo plain. Douglas J. MacEachin, *The Final Months of the War with Japan*. Central Intelligence Agency (2007), 9, accessed February 1, 2017, www.cia.gov/library/center-for-the-study-of-intelligence/csi-pub; Stimson, "The Decision," 103–4; McCullough, *Truman*, 400–401.

58 Stimson, "The Decision," 103–4.

59 McCullough, *Truman*, 428, 430–31, 435–37.

60 *The Potsdam Declaration*, July 26, 1945, 1–2, accessed February 1, 2017, www.ndl.go/constitution/e/etc./c06.html.

61 Eiji, *Inside GHQ*, 42, 44.

62 State-War-Navy Coordinating Committee, *Politico-Military Problems in the Far East: United States Initial Post-Defeat Policy Relating to Japan* (SWNCC

214   *David M. Crowe*

150/4), 21 September 1945, 1–4, accessed February 1, 2017, www.ndl.go.jp/constitution/e/shiryo/01/022_2tx.html.

63 State-War-Navy Coordinating Committee, *Politico-Military Problems in the Far East: United States Initial Post-Defeat Policy Relating to Japan* (SWNCC 150), 11 June 1945, 2, accessed February 1, 2017, www.ndl.go.jp/constitution/e/shiryo/01/009/009tx.html.

64 Douglas MacArthur Archives. SWNCC, "Identification, Apprehension, and Trial of Persons Suspected of War Crimes," 22 September 1945, RG9, Box 159, Folder, "War Crimes, September 45–June 46," 1–2.

65 McCullough, *Truman*, 436.

66 MacArthur, *Reminiscences*, 288.

67 Joint Chiefs of Staff, *Basic Directive for Post-Surrender Military Government in Japan Proper*, J.C.S. 1380/15, 3 November 1945, 1–9, accessed on December 29, 2016, www.ndl.go.jp/constitution/shiryo/01/036/036tx.html.

68 Dower, *Embracing Defeat*, 78–79.

69 Office of the Supreme Commander for the Allied Powers, *Removal of Restrictions on Political, Civil, and Religious Liberties* (SCAPIN 93), 4 October 1945, in Report of Government Section Supreme Commander for the Allied Powers, *Political Reorientation of Japan: September 1945 to September 1948.* Appendices, vol. 2 (Washington, DC: U.S. Government Printing Office, 1949), 463–65.

70 Ibid., 741.

71 Ibid., 742; Office of the Supreme Commander for the Allied Powers, Directive No. 1 and Directive No. 2, September 2–3, 1945, in *Political Reorientation of Japan: September 1945 to September 1948.* vol. VI, Report of Government Section, Supreme Commander for the Allied Forces (Washington, DC: U.S. Government Printing Office, 1949), 442–52. When the war ended, there were almost 7 million Japanese soldiers under arms throughout the Pacific and East Asia; *Reports of General MacArthur: MacArthur in Japan: The Occupation: Military Phase*, vol. I, Supplement (Washington, DC: U.S. Government Printing Office, 1994), 117–34.

72 The Department of State, *Occupation of Japan: Policy and Progress* (Washington, DC: U.S. Government Printing Office, 1946), 40.

73 *Political Reorientation of Japan*, Appendices, 2, 749.

74 Eiji, *Inside GHQ*, 78–79.

75 Ray Salvatore Jennings, *The Road Ahead: Lessons in Nation Building from Japan, Germany, and Afghanistan for Postwar Iraq* (Washington, DC: United States Institute of Peace, 2003), 16–17.

76 *The Constitution of Japan* (1948), in *Political Reorientation of Japan*, Appendices, 2, 671–77.

77 Ibid., 776–77.

78 Ibid., 479–81.

79 Ibid., 489, 501–7.

80 *Political Reorientation of Japan*, VI, 27, 29, 36–37, 39, 41, 47, 56–57.

81 Eiji, *Inside GHQ*, 334, 336–37.

82 Dower, *Embracing Defeat*, 533, 540, 541.

83 MacArthur Archives, "Identification, Apprehension and Trial of Persons Suspected of War Crimes," 1–2; MacArthur Archives, Bonner F. Fellers, "Memorandum to the Commander – in-Chief," 2 October 1945, RG5, Box 2, Folder 2, "O.C., 45," 1 p.

84 MacArthur Archives, "MacArthur to WARCOS," October 7, 1945, RG9, Box 159, Folder "War Crimes, September 45–June 46," 1 p.; "Washington to CINCAFPAC [MacArthur]," 11 October 1945, RG9, Box 159, Folder, "War Crimes, September 45–June 46," 1 p.

85 MacArthur, *Reminisces*, 146; UNWCC, *Law Reports*, IV, 3–4, 37–63; Gary D. Solis, *The Law of Armed Conflict: International Humanitarian Law in War*

(Cambridge: Cambridge University Press, 2010), 383; Peter Macguire, *Law and War: International Law & American History*, Revised ed. (New York: Columbia University Press, 2010), 107; Hampton Sides, "The Trial of General Homma," *American Heritage Magazine* 58, no. 1 (February/March 2007): 2, 17–19, accessed August 4, 2007), www.americanheritage.com/print/61812; Crowe, *War Crimes*, 133–34, 198–99, 221, 222, 252, 274, 284.

86 MacArthur Archives, "CINCAFPAC ADV to WARCOS (JOINT CHIEFS OF STAFF)," 9 December 1945, RG9, Folder, "War Crimes, September 45–June 46," 1–2; Joseph B. Keenan Papers, Harvard Law School Library, "Joseph B. Keenan Biography," Box 2, n.d., 1–8; Ibid., "Joseph B. Keenan to Kenneth McKellar," December 26, 1945, Box 2, 1–2.

87 Crowe, *War Crimes*, 202–3, 210–12; the court's president, William Webb, was equally controversial, and considered "arrogant and dictatorial" by his peers. B.V.A. Röling and Antonio Cassese, *The Tokyo Trial and Beyond* (Cambridge: Polity Press, 1993), 30. This is the memoir of Judge Röling, the highly respected Dutch judge on the tribunal.

88 Crowe, *War Crimes*, 202–3, 204, 205, 206–7, 209–12, 216–17, 225–41.

89 Eiji, *Inside GHQ*, 485.

90 Ibid., 503–6.

11 War by other means
Dynamics of sport in divided Germany and divided Korea

Aaron D. Horton

Modern spectator sports emerged in the nineteenth century alongside industrialization and urbanization. Team sports in particular, such as baseball in the United States and soccer in Europe, helped build a sense of collective identity and belonging among fans, whose teams typically represented particular towns or communities. Sports rivalries began to take on the characteristics of other conflicts, especially when significant political, social, or cultural divisions were involved. For example, the historic rivalry between Glasgow soccer clubs Rangers and Celtic revolves around sectarian divisions: Rangers has traditionally represented the city's Protestants, and Celtic its Catholics. Through a mixture of imperialism, war, immigration, and economic or cultural interactions, several Western spectator sports, especially soccer, were introduced and popularized across the world. While baseball (Japan, South Korea, and Latin America), cricket (India, Pakistan, and other British colonies and dominions), and rugby (Latin America, South Africa, and various Pacific Islands) were embraced in various parts of the world, soccer had the broadest global appeal by far. The game itself is simple and requires little equipment (a round object to kick around and any number of possible ways of marking goalposts), particularly appealing in regions suffering from widespread poverty.

International competition offers frequent opportunity for nationalism to manifest itself. The modern Olympics began in 1896 during a period of high diplomatic tension in Europe. Modern Olympic founder Pierre de Coubertin hoped that nationalist braggadocio could be resolved through sports, that the games could help promote peace around the world.[1] Of course, the games did nothing of the sort, and the world would soon endure the most destructive conflict to that point in history. Despite the Olympic ideal of using sports to promote international understanding and peace, sporting events are often "war by other means," to borrow a concept from German military strategist Carl von Clausewitz, who once claimed that war was "politics by other means." Fans often identify their regional or national aspirations with the fortunes of their sports teams, and athletic encounters can become venues for the public expression, sometimes peaceful, sometimes not, of overlapping identities and sentiments. For example, cricket matches between India and Pakistan regularly draw hundreds of millions of television viewers; nearly a billion people watched their February 2015 Cricket World Cup encounter.[2] These encounters are charged with political and cultural tensions, though the matches themselves have typically seen little violence in recent years. In soccer, international friendlies can sometimes be occasions for nationalist rhetoric or even violence, and in major international competitions such as regional championships or the World Cup, the stakes, and therefore fan passions, are even higher.

Beyond fans themselves, governments and state agencies have often had a tremendous interest in sports. Success in international athletic competitions can be used as a means of self-promotion, theoretically demonstrating the superiority of one's society, culture, or political system both to one's own citizens and to the rest of the world. Heavy government involvement in sports has featured prominently, though not exclusively, in communist nations seeking to validate socialist principles of collective unity, strength, and conformity against non-communist opposition. Throughout the Cold War, the global rivalry between the United States and Soviet Union manifested frequently in the Olympics, as each nation hoped to prove, through its athletes, that its political system was superior to the other. Outside tensions spilled over to the games; for example, the United States led a boycott of the 1980 summer Olympics in Moscow to protest the Soviet war in Afghanistan, and the Soviets retaliated with their own boycott of the 1984 summer games in Los Angeles.

Because of their recent political divisions, Germany and Korea offer a particularly fascinating study of the dynamics of sports and identity. While the sports rivalry between the United States and Soviet Union was intense, the linguistic, cultural, and social similarities in the two Germanys and two Koreas meant their encounters in sports would have much different dynamics. The divisions of Germany and Korea were consequences of World War II and Cold War maneuvering, and all four young nations would use sports to validate and promote their particular political, economic, and cultural systems in direct contrast to their neighboring rival. In West Germany, soccer in particular was a means of restoring "normality" and achieving acceptance back into the international community. The national team's 3–2 victory over heavily favored Hungary in the 1954 World Cup final in Bern (*Das Wünder von Bern*, "The Miracle of Bern") was, for many, an occasion that signified Germany's official return to the international community, a turning point in the new Federal Republic's brief history.[3] Similarly, South Korea has used sports to advertise its arrival as a major player in global affairs, especially via its booming economy. Seoul hosted the 1988 Summer Olympics, and Korea jointly hosted the 2002 World Cup with Japan. The South Korean national soccer team is consistently one of the best sides in Asia, and the country's domestic K-League is among the best in the region.

East Germany and North Korea, like many other totalitarian states, viewed sports primarily as a means of promoting the superiority of communist political, economic, and cultural values. Little to no emphasis was placed on individual achievement, as is often the case in Western sports, but rather on sports' apparent ability to foster greater conformity and collective strength, a strength that could ideally be demonstrated through international victories against "morally corrupt" non-communist nations. Whether in East Germany's shocking 1–0 upset of West Germany in the opening match of the 1974 World Cup and dominance in certain individual Olympic events, such as swimming, or North Korea's hopeful but ultimately disastrous participation in the 2010 World Cup, these nations' communist regimes sought to maximize the potential propaganda value of their success on the field.

With their opposing ideologies deeply imbedded in their sporting traditions, it is unsurprising that events involving the two Germanys or two Koreas have frequently been occasions invested with deep political and cultural significance. By approaching the dynamics of divided nations from this particular angle, we will arrive at a more complete understanding of how sports often embody political, social, and cultural aspirations. We will begin by examining the early development of spectator sports in Germany and Korea and the nations' involvement in the Olympics before discussing their encounters in soccer.

Early development and the Olympics

As was the case throughout the Western world, modern spectator sports in Germany emerged due to the rapid growth of industry and urbanization in the latter half of the nineteenth century. Soccer, an English import, was widely popular by the beginning of the twentieth century, but *Kaiserreich* elites, interested primarily in fostering a sense of national unity and conformity in their newly unified nation (1871), distrusted it and other sports that encouraged individualism and competitiveness. As a result, gymnastics, particularly the synchronized variety, were widely supported and promoted by the regime as an activity that encouraged and demonstrated national unity. This is why, for example, numerous soccer clubs in Germany bear the prefix "TSV" (*Turn- und Sportverein*, "Gymnastics and sport club), indicating a clear preference for gymnastics above other activities. Despite official disdain, soccer emerged as the most popular sport in Germany, as it had throughout most of Europe and the world. The Nazi regime embraced sports as a means of self-promotion, most evident in the spectacle of the 1936 Berlin Olympics, which saw thousands of German spectators singing, chanting, and performing the Nazi salute in unison in the 100,000-seat Olympiastadion. World War II disrupted international sporting events, as both the Olympics and FIFA World Cup were suspended during the conflict. After the war, however, sports would play a major role in both Germanys' efforts to establish new, internationally acceptable identities.

In Korea, traditional sports included the martial art Taekwondo, which has become popular throughout the Western world and was adopted as an

War by other means 219

Olympic sport beginning in 1992 at the summer games in Barcelona. Soccer was supposedly introduced into Korea at Incheon in 1882 by the crew of the HMS *Flying Fish*, though there is little documentary evidence to support the oft-repeated claim. The first verifiable organized international soccer match in Korea was played on March 26, 1897 between the crew of the HMS *Narcissus* and students from the Royal English School in Seoul.[4] In addition to soccer's apparent introduction decades earlier, baseball, believed to have been introduced by American missionaries in 1905, also gained widespread popularity there.[5] Japanese occupation and colonization did little to dampen Korean enthusiasm for soccer and baseball, and after World War II sports would, as in Germany, offer both Koreas a means of self-promotion and the construction of positive national identities.

Pierre de Coubertin, the driving force behind the establishment of the modern Olympics, first held in Athens in 1896, believed that athletic competition would divert political tensions into a peaceful venue, allowing nations to prove their superiority on the playing field rather than the battlefield. Its founder's vision is reflected on the modern International Olympic Committee's (IOC) homepage, which states that its primary purpose is to "build a better world through sport."[6] Indeed, the Olympics, both summer and winter, have provided many moments of positive, peaceful interaction between athletes from rival nations, but they have also seen political conflicts taint their founder's vision for promoting peace and understanding through sport. German and Korean involvement in the Olympics have involved their fair share of both.

In 1951, the IOC recognized the West German Olympic committee while rejecting its East German counterpart's application for membership. The West Germans sent a team to the 1952 Summer Olympics in Helsinki, but the East Germans were excluded. In 1955, the IOC recognized the East German Olympic committee, but with a caveat: the two Germanys had to field a joint team. The East German government chafed at this, and worked diligently to acquire recognition as a separate nation in order to field its own Olympic team.[7] In 1955, GDR leader Walter Ulbricht made clear the importance of sports to his young nation, stating that "it is necessary to raise sporting performances dramatically in order to help strengthen and solidify the reputation of our German Democratic Republic."[8] In 1952, East Germany had been granted membership in FIFA and FIBA, the international governing bodies of soccer and basketball, respectively. The West German government consistently supported the continuation of the joint Olympic team, despite its unpopularity among its public, as a post–Berlin Wall insistence of its own legitimacy and denial of the GDR's. Due partly to West Germany's politicizing of the issue, attempting to use the joint team as a demonstration of its status as the "real" Germany, the IOC voted, at a meeting in Madrid in October 1965, to grant East Germany full recognition as a separate nation, allowing it to field its own team at the 1968 Summer Games in México City.[9] Beginning with the 1968 Games, the East

220   *Aaron D. Horton*

German government would concentrate the majority of its sports budget on developing athletes to excel in individual competitions such as swimming and various track-and-field events. Though tainted by later revelations of comprehensive doping programs, this policy was wildly successful, as GDR athletes won a disproportionately high number of gold medals for a nation of its size (one gold per 425,000 people, compared with one per 6.5 million for the United States).[10] Indeed, East Germany consistently outperformed West Germany in Olympic competition,[11] though as we will see shortly, the same could not be said of their fortunes in soccer.

In 1972, West Germany hosted the Summer Olympics in Munich. The process of bidding for the Games was complicated by the country's tenuous and often contentious relationship with East Germany. Prior sports encounters between the Germanys had been rife with tension; the East had long sought separate international recognition from the IOC (granted in 1965), while the West refused repeatedly to acknowledge its counterpart's legitimacy, on or off the field, going so far as to ban the display of GDR symbols in 1959.[12] In 1961 at the World Hockey Championships in Switzerland, the West German team withdrew from the competition rather than risk playing and losing to East Germany, a possibility that could lend more credibility to the GDR's validity as a separate state.[13] One idea, under consideration in the early to mid-1960s, was to host a future Summer Olympics in Berlin, a gesture that would, in theory, promote cooperation and understanding in the divided city. Ultimately, the prospect of a Berlin Olympics evaporated due to ongoing clashes between East and West German representatives over, among other matters, issues of flag and anthem recognition. The IOC feared that granting (West) Berlin hosting rights would be seen as an antagonistic gesture, an intentional insult to East Germany.[14] Instead, in 1966, the IOC awarded the 1972 Summer Games to Munich, though this in no way solved the ongoing problem of West Germany's ban on East German national symbols. In 1969, Willy Brandt of the Social Democratic Party (SPD) became chancellor, and his *Ostpolitik* policy of increased détente with the Communist Bloc combined with pressure from the IOC on West Germany to remove its restrictions on the flying of the East German flag or the playing of its anthem led, finally, to the lifting of the 1959 ban in 1970, ensuring their use in the 1972 Games and beyond. The Games themselves were a tremendous success for East Germany, whose team finished third, one place ahead of the West, in the overall medal count, fulfilling the concept of "allowing" the West to pay for staging the event while the East focused entirely on winning.[15] Aided by its extensive talent-selection and doping programs, East Germany would improve upon its 1972 performance at the 1976 Games in Montreal, where it finished second to the Soviet Union in the medal count.[16] Olympic success was powerful fuel for GDR anti-Western propaganda and claims of the superiority of its political and economic system, despite later revelations of widespread use of performance-enhancing drugs among its athletes.

War by other means 221

The Koreas, on the other hand, never fielded a joint team, though they marched together in the opening ceremonies of the 2000 Games in Sydney, Australia as part of a broader détente stemming from ROK president Kim Dae-jung's "Sunshine Policy" of dialogue and reconciliation with the DPRK. Before World War II, Korean athletes occasionally competed in the Olympics as part of the Japanese team. South Korea first participated in the 1948 Winter Olympics in Saint-Moritz, Switzerland and the 1948 Summer Olympics in London. North Korea, though first recognized by the IOC in 1957, did not send a team to the Olympics until the 1964 Winter Games in Innsbruck, Austria. In the soccer qualifiers for the 1964 Summer Games, the DPRK team withdrew from the competition, despite having won several matches, to avoid playing the ROK,[17] an action reminiscent of West Germany's withdrawal from the 1961 World Hockey Championship. South Korean athletes have excelled in certain events, such as speed skating, while North Korea's participation has been comparatively lackluster.

For South Korea, the pinnacle of their Olympic involvement came in 1988, when the nation hosted the Summer Olympics in Seoul. True to its stated purpose of "building a better world through sport," the IOC awarded hosting rights to Seoul in 1981, partly in hopes of fostering greater dialogue and peace between the two Koreas. Indeed, by 1985 the two countries became engaged in serious discussions to host the games jointly; the proposed plan would have seen half of the events hosted in Seoul, and half in Pyongyang. The concept, proposed by North Korea, may have been a clever political maneuver intended to present South Korea with the difficult choice of either rejecting joint games and appearing hostile and uncooperative, or allowing them, which would amount at the very least to a tacit diplomatic recognition of the North's legitimacy. As part of their proposal, the North Korean Olympic Committee demanded that the title of the games be changed to the "Korea Pyongyang Seoul Olympic Games." Negotiations spanned most of 1985 and 1986, but ultimately, the two sides, along with IOC president Juan Antonio Samaranch, could not manage an arrangement acceptable to all parties. Among other issues, the countries' committees could not agree on which or how many events each would host, and the North had insisted on having its own separate organizing committee.[18]

Having failed to secure co-hosting rights, North Korea boycotted the games, their second consecutive abstention from the Summer Olympics, because their participation would have been seen as a tacit acknowledgment of their counterpart's national legitimacy.[19] DPRK leader Kim Il-sung attempted, unsuccessfully, to convince major allies such as the Soviet Union and China to boycott the games, which surely added to the North's frustration.[20] This frustration and failure either to co-host or to lead a mass boycott may well have led to the events of November 29, 1987, when a bomb placed by North Korean agents destroyed Korean Airlines Flight 858, in transit from Baghdad to Seoul, killing over 100 people. This was evidently an attempt to sabotage the Seoul Games by scaring away attendees, though

North Korea denied any involvement with the attack.[21] Despite the bombing, the games were a great success that advertised South Korea's modernity to the international community, in stark contrast to the increasingly desperate fortunes of its northern neighbor. Indeed, mass protests in June 1987 against President Chun Doo-hwan's authoritarian regime, combined with concerns that the demonstrations would interfere with or tarnish the Summer Games, contributed to the country's peaceful transition to democracy with the December 1987 election of President Roh Tae-woo.[22]

For the Germanys and Koreas, as well as numerous other nations (such as the United States and the Soviet Union), the Olympics offered relatively peaceful opportunities to promote one's nation and its values either by hosting the Games or via success in various events. Of course, political conflicts often spilled over into the Games despite their founder's intention of using them as a means of promoting greater international understanding and cooperation. West Germany attempted to block East German efforts to achieve IOC recognition, fearing that it would undermine the Federal Republic's ongoing insistence that the GDR was an illegitimate state. East Germany used its eventual IOC membership and surprising, drug-fueled success at the Games as a demonstration of socialist unity and strength as well as a means of validating its legitimacy as a sovereign state. Similarly, South Korea's hosting of the 1988 Games was a powerful benchmark in the nation's brief history; it not only coincided with the ROK's transition to genuine democracy, but also served as a showcase for an emerging economic powerhouse. North Korea, on the other hand, tried and failed either to hijack or sabotage the Seoul Games, and the failure of its attempted mass boycott would be a powerful portent of its increasing isolation from the international community.

Soccer encounters between the divided nations

In contrast to the Olympics, which primarily (though not exclusively) features individual competitions, team sports can offer a powerful analogue to the battlefield, a binary contest in which two sides, clad in their respective uniforms, seek victory. Accordingly, soccer encounters involving rival nations, provinces, cities, or other perceived or actual communities, often take on the character of a military engagement, stirring up powerful feelings of nationalism and belonging (or opposition and antagonism) among athletes and fans alike. From the playing and singing of national anthems to the widespread display of national imagery on the field and in the stands, team sports offer a venue for the public expression and validation of nationalist sentiments and aspirations. Sometimes these encounters are relatively uneventful; for example, the United States–Iran group match on June 21, 1998 at the World Cup in France was characterized by good sportsmanship that saw the sides share pre-match handshakes and pose for a group photo.[23] Others, such as the October 14, 2014 European Championship qualifier between Albania and Serbia in Belgrade, can descend quickly into complete chaos; when a drone flew over the field flying a "greater Albania" flag that included Kosovo, a region once claimed by both Albania and Serbia, a Serbian player pulled down the flag. This incident led to violent clashes among both players and fans, and the match was quickly abandoned.[24] In Germany and Korea, soccer offered a proxy battlefield that often blurred the line between politics and sport.

German soccer encounters: the 1974 World Cup

Two years after hosting the Summer Olympics in Munich, West Germany hosted the 1974 FIFA World Cup, twenty years after *Die Mannschaft* defeated Hungary in Switzerland to claim their first world championship in 1954. The 1954 World Cup victory helped signal (West) Germany's rehabilitation and acceptance back into the international community (it was banned from the 1950 World Cup in Brazil), and the 1974 version, much like the 1972 Olympics, offered the nation an opportunity to showcase its modernity and economic strength. The Munich Olympics had been marred by a hostage crisis in which eleven Israeli athletes were taken hostage and eventually murdered by members of Black September, a Palestinian terrorist organization,[25] so the 1974 World Cup took on an even greater importance for its organizers, as it would reassure the world that the hostage crisis was a one-off incident and that West Germany was a stable, modern, and safe country. German authorities were also deeply concerned about the so-called Baader-Meinhof Gang, also known as the Red Army Faction, a domestic terrorist organization. Tensions and security were high during the competition, which the USSR boycotted via its refusal to play a play-off qualifier against Chile, then led by right-wing dictator Augusto Pinochet. Despite a swarm of concerns and distractions, Germans on both sides of the Iron Curtain were, above all else, eagerly anticipating the group stage match between East and West Germany on June 22.[26]

The two sides had never met before, but West Germany had enjoyed far more success in soccer, through both its national and club teams, which included multiple-European championship winners FC Bayern München, who had defeated Athlético Madrid in the Champions Cup (now the Champions League) final the month prior to the World Cup.[27] Soccer was by far the most popular sport in both Germanys, despite the Eastern regime's lack of interest or financial support. Indeed, Manfred Ewald, head of the GDR's Gymnastics and Sport Union (DTSB), and other high-ranking sports officials apparently feared that the binary nature of team sports carried too much potential for embarrassment at the hands of Western rivals when, for example, East German clubs entered the European Champions' Cup or the national side played friendlies, Euro Cup, or World Cup qualifiers against Western nations.[28] East German soccer fans nonetheless avidly followed both their own teams and those from the West. National team and

224   *Aaron D. Horton*

major club matches were generally well attended; for example, on June 2, 1966, ninety thousand fans packed Leipzig's *Zentralstadion* for a friendly against England (who won 2–1).[29] East Germany's travel restrictions rarely allowed visits to the West, but many soccer fans took advantage of their ability to travel within the Soviet bloc; it was not uncommon for hundreds or even thousands of GDR fans to travel to away games throughout Eastern Europe, especially when they had the opportunity to see teams from the *Bundesliga*, West Germany's top-tier league.[30]

Despite official preference for individual sports, soccer in the GDR had powerful supporters, including Erich Mielke, head of the Stasi. Mielke used his considerable power and influence to manipulate the *Oberliga*, the GDR's top league, to ensure that the vast majority of star players were concentrated in a handful of teams, especially Dynamo Berlin, his club of choice. Dynamo Dresden was, arguably, the most popular club in the history of the *Oberliga*, having won several league titles in the 1960s and 1970s, but Mielke, believing that the nation's top club should be from its capital, frequently diverted top players to Berlin while also using his ability to approve or deny travel to the West for East German referees to ensure that his club regularly received favorable calls. Accordingly, Dynamo Berlin won ten consecutive league championships from 1979 to 1988, killing much fan enthusiasm in the process, since many East German fans soon realized that the fix was in, season after season.[31] Overall attendance at domestic club matches declined sharply from a high of over 2.5 million in the 1976–1977 season to less than two million per year throughout most of the 1980s, when Mielke's "chosen" squad dominated, year after year.[32]

In the weeks and months leading up to the first-ever soccer match between East and West Germany, Western players and fans were extremely confident that the GDR side would pose little threat to them. Such confidence was understandable, given the East German national team's mediocre history. East German youth teams performed reasonably well, and the Olympic squad took bronze at the 1972 Olympics (and gold at the 1976 Games). The senior national side was, however, widely known among East Germans as the "*Weltmeister der Freundschaftsspiele*," the world champion of friendlies.[33] The team was often competitive in exhibitions, but not in "meaningful" matches. Indeed, the team had never qualified for a Euro or World Cup prior to 1974, which would be their only appearance in a major tournament.

A mere 1,800 "politically reliable" fans were allowed to follow the East German team at the World Cup,[34] likely due to fears that less "patriotic" individuals may not return home afterward, much like the numerous Cuban athletes who have defected over the years during sporting events held in the United States. The match itself was a plodding, defensive affair until East German and FC Magdeburg striker Jürgen Sparwasser sprinted into a gap between two defenders and slotted the ball into the net in the seventy-seventh minute. The surprising 1–0 victory won the group for East Germany, but the West Germans would still go on to win the tournament.[35] The East German government touted the victory extensively in all available media, though some of its citizens were ambivalent about the result. East German–born contemporary author Thomas Brussig recalled that many Easterners had mixed feelings about the match and that some even cheered for their Western opponents: "Some were all for Western footballers, some totally against them. Naturally, it was for political reasons. The [GDR] defined itself through success in sport."[36] Superfan Helmut Klopfleisch, who defiantly supported the West German national side and various Western clubs, often traveling to see them play when they visited opponents in Eastern Europe, was disgusted by East Germany's victory: "It was a day of mourning in our house. . . . The worst of it all was the 300 Party bosses in the stands, waving their little flags . . . clapping at all the wrong movements because they knew nothing about soccer."[37] Despite such mixed feelings among some fans, the win was a tremendous propaganda victory for the GDR regime, which would avoid arranging any further national soccer matches against their counterpart to preserve their "bragging rights."

Korean soccer encounters

Unlike the two Germanys, the Koreas have played each other numerous times in soccer, and the matches have often been affected by politics. Beginning in the 1980s, South Korea has featured one of the premier professional soccer leagues in Asia, the K-League (founded as the "Super League" in 1983),[38] and its national squad is consistently competitive, having played in every World Cup since 1986 and finishing fourth at the 2002 event, when the country co-hosted the tournament with Japan. North Korea, on the other hand, has only appeared in two World Cups (1966 and 2010), and its domestic league is semi-amateur at best. The DPRK's qualification for the 1966 tournament was due to a boycott (by the other teams in the Asian zone), protesting that the region was allotted only one spot (shared with Africa) at the finals. Ever the contrarians, the DPRK did not join the protest, greatly increasing their chances of qualification because they only needed to defeat Australia in a play-off to reach the tournament finals in England.[39] The North Korean team had a surprising run at the 1966 Cup in England, including a 1–0 upset of Italy and a thrilling 5–3 quarterfinal loss against Portugal, progressing further than any previous Asian side and in the process convincing FIFA to expand the number of Asian teams in future tournaments. North Korea's 2010 campaign in South Africa was, however, a complete disaster, from its embarrassing 7–0 loss to Portugal to the Chinese actors in identical garb who cheered the team in lieu of actual North Korean fans, to coach Kim Jong-hun's claim that DPRK leader Kim Jong-il used an invisible phone to advise him on tactics, and to unconfirmed reports that the team and coach had been subjected to public humiliation upon return to the country.

226 *Aaron D. Horton*

Like the Germanys' sole meeting in the 1974 World Cup, the Korean teams' encounters were typically due to participation in various tournaments rather than mutually agreed-upon friendlies. The teams' first encounter was at the 1978 Asian Games in Thailand, and resulted in a 0–0 draw. The teams would meet most frequently on neutral ground, though in 1990 they played a pair of friendlies, a 2–1 North Korean victory in Pyongyang and a 1–0 South Korean victory in Seoul. These inter-Korean matches often mirrored the status of their governments' diplomatic relationship at any given time. For example, in 2005, the nations' men's and women's teams played a pair of friendlies in the South to commemorate the sixtieth anniversary of their liberation from Japanese occupation at the end of World War II. This unusual occasion was made possible by the countries' improved relations due to the "Sunshine Policy" of President Kim Dae-jung (who left office in 2003).

Since 2005, matches between the Koreas have frequently been marred by political tensions. One recurring issue was that FIFA requires the playing of national anthems at international matches. The North in particular has been obstinate in its refusal to play the South's anthem or display its flag, as doing so could constitute at least a tacit recognition of the ROK's legitimacy. This explains why the sides have only played once, in Pyongyang in 1990. In 2008–2009, when the two teams were drawn twice into the same qualifying groups for the 2010 World Cup, necessitating four matches between them, the two matches to be hosted by the North were held in Shanghai, China, due to the DPRK's refusal to display the ROK flag or play its anthem.[40] After a 1–0 loss in Seoul on April 1, 2009, the North accused South Korean president Lee Myung-bak of poisoning its players prior to the match, and demanded that FIFA investigate its accusation. Not coincidentally, Lee (inaugurated in 2008) had taken a firm stance against North Korean demands for aid, insisting that the DPRK make political concessions in exchange for continuing financial and material support from the South.[41] Matches between North and South Korean women's teams have been more frequent and relatively uneventful, possibly because the Northern team has largely dominated its Southern counterpart, likely due to a lack of institutional and financial support for the development of women's soccer in the ROK.

Sport and "legitimacy": did it work?

As discussed above, success in sports and the hosting of major events became ways for leaders of divided nations to demonstrate their nation's legitimacy in contrast to their counterparts. For the non-communist nations, such efforts have been largely successful. West Germany's World Cup victories in 1954 and 1974 were touted as evidence of the country's recovery and reacceptance into the international community (1954) and emergence as one of the world's leading economic powers (1974), presenting a seemingly stark contrast to its Eastern neighbor's repressive regime. Competing as a

War by other means 227

separate country, West Germany won three World Cups in total (the third in Italy in 1990). The Federal Republic's staging of the 1972 Munich Olympics and the 1974 World Cup, despite the hostage crisis at the former, further advertised to the world that West Germany was a modern, progressive, and successful country.

Like West Germany, South Korea hosted a pair of major sporting events: the 1988 Seoul Olympics and the 2002 World Cup (co-hosted with Japan), which both accelerated its transition to democracy (1988) and demonstrated the nation's modernity and growth, both economic and technological, to the wider world (2002). Many Koreans believed that hosting the 2002 World Cup would help dispel the ongoing international misconception of the country as a "poor peasant" society, while President Kim Dae-jung proclaimed that the tournament was a "chance to make the country prosper diplomatically, economically and culturally, in sectors like tourism and science."[42] At the 2002 tournament, the "Red Devils" made it all the way to the semifinal, where they lost a close 1–0 match to Germany, while droves of fans, clad in team and national colors, gathered across the country to watch matches. The event projected a positive image of modern Korean identity, a blend of traditional (via the playing of folk musical instruments, for example) and cosmopolitan (via widespread use of English and Chinese signs and street vendors serving "Western" foods) elements.[43] South Korea's international success in other sports, such as Olympic speed skating, provides a further means of self-promotion via sports victories and fandom.

The communist counterparts' efforts to use sports as a means of legitimation met with mixed results. East Germany also sought legitimacy both by attaining membership in various sports governing bodies such as the IOC and FIFA as well as through its surprising, drug-fueled dominance in various Olympic sports (and its upset victory against West Germany in the 1974 World Cup). However, East Germany's overwhelming Olympic successes largely failed to inspire confidence in the regime among its citizens, partly because soccer was, by far, the country's most popular sport despite the government's decision to channel the bulk of its sports budget into developing and supporting Olympic athletes.[44]

In contrast to East Germany's various sporting successes, North Korea's involvement in international sports has been sporadic and largely unsuccessful, a reflection of its regime's erratic and isolationist policies. While its surprising run to the quarterfinals at the 1966 World Cup captured the imaginations of soccer fans around the world, its 2010 campaign was a disaster of epic proportions both on and off the field, a clear reminder of the DPRK's modern status as an erratic, isolated, and belligerent pariah nation. For example, when the North Korean team played well against Brazil, only losing 2–1, the regime decided to televise its next match, against Portugal, which it lost 7–0, an embarrassing result that saw the television feed cut abruptly to footage of factory workers singing the praises of Kim Il-sung. The nation's *Juche* philosophy of self-reliance, first promoted by

228   *Aaron D. Horton*

Kim Il-sung as the lynchpin of his regime's legitimacy, theoretically meant that North Korea neither needed nor wanted to engage with the outside world. Udo Merkel argues, however, that its membership in the IOC, FIFA, and various other international sports governing bodies contradicts and potentially undermines *Juche*,[45] though a lack of sources prevents us from exploring average North Koreans' perspectives on sport and national legitimacy. Both East Germany and North Korea largely failed to use sports as a means of establishing and promoting national legitimacy either through emphasizing the wrong sports (East Germany) or poor and erratic decision making (North Korea), but we should also consider another factor, unique to divided nations: the potential for fandom to transcend political boundaries.

Fandom across borders? The unifying potential of sport

While the governments and sports ministries of the four nations all sought, to one extent or another, to utilize sports as a vehicle of self-promotion, an extension of political and diplomatic efforts to de-legitimize their counterparts, average citizens' perspectives often differed from official narratives. The East German government attempted to rally its citizens around its various sports endeavors, but many of its citizens defiantly supported West German soccer clubs and the Western national team. Thousands of East German fans traveled to see Bundesliga clubs and the West German national team when they played matches in Eastern Europe; for example, 1,303 Easterners traveled to Warsaw to see West Germany play Poland on October 10, 1971.[46] Inversely, few West Germans followed East German club soccer or its national team; after all, the West German Bundesliga was (and still is) one of the top professional leagues in Europe, and the men's national team is consistently among the best in the world, having won four World Cups (three as West Germany: 1954, 1974, 1990, and a fourth in 2014). Domestic club matches in East Germany, marred by government interference by Erich Mielke and others, were often occasions for fans to vent their frustrations with the regime; the relative anonymity offered in the stadium stands led to frequent chants of "Stasi out!" and other anti-regime sentiments.[47] Such behavior was a source of concern for the Stasi, who closely monitored the activities of both "troublesome" domestic and traveling fans, but ongoing East German support for West German soccer teams clearly demonstrated the GDR's failure to convince many of its citizens to accept the concept of a separate, socialist Germany, as many continued to identify with their fellow Germans across the border. Sheldon Anderson argues that government interference and coercion in sports (funneling talented youth into particular sports, underfunding soccer despite its popularity, etc.) actually diminished fan interest in sports, undermining its potential as a means of promoting national identity and legitimacy among its own citizens despite East Germany's impressive Olympic successes.[48]

In Korea, sports often (though not always) transcend political division and tension among average fans, though our knowledge of average North Koreans' attitudes is severely limited by their government's repressive and isolationist policies. While there have been numerous instances of official conflict over sports, such as North Korea's alleged involvement in the 1987 airline bombing ahead of the 1988 Seoul Olympics or its accusations of poisoning after their 2009 loss to South Korea in a World Cup qualifier, fans in South Korea tend to support North Korea in international competitions, built on a deeply rooted concept of racial and national unity that transcends current political boundaries. For example, when North Korea qualified for the 2010 World Cup, many South Koreans declared that they would support both Korean teams in the tournament, despite the recent sinking of a ROK naval vessel, the *Cheonan*, by North Korea. Oh Kyu-wook of the *Korea Herald* said he would cheer for the North because "they are part of Korea."[49] South Korean striker Park Si-jung told the Western media that "[we] speak the same language and are actually the same country" when declaring his support for the North's team.[50] One also finds this sense of solidarity outside of sports; in 2006, when the South Korean government interrupted television broadcasts to announce and condemn a North Korean missile test, Udo Merkel spoke with numerous Southerners who calmly and confidently declared that the North "would not use such weapons against *its own people* in the South."[51] Such declarations, both inside and outside the realm of sport, suggest a clear distinction in the minds of many Koreans between nation and politics; while South Koreans may largely view the DPRK regime as illegitimate, they maintain a powerful sense of solidarity with the people of the North, a concept of ethnic and national unity that transcends political boundaries. This trend has occasionally, though less often, manifested in the North; its tightly controlled state media reported frequently and positively on the South Korean team's impressive semi-final run at the 2002 World Cup, another example of ethnic nationalism trumping political division.[52] Of course, this occurred during the height of the "Sunshine Policy" era of détente; a few years later, the North would have its home qualifiers against the South moved to China due to its obstinate refusal to play the ROK anthem, as well as hurl ludicrous accusations as excuses for losing to their counterpart.

Conclusion

Though a largely nonviolent endeavor, sports are inextricably linked to regional, national, ethnic, and other identities. Accordingly, political conflicts and aspirations often manifest on the playing fields (or track, or pool, or court, or ring, etc.), adding a further dimension to athletic competitions. In the cases of divided Germany and Korea, sports were often utilized for political purposes, though such efforts did not always achieve the intended results among the countries' populations. West Germany and South Korea utilized sports as self-promotion, a means of advertising the virtues of their respective nations to the world. By hosting Olympics (Munich 1974, Seoul 1988) and World Cups (West Germany 1974, South Korea/Japan 2002), the nations sought to escape negative perceptions from the past. Both nations used these events to demonstrate their modernity and economic progress, while implicitly undermining their rivals' legitimacy. East Germany and North Korea used sports as a vehicle of nationalist legitimation, hoping that success on the athletic field would inspire a greater sense of national unity among their citizens and achieve greater legitimacy in the eyes of the international community. While East Germany was extremely successful in the Olympics, the controlled, artificial nature of its sports culture largely failed to inspire or unite its people, many of whom continued to identify strongly with West Germany. Despite sporadic successes, most notably the 1966 World Cup, North Korea's attempts to use sports as a means of self-promotion has largely been unsuccessful. Instead of fostering legitimacy in the eyes of the world, North Korean participation in sports has led most often to derision bordering on the absurd, as in their bizarre and disastrous 2010 World Cup campaign.

Properly utilized, success in sports and the hosting of major events offer a powerful and highly visible means of promoting the positive virtues of one's country. Sports are a near-universal language that transcends political and cultural boundaries, inspiring passions among millions upon millions in a way that the intricacies of political, diplomatic, and economic competition cannot. The Germanys and Koreas invested tremendous resources in developing and promoting athletic endeavors, and political tensions often manifested in the realm of sport. Despite governments' efforts to use sports as a vehicle for nationalist aspirations, average citizens sometimes rejected official narratives and political stances by choosing to support teams across borders, as in East Germans' widespread support for West German soccer teams or in South Koreans' sense of solidarity with the North Korean national team. The cases of divided Germany and Korea demonstrate that sports, easily and often dismissed by many as a significant factor in politics and diplomacy, carry immense potential to serve as war by other means.

Notes

1 Christopher Hill, *Olympic Politics* (Manchester: Manchester University Press, 1996), 7–8.
2 Scyld Berry, "India Beat Pakistan by 76 Runs as Estimated One Billion Viewers Tune in to World Cup Clash," *The Telegraph*, February 15, 2015, accessed March 14, 2016, www.telegraph.co.uk/sport/cricket/cricket-world-cup/11413995/India-beat-Pakistan-by-76-runs-as-estimated-one-billion-viewers-tune-in-to-World-Cup-clash.html.
3 Ulrich Hesse-Lichtenberger, *Tor! The Story of German Football* (London: WSC Books, 2003), 125.

War by other means 231

4 Robert Neff, "The Origins of Korean Soccer: The Myth and Reality of the Beautiful Game's Arrival on the Peninsula," *OhmyNews*, February 2, 2007, accessed July 14, 2016, http://english.ohmynews.com/ArticleView/article_view.asp?no=344165&rel_no=1.

5 Andrew Wong, "A Short History of Korean Baseball," *Asian Baseball Committee*, December 31, 2010, accessed July 14, 2016, http://research.sabr.org/asianbb/south-korean/history.

6 "The International Olympic Committee," accessed July 20, 2016, www.olympic.org/the-ioc.

7 Kay Schiller and Christopher Young, *The 1972 Munich Olympics and the Making of Modern Germany* (Berkeley: University of California Press, 2010), Kindle ed., loc. 159–60.

8 Sheldon Anderson, "Soccer and the Failure of East German Sports Policy," *Soccer & Society* 12, no. 5 (September 2011): 653.

9 Schiller and Young, *The 1972 Munich Olympics*, 158–63.

10 Anderson, "Soccer and the Failure of East German Sports Policy," 653.

11 East Germany finished ahead of West Germany in the overall medal count in every Summer Olympics in whicn both countries participated: 1968 (Mexico City), 1972 (Munich), 1976 (Montreal), and 1988 (Seoul). West Germany joined the United States' boycott of the 1980 Games in Moscow, and East Germany joined the Soviet Union in boycotting the 1984 Games in Los Angeles. East Germany also finished ahead of West Germany in the 1972 (Sapporo), 1976 (Innsbruck), 1980 (Lake Placid, NY), 1984 (Sarajevo), and 1988 (Calgary) Winter Games. Jutta Braun, "The People's Sport? Popular Sport and Fans in the Later Years of the German Democratic Republic," *German History* 27, no. 3: 416.

12 Schiller and Young, *The 1972 Munich Olympics*, 158.

13 Anderson, "Soccer and the Failure of East German Sports Policy," 653.

14 Schiller and Young, *The 1972 Munich Olympics*, 24.

15 Ibid., 174–75.

16 Steven Ungerleider, *Faust's Gold: Inside the East German Doping Machine* (New York: St. Martin's, 2001), Kindle ed., loc. 333.

17 Bill Murray, "Cultural Revolution? Football in the Societies of Asia and the Pacific," in *Giving the Game Away: Football, Politics and Culture on Five Continents*, ed. Stephen Wagg (London: Leicester University Press, 1995), 143.

18 Sergey Radchenko, "Sport and Politics on the Korean Peninsula: North Korea and the 1988 Seoul Olympics," *North Korea International Documentation Project*, accessed July 24, 2016, www.wilsoncenter.org/publication/nkidp-e-dossier-no-3-sport-and-politics-the-korean-peninsula-north-korea-and-the-1988.

19 They had also boycotted the 1984 Los Angeles Games, along with the Soviet Union and several other members of the communist bloc in retaliation for the United States' and others' boycott of the 1980 Moscow Games.

20 Radchenko, "Sport and Politics on the Korean Peninsula."

21 Bruce Cumings, "Despite an Air of Mystery, Downing of Korean Jetliner Puts a Chill on Peninsula," *Los Angeles Times*, February 11, 1988, accessed July 20, 2016, http://articles.latimes.com/1988-02-11/local/me-41784_1_north-korean.

22 George Katsiaficas, *Asia's Unknown Uprisings*, Volume 1 of *South Korean Social Movements in the 20th Century* (Oakland, CA: PM Press, 2012), 277–78.

23 Neil Billingham, "98: The Most Politically Charged Game in World Cup History," *Four Two*, June 6, 2014, accessed July 24, 2016, www.fourfourtwo.com/features/98-most-politically-charged-game-world-cup-history.

24 Nick Ames, "Serbia v Albania: Drones, Flags and Violence in Abandoned Match," *BBC*, October 15, 2014, accessed July 24, 2016, www.bbc.com/sport/football/29624259.

232 *Aaron D. Horton*

25 Simon Reeve, "Olympics Massacre: Munich—the Real Story," *The Independent*, January 22, 2006, accessed July 24, 2016, https://web.archive.org/web/20120316084844/www.independent.co.uk/news/world/europe/olympics-massacre-munich—the-real-story-524011.html.

26 Erik E. Cleves, "East Germany v West Germany – Football and the Cold War," *History in an Hour*, July 1, 2012, accessed July 25, 2016, www.historyinanhour.com/2012/07/01/east-germany-v-west-germany-world-cup/.

27 Ibid.

28 Hesse-Lichtenberger, *Tor!* 223–24.

29 David Downing, *The Best of Enemies: England v Germany* (London: Bloomsbury, 2001), 96.

30 Markus Hesselmann and Robert Ide, "A Tale of Two Germanys: Football Culture and National Identity in the German Democratic Republic," in *German Football: History, Culture, Society*, ed. Alan Tomlinson and Christopher Young (London: Routledge, 2006), 42.

31 Hesse-Lichtenberger, *Tor!* 231.

32 Mike Dennis, "Soccer Hooliganism in the German Democratic Republic," in *German Football: History, Culture, Society*, ed. Alan Tomlinson and Christopher Young (London: Routledge, 2006), 53.

33 Frank Willmann, ed., *Fußball-Land DDR: Anstoß, Abpfiff, Aus* (Berlin: Eulenspiegel Verlag, 2004), 139.

34 Anderson, "Soccer and the Failure of East German Sports Policy," 652.

35 Cleves, "East Germany v West Germany."

36 "'Sich die ganze Welt vom Fußball her erklären': Thomas Brussig im Gespräch mit Stefan Hermanns und Markus Hesselmann," in *Querpässe: Beiträge zur Literatur-, Kultur- und Mediengeschichte des Fußballs*, ed. Ralf Adelmann, Rolf Parr, and Thomas Schwarz (Heidelberg: Synchron, 2003), 171.

37 Simon Kuper, *Soccer Against the Enemy: How the World's Most Popular Sport Starts and Fuels Revolutions and Keeps Dictators in Power* (New York: Nation Books, 2006), 24.

38 Lee Jong-Young, "The Development of Football in Korea," in *Japan, Korea and the 2002 World Cup*, ed. John Horne and Wolfram Manzenreiter (London: Routledge, 2002), 79.

39 Murray, "Cultural Revolution? Football in the Societies of Asia and the Pacific," 144.

40 Mark Ledsom, "Koreas Match Moved to Shanghai After Anthem Row," *Reuters*, March 7, 2008, accessed July 16, 2014, http://uk.reuters.com/article/2008/03/07/uk-soccer-fifa-koreas-idUKL0789295820080307.

41 Andrei Lankov, *The Real North Korea: Life and Politics in the Failed Stalinist Utopia* (Oxford: Oxford University Press, 2013), 174.

42 Choi Yoon-Sung, "Football and the South Korean Imagination: South Korea and the 2002 World Cup Tournaments," in *Football Goes East: Business, Culture and the People's Game in China, Japan and South Korea*, ed. Wolfram Manzenreiter and John Horne (New York: Routledge, 2004), 143.

43 Ibid., 142–43.

44 Hesselmann, and Ide, "A Tale of Two Germanys," 40.

45 Udo Merkel, "Sport and Physical Culture in North Korea: Resisting, Recognizing and Relishing Globalization," *Sociology of Sport Journal* 29 (2012): 521.

46 Braun, "The People's Sport?" 425.

47 Dennis, "Soccer Hooliganism in the German Democratic Republic," 57.

48 Anderson, "Soccer and the Failure of East German Sports Policy," 660.

49 Rose Raymond, "South and North Korea Both Made History This World Cup," *National Public Radio*, June 22, 2010.

War by other means   233

50 John Duerden, "Park Ji-sung Hopes World Cup Can Help Unite a Divided Korea," *The Guardian*, May 27, 2010, accessed January 24, 2014, www.theguardian.com/football/2010/may/28/park-ji-sung-south-korea?INTCMP=ILCNETTXT3487.

51 Merkel, "Sport and Physical Culture in North Korea," 509–10.

52 Udo Merkel, "The Politics of Sport Diplomacy and Reunification in Divided Korea: One Nation, Two Countries and Three Flags," *International Review for the Sociology of Sport* 43, no. 3 (2008): 292.

Index

Note: Page numbers in *italic* indicate a figure on the corresponding page.

Adickes, Franz 101, 103, 105–107; *see also* Lex Adickes
Allies *see* occupation; World War II; *and individual nations*
anti-nuclear movement 14, 128–35, 141n43, 142n51
Aoki Shūzō 86–7
Asian values 15, 145–46, 153–56
attitudes *see* images, Japanese

Balzac, Honoré de 165, 170–71
Berlin Women's Missionary Association for China (BFM) *see* Findelhaus Bethesda
Bethesda *see* Findelhaus Bethesda
Big Sword Society 46, 51
Bildung 87, 89; *see also kyōyōshugi*
biography 15, 166–73; *see also* Zweig, Stefan
Bismarck, Otto von 3, 126, 138n11
Blumhardt, Christoph 49–50
Boxer Rebellion *see* Boxer Uprising
Boxer Uprising 3, 12, 26, 28, 58, 59n7; challenge to Weimar Mission 45–46, 47–49; historical background 46–47, 58n2; *see also* Schüler, Wilhelm; Wilhelm, Richard
Britain: and Fukushima nuclear incident 125, 130; GNP of 4; Japanese view of 85, 86; and Treaty of Tianjin 2–3; and victory in Opium Wars 62; *see also* occupation; World War II
Buddhism 43n71, 145, 148, 154

capitalism: East Asian 14–15; transition to 176, 182, 184, 187; *see* Weber, Max
censorship 15, 50, 52, 171–72, 178
Chen Ran 15, 176, 183–88

Chiang Kai-shek 3
China: role in Allied occupation 193, 194, 202, 210; *see also* biography; family; German-Chinese relations; German-East Asian relations; Jews; Kiaochow; Manchukuo; modernization; New Culture Movement; People's Republic of China (PRC); Shanghai; Weber, Max; Zweig, Stefan
Christianity *see* Findelhaus Bethesda; Schüler, Wilhelm; Weber, Max; Weimar Mission; Wilhelm, Richard
Churchill, Winston 193–96
Clay, General Lucius 198
Cold War: and Allied occupation of Japan 206–207; and history 7; and relationship of Germany and Japan 91, 94, 107, 136; and sports 217
colonialism: in China 66; German 55; and the Holocaust 65; *see also* occupation; *and individual nations*
communism 15, 16; and censorship 15; Chinese 3, 162; German 6, 127; Korean 6; United States approach to 16; *see also* Cold War; Germany; Korea; People's Republic of China (PRC); Soviet Union; Wolf, Christa; Zweig, Stefan
Confucianism: and Boxer Uprising 48; and Max Weber 145, 147–50, 153–56; and New Culture Movement 167–68; *see also* family
cultural flows 1, 5, 7–8, 16–17
Cultural Revolution 6, 154–55, 172, 183–84, 187
culture 15; *see also* Asian values; cultural flows; images, Japanese; popular culture; Weber, Max

236 Index

democracy: and Allied occupation 16; and Japan 93; in People's Republic of China (PRC) 186; and sports 222, 227
denazification 127, 198–99, 209
Deng Xiaoping 4, 172, 182–83
development *see* economy
documentary film see *Exil Shanghai*; *Shanghai Ghetto*

economy 1, 4, 14, 127, 150–58; *see also* capitalism; communism; culture; industrialization; land readjustment; Weber, Max; *and individual nations*
Eulenburg Expedition 2–3
Exil Shanghai 13, 63, 71–8, 80n35

family: in 1990s China 182–84; Confucian model 12–13, 23–30, 33–8, 148, 153, 184; and entrepreneurship 149; Japanese image of German 95; nuclear (*xiao jiating*) 13, 23–6, 30, 35, 37, 39; in Weber 147–49, 153; *see also* Findelhaus Bethesda
Federal Republic of Germany (FRG) 201; *see also* Cold War
Findelhaus Bethesda 12–13, 23–7, 39n8, 39n10; Christian inculcation at 40n31; economic aspect of 28–30, 41n39; and marriage 42n60, 43n71; religious aspect of 27–8; and social networks 31–3, 41n45, 43n73, 43n74; social security aspect of 30–1, 41n44; spaces and 33–6; and transnational forces 36–8
France: electricity imports from 134; and Fukushima nuclear incident 125, 130; GNP of 4; Japanese view of 85, 86; and Treaty of Tianjin 2–3; and Triple Intervention 87–88; and victory in Opium Wars 62; World Cup in 222; *see also* Balzac, Honoré de; occupation; World War II
Franco-Prussian War 3
French Concession 62
Fukushima nuclear incident 14, 123–25, 128–36, 139n31, 139–40n32

Gao Mingkai 170–71
German-Chinese relations 2–4, 136; *see also* Findelhaus Bethesda
German Democratic Republic (GDR) 201; *see also* Cold War; sports; Wolf, Christa

German-East Asian relations 2–7; *see also* Weber, Max
German-Japanese relations 4–5, 123, 125–27, 141n43; *see also* Fukushima nuclear incident
German-Korean relations 5–7; *see also* sports
Germany: *see* Cold War; Federal Republic of Germany (FRG); German-Chinese relations; German Democratic Republic (GDR); German-East Asian relations; German-Japanese relations; German-Korean relations; images, Japanese; Lex Adickes; modernization; Nazi Germany; occupation; Sinophobia; sports; Weber, Max; Wolf, Christa; World War II
Goethe, Johann Wolfgang von 5, 164, 168
Gotō Shinpei 110–12, 114
Great Britain *see* Britain

Hiroshima 16, 135, 203, 210
history: comparative approach to 9; global history 7–9; social history 8; transnational history 7–9, 24; *see also* cultural flows; *Exil Shanghai*; *Shanghai Ghetto*; Zweig, Stefan
historiography 9–12
Hitler Jugend 90
Hitler-Stalin Pact 4, 90
Howard, Ebenezer 109, 116

images, Japanese 13–14, 85–6; 1871–1918 86–8; 1919–1945 88–90; 1945–1970s 91–2; 1980s 92–4; in the present 96–7; since the 1980s 94–6
Imperial University (Tokyo) 87, 88, 89
individualism 37, 152, 154, 167, 169, 176, 218
industrialization 6, 101, 148, 150, 151, 154; *see also* sports
International Settlement 62, 66–7, 74
Iwakura Mission 86, 126

Janklowicz-Mann, Dana see *Shanghai Ghetto*
Japan: Meiji government 18n20, 85–9, 102, 107–108, 126, 150, 153, 206; relations with neighbors 5, 136; Taishō era 5, 109; Westernization of 14, 102, 108; *see also* Fukushima nuclear incident; German-East Asian relations; German-Japanese relations;

Index   237

Hiroshima; images, Japanese; land readjustment; modernization; Nagasaki; occupation; urban planning; war guilt; Weber, Max
Jews 12, 13, 62–3, 80n32, 90, 199; Committee for the Assistance of European Jewish Refugees 80n31; as survivors 79n21; *see also Exil Shanghai; Shanghai Ghetto*; Zweig, Stefan

Kafka, Franz 177
Kiaochow 3, 45–49, 50, 88
Kiautschou Bay *see* Kiaochow
Kim Dae-Jung 6, 11–12, 221, 226, 227; *see also* Sunshine Policy
Kim Il-Sung 6, 221, 227–28
Kohl, Helmut 6, 129
Korea: colonization of 1; diplomatic relations with Germany 5–7; division into North and South 6–7; historiography of 11–12; relations with Japan 5; *see also* economy; German-East Asian relations; German-Korean relations; Korean War; land readjustment; modernization; sports; Weber, Max
Korean War 116–17, 209
Kristallnacht 66, 72
Kwon, Keedon 153, 155
kyōyōshugi 87, 89, 91, 95

land readjustment 14, 101–103; in Japan 107–11, 118–19; in Seoul 112–19, *117; see also* Lex Adickes
League of Nations 89, 138n13
Leibniz, Gottfried 2
Lex Adickes 118–19; features of 105–107; Prussian Building Line Act as springboard to 103–104
Li Hongzhang 3
literature: in 20th and 21st century China 182–88; genre 15, 162–66, 166–69, 171–73; socialist realism 177–78; *see also* biography; Chen Ran; transreading; Wolf, Christa; Zweig, Stefan

MacArthur, General Douglas 16, 201, 203, 205–208
Manchukuo 3, 90, 112
Maoism 162, 168–73, 183
Mao Zedong 3, 169, 182; *see also* Maoism; People's Republic of China (PRC)
Marxism 39n4, 89, 146, 169, 170
McCloy, John J. 198

memory 13; models of 63–65; *see also Exil Shanghai; Shanghai Ghetto*
Merkel, Angela 6, 128–29
migration *see* Findelhaus Bethesda; Jews; urbanization
missionaries *see* Findelhaus Bethesda
modernization: of China 3, 39n4, 48, 155, 168; of Germany 85, 96, 126–27; of Japan 85, 89, 94, 96, 126–27, 153; of South Korea 153; *see also* land readjustment
Morgenthau, Henry 195–96

Nagasaki 16, 135, 203, 210
Nazi Germany: alliance with Japan 1; cooperation with China 3; Japanese image of 90; and literature 187; rise of 8; and sports 218; *see also* denazification; Jews; occupation; World War II
New Culture Movement 23, 26, 39n11, 166–68, 172
Nietzsche, Friedrich 5, 163
nuclear technology 96, 141n45, 202; *see also* anti-nuclear movement; Fukushima nuclear incident
Nuremberg Trials 4, 199–200, 208

occupation: by Allies 4, 16, *197*; and Boxer Uprising 47–8, 51–2, 54–8; of Korean peninsula by Japan 112–13, 219, 226; of Shanghai by Japan 70, 79n21; Stalinist 16; *see also* World War II
October Revolution of 1917 62
Opium Wars 2–3, 62
Ottinger, Ulrike *see Exil Shanghai*

pedagogy 176–88
People's Republic of China (PRC): relations with Germany 3–4, 10, 15; women and 176, 182–88; *see also* Maoism; Mao Zedong
popular culture 85; *see also* sports
POW camps 3, 198
propaganda: Boxer Uprising 59n7; Maoist 169, 172; sports as 218, 220, 225; World War II 85, 90, 126
Prussia *see* Germany

Qingdao *see* Boxer Uprising; Weimar Mission
Qing empire *see* China

racism 4, 13, 45, 48, 70; *see also* Sinophobia
rationality 15, 54; and colonialism 113–14; German 94–6; and economic

238 *Index*

development 152, 156, 157; and land readjustment 102, 104–107, 115; Max Weber on 145–50, 157, 159n4; women and 180, 185–86

reading *see* transreading

refugees 13, 55, 79n26, 127, 198; *see also* Jews

representation *see* images, Japanese

Roosevelt, Franklin 193–95, 202

Schüler, Wilhelm 13, 45, 48–9, 52, 54–8, 60n34

Shanghai 62–3, 65, 167, 169, 170, 226; *see also Exil Shanghai*; Findelhaus Bethesda; Jews; *Shanghai Ghetto*

Shanghai Ghetto 13, 63, 65–71, 76–7; *see also Exil Shanghai*

Sima Qian 166

Sino-German relations *see* German-Chinese relations

Sino-Japanese War 88

Sinophobia 159n19

sociology *see* Weber, Max

Soviet Union 3, 6, 7; and Fukushima nuclear incident 127, 133; and Japan 90; and occupations of Germany and Japan 193; socialist realism 177–78, 181; sports and 220–22, 231n11; *see also* Cold War; Stalin, Joseph; World War II

space 39n4; *see also* Findelhaus Bethesda

sports 16, 216; baseball 87, 216, 219; cricket 216–17; modern Olympics 216–22, 223–24, 227, 229, 230, 231n11; soccer 16, 95, 216–18, 218–21, 222–26, 227, 228–30

Stalin, Joseph 16, 177–78, 194–95, 201, 209; *see also* Hitler-Stalin Pact

stereotype *see* images, Japanese

Stimson, Henry 195, 202

Strachey, Lytton 162, 167

Sunshine Policy 6, 221, 226, 229

survivors *see* Jews

Tokyo Trials 4, 208

Tolstoy, Leo 163, 168, 170

transreading 15, 176, 177–82, 184–88

Treaty of Tianjin 2–3

trials *see* war crimes trials

Triple Intervention 4, 87–8

Ugaki Kazushige 87, 114

United Kingdom (UK) *see* Britain

United States (US): American exceptionalism 8; dominance in Asia Pacific 126; Japanese images of 85; *see also* Cold War; occupation; popular culture; World War II

urbanization 101, 103, 114, 118, 216, 218; *see also* land readjustment; Lex Adickes; sports

urban planning 13, 14; *see also* land readjustment; Lex Adickes

USSR *see* Soviet Union

Verstehen 147, 157

war crimes trials 195–96, 199–200, 203, 206–209; *see also* Nuremberg Trials; Tokyo Trials

war guilt 5, 16, 210

Weber, Max 15, 145–46, 159n4, 161n44; and East Asian model of development 150–58; his study of Asian societies 146–50

Weimar Mission 12, 13, 45, 47–9; *see also* Schüler, Wilhelm; Wilhelm, Richard

Westernization *see under* Japan

widowhood 23, 30–1, 40n35, 42n62, 44n87

Wilhelm, Richard 13, 46, 48–55, 58, 149, 160n19

Wolf, Christa 15, 176–82, 185, 187

women: delayed transfer practice 43n76; in Republican China 13, 15; and self-definition in the 21st century 176–88; *see also* Chen Ran; family; Findelhaus Bethesda; widowhood; Wolf, Christa

World War II: Allied occupation of Germany 193–200, *197*; Allied occupation of Japan 193–194, 201–210, *204*

Zeitschrift für Missionskunde und Religionswissenschaft (ZMR) *see* Weimar Mission

Zweig, Stefan 15; poetology of 162–66; works in China 167–73